Pedro and Me

Pedro and Me

Friendship, Loss, and What I Learned

JUDD WINICK

HENRY HOLT AND COMPANY / NEW YORK

This book is dedicated to my fellow travelers:

Sean Sasser,
Cory Murphy,
and Pam Ling.

I love you with all my heart.

Henry Holt and Company, LLC
Publishers since 1866
115 West 18th Street
New York, New York 10011

Henry Holt is a registered trademark of Henry Holt and Company, LLC

Published in Canada by Fitzhenry & Whiteside Ltd., 195 Allstate Parkway,
Markham, Ontario L3R 4T8.

Library of Congress Cataloging-in-Publication Data
Winick, Judd
Pedro and me: friendship, loss, and what I learned / by Judd Winick of MTV's *The Real World*
p. cm.
Summary: In graphic format, this book describes the friendship between two roommates on the MTV show *The Real World*, one of whom died of AIDS.
1. Zamora, Pedro, 1972—Health—Comic books, strips, etc.
2. Winick, Judd—Comic books, strips, etc.
3. AIDS (Disease)—Patients—United States—Biography—Comic books, strips, etc.
4. AIDS activists—United States—Biography—Comic books, strips, etc.
5. Real World (Television program: United States)—Juvenile literature.
[1. Zamora, Pedro, 1972—Cartoons and comics. 2. Winick, Judd—Cartoons and comics.
3. AIDS (Disease)—Cartoons and comics. 4. Diseases—Cartoons and comics.
5. Real World (Television program: United States)—Cartoons and comics.] I. Title.
RC607.A26 W5726 2000 362.1'969792'0092—dc21 99-40729

ISBN 0-8050-6403-6
First Edition—2000
Printed in the United States of America on acid-free paper. ∞
1 3 5 7 9 10 8 6 4 2

Permission for the use of the following is gratefully acknowledged:

Sixty-six word excerpt from *A Prayer for Owen Meany* by John Irving
Copyright © 1989 by John Irving
Reprinted by permission of HarperCollins Publishers, Inc.
William Morrow

CONTENTS

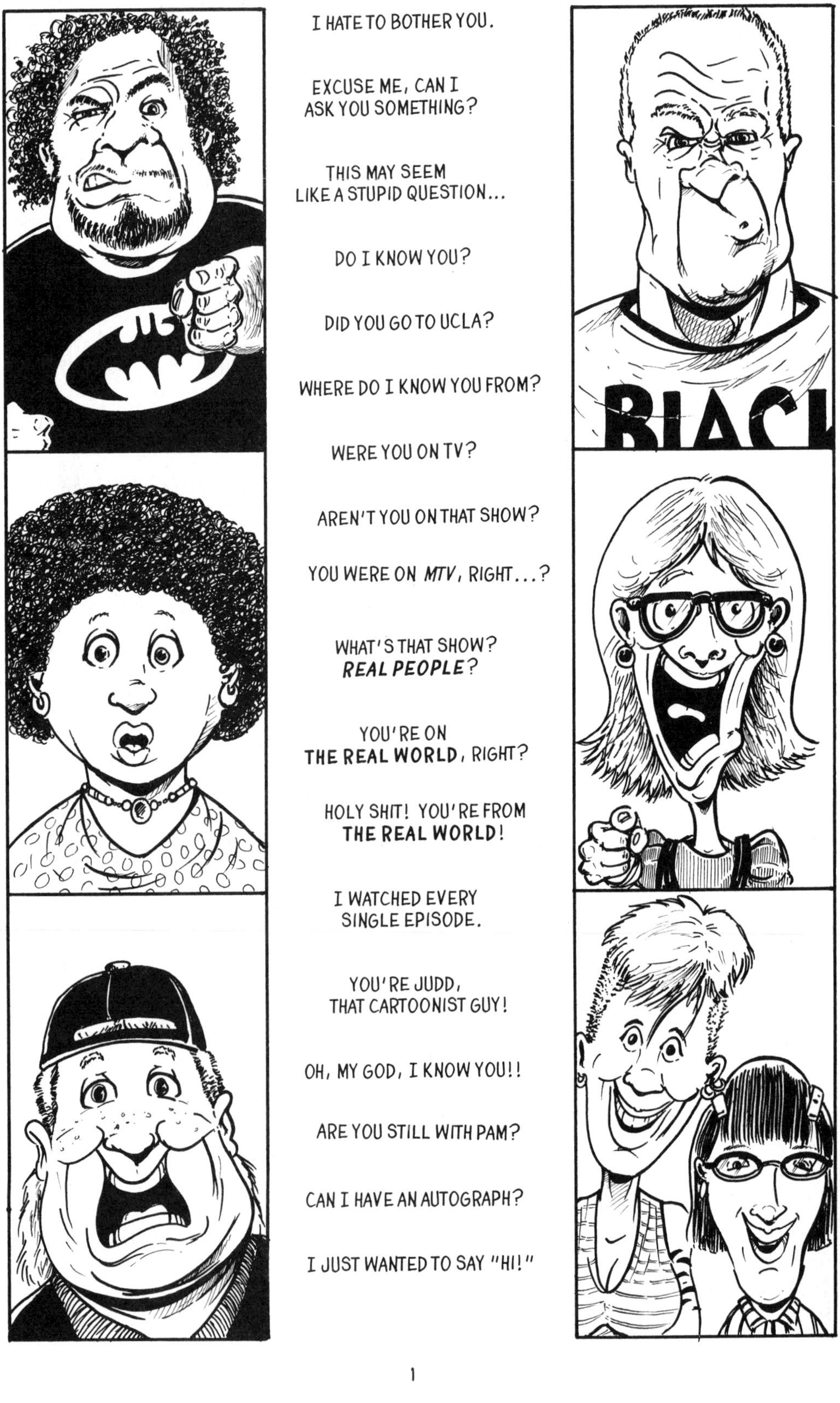
I HATE TO BOTHER YOU.
EXCUSE ME, CAN I ASK YOU SOMETHING?
THIS MAY SEEM LIKE A STUPID QUESTION...
DO I KNOW YOU?
DID YOU GO TO UCLA?
WHERE DO I KNOW YOU FROM?
WERE YOU ON TV?
AREN'T YOU ON THAT SHOW?
YOU WERE ON *MTV*, RIGHT...?
WHAT'S THAT SHOW? ***REAL PEOPLE***?
YOU'RE ON **THE REAL WORLD**, RIGHT?
HOLY SHIT! YOU'RE FROM **THE REAL WORLD**!
I WATCHED EVERY SINGLE EPISODE.
YOU'RE JUDD, THAT CARTOONIST GUY!
OH, MY GOD, I KNOW YOU!!
ARE YOU STILL WITH PAM?
CAN I HAVE AN AUTOGRAPH?
I JUST WANTED TO SAY "HI!"

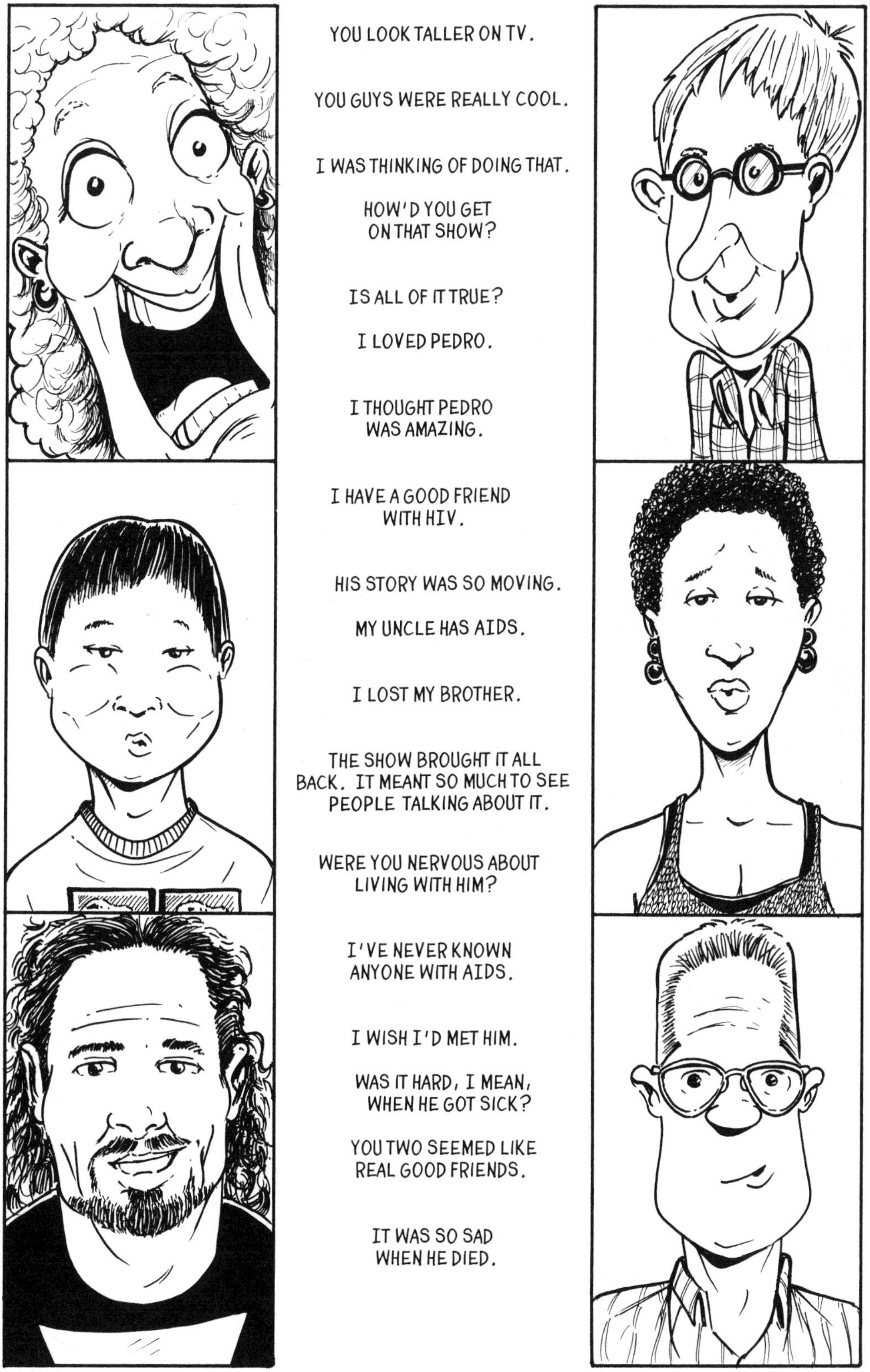
YOU LOOK TALLER ON TV.
YOU GUYS WERE REALLY COOL.
I WAS THINKING OF DOING THAT.
HOW'D YOU GET ON THAT SHOW?
IS ALL OF IT TRUE?
I LOVED PEDRO.
I THOUGHT PEDRO WAS AMAZING.
I HAVE A GOOD FRIEND WITH HIV.
HIS STORY WAS SO MOVING.
MY UNCLE HAS AIDS.
I LOST MY BROTHER.
THE SHOW BROUGHT IT ALL BACK. IT MEANT SO MUCH TO SEE PEOPLE TALKING ABOUT IT.
WERE YOU NERVOUS ABOUT LIVING WITH HIM?
I'VE NEVER KNOWN ANYONE WITH AIDS.
I WISH I'D MET HIM.
WAS IT HARD, I MEAN, WHEN HE GOT SICK?
YOU TWO SEEMED LIKE REAL GOOD FRIENDS.
IT WAS SO SAD WHEN HE DIED.

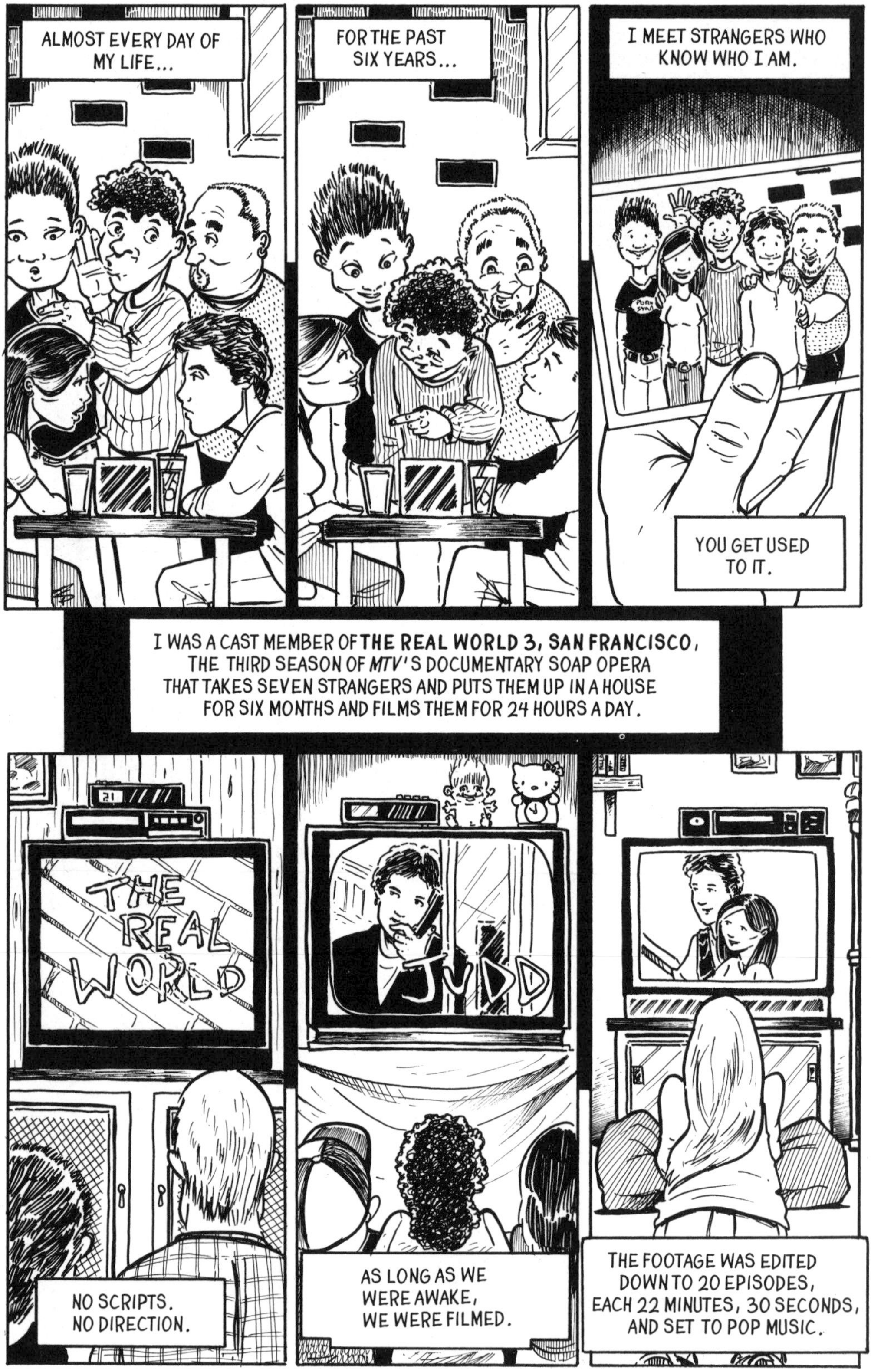
ALMOST EVERY DAY OF MY LIFE...
FOR THE PAST SIX YEARS...
I MEET STRANGERS WHO KNOW WHO I AM.
YOU GET USED TO IT.
I WAS A CAST MEMBER OF **THE REAL WORLD 3, SAN FRANCISCO**, THE THIRD SEASON OF *MTV*'S DOCUMENTARY SOAP OPERA THAT TAKES SEVEN STRANGERS AND PUTS THEM UP IN A HOUSE FOR SIX MONTHS AND FILMS THEM FOR 24 HOURS A DAY.
THE REAL WORLD
NO SCRIPTS. NO DIRECTION.
JUDD
AS LONG AS WE WERE AWAKE, WE WERE FILMED.
THE FOOTAGE WAS EDITED DOWN TO 20 EPISODES, EACH 22 MINUTES, 30 SECONDS, AND SET TO POP MUSIC.

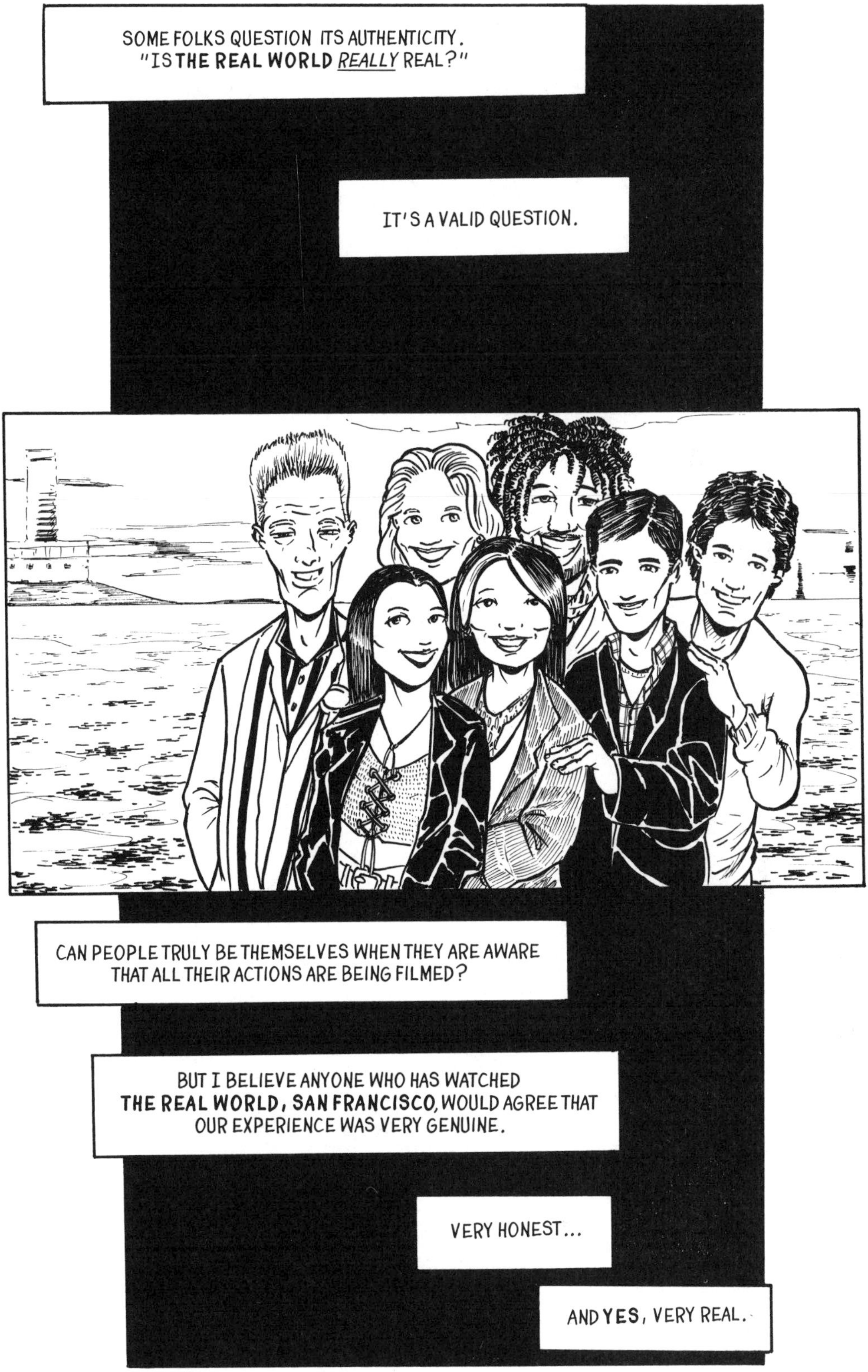
SOME FOLKS QUESTION ITS AUTHENTICITY.
"IS THE REAL WORLD REALLY REAL?"
IT'S A VALID QUESTION.
CAN PEOPLE TRULY BE THEMSELVES WHEN THEY ARE AWARE THAT ALL THEIR ACTIONS ARE BEING FILMED?
BUT I BELIEVE ANYONE WHO HAS WATCHED THE REAL WORLD, SAN FRANCISCO, WOULD AGREE THAT OUR EXPERIENCE WAS VERY GENUINE.
VERY HONEST...
AND YES, VERY REAL.

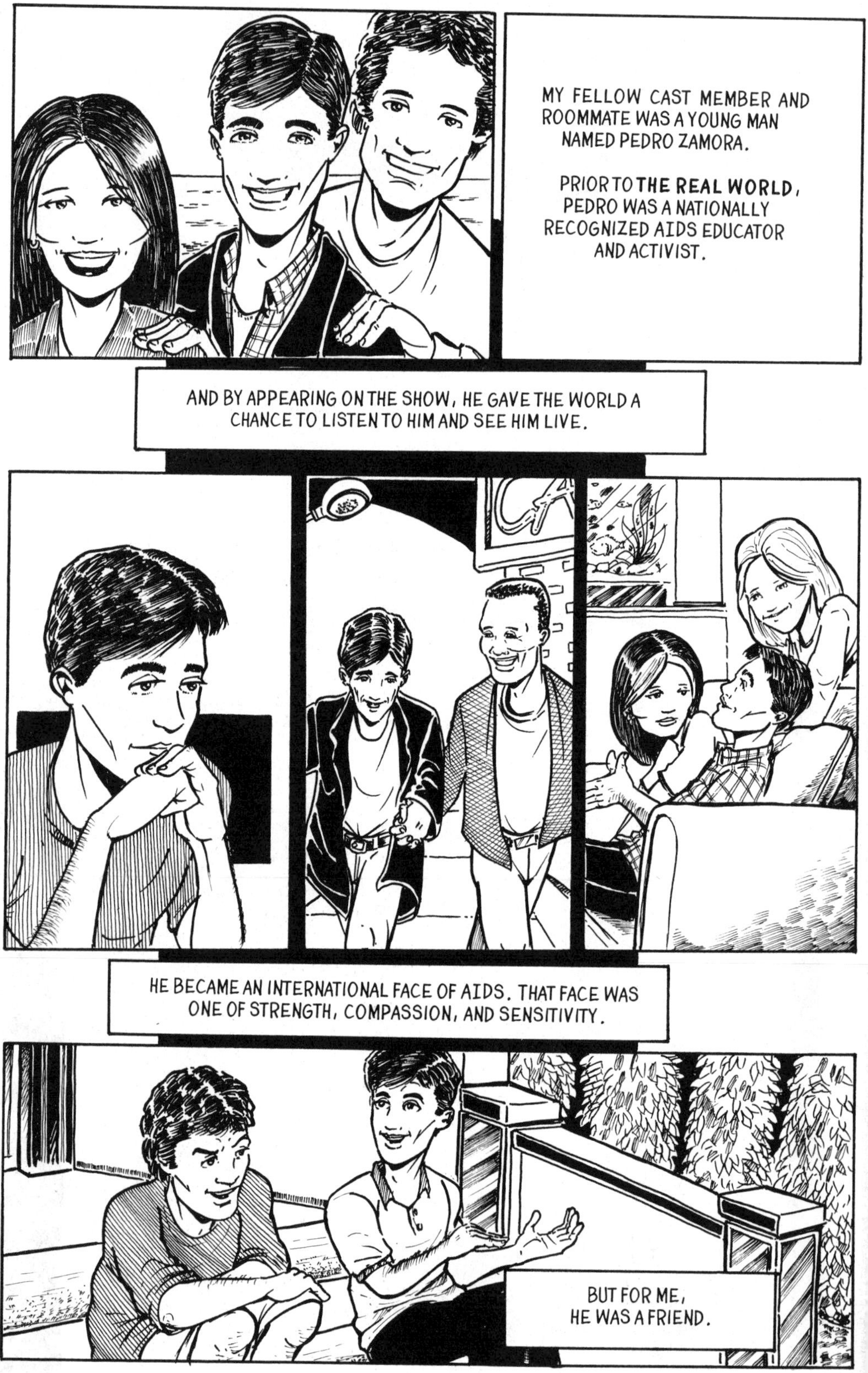
MY FELLOW CAST MEMBER AND ROOMMATE WAS A YOUNG MAN NAMED PEDRO ZAMORA.
PRIOR TO **THE REAL WORLD**, PEDRO WAS A NATIONALLY RECOGNIZED AIDS EDUCATOR AND ACTIVIST.
AND BY APPEARING ON THE SHOW, HE GAVE THE WORLD A CHANCE TO LISTEN TO HIM AND SEE HIM LIVE.
HE BECAME AN INTERNATIONAL FACE OF AIDS. THAT FACE WAS ONE OF STRENGTH, COMPASSION, AND SENSITIVITY.
BUT FOR ME, HE WAS A FRIEND.

CHAPTER ONE

THE SHUTTLE GUY

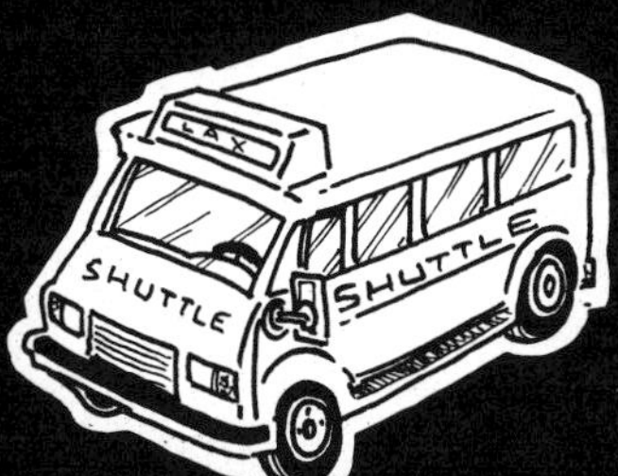
LAX
SHUTTLE
SHUTTLE

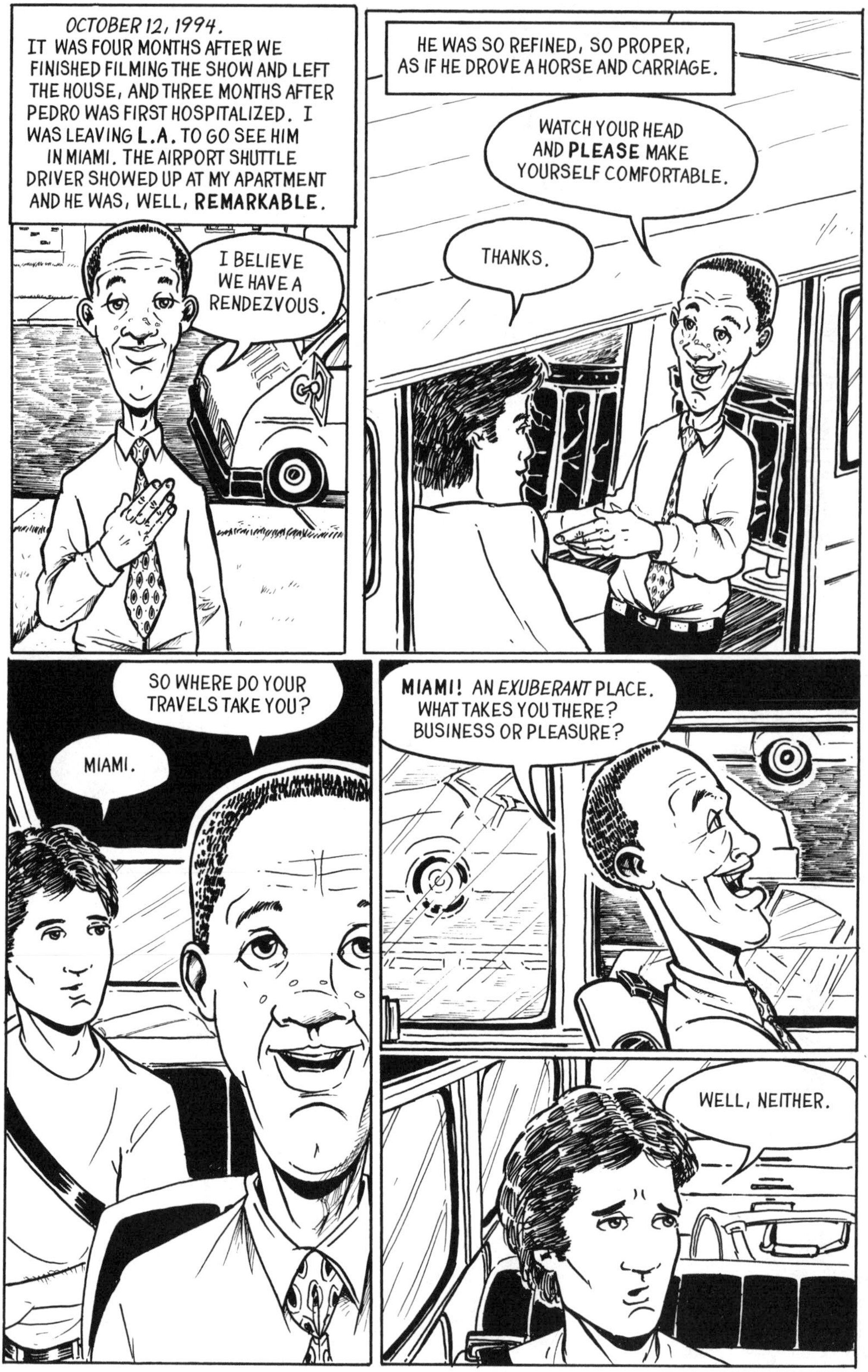
OCTOBER 12, 1994.
IT WAS FOUR MONTHS AFTER WE FINISHED FILMING THE SHOW AND LEFT THE HOUSE, AND THREE MONTHS AFTER PEDRO WAS FIRST HOSPITALIZED. I WAS LEAVING L.A. TO GO SEE HIM IN MIAMI. THE AIRPORT SHUTTLE DRIVER SHOWED UP AT MY APARTMENT AND HE WAS, WELL, REMARKABLE.
I BELIEVE WE HAVE A RENDEZVOUS.
HE WAS SO REFINED, SO PROPER, AS IF HE DROVE A HORSE AND CARRIAGE.
WATCH YOUR HEAD AND PLEASE MAKE YOURSELF COMFORTABLE.
THANKS.
SO WHERE DO YOUR TRAVELS TAKE YOU?
MIAMI.
MIAMI! AN EXUBERANT PLACE. WHAT TAKES YOU THERE? BUSINESS OR PLEASURE?
WELL, NEITHER.

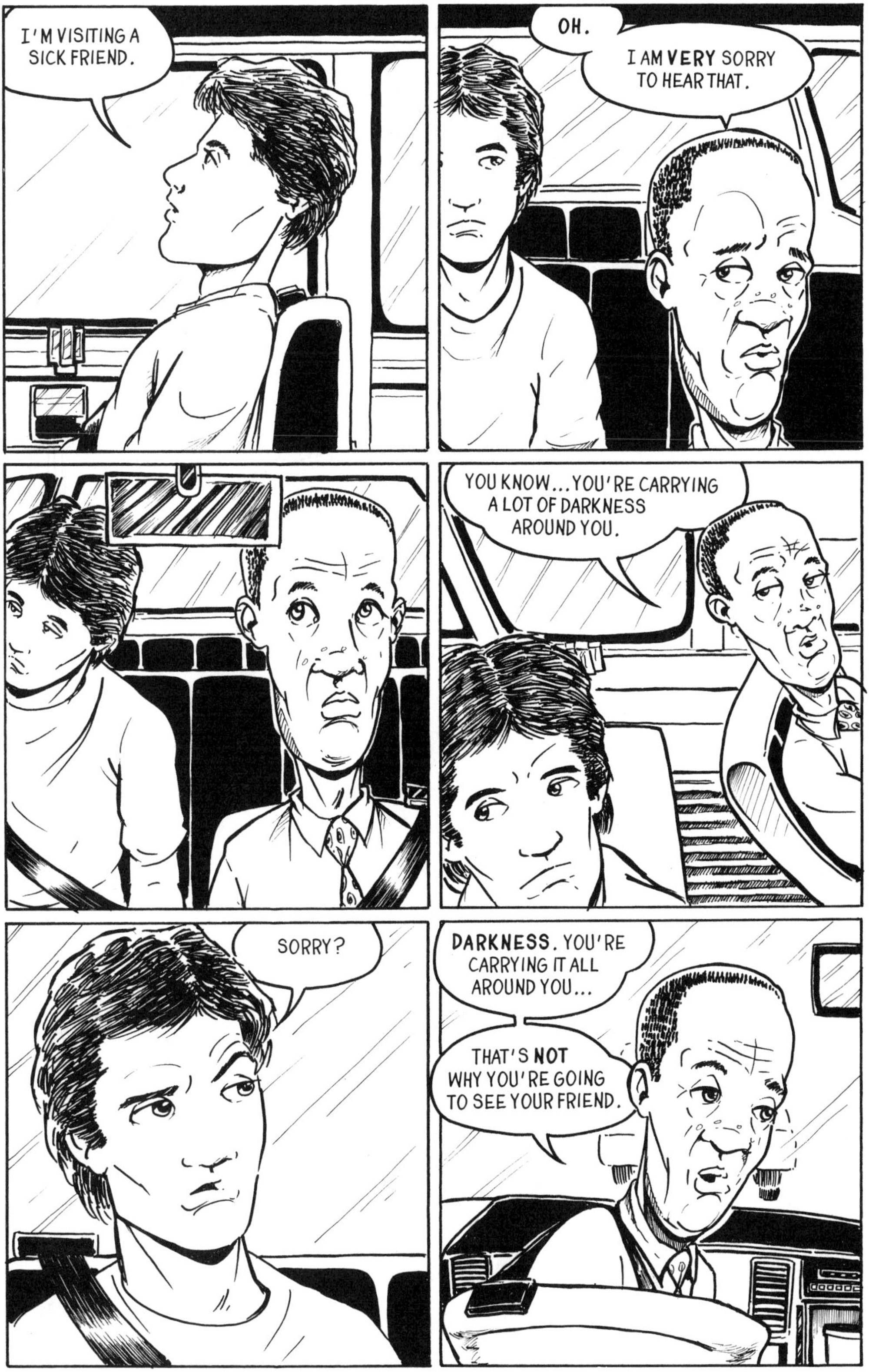
I'M VISITING A SICK FRIEND.
OH.
I AM **VERY** SORRY TO HEAR THAT.
YOU KNOW...YOU'RE CARRYING A LOT OF DARKNESS AROUND YOU.
SORRY?
DARKNESS. YOU'RE CARRYING IT ALL AROUND YOU...
THAT'S **NOT** WHY YOU'RE GOING TO SEE YOUR FRIEND.

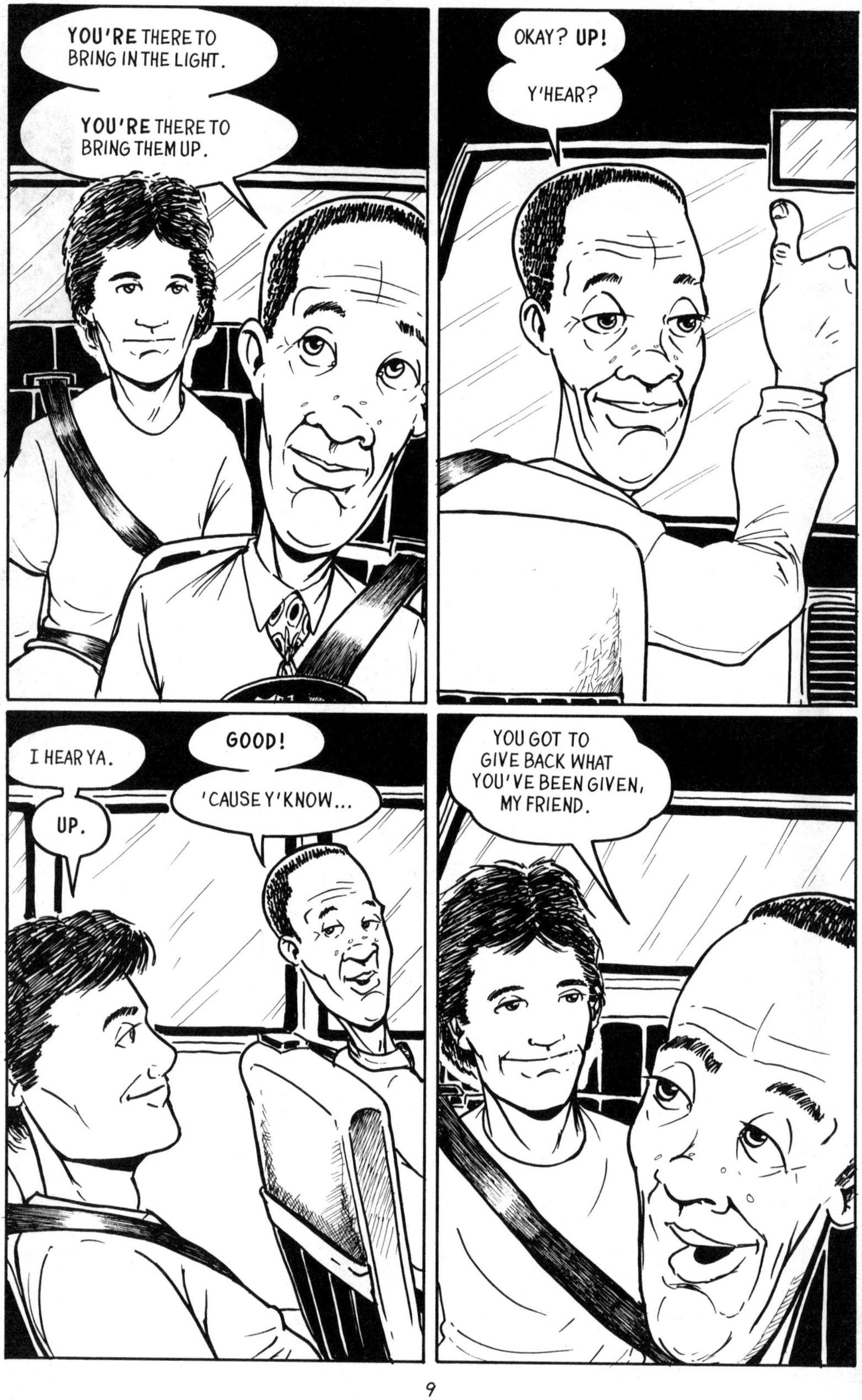
YOU'RE THERE TO BRING IN THE LIGHT.
YOU'RE THERE TO BRING THEM UP.
OKAY? UP!
Y'HEAR?
I HEAR YA.
UP.
GOOD!
'CAUSE Y'KNOW...
YOU GOT TO GIVE BACK WHAT YOU'VE BEEN GIVEN, MY FRIEND.

CHAPTER TWO

THIS IS WHERE I COME FROM: PART ONE

JUDD: PORTRAIT OF A CRANKY CARTOONIST AS A YOUNG MAN

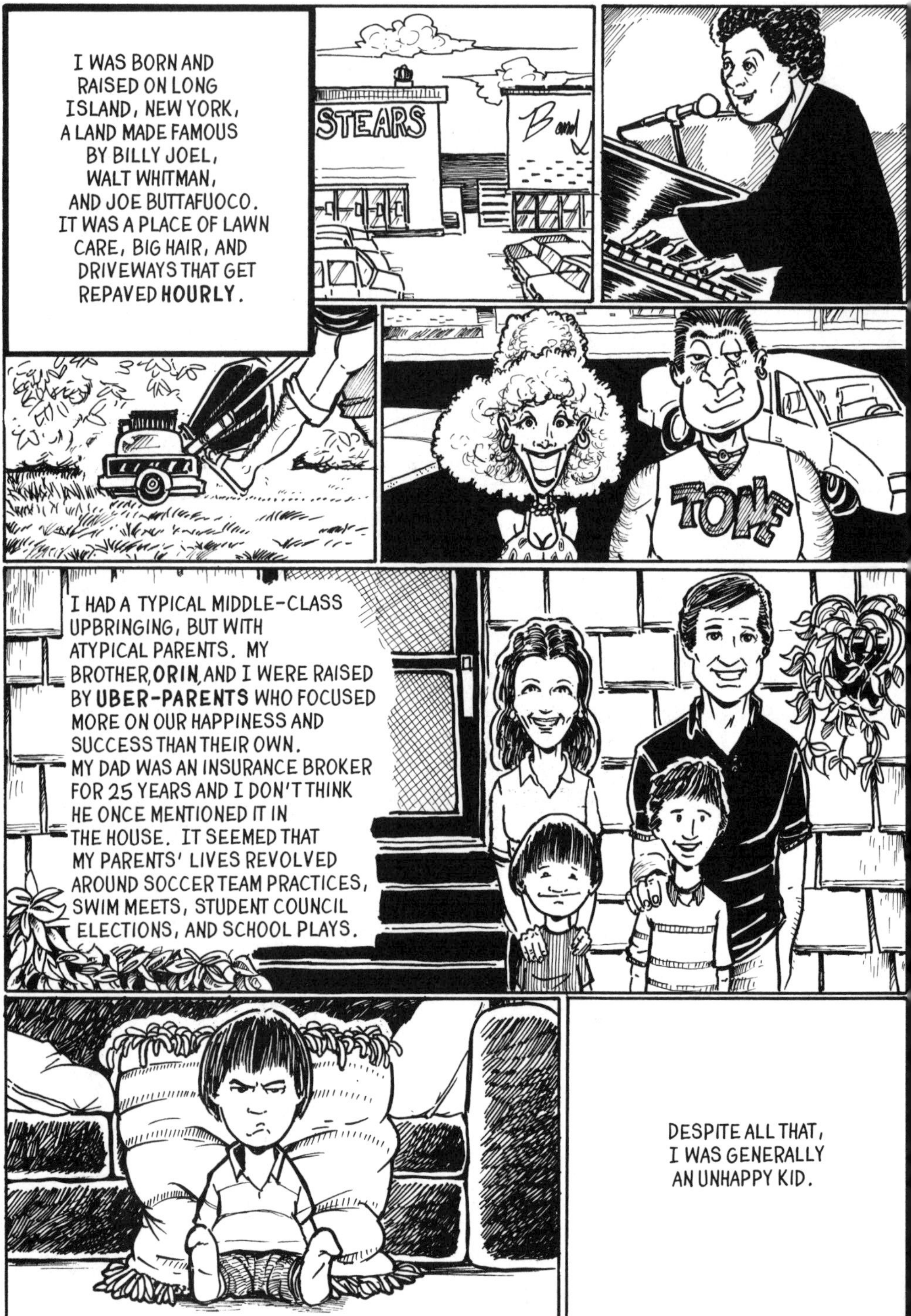
I WAS BORN AND RAISED ON LONG ISLAND, NEW YORK, A LAND MADE FAMOUS BY BILLY JOEL, WALT WHITMAN, AND JOE BUTTAFUOCO. IT WAS A PLACE OF LAWN CARE, BIG HAIR, AND DRIVEWAYS THAT GET REPAVED **HOURLY**.
STEARS
I HAD A TYPICAL MIDDLE-CLASS UPBRINGING, BUT WITH ATYPICAL PARENTS. MY BROTHER, **ORIN**, AND I WERE RAISED BY **UBER-PARENTS** WHO FOCUSED MORE ON OUR HAPPINESS AND SUCCESS THAN THEIR OWN. MY DAD WAS AN INSURANCE BROKER FOR 25 YEARS AND I DON'T THINK HE ONCE MENTIONED IT IN THE HOUSE. IT SEEMED THAT MY PARENTS' LIVES REVOLVED AROUND SOCCER TEAM PRACTICES, SWIM MEETS, STUDENT COUNCIL ELECTIONS, AND SCHOOL PLAYS.
DESPITE ALL THAT, I WAS GENERALLY AN UNHAPPY KID.

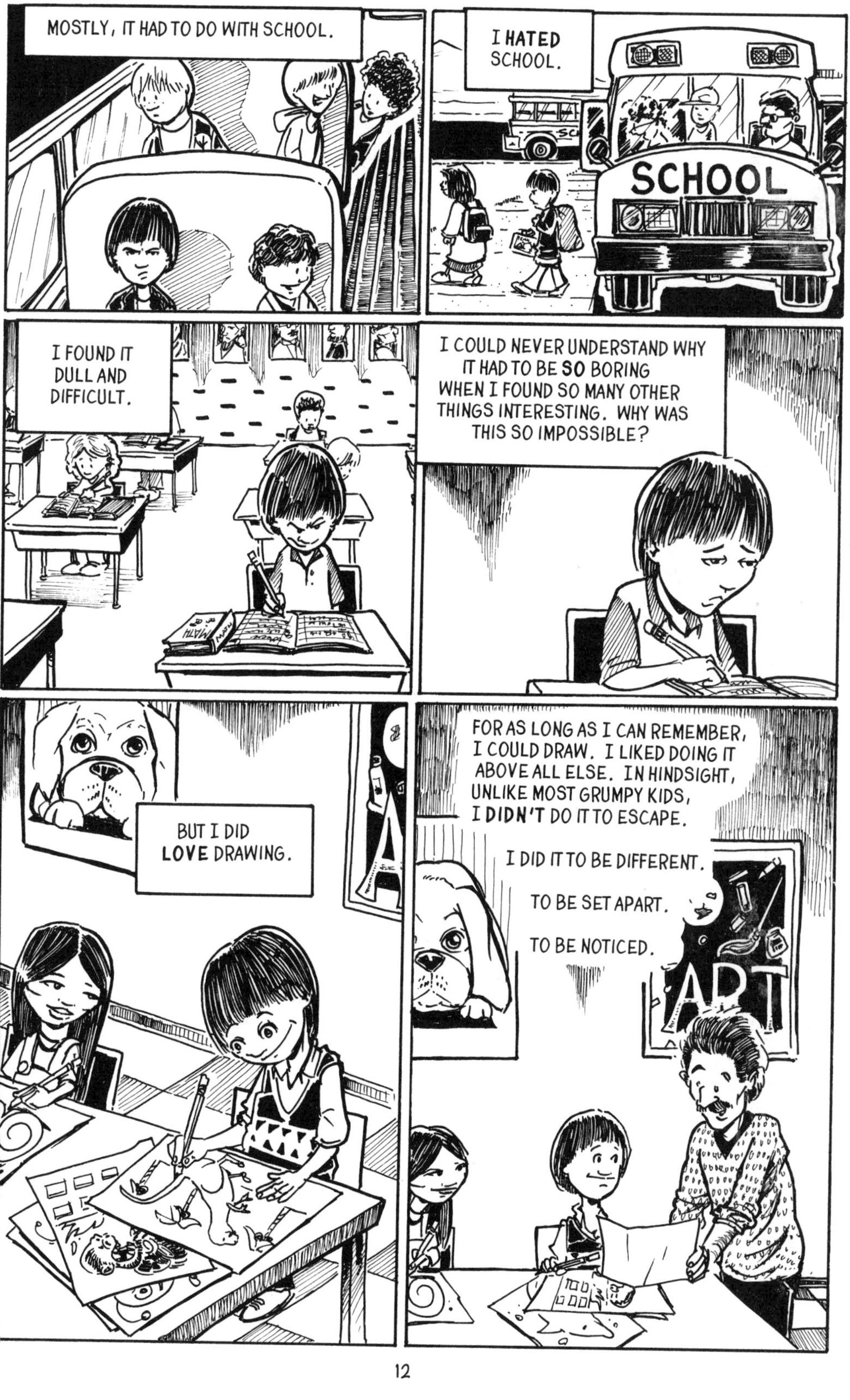
MOSTLY, IT HAD TO DO WITH SCHOOL.
I **HATED** SCHOOL.
SCHOOL
I FOUND IT DULL AND DIFFICULT.
MATH
I COULD NEVER UNDERSTAND WHY IT HAD TO BE **SO** BORING WHEN I FOUND SO MANY OTHER THINGS INTERESTING. WHY WAS THIS SO IMPOSSIBLE?
BUT I DID **LOVE** DRAWING.
FOR AS LONG AS I CAN REMEMBER, I COULD DRAW. I LIKED DOING IT ABOVE ALL ELSE. IN HINDSIGHT, UNLIKE MOST GRUMPY KIDS, I **DIDN'T** DO IT TO ESCAPE.
I DID IT TO BE DIFFERENT.
TO BE SET APART.
TO BE NOTICED.
ART

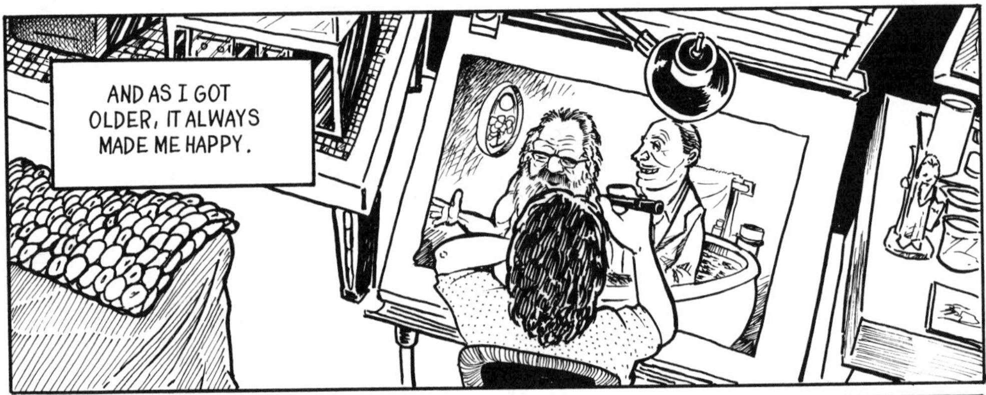
AND AS I GOT OLDER, IT ALWAYS MADE ME HAPPY.

I GREW UP IN A HOUSE OF ENCOURAGEMENT AND PASSIVE SENSITIVITY.

THE GENERAL RULE WAS TO BE NICE TO PEOPLE AND WORK HARD.

I DID BOTH. I WAS AN A-/B+ STUDENT, ON THE STUDENT COUNCIL, ON THE SOCCER TEAM, RAN TRACK, DID THE SCHOOL PLAYS, AND DID ART.

THERE WAS **ALWAYS** ART.

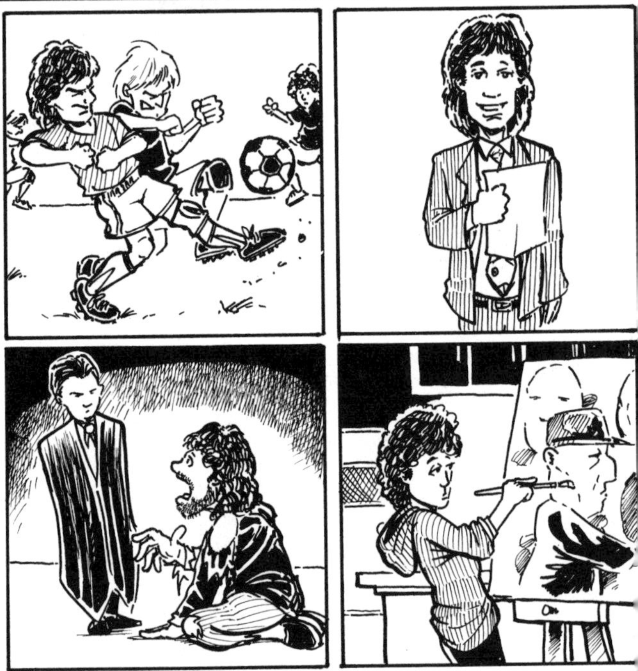

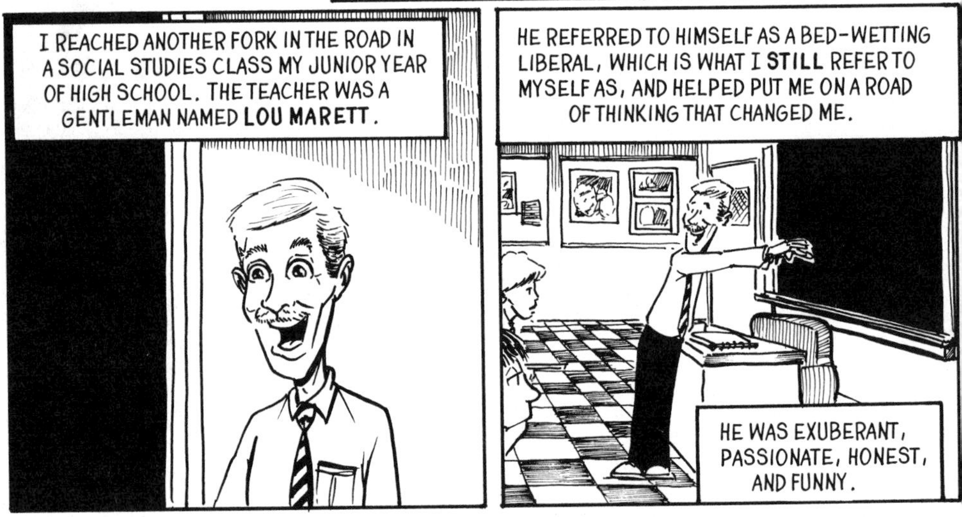
I REACHED ANOTHER FORK IN THE ROAD IN A SOCIAL STUDIES CLASS MY JUNIOR YEAR OF HIGH SCHOOL. THE TEACHER WAS A GENTLEMAN NAMED LOU MARETT.
HE REFERRED TO HIMSELF AS A BED-WETTING LIBERAL, WHICH IS WHAT I STILL REFER TO MYSELF AS, AND HELPED PUT ME ON A ROAD OF THINKING THAT CHANGED ME.
HE WAS EXUBERANT, PASSIONATE, HONEST, AND FUNNY.

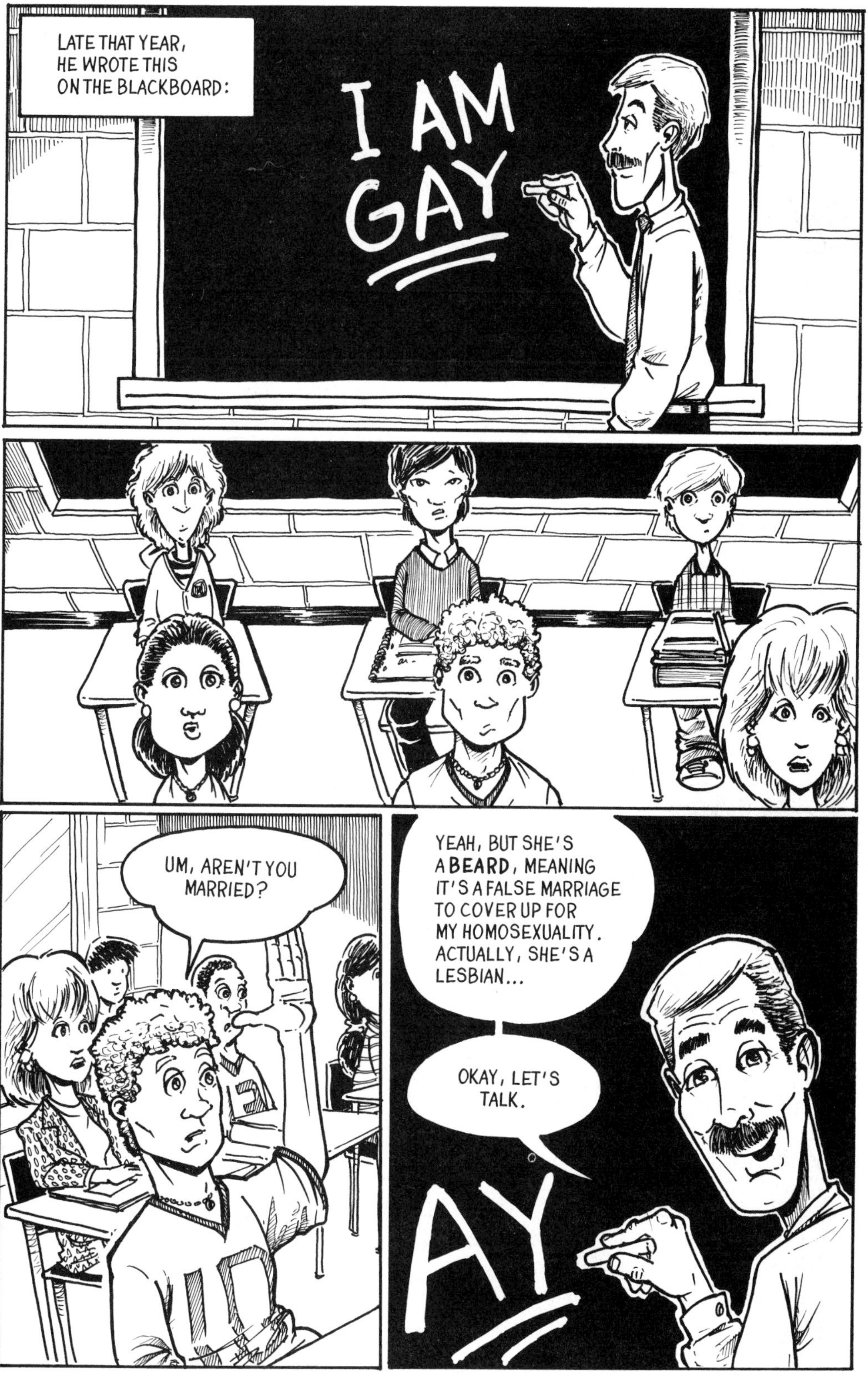

LATE THAT YEAR, HE WROTE THIS ON THE BLACKBOARD:
I AM GAY
UM, AREN'T YOU MARRIED?
YEAH, BUT SHE'S A **BEARD**, MEANING IT'S A FALSE MARRIAGE TO COVER UP FOR MY HOMOSEXUALITY. ACTUALLY, SHE'S A LESBIAN...
OKAY, LET'S TALK.

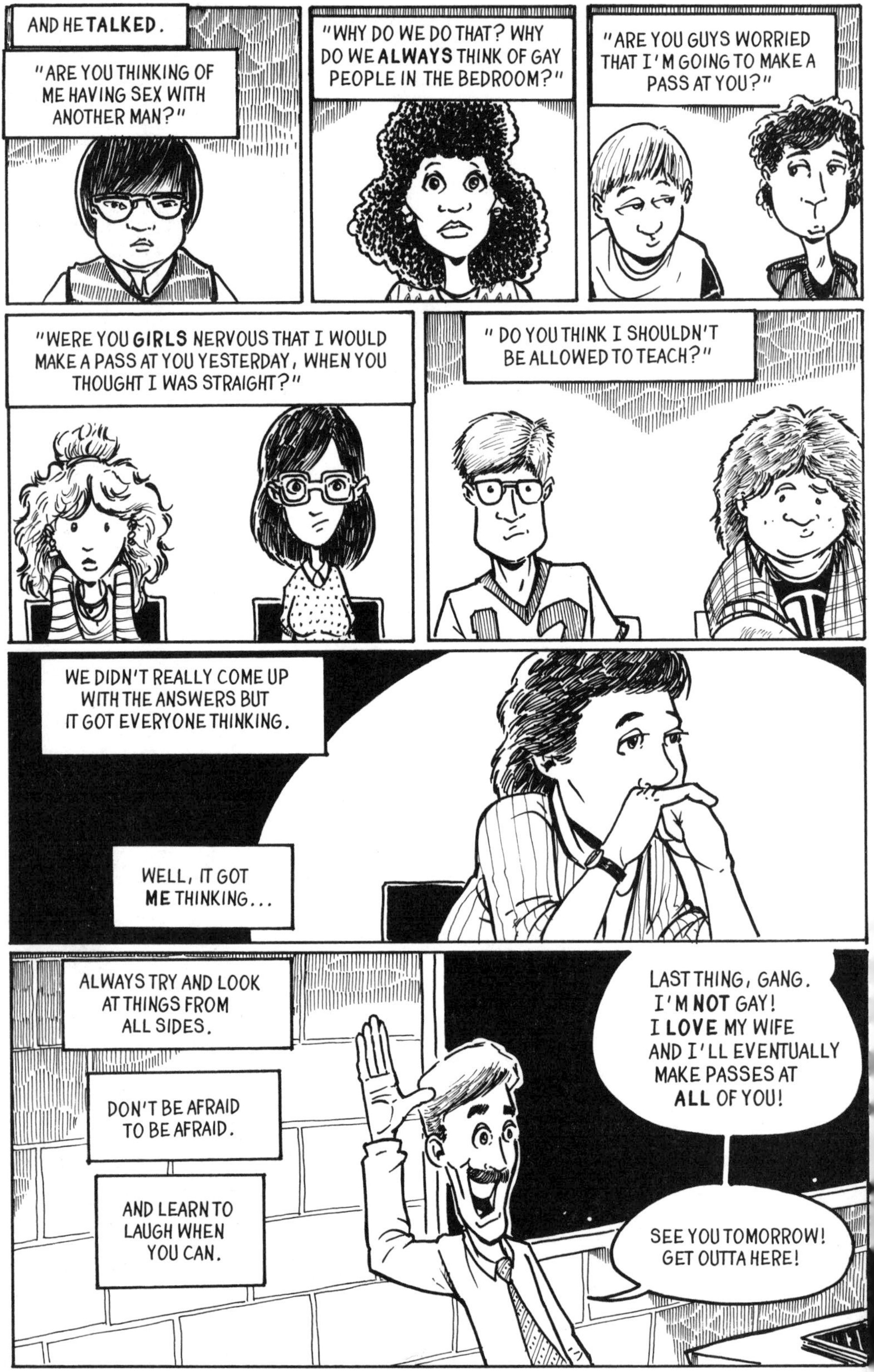
AND HE **TALKED**.
"ARE YOU THINKING OF ME HAVING SEX WITH ANOTHER MAN?"
"WHY DO WE DO THAT? WHY DO WE **ALWAYS** THINK OF GAY PEOPLE IN THE BEDROOM?"
"ARE YOU GUYS WORRIED THAT I'M GOING TO MAKE A PASS AT YOU?"
"WERE YOU **GIRLS** NERVOUS THAT I WOULD MAKE A PASS AT YOU YESTERDAY, WHEN YOU THOUGHT I WAS STRAIGHT?"
"DO YOU THINK I SHOULDN'T BE ALLOWED TO TEACH?"
WE DIDN'T REALLY COME UP WITH THE ANSWERS BUT IT GOT EVERYONE THINKING.
WELL, IT GOT **ME** THINKING...
ALWAYS TRY AND LOOK AT THINGS FROM ALL SIDES.
DON'T BE AFRAID TO BE AFRAID.
AND LEARN TO LAUGH WHEN YOU CAN.
LAST THING, GANG. I'M **NOT** GAY! I **LOVE** MY WIFE AND I'LL EVENTUALLY MAKE PASSES AT **ALL** OF YOU!
SEE YOU TOMORROW! GET OUTTA HERE!

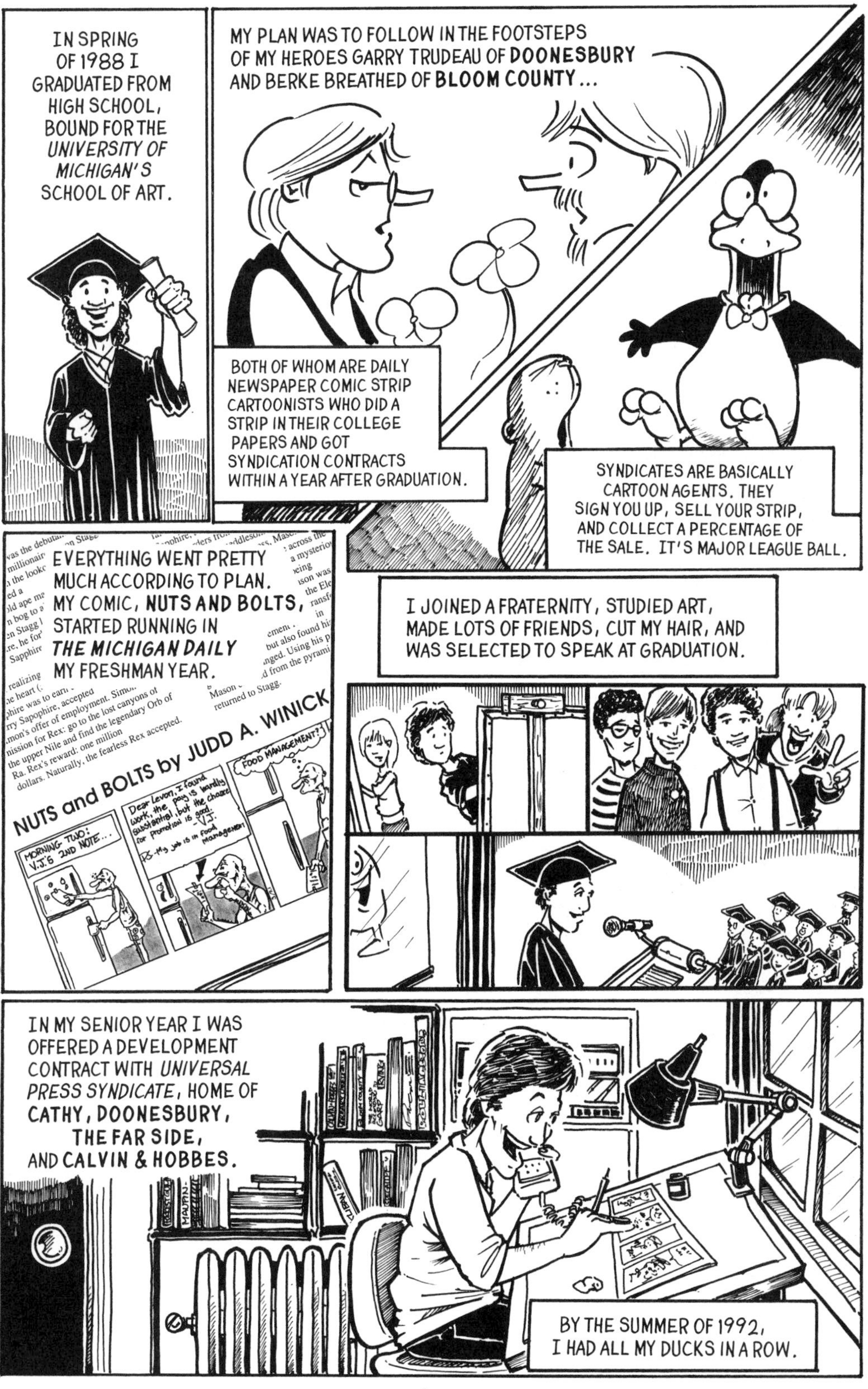

IN SPRING OF 1988 I GRADUATED FROM HIGH SCHOOL, BOUND FOR THE *UNIVERSITY OF MICHIGAN'S* SCHOOL OF ART.
MY PLAN WAS TO FOLLOW IN THE FOOTSTEPS OF MY HEROES GARRY TRUDEAU OF **DOONESBURY** AND BERKE BREATHED OF **BLOOM COUNTY**...
BOTH OF WHOM ARE DAILY NEWSPAPER COMIC STRIP CARTOONISTS WHO DID A STRIP IN THEIR COLLEGE PAPERS AND GOT SYNDICATION CONTRACTS WITHIN A YEAR AFTER GRADUATION.
SYNDICATES ARE BASICALLY CARTOON AGENTS. THEY SIGN YOU UP, SELL YOUR STRIP, AND COLLECT A PERCENTAGE OF THE SALE. IT'S MAJOR LEAGUE BALL.
EVERYTHING WENT PRETTY MUCH ACCORDING TO PLAN. MY COMIC, **NUTS AND BOLTS,** STARTED RUNNING IN ***THE MICHIGAN DAILY*** MY FRESHMAN YEAR.
NUTS and BOLTS by JUDD A. WINICK
MORNING TWO: V.J.'S 2ND NOTE...
Dear Levon, I found work, the pay is hardly substantial but the chance for promotion is good. -V.J.
P.S.-My job is in food management
FOOD MANAGEMENT?
I JOINED A FRATERNITY, STUDIED ART, MADE LOTS OF FRIENDS, CUT MY HAIR, AND WAS SELECTED TO SPEAK AT GRADUATION.
IN MY SENIOR YEAR I WAS OFFERED A DEVELOPMENT CONTRACT WITH *UNIVERSAL PRESS SYNDICATE*, HOME OF **CATHY, DOONESBURY, THE FAR SIDE,** AND **CALVIN & HOBBES.**
BY THE SUMMER OF 1992, I HAD ALL MY DUCKS IN A ROW.

1993: JUDD

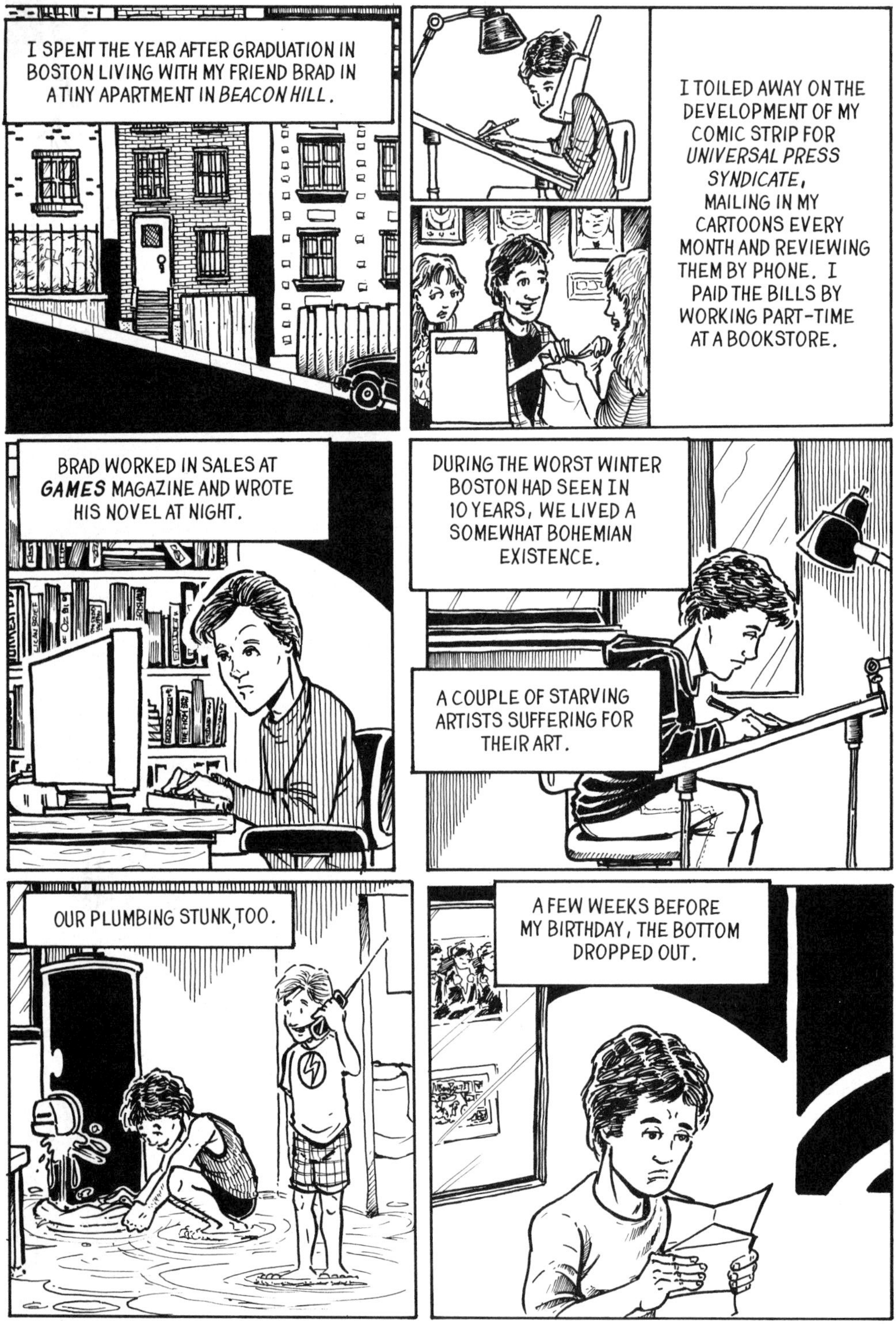
I SPENT THE YEAR AFTER GRADUATION IN BOSTON LIVING WITH MY FRIEND BRAD IN A TINY APARTMENT IN *BEACON HILL*.
I TOILED AWAY ON THE DEVELOPMENT OF MY COMIC STRIP FOR *UNIVERSAL PRESS SYNDICATE*, MAILING IN MY CARTOONS EVERY MONTH AND REVIEWING THEM BY PHONE. I PAID THE BILLS BY WORKING PART-TIME AT A BOOKSTORE.
BRAD WORKED IN SALES AT ***GAMES*** MAGAZINE AND WROTE HIS NOVEL AT NIGHT.
DURING THE WORST WINTER BOSTON HAD SEEN IN 10 YEARS, WE LIVED A SOMEWHAT BOHEMIAN EXISTENCE.
A COUPLE OF STARVING ARTISTS SUFFERING FOR THEIR ART.
OUR PLUMBING STUNK, TOO.
A FEW WEEKS BEFORE MY BIRTHDAY, THE BOTTOM DROPPED OUT.

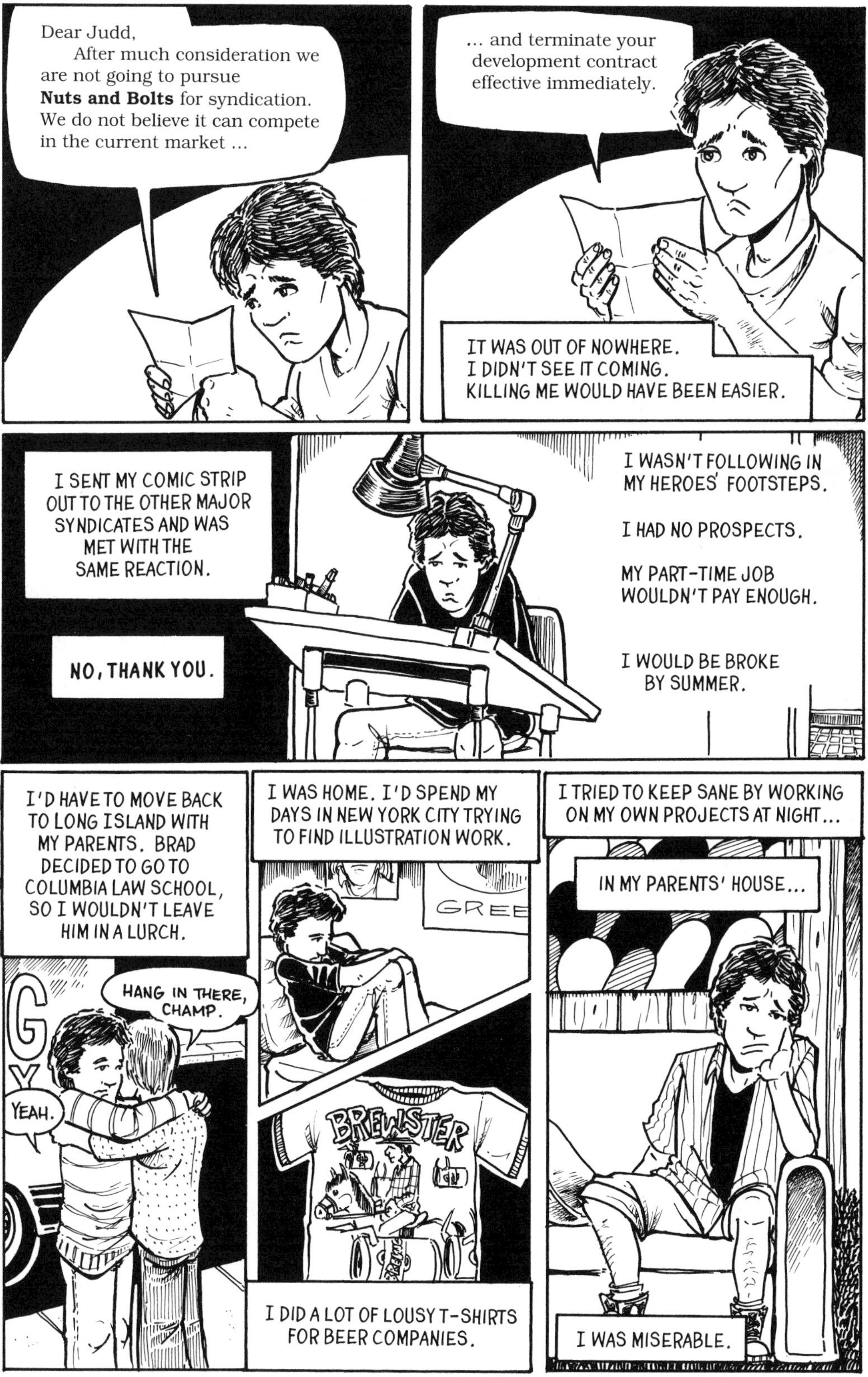

Dear Judd,
After much consideration we are not going to pursue **Nuts and Bolts** for syndication. We do not believe it can compete in the current market ...
... and terminate your development contract effective immediately.
IT WAS OUT OF NOWHERE. I DIDN'T SEE IT COMING. KILLING ME WOULD HAVE BEEN EASIER.
I SENT MY COMIC STRIP OUT TO THE OTHER MAJOR SYNDICATES AND WAS MET WITH THE SAME REACTION.
NO, THANK YOU.
I WASN'T FOLLOWING IN MY HEROES' FOOTSTEPS.
I HAD NO PROSPECTS.
MY PART-TIME JOB WOULDN'T PAY ENOUGH.
I WOULD BE BROKE BY SUMMER.
I'D HAVE TO MOVE BACK TO LONG ISLAND WITH MY PARENTS. BRAD DECIDED TO GO TO COLUMBIA LAW SCHOOL, SO I WOULDN'T LEAVE HIM IN A LURCH.
HANG IN THERE, CHAMP.
YEAH.
I WAS HOME. I'D SPEND MY DAYS IN NEW YORK CITY TRYING TO FIND ILLUSTRATION WORK.
GREE
BREWSTER
I DID A LOT OF LOUSY T-SHIRTS FOR BEER COMPANIES.
I TRIED TO KEEP SANE BY WORKING ON MY OWN PROJECTS AT NIGHT...
IN MY PARENTS' HOUSE...
I WAS MISERABLE.

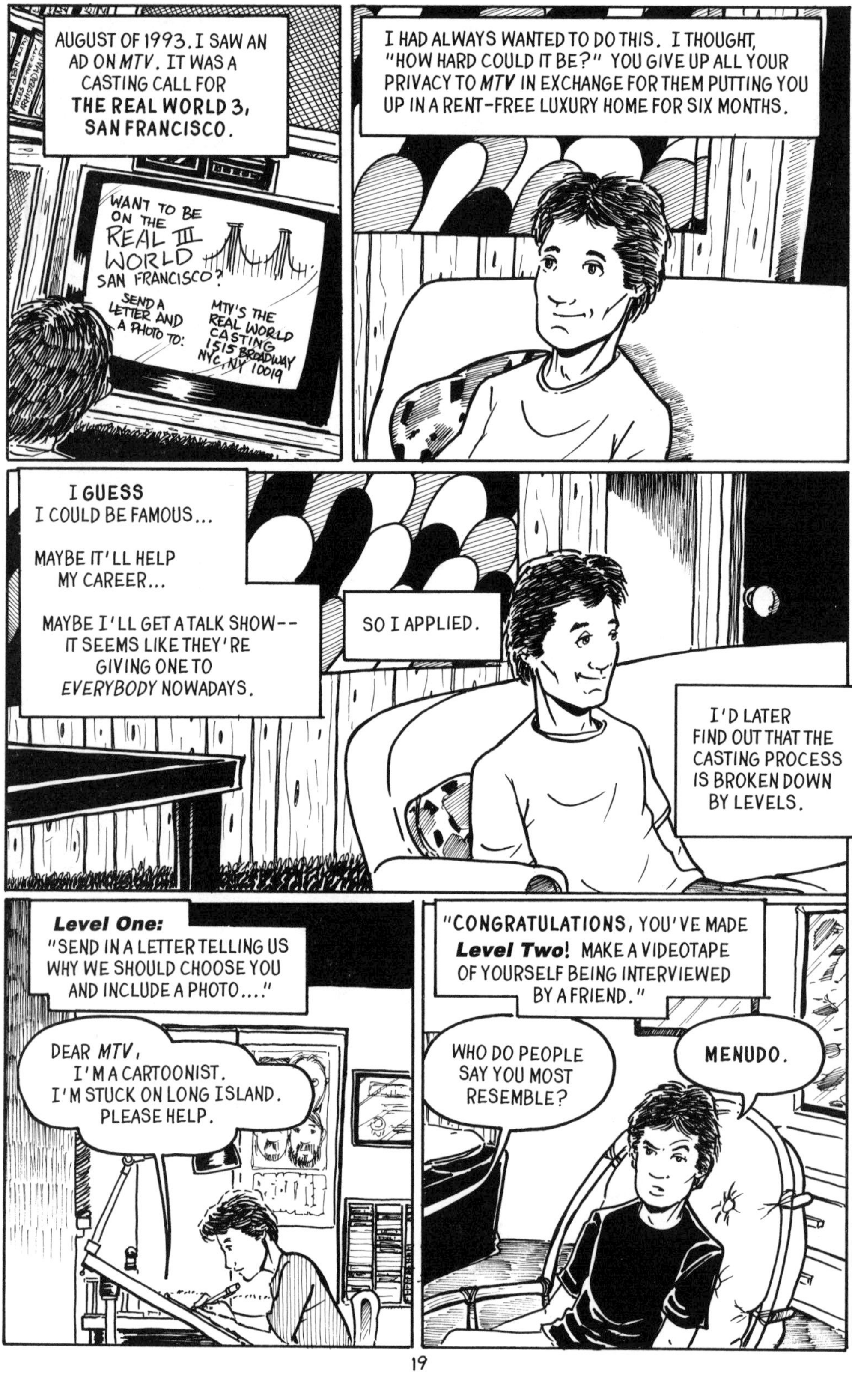
AUGUST OF 1993. I SAW AN AD ON *MTV*. IT WAS A CASTING CALL FOR **THE REAL WORLD 3, SAN FRANCISCO**.
WANT TO BE ON THE REAL III WORLD SAN FRANCISCO?
SEND A LETTER AND A PHOTO TO:
MTV'S THE REAL WORLD CASTING 1515 BROADWAY NYC, NY 10019
I HAD ALWAYS WANTED TO DO THIS. I THOUGHT, "HOW HARD COULD IT BE?" YOU GIVE UP ALL YOUR PRIVACY TO *MTV* IN EXCHANGE FOR THEM PUTTING YOU UP IN A RENT-FREE LUXURY HOME FOR SIX MONTHS.
I **GUESS** I COULD BE FAMOUS...
MAYBE IT'LL HELP MY CAREER...
MAYBE I'LL GET A TALK SHOW-- IT SEEMS LIKE THEY'RE GIVING ONE TO *EVERYBODY* NOWADAYS.
SO I APPLIED.
I'D LATER FIND OUT THAT THE CASTING PROCESS IS BROKEN DOWN BY LEVELS.
Level One: "SEND IN A LETTER TELLING US WHY WE SHOULD CHOOSE YOU AND INCLUDE A PHOTO...."
DEAR *MTV*, I'M A CARTOONIST. I'M STUCK ON LONG ISLAND. PLEASE HELP.
"**CONGRATULATIONS**, YOU'VE MADE ***Level Two***! MAKE A VIDEOTAPE OF YOURSELF BEING INTERVIEWED BY A FRIEND."
WHO DO PEOPLE SAY YOU MOST RESEMBLE?
MENUDO.

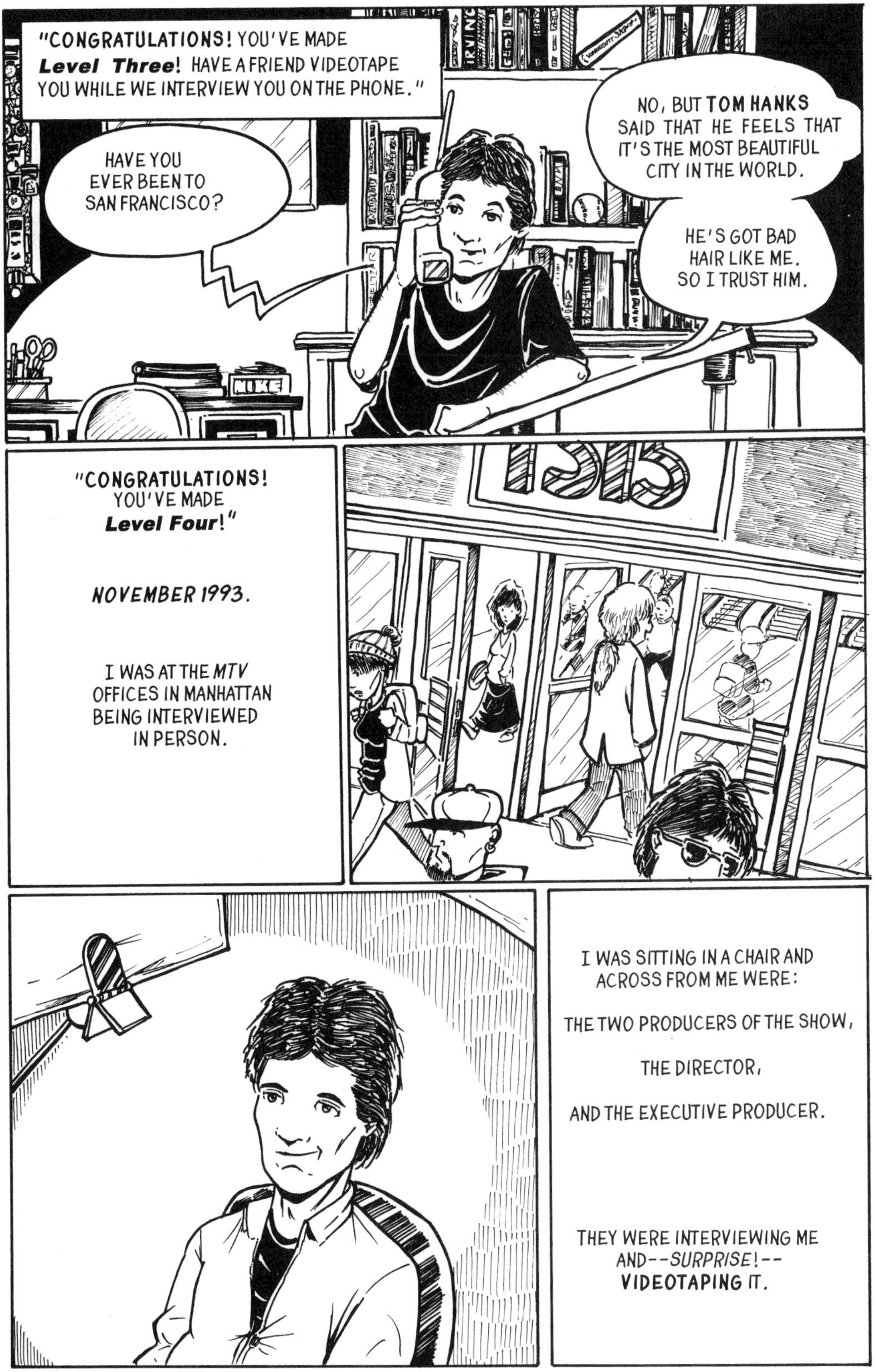
"CONGRATULATIONS! YOU'VE MADE **Level Three**! HAVE A FRIEND VIDEOTAPE YOU WHILE WE INTERVIEW YOU ON THE PHONE."
HAVE YOU EVER BEEN TO SAN FRANCISCO?
NO, BUT **TOM HANKS** SAID THAT HE FEELS THAT IT'S THE MOST BEAUTIFUL CITY IN THE WORLD.
HE'S GOT BAD HAIR LIKE ME. SO I TRUST HIM.
NIKE
"CONGRATULATIONS! YOU'VE MADE **Level Four**!"
NOVEMBER 1993.
I WAS AT THE *MTV* OFFICES IN MANHATTAN BEING INTERVIEWED IN PERSON.
1515
I WAS SITTING IN A CHAIR AND ACROSS FROM ME WERE:
THE TWO PRODUCERS OF THE SHOW,
THE DIRECTOR,
AND THE EXECUTIVE PRODUCER.
THEY WERE INTERVIEWING ME AND--*SURPRISE*!-- **VIDEOTAPING** IT.

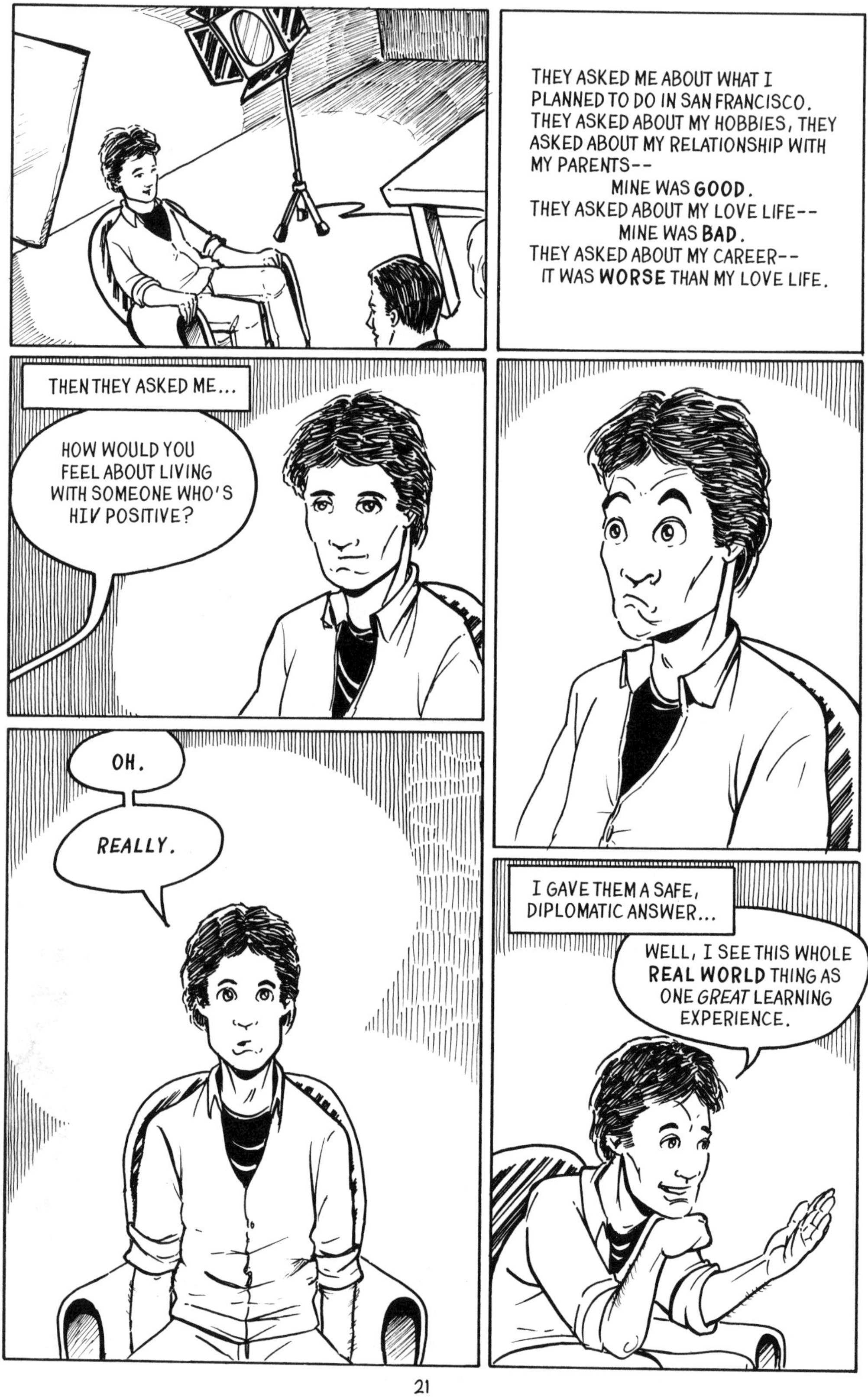
THEY ASKED ME ABOUT WHAT I PLANNED TO DO IN SAN FRANCISCO. THEY ASKED ABOUT MY HOBBIES, THEY ASKED ABOUT MY RELATIONSHIP WITH MY PARENTS--
MINE WAS **GOOD**.
THEY ASKED ABOUT MY LOVE LIFE--
MINE WAS **BAD**.
THEY ASKED ABOUT MY CAREER--
IT WAS **WORSE** THAN MY LOVE LIFE.
THEN THEY ASKED ME...
HOW WOULD YOU FEEL ABOUT LIVING WITH SOMEONE WHO'S HIV POSITIVE?
OH.
REALLY.
I GAVE THEM A SAFE, DIPLOMATIC ANSWER...
WELL, I SEE THIS WHOLE **REAL WORLD** THING AS ONE *GREAT* LEARNING EXPERIENCE.

AND I'M GOING TO BE LIVING WITH SIX OTHER PEOPLE FROM DIVERSE BACKGROUNDS...

SO I'LL OBVIOUSLY HAVE HAD **DIFFERENT** EXPERIENCES.

AND I DON'T REALLY KNOW ANYONE WHO'S HIV POSITIVE, AT LEAST **PERSONALLY**. SO THAT SORT OF LIFE EXPERIENCE IS SOMETHING THAT I'M MORE THAN WILLING TO LEARN --

I CA
BUT
NE

BLAH, BLAH, BLAH, BLAH!

BLAH! BLAH! BLAH!
BLAH! BLAH! BLA
BLAH! BLAH! BLA
BLAH! BLAH! BLA

WHAT I'M ACTUALLY THINKING IS...

JESUS H. CHRIST. I'M GOING TO BE LIVING WITH SOMEONE WHO HAS **AIDS**...

BLAH
BLAH BL
BLAH BL
BLAH BLA

I HAD NOT FIGURED ON THIS.

22

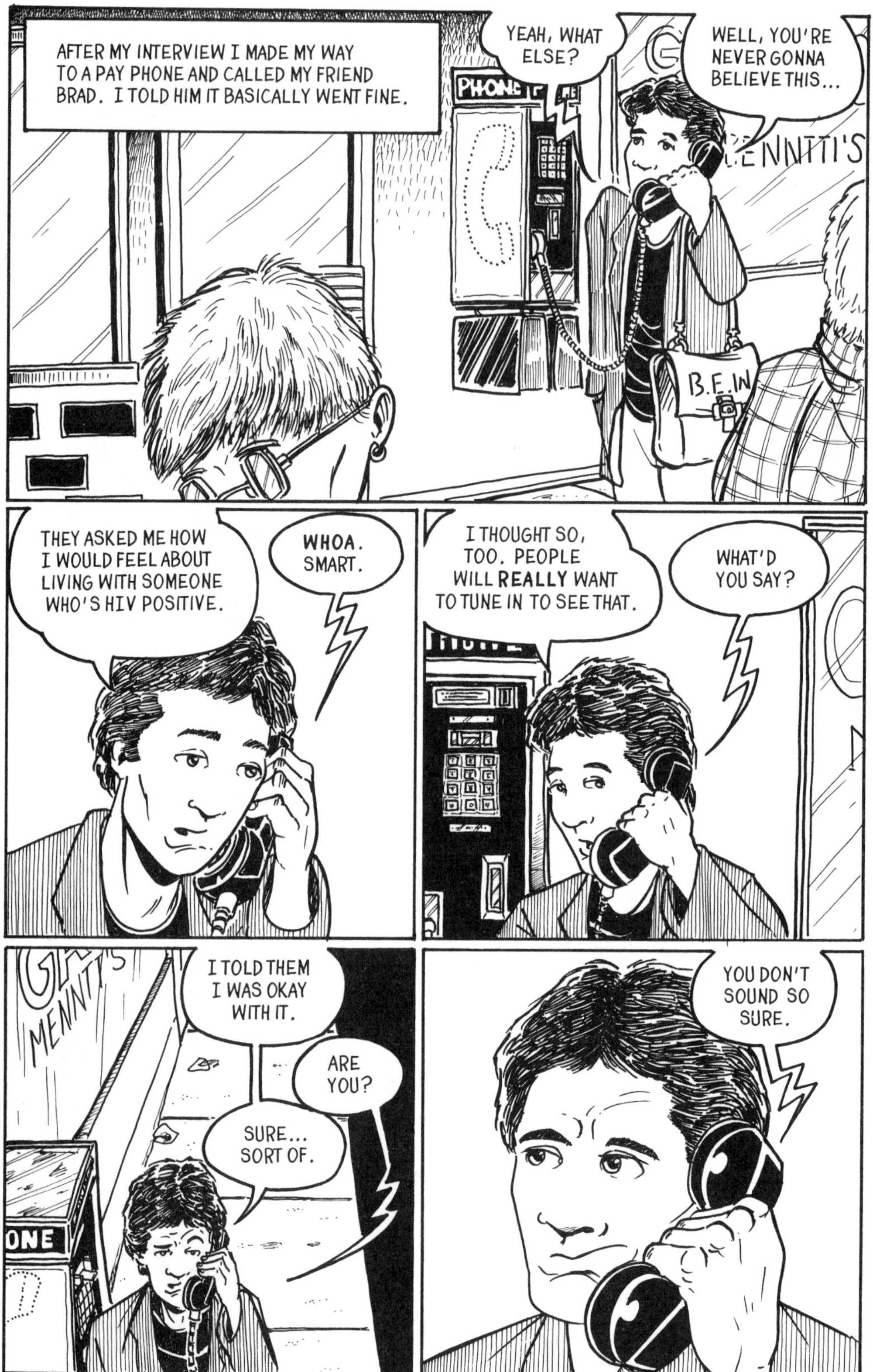
AFTER MY INTERVIEW I MADE MY WAY TO A PAY PHONE AND CALLED MY FRIEND BRAD. I TOLD HIM IT BASICALLY WENT FINE.
YEAH, WHAT ELSE?
WELL, YOU'RE NEVER GONNA BELIEVE THIS...
PHONE
B.E.W.
THEY ASKED ME HOW I WOULD FEEL ABOUT LIVING WITH SOMEONE WHO'S HIV POSITIVE.
WHOA. SMART.
I THOUGHT SO, TOO. PEOPLE WILL REALLY WANT TO TUNE IN TO SEE THAT.
WHAT'D YOU SAY?
I TOLD THEM I WAS OKAY WITH IT.
ARE YOU?
SURE... SORT OF.
YOU DON'T SOUND SO SURE.

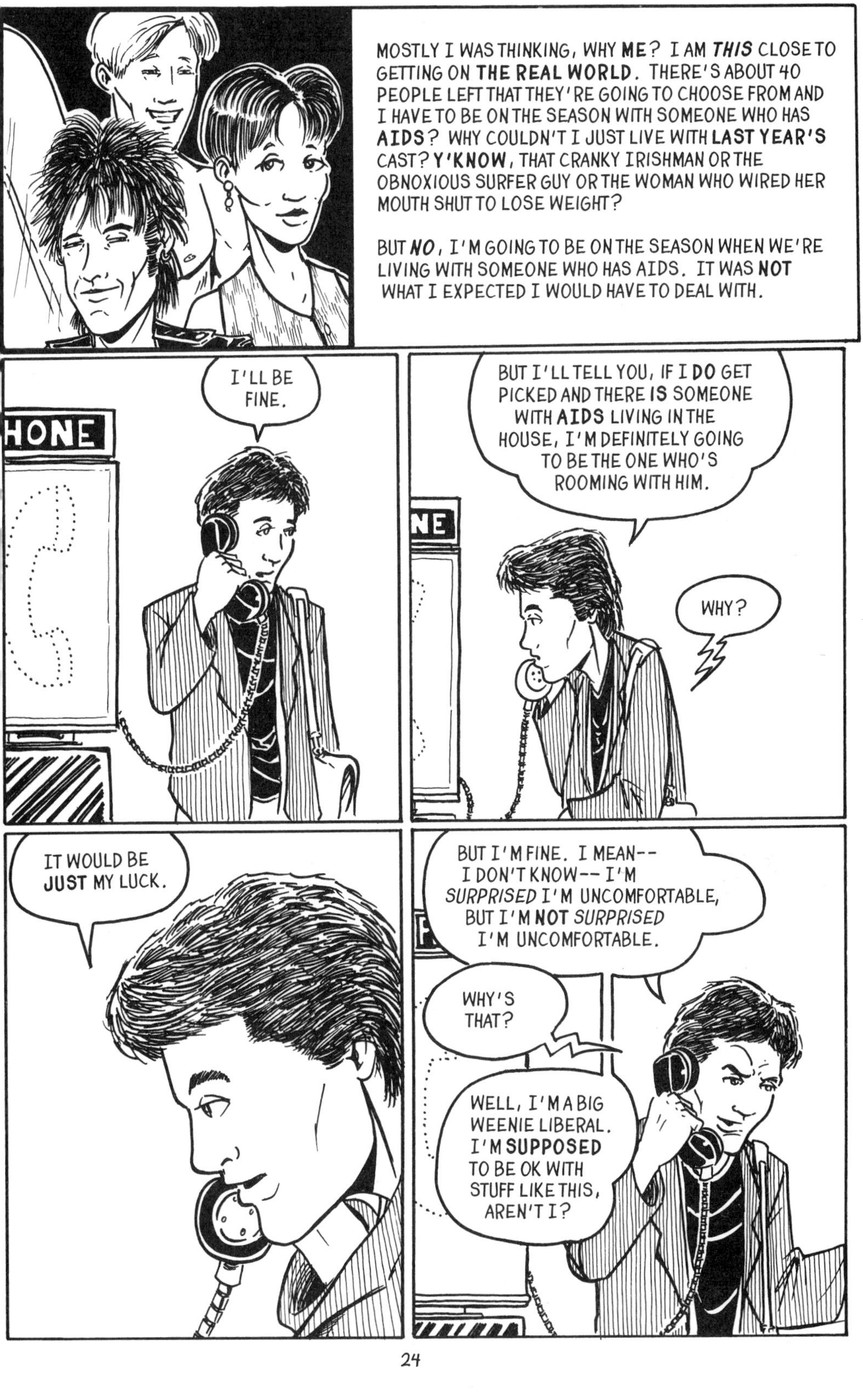
MOSTLY I WAS THINKING, WHY ME? I AM THIS CLOSE TO GETTING ON THE REAL WORLD. THERE'S ABOUT 40 PEOPLE LEFT THAT THEY'RE GOING TO CHOOSE FROM AND I HAVE TO BE ON THE SEASON WITH SOMEONE WHO HAS AIDS? WHY COULDN'T I JUST LIVE WITH LAST YEAR'S CAST? Y'KNOW, THAT CRANKY IRISHMAN OR THE OBNOXIOUS SURFER GUY OR THE WOMAN WHO WIRED HER MOUTH SHUT TO LOSE WEIGHT?
BUT NO, I'M GOING TO BE ON THE SEASON WHEN WE'RE LIVING WITH SOMEONE WHO HAS AIDS. IT WAS NOT WHAT I EXPECTED I WOULD HAVE TO DEAL WITH.
HONE
I'LL BE FINE.
BUT I'LL TELL YOU, IF I DO GET PICKED AND THERE IS SOMEONE WITH AIDS LIVING IN THE HOUSE, I'M DEFINITELY GOING TO BE THE ONE WHO'S ROOMING WITH HIM.
NE
WHY?
IT WOULD BE JUST MY LUCK.
BUT I'M FINE. I MEAN-- I DON'T KNOW-- I'M SURPRISED I'M UNCOMFORTABLE, BUT I'M NOT SURPRISED I'M UNCOMFORTABLE.
WHY'S THAT?
WELL, I'M A BIG WEENIE LIBERAL. I'M SUPPOSED TO BE OK WITH STUFF LIKE THIS, AREN'T I?

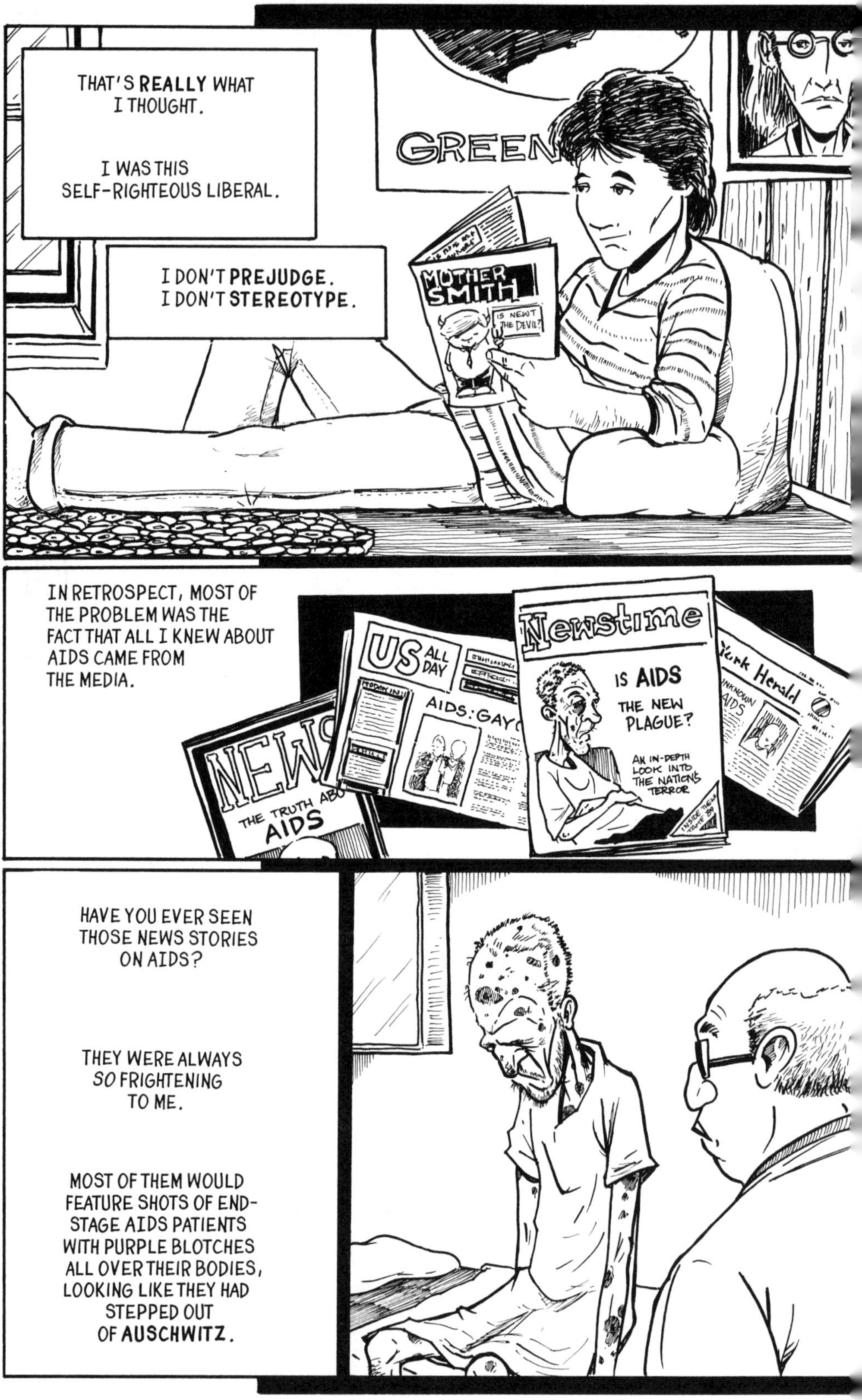

THAT'S **REALLY** WHAT I THOUGHT.
I WAS THIS SELF-RIGHTEOUS LIBERAL.
I DON'T **PREJUDGE**. I DON'T **STEREOTYPE**.
GREEN
MOTHER SMITH
IS NEWT THE DEVIL?
IN RETROSPECT, MOST OF THE PROBLEM WAS THE FACT THAT ALL I KNEW ABOUT AIDS CAME FROM THE MEDIA.
NEWS
THE TRUTH ABO
AIDS
US ALL DAY
AIDS: GAY
Newstime
IS AIDS THE NEW PLAGUE?
AN IN-DEPTH LOOK INTO THE NATION'S TERROR
York Herald
UNKNOWN AIDS
HAVE YOU EVER SEEN THOSE NEWS STORIES ON AIDS?
THEY WERE ALWAYS *SO* FRIGHTENING TO ME.
MOST OF THEM WOULD FEATURE SHOTS OF END-STAGE AIDS PATIENTS WITH PURPLE BLOTCHES ALL OVER THEIR BODIES, LOOKING LIKE THEY HAD STEPPED OUT OF **AUSCHWITZ**.

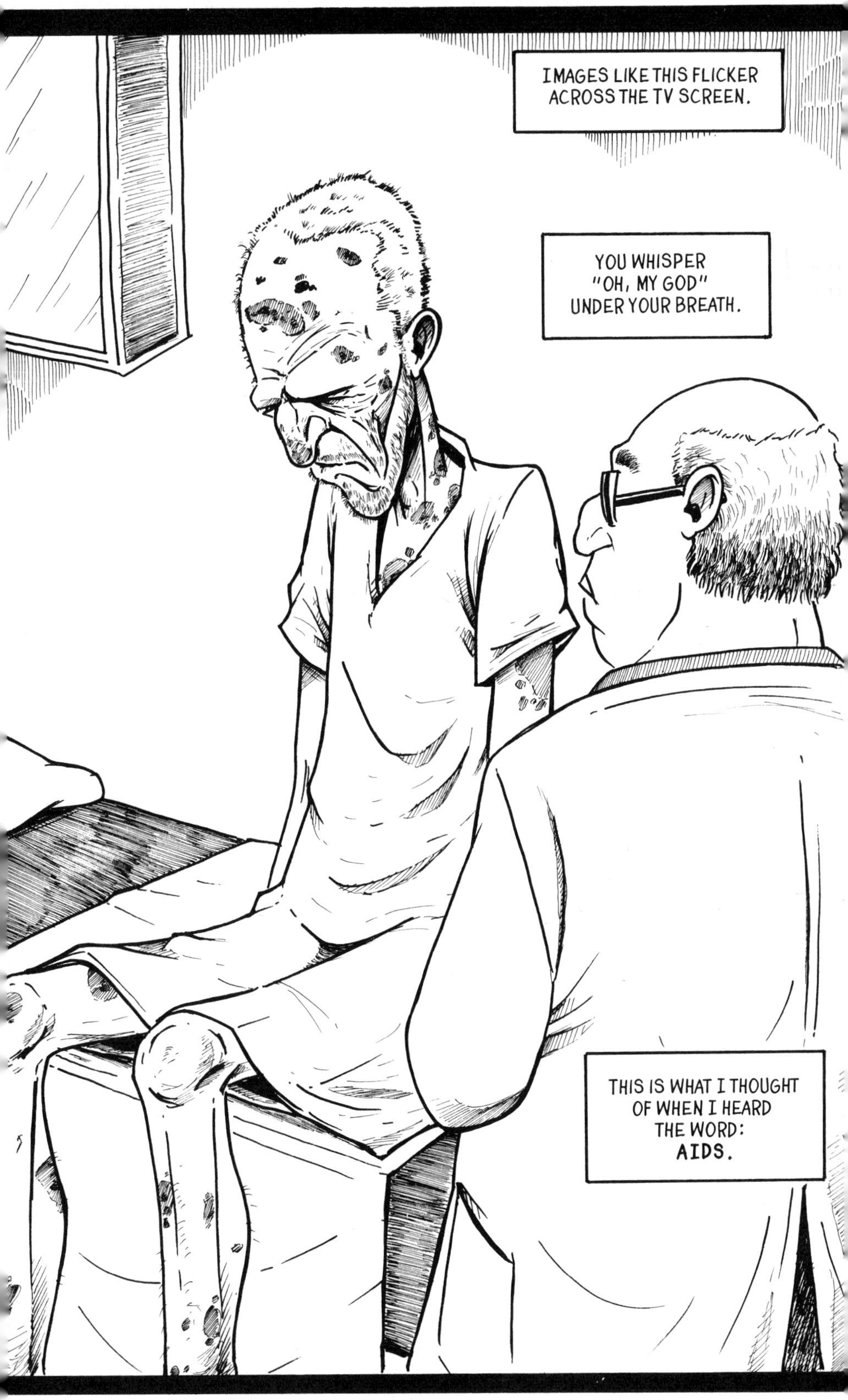
IMAGES LIKE THIS FLICKER ACROSS THE TV SCREEN.
YOU WHISPER "OH, MY GOD" UNDER YOUR BREATH.
THIS IS WHAT I THOUGHT OF WHEN I HEARD THE WORD: AIDS.

THE OTHER IMAGES OF AIDS I GOT WERE THE DRAMATIZED ONES, THE ONE OR TWO TV MOVIES OR PLOT LINES ON SHOWS THAT INVOLVED AIDS.

THEY WERE ALWAYS SO WEIRD. THEY HAD THIS CONSTANT AIR OF DOOM AND DESOLATION. THIS COMBINED WITH THE FACT THAT THE CHARACTERS (ALWAYS GAY MEN) **NEVER** TOUCHED EACH OTHER.

OR ANYONE ELSE...

IT CREATED DISTANCE.

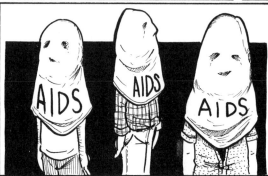

AIDS

AIDS

AIDS

ALL THIS WAS FURTHERED BY THE FACT THAT I DIDN'T KNOW ANYONE WITH HIV. WHEN I THOUGHT OF PEOPLE WITH AIDS, THAT'S ALL I SAW:

AIDS.
LIKE A *SHROUD.*

MORNIN'.

HEY.

WHEN I THOUGHT OF LIVING WITH SOMEONE WHO HAD HIV, I ENVISIONED LIVING WITH THE AIDS VIRUS WALKING AROUND ON TWO LEGS.

STEREOTYPES

SO THE BLEEDING HEART LIBERAL WAS WALKING AROUND WITH BIG BAGFULS OF STEREOTYPES.

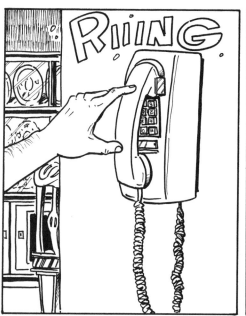

RIIING.

HELLO?

IN JANUARY OF 1994 I GOT *THE* CALL. ON THE PHONE WERE THE PRODUCERS AND THEY INVITED ME--

INVITED,

LIKE YOU'RE GONNA SAY **NO**--

THEY INVITED ME TO BECOME A CAST MEMBER OF *THE REAL WORLD 3, SAN FRANCISCO.*

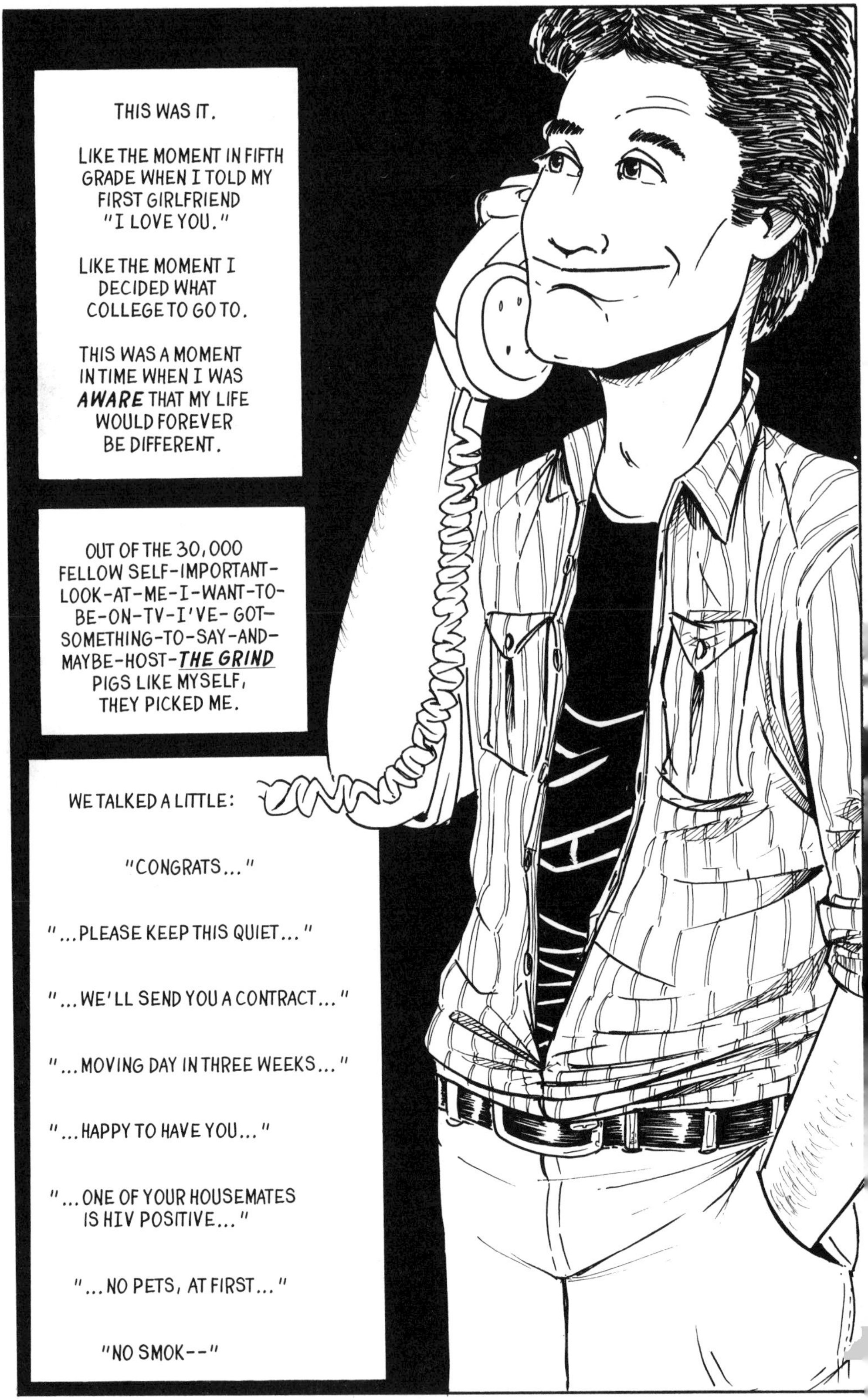
THIS WAS IT.
LIKE THE MOMENT IN FIFTH GRADE WHEN I TOLD MY FIRST GIRLFRIEND "I LOVE YOU."
LIKE THE MOMENT I DECIDED WHAT COLLEGE TO GO TO.
THIS WAS A MOMENT IN TIME WHEN I WAS *AWARE* THAT MY LIFE WOULD FOREVER BE DIFFERENT.
OUT OF THE 30,000 FELLOW SELF-IMPORTANT-LOOK-AT-ME-I-WANT-TO-BE-ON-TV-I'VE-GOT-SOMETHING-TO-SAY-AND-MAYBE-HOST-*THE GRIND* PIGS LIKE MYSELF, THEY PICKED ME.
WE TALKED A LITTLE:
"CONGRATS..."
"...PLEASE KEEP THIS QUIET..."
"...WE'LL SEND YOU A CONTRACT..."
"...MOVING DAY IN THREE WEEKS..."
"...HAPPY TO HAVE YOU..."
"...ONE OF YOUR HOUSEMATES IS HIV POSITIVE..."
"...NO PETS, AT FIRST..."
"NO SMOK--"

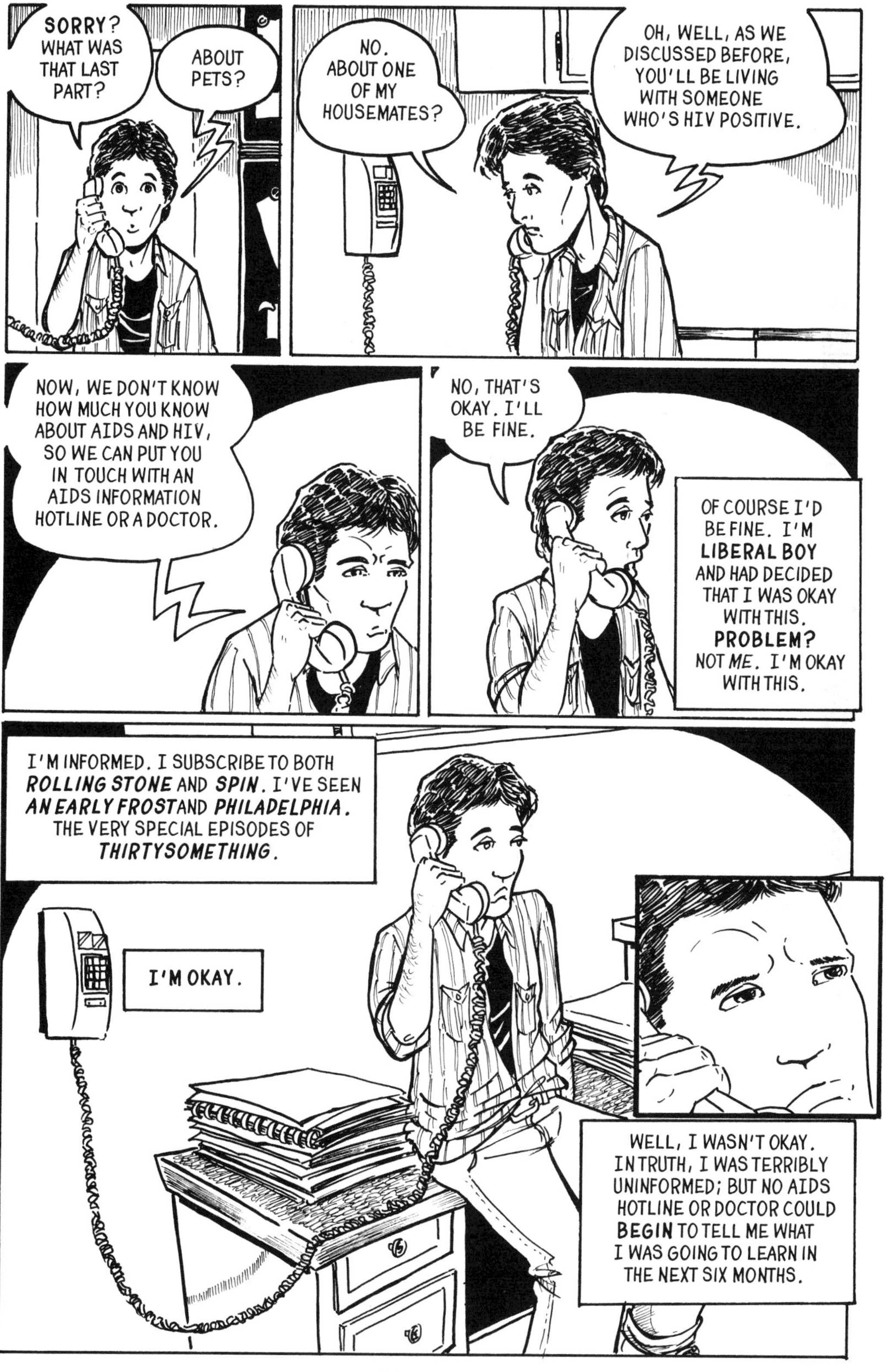
SORRY? WHAT WAS THAT LAST PART?
ABOUT PETS?
NO. ABOUT ONE OF MY HOUSEMATES?
OH, WELL, AS WE DISCUSSED BEFORE, YOU'LL BE LIVING WITH SOMEONE WHO'S HIV POSITIVE.
NOW, WE DON'T KNOW HOW MUCH YOU KNOW ABOUT AIDS AND HIV, SO WE CAN PUT YOU IN TOUCH WITH AN AIDS INFORMATION HOTLINE OR A DOCTOR.
NO, THAT'S OKAY. I'LL BE FINE.
OF COURSE I'D BE FINE. I'M LIBERAL BOY AND HAD DECIDED THAT I WAS OKAY WITH THIS. PROBLEM? NOT ME. I'M OKAY WITH THIS.
I'M INFORMED. I SUBSCRIBE TO BOTH ROLLING STONE AND SPIN. I'VE SEEN AN EARLY FROST AND PHILADELPHIA. THE VERY SPECIAL EPISODES OF THIRTYSOMETHING.
I'M OKAY.
WELL, I WASN'T OKAY. IN TRUTH, I WAS TERRIBLY UNINFORMED; BUT NO AIDS HOTLINE OR DOCTOR COULD BEGIN TO TELL ME WHAT I WAS GOING TO LEARN IN THE NEXT SIX MONTHS.

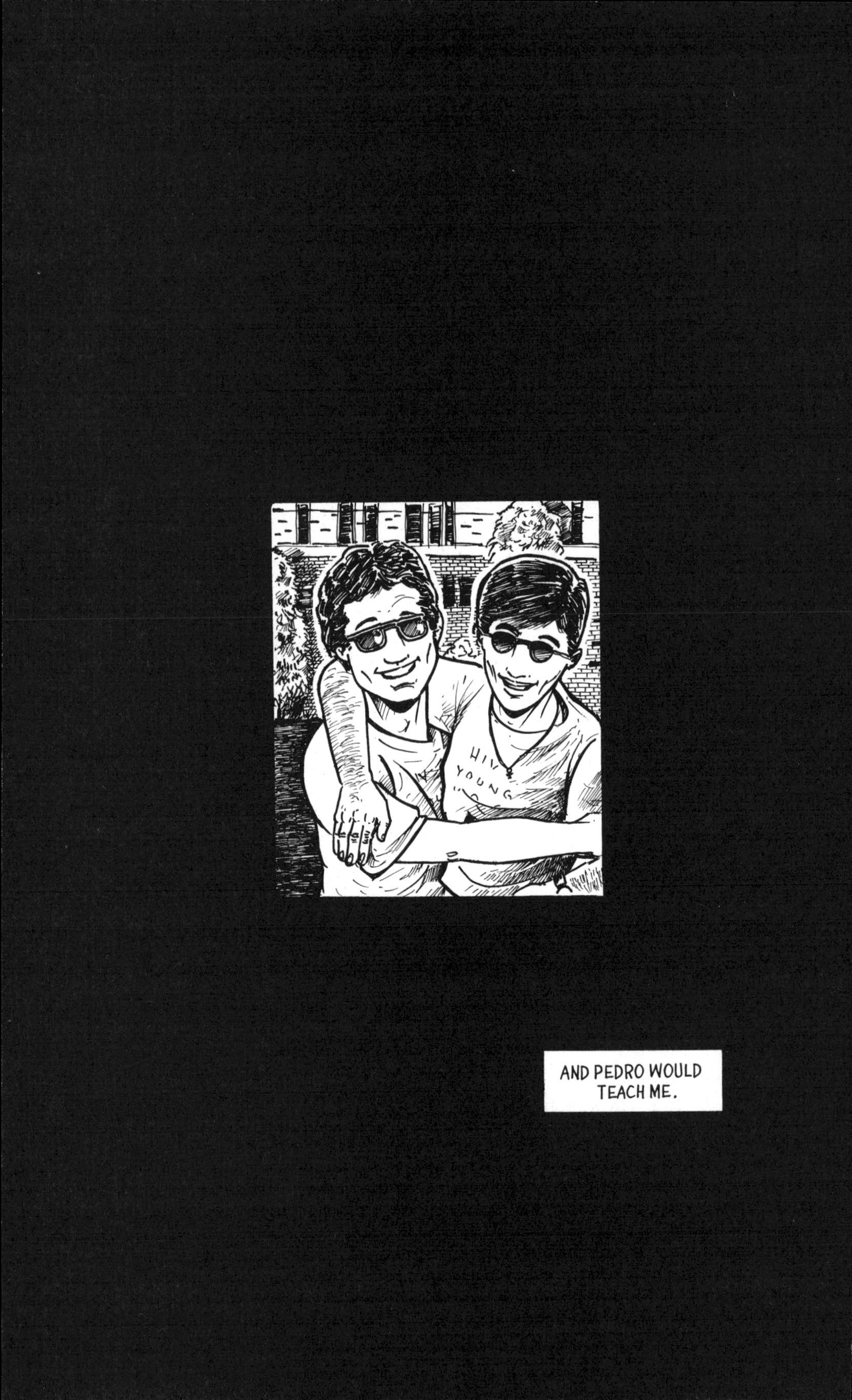
HIV
YOUNG
AND PEDRO WOULD TEACH ME.

CHAPTER THREE

THIS IS WHERE I COME FROM: PART TWO

PEDRO: WALKING UPHILL

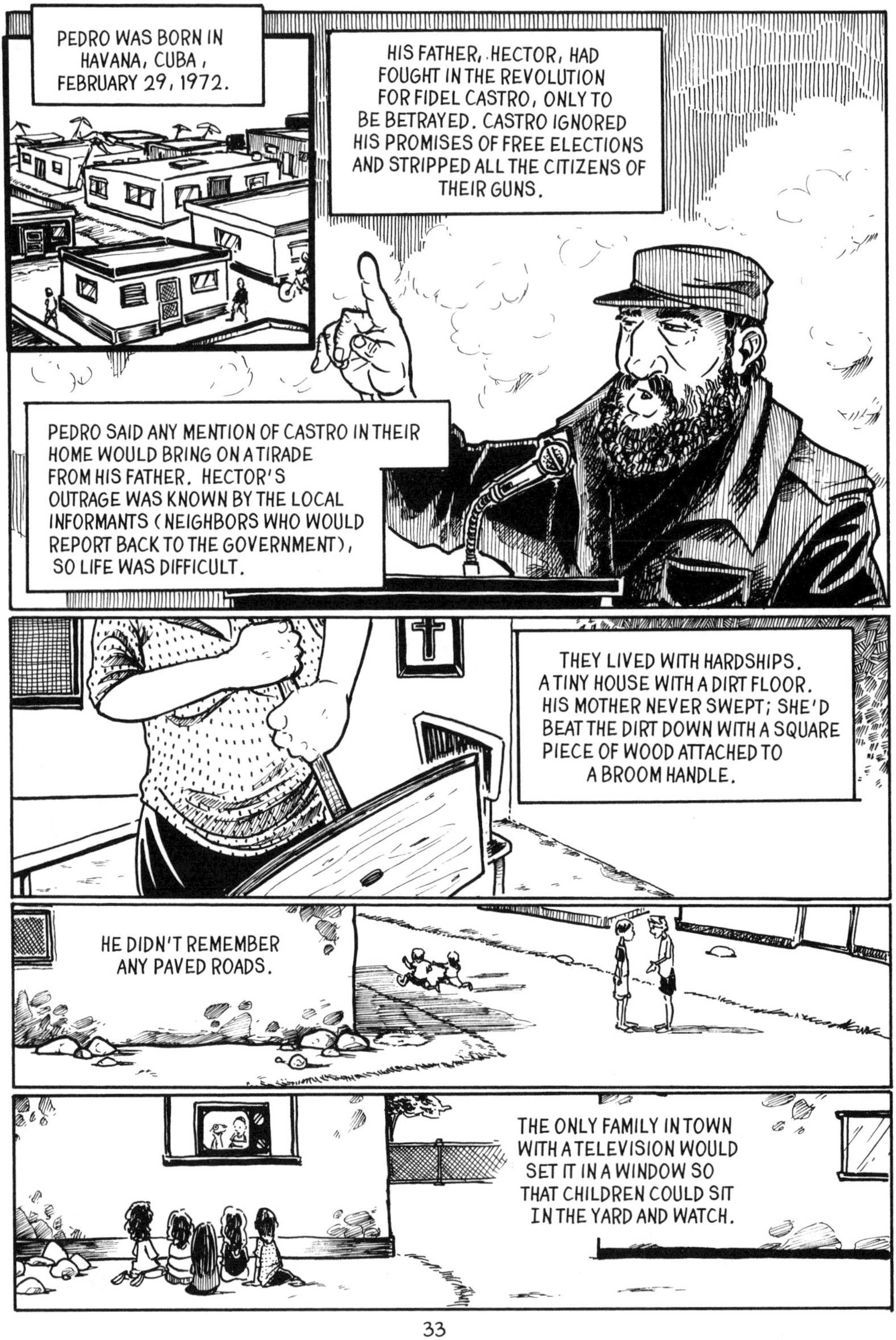
PEDRO WAS BORN IN HAVANA, CUBA, FEBRUARY 29, 1972.
HIS FATHER, HECTOR, HAD FOUGHT IN THE REVOLUTION FOR FIDEL CASTRO, ONLY TO BE BETRAYED. CASTRO IGNORED HIS PROMISES OF FREE ELECTIONS AND STRIPPED ALL THE CITIZENS OF THEIR GUNS.
PEDRO SAID ANY MENTION OF CASTRO IN THEIR HOME WOULD BRING ON A TIRADE FROM HIS FATHER. HECTOR'S OUTRAGE WAS KNOWN BY THE LOCAL INFORMANTS (NEIGHBORS WHO WOULD REPORT BACK TO THE GOVERNMENT), SO LIFE WAS DIFFICULT.
THEY LIVED WITH HARDSHIPS. A TINY HOUSE WITH A DIRT FLOOR. HIS MOTHER NEVER SWEPT; SHE'D BEAT THE DIRT DOWN WITH A SQUARE PIECE OF WOOD ATTACHED TO A BROOM HANDLE.
HE DIDN'T REMEMBER ANY PAVED ROADS.
THE ONLY FAMILY IN TOWN WITH A TELEVISION WOULD SET IT IN A WINDOW SO THAT CHILDREN COULD SIT IN THE YARD AND WATCH.

FOOD WAS SCARCE. AFTER WORKING SINCE DAWN, HECTOR WOULD COME HOME WITH WHATEVER GOODS HE WAS ABLE TO GET.

PEDRO'S MOTHER WOULD GO TRADE ON THE BLACK MARKET FOR FOOD.

AND WHEN SHE RETURNED, THE FAMILY WOULD FINALLY EAT.

BUT CONTRARY TO ALL THAT, PEDRO SAID HE WAS A HAPPY KID.

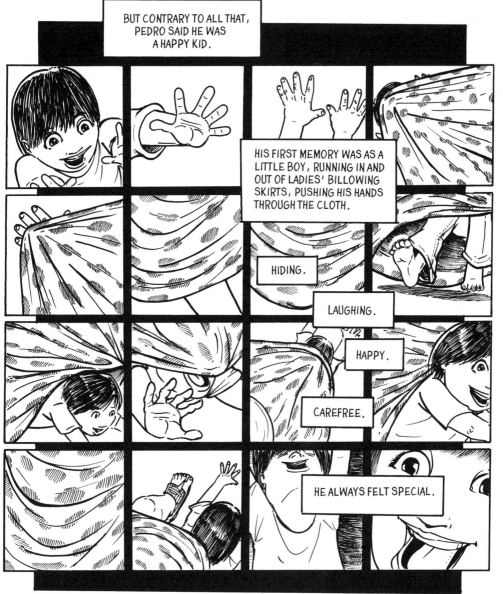

HIS FIRST MEMORY WAS AS A LITTLE BOY, RUNNING IN AND OUT OF LADIES' BILLOWING SKIRTS, PUSHING HIS HANDS THROUGH THE CLOTH.

HIDING.

LAUGHING.

HAPPY.

CAREFREE.

HE ALWAYS FELT SPECIAL.

34

IN HIS ENTIRE LIFE THERE WAS ALWAYS
SOMETHING CHARMED ABOUT PEDRO.

AND MAYBE IT WAS **NEVER** MORE
OBVIOUS THAN IN HIS CHILDHOOD.

HIS FAMILY CALLED HIM A *SURPRISE CHILD*.
HIS MOTHER, ZORAIDA, HAD BEEN TOLD AFTER
THE BIRTH OF HER SEVENTH CHILD
THAT SHE WOULDN'T BE ABLE TO
HAVE ANOTHER.

PEDRO WAS BORN
ON FEBRUARY 29.

THE LEAP DAY OF
THE LEAP YEAR.

HE CAME OUT FEET FIRST.

A RELIGIOUS SAGE OF **SANTERIA**, WHICH IS A FAITH COMBINING CATHOLIC AND AFRICAN BELIEFS, TOLD PEDRO'S MOTHER THAT HE WAS A *GRANDE CABEZA*--

A WISE ONE--

HE WAS BORN TO SAVE LIVES.

AND HE WAS HONORED.

ONLY MEN WERE PERMITTED TO CUT HIS HAIR.

WOMEN KNELT IN HIS PRESENCE.

HE WAS ALLOWED TO ATTEND RELIGIOUS CEREMONIES MEANT ONLY FOR ADULTS.

HE WAS COVERED IN A SHOWER OF WHITE FLOWERS AND COLOGNE.

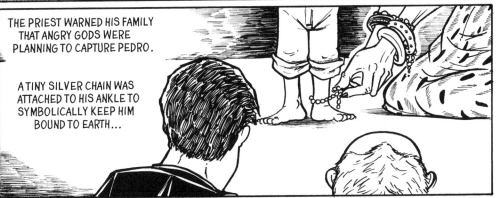

THE PRIEST WARNED HIS FAMILY THAT ANGRY GODS WERE PLANNING TO CAPTURE PEDRO.

A TINY SILVER CHAIN WAS ATTACHED TO HIS ANKLE TO SYMBOLICALLY KEEP HIM BOUND TO EARTH...

SO THE ANGELS WOULDN'T SPIRIT HIM AWAY.

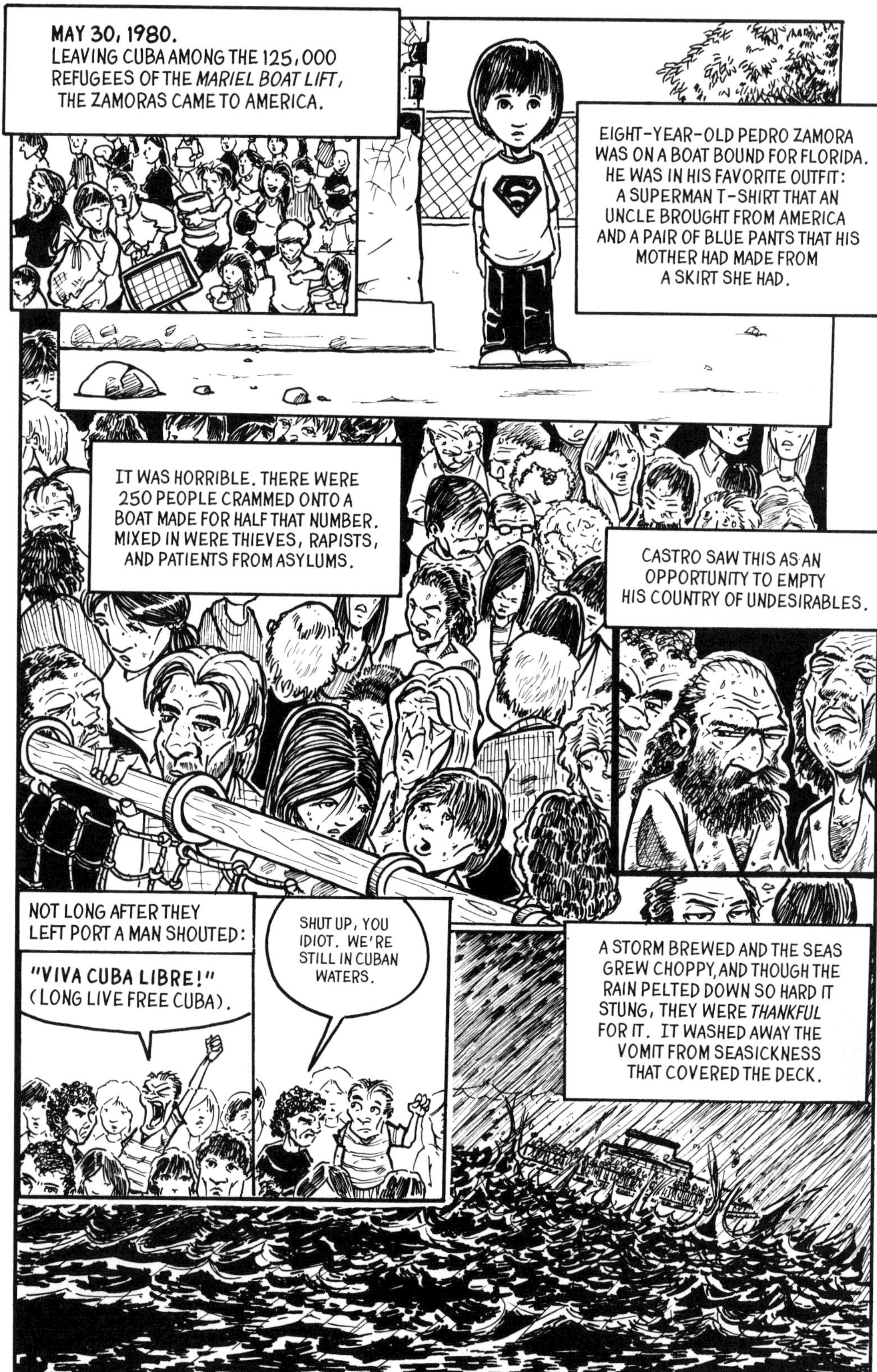
MAY 30, 1980.
LEAVING CUBA AMONG THE 125,000 REFUGEES OF THE *MARIEL BOAT LIFT*, THE ZAMORAS CAME TO AMERICA.
EIGHT-YEAR-OLD PEDRO ZAMORA WAS ON A BOAT BOUND FOR FLORIDA. HE WAS IN HIS FAVORITE OUTFIT: A SUPERMAN T-SHIRT THAT AN UNCLE BROUGHT FROM AMERICA AND A PAIR OF BLUE PANTS THAT HIS MOTHER HAD MADE FROM A SKIRT SHE HAD.
IT WAS HORRIBLE. THERE WERE 250 PEOPLE CRAMMED ONTO A BOAT MADE FOR HALF THAT NUMBER. MIXED IN WERE THIEVES, RAPISTS, AND PATIENTS FROM ASYLUMS.
CASTRO SAW THIS AS AN OPPORTUNITY TO EMPTY HIS COUNTRY OF UNDESIRABLES.
NOT LONG AFTER THEY LEFT PORT A MAN SHOUTED:
"VIVA CUBA LIBRE!" (LONG LIVE FREE CUBA).
SHUT UP, YOU IDIOT. WE'RE STILL IN CUBAN WATERS.
A STORM BREWED AND THE SEAS GREW CHOPPY, AND THOUGH THE RAIN PELTED DOWN SO HARD IT STUNG, THEY WERE *THANKFUL* FOR IT. IT WASHED AWAY THE VOMIT FROM SEASICKNESS THAT COVERED THE DECK.

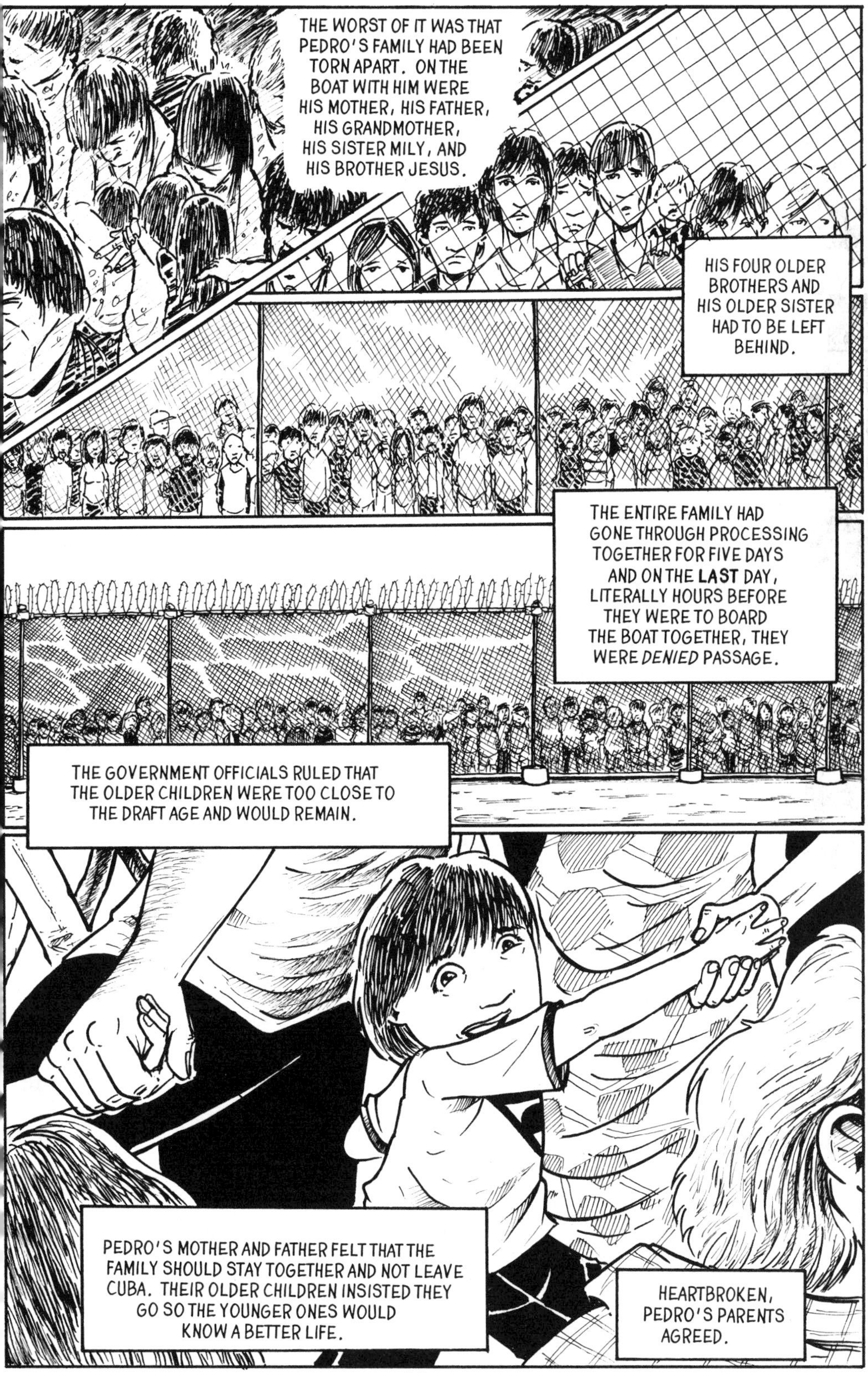
THE WORST OF IT WAS THAT PEDRO'S FAMILY HAD BEEN TORN APART. ON THE BOAT WITH HIM WERE HIS MOTHER, HIS FATHER, HIS GRANDMOTHER, HIS SISTER MILY, AND HIS BROTHER JESUS.
HIS FOUR OLDER BROTHERS AND HIS OLDER SISTER HAD TO BE LEFT BEHIND.
THE ENTIRE FAMILY HAD GONE THROUGH PROCESSING TOGETHER FOR FIVE DAYS AND ON THE **LAST** DAY, LITERALLY HOURS BEFORE THEY WERE TO BOARD THE BOAT TOGETHER, THEY WERE *DENIED* PASSAGE.
THE GOVERNMENT OFFICIALS RULED THAT THE OLDER CHILDREN WERE TOO CLOSE TO THE DRAFT AGE AND WOULD REMAIN.
PEDRO'S MOTHER AND FATHER FELT THAT THE FAMILY SHOULD STAY TOGETHER AND NOT LEAVE CUBA. THEIR OLDER CHILDREN INSISTED THEY GO SO THE YOUNGER ONES WOULD KNOW A BETTER LIFE.
HEARTBROKEN, PEDRO'S PARENTS AGREED.

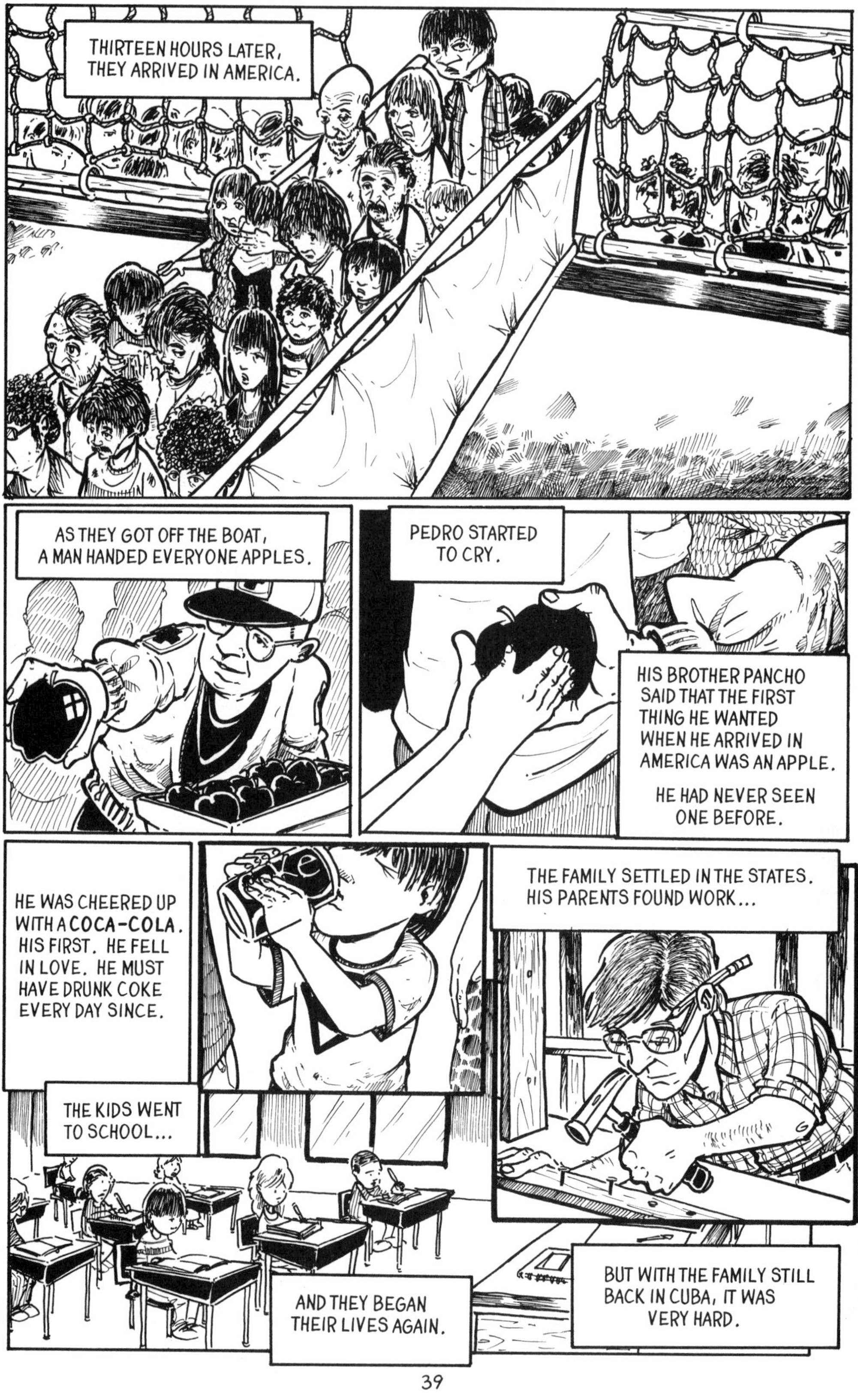
THIRTEEN HOURS LATER, THEY ARRIVED IN AMERICA.
AS THEY GOT OFF THE BOAT, A MAN HANDED EVERYONE APPLES.
PEDRO STARTED TO CRY.
HIS BROTHER PANCHO SAID THAT THE FIRST THING HE WANTED WHEN HE ARRIVED IN AMERICA WAS AN APPLE.
HE HAD NEVER SEEN ONE BEFORE.
HE WAS CHEERED UP WITH A COCA-COLA. HIS FIRST. HE FELL IN LOVE. HE MUST HAVE DRUNK COKE EVERY DAY SINCE.
THE FAMILY SETTLED IN THE STATES. HIS PARENTS FOUND WORK...
THE KIDS WENT TO SCHOOL...
AND THEY BEGAN THEIR LIVES AGAIN.
BUT WITH THE FAMILY STILL BACK IN CUBA, IT WAS VERY HARD.

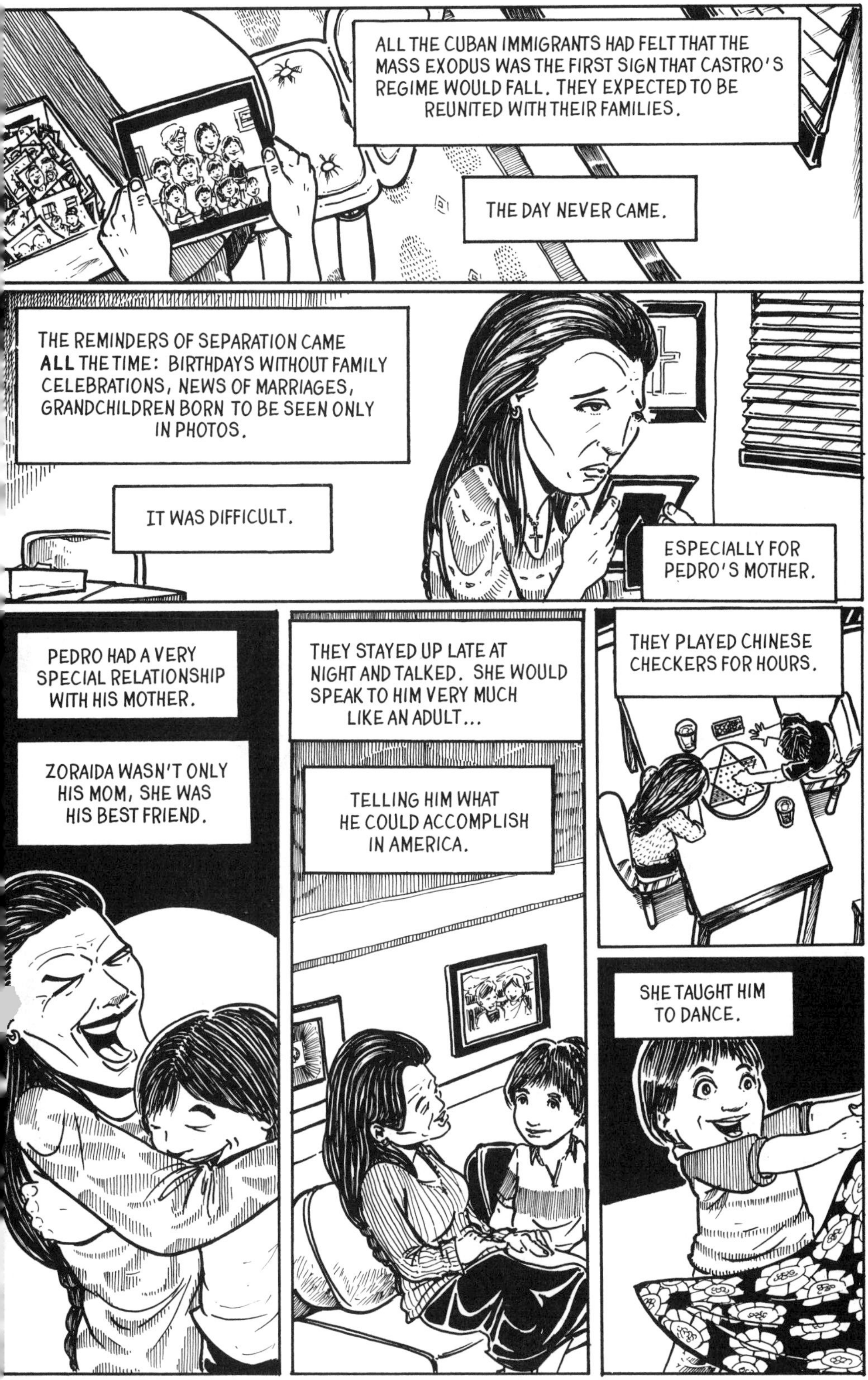
ALL THE CUBAN IMMIGRANTS HAD FELT THAT THE MASS EXODUS WAS THE FIRST SIGN THAT CASTRO'S REGIME WOULD FALL. THEY EXPECTED TO BE REUNITED WITH THEIR FAMILIES.
THE DAY NEVER CAME.
THE REMINDERS OF SEPARATION CAME **ALL** THE TIME: BIRTHDAYS WITHOUT FAMILY CELEBRATIONS, NEWS OF MARRIAGES, GRANDCHILDREN BORN TO BE SEEN ONLY IN PHOTOS.
IT WAS DIFFICULT.
ESPECIALLY FOR PEDRO'S MOTHER.
PEDRO HAD A VERY SPECIAL RELATIONSHIP WITH HIS MOTHER.
ZORAIDA WASN'T ONLY HIS MOM, SHE WAS HIS BEST FRIEND.
THEY STAYED UP LATE AT NIGHT AND TALKED. SHE WOULD SPEAK TO HIM VERY MUCH LIKE AN ADULT...
TELLING HIM WHAT HE COULD ACCOMPLISH IN AMERICA.
THEY PLAYED CHINESE CHECKERS FOR HOURS.
SHE TAUGHT HIM TO DANCE.

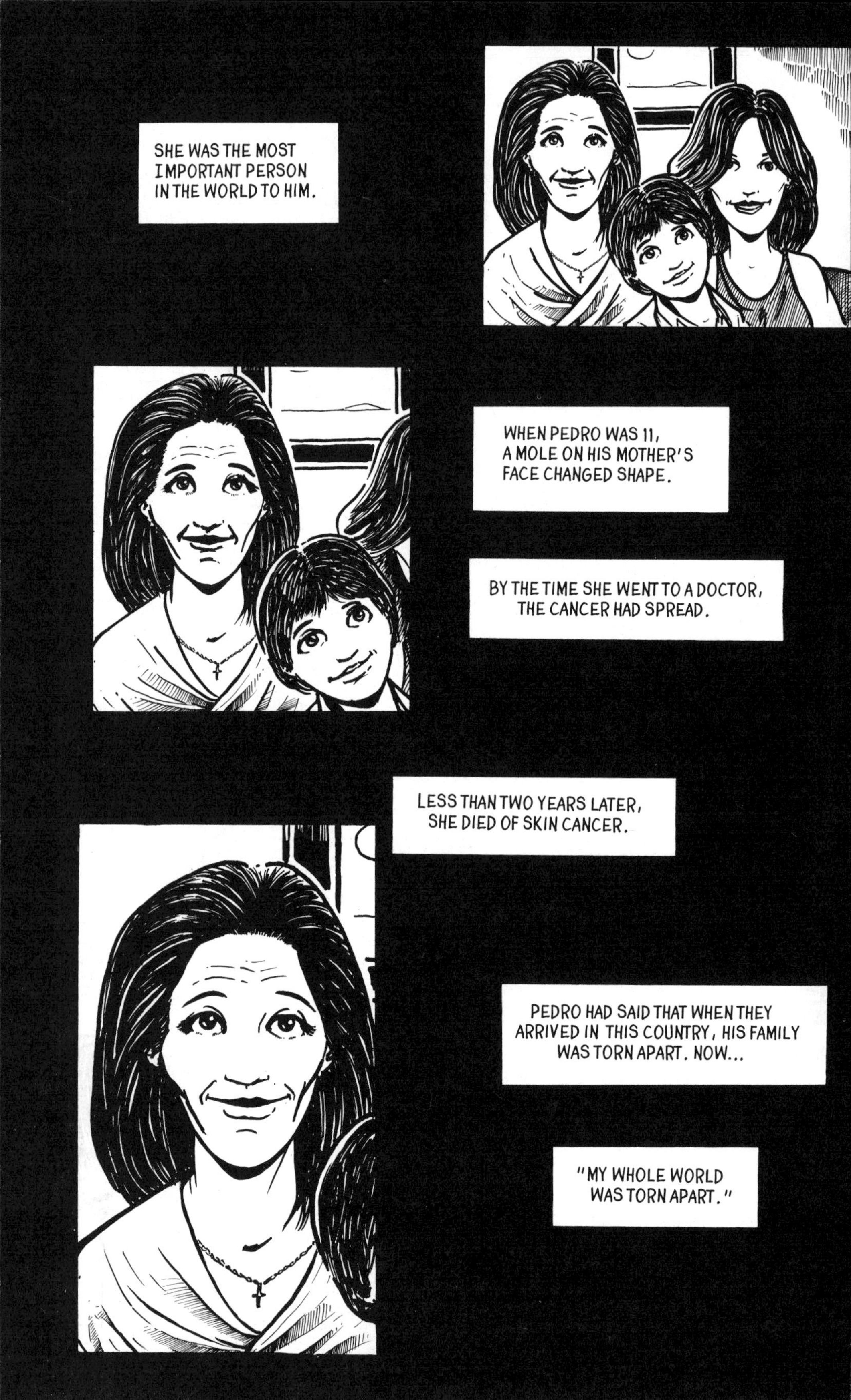
SHE WAS THE MOST IMPORTANT PERSON IN THE WORLD TO HIM.
WHEN PEDRO WAS 11, A MOLE ON HIS MOTHER'S FACE CHANGED SHAPE.
BY THE TIME SHE WENT TO A DOCTOR, THE CANCER HAD SPREAD.
LESS THAN TWO YEARS LATER, SHE DIED OF SKIN CANCER.
PEDRO HAD SAID THAT WHEN THEY ARRIVED IN THIS COUNTRY, HIS FAMILY WAS TORN APART. NOW...
"MY WHOLE WORLD WAS TORN APART."

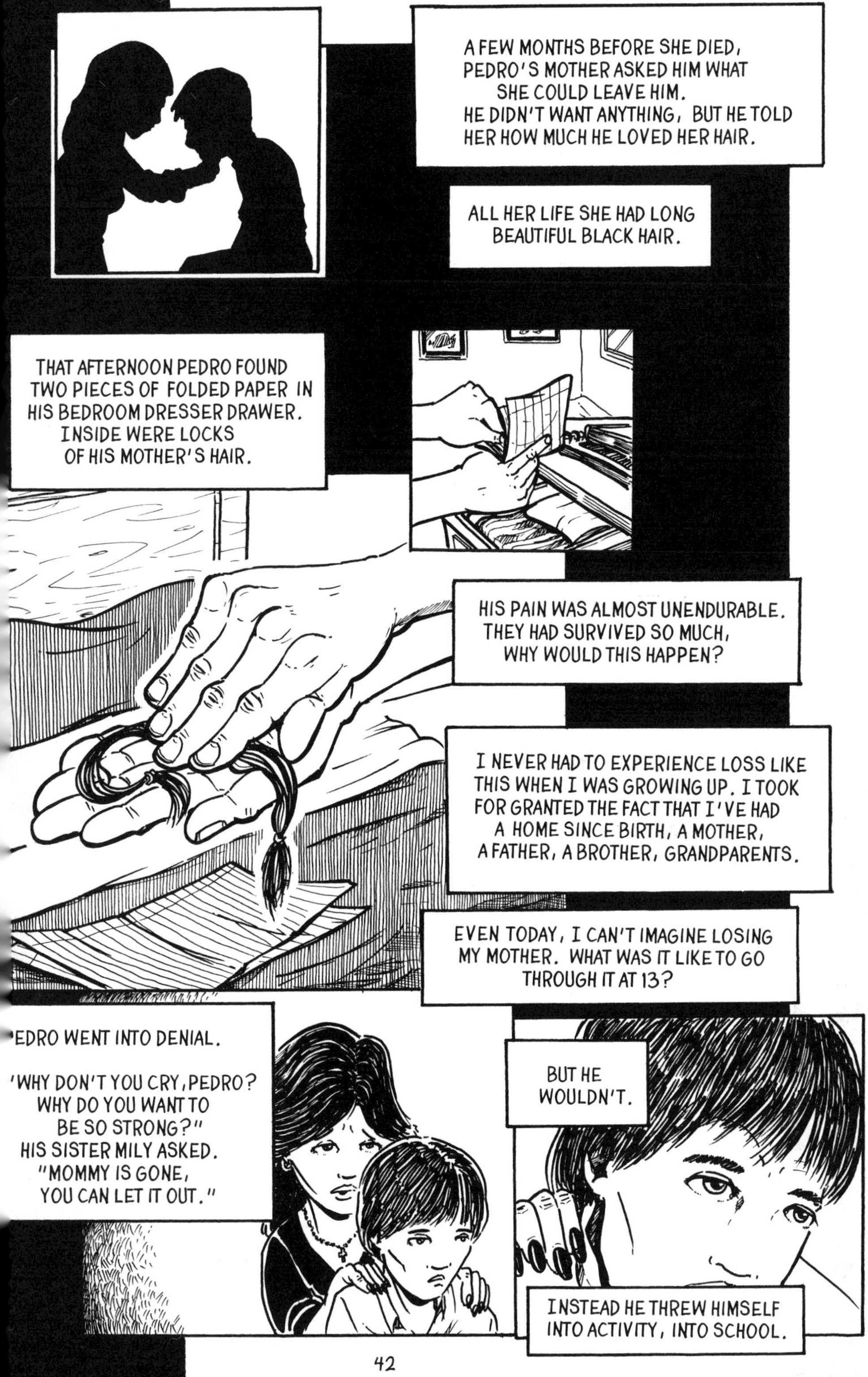

A FEW MONTHS BEFORE SHE DIED, PEDRO'S MOTHER ASKED HIM WHAT SHE COULD LEAVE HIM. HE DIDN'T WANT ANYTHING, BUT HE TOLD HER HOW MUCH HE LOVED HER HAIR.
ALL HER LIFE SHE HAD LONG BEAUTIFUL BLACK HAIR.
THAT AFTERNOON PEDRO FOUND TWO PIECES OF FOLDED PAPER IN HIS BEDROOM DRESSER DRAWER. INSIDE WERE LOCKS OF HIS MOTHER'S HAIR.
HIS PAIN WAS ALMOST UNENDURABLE. THEY HAD SURVIVED SO MUCH, WHY WOULD THIS HAPPEN?
I NEVER HAD TO EXPERIENCE LOSS LIKE THIS WHEN I WAS GROWING UP. I TOOK FOR GRANTED THE FACT THAT I'VE HAD A HOME SINCE BIRTH, A MOTHER, A FATHER, A BROTHER, GRANDPARENTS.
EVEN TODAY, I CAN'T IMAGINE LOSING MY MOTHER. WHAT WAS IT LIKE TO GO THROUGH IT AT 13?
EDRO WENT INTO DENIAL.
'WHY DON'T YOU CRY, PEDRO? WHY DO YOU WANT TO BE SO STRONG?" HIS SISTER MILY ASKED. "MOMMY IS GONE, YOU CAN LET IT OUT."
BUT HE WOULDN'T.
INSTEAD HE THREW HIMSELF INTO ACTIVITY, INTO SCHOOL.

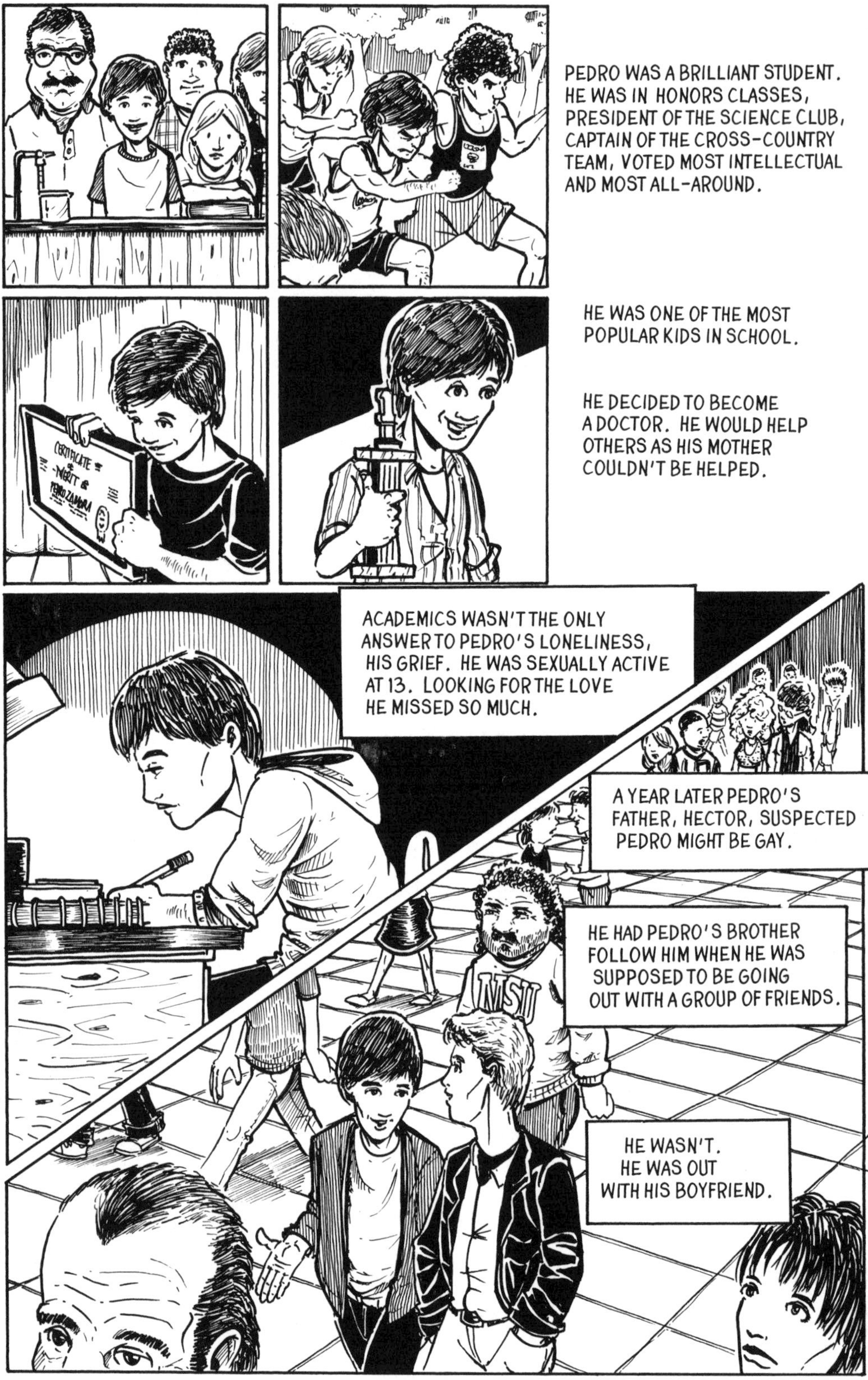
PEDRO WAS A BRILLIANT STUDENT. HE WAS IN HONORS CLASSES, PRESIDENT OF THE SCIENCE CLUB, CAPTAIN OF THE CROSS-COUNTRY TEAM, VOTED MOST INTELLECTUAL AND MOST ALL-AROUND.
HE WAS ONE OF THE MOST POPULAR KIDS IN SCHOOL.
HE DECIDED TO BECOME A DOCTOR. HE WOULD HELP OTHERS AS HIS MOTHER COULDN'T BE HELPED.
ACADEMICS WASN'T THE ONLY ANSWER TO PEDRO'S LONELINESS, HIS GRIEF. HE WAS SEXUALLY ACTIVE AT 13. LOOKING FOR THE LOVE HE MISSED SO MUCH.
A YEAR LATER PEDRO'S FATHER, HECTOR, SUSPECTED PEDRO MIGHT BE GAY.
HE HAD PEDRO'S BROTHER FOLLOW HIM WHEN HE WAS SUPPOSED TO BE GOING OUT WITH A GROUP OF FRIENDS.
HE WASN'T. HE WAS OUT WITH HIS BOYFRIEND.

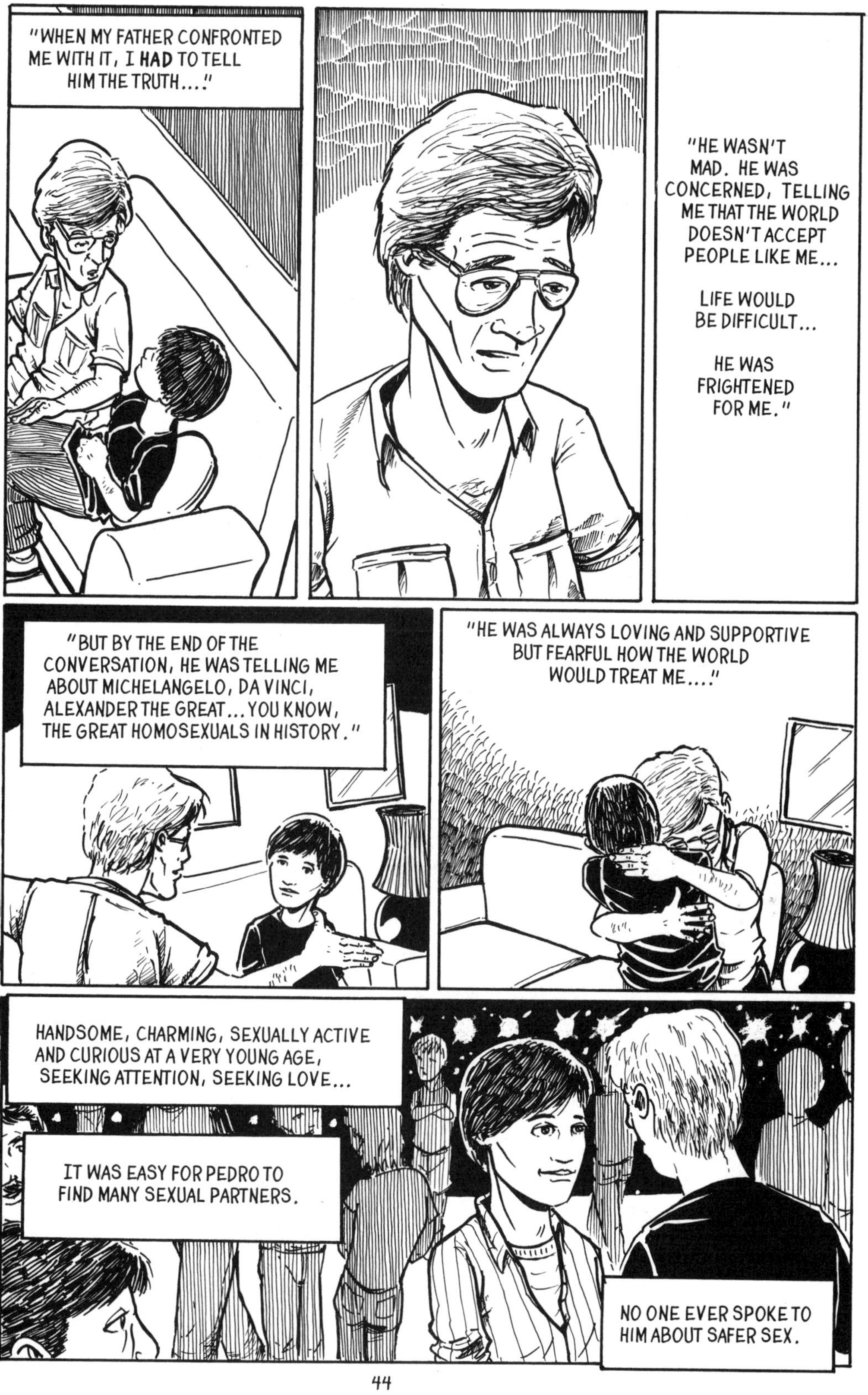
"WHEN MY FATHER CONFRONTED ME WITH IT, I **HAD** TO TELL HIM THE TRUTH...."
"HE WASN'T MAD. HE WAS CONCERNED, TELLING ME THAT THE WORLD DOESN'T ACCEPT PEOPLE LIKE ME...
LIFE WOULD BE DIFFICULT...
HE WAS FRIGHTENED FOR ME."
"BUT BY THE END OF THE CONVERSATION, HE WAS TELLING ME ABOUT MICHELANGELO, DA VINCI, ALEXANDER THE GREAT... YOU KNOW, THE GREAT HOMOSEXUALS IN HISTORY."
"HE WAS ALWAYS LOVING AND SUPPORTIVE BUT FEARFUL HOW THE WORLD WOULD TREAT ME...."
HANDSOME, CHARMING, SEXUALLY ACTIVE AND CURIOUS AT A VERY YOUNG AGE, SEEKING ATTENTION, SEEKING LOVE...
IT WAS EASY FOR PEDRO TO FIND MANY SEXUAL PARTNERS.
NO ONE EVER SPOKE TO HIM ABOUT SAFER SEX.

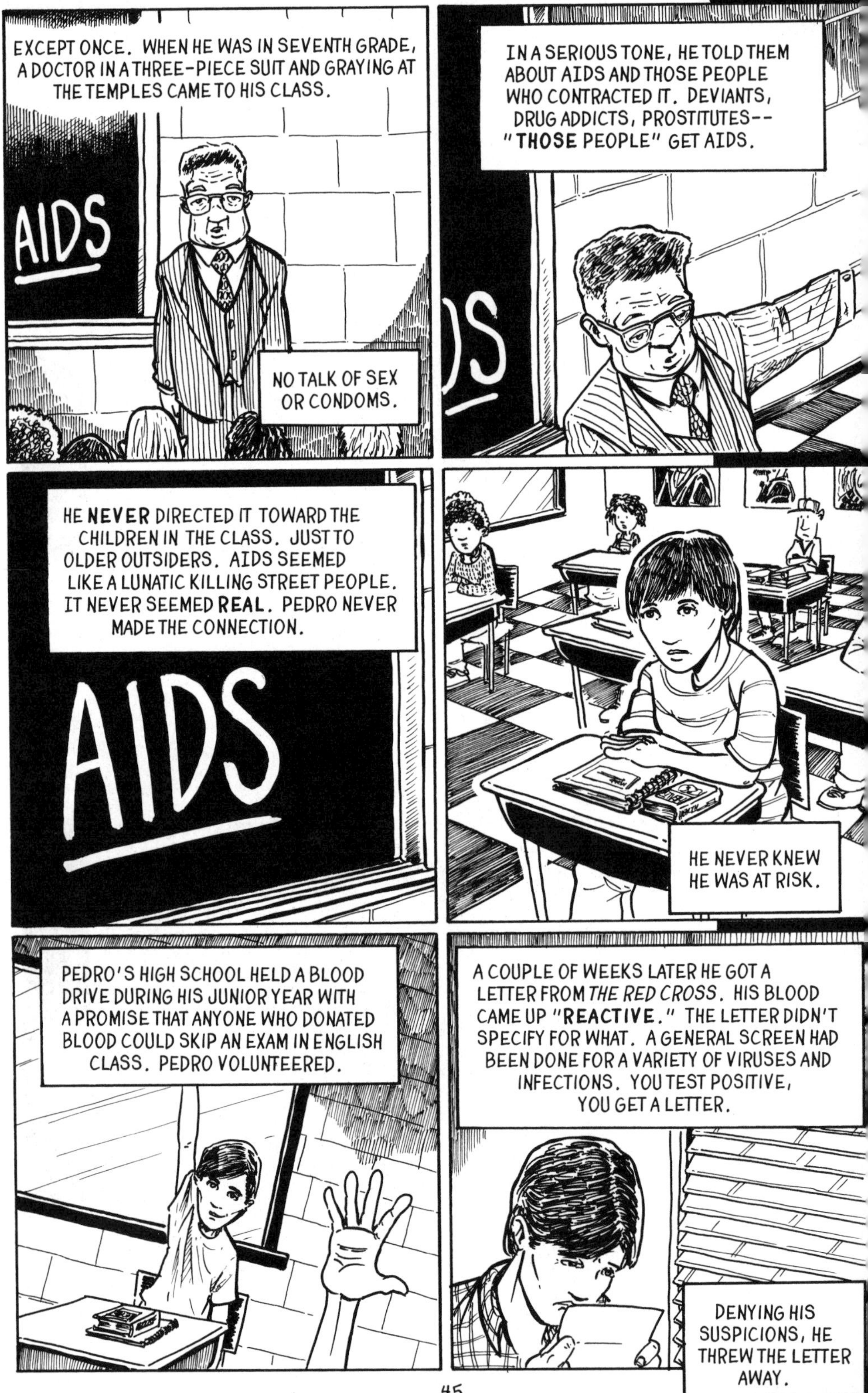
EXCEPT ONCE. WHEN HE WAS IN SEVENTH GRADE, A DOCTOR IN A THREE-PIECE SUIT AND GRAYING AT THE TEMPLES CAME TO HIS CLASS.
AIDS
NO TALK OF SEX OR CONDOMS.
IN A SERIOUS TONE, HE TOLD THEM ABOUT AIDS AND THOSE PEOPLE WHO CONTRACTED IT. DEVIANTS, DRUG ADDICTS, PROSTITUTES-- "THOSE PEOPLE" GET AIDS.
HE NEVER DIRECTED IT TOWARD THE CHILDREN IN THE CLASS. JUST TO OLDER OUTSIDERS. AIDS SEEMED LIKE A LUNATIC KILLING STREET PEOPLE. IT NEVER SEEMED REAL. PEDRO NEVER MADE THE CONNECTION.
AIDS
HE NEVER KNEW HE WAS AT RISK.
PEDRO'S HIGH SCHOOL HELD A BLOOD DRIVE DURING HIS JUNIOR YEAR WITH A PROMISE THAT ANYONE WHO DONATED BLOOD COULD SKIP AN EXAM IN ENGLISH CLASS. PEDRO VOLUNTEERED.
A COUPLE OF WEEKS LATER HE GOT A LETTER FROM THE RED CROSS. HIS BLOOD CAME UP "REACTIVE." THE LETTER DIDN'T SPECIFY FOR WHAT. A GENERAL SCREEN HAD BEEN DONE FOR A VARIETY OF VIRUSES AND INFECTIONS. YOU TEST POSITIVE, YOU GET A LETTER.
DENYING HIS SUSPICIONS, HE THREW THE LETTER AWAY.

TWO WEEKS LATER ANOTHER
LETTER ARRIVED RESTATING
THE RESULTS AND
REQUESTING ADDITIONAL TESTS.

HE THREW IT AWAY.

TWO MORE WEEKS ANOTHER
LETTER. THEN ANOTHER.
THEN ANOTHER.

MANY WEEKS AND
MANY LETTERS LATER,
PEDRO GOT HIMSELF TESTED.

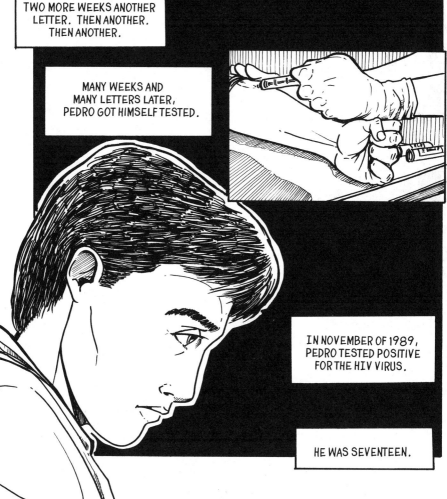

IN NOVEMBER OF 1989,
PEDRO TESTED POSITIVE
FOR THE HIV VIRUS.

HE WAS SEVENTEEN.

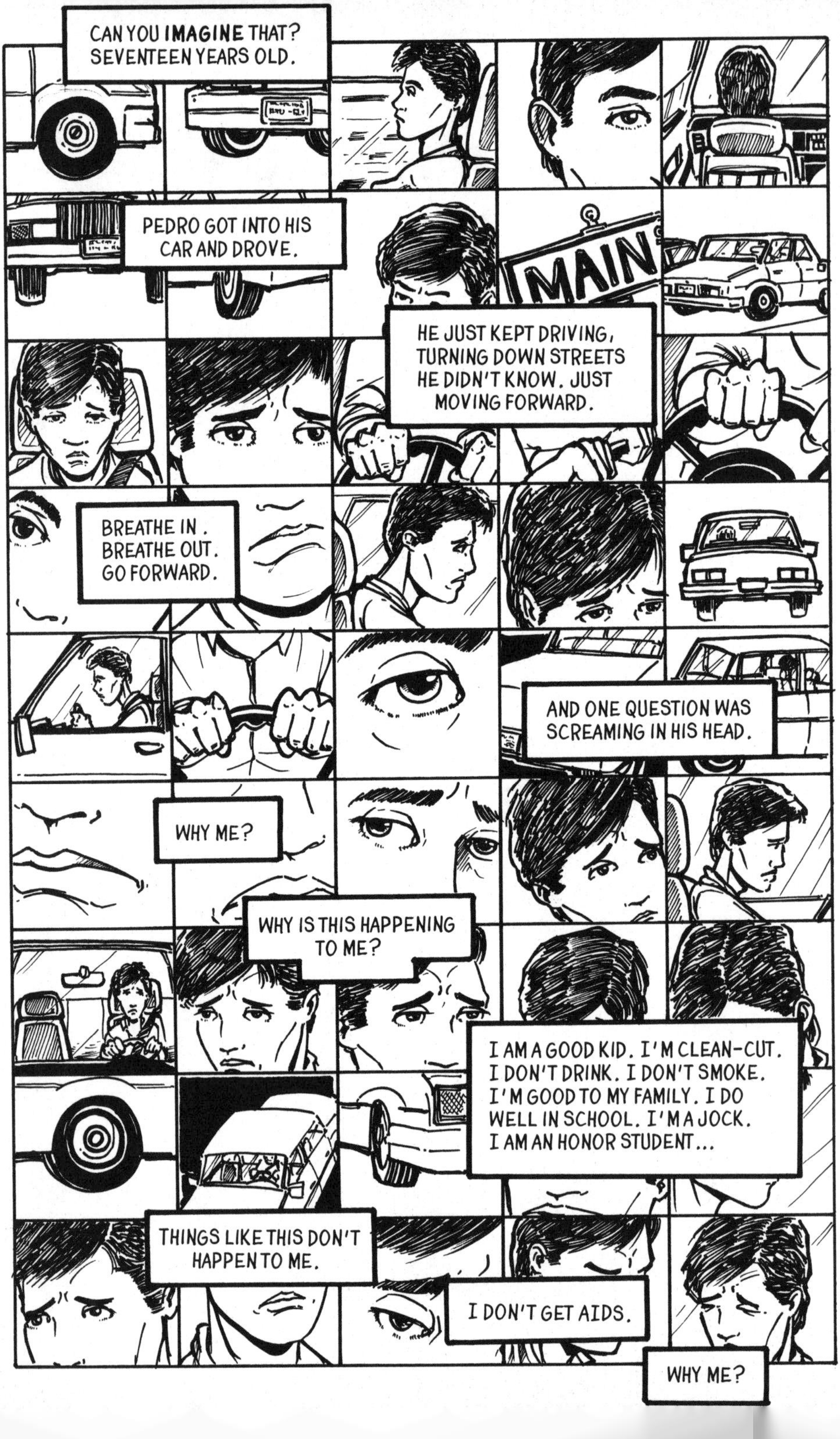
CAN YOU IMAGINE THAT? SEVENTEEN YEARS OLD.
PEDRO GOT INTO HIS CAR AND DROVE.
MAIN
HE JUST KEPT DRIVING, TURNING DOWN STREETS HE DIDN'T KNOW. JUST MOVING FORWARD.
BREATHE IN. BREATHE OUT. GO FORWARD.
AND ONE QUESTION WAS SCREAMING IN HIS HEAD.
WHY ME?
WHY IS THIS HAPPENING TO ME?
I AM A GOOD KID. I'M CLEAN-CUT. I DON'T DRINK. I DON'T SMOKE. I'M GOOD TO MY FAMILY. I DO WELL IN SCHOOL. I'M A JOCK. I AM AN HONOR STUDENT...
THINGS LIKE THIS DON'T HAPPEN TO ME.
I DON'T GET AIDS.
WHY ME?

BEFORE THAT DAY HIS DECISIONS,
HIS GOALS, HIS OBSTACLES WERE CLEAR
AND SIMPLE.

"WHAT COLLEGE AM I GOING
TO GO TO?"

"SHOULD I GO PRE-MED
OR MAYBE STUDY LAW?

"WILL I TAKE THE
CAR WITH ME?"

"DO I GO TO A NORTHERN SCHOOL?
I'LL BE AWAY FROM MY FAMILY,
IT'LL BE COLD, BUT WHY LIMIT
MY OPTIONS?"

THESE ARE THE QUESTIONS AND
THOUGHTS OF A
SEVENTEEN-YEAR-OLD.

BUT NOW THAT HAD CHANGED.
PEDRO WAS JUST
THINKING ONE THING.

"... I HAVE AIDS ... "

"... I AM GOING TO DIE. "

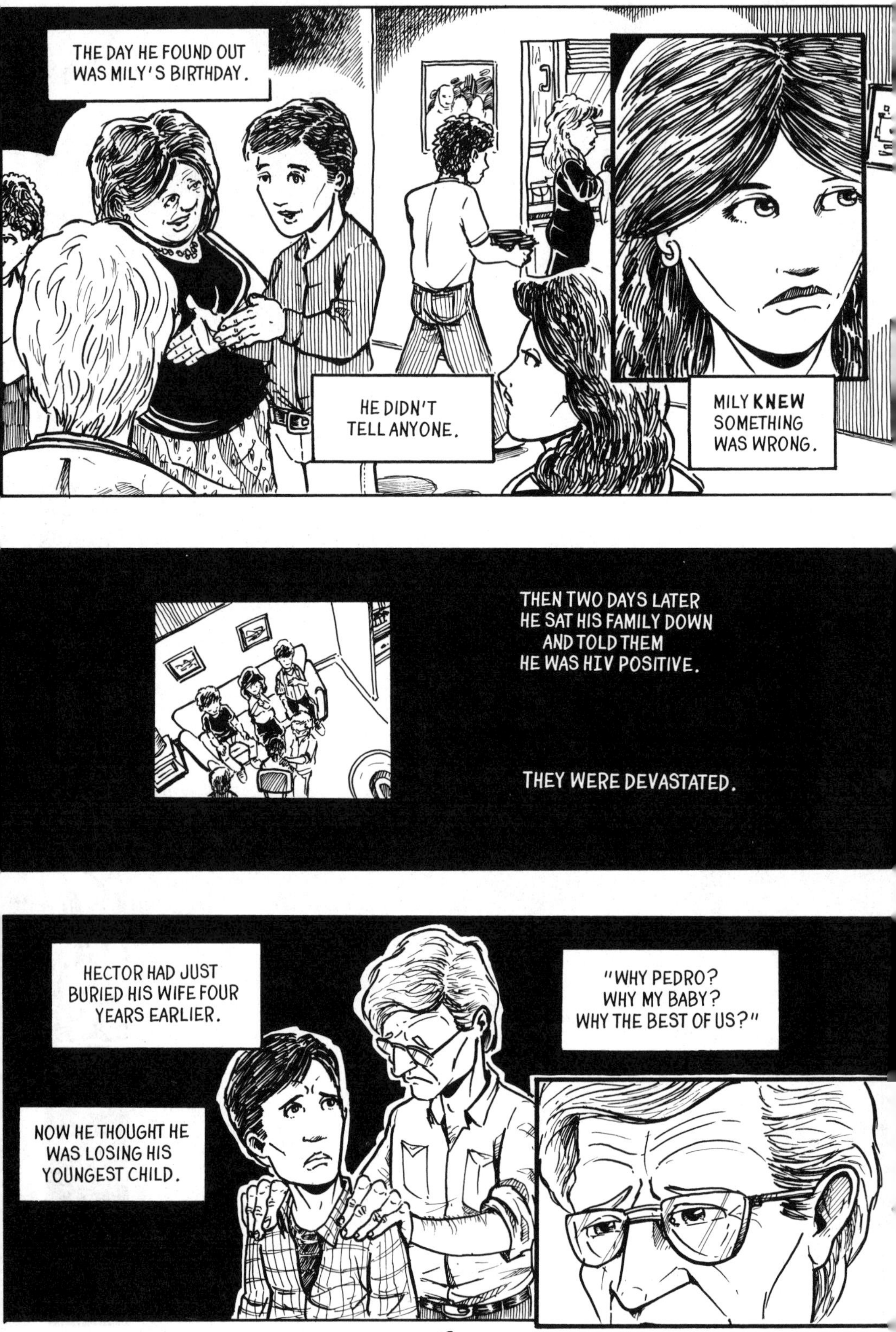
THE DAY HE FOUND OUT WAS MILY'S BIRTHDAY.
HE DIDN'T TELL ANYONE.
MILY KNEW SOMETHING WAS WRONG.
THEN TWO DAYS LATER HE SAT HIS FAMILY DOWN AND TOLD THEM HE WAS HIV POSITIVE.
THEY WERE DEVASTATED.
HECTOR HAD JUST BURIED HIS WIFE FOUR YEARS EARLIER.
NOW HE THOUGHT HE WAS LOSING HIS YOUNGEST CHILD.
"WHY PEDRO? WHY MY BABY? WHY THE BEST OF US?"

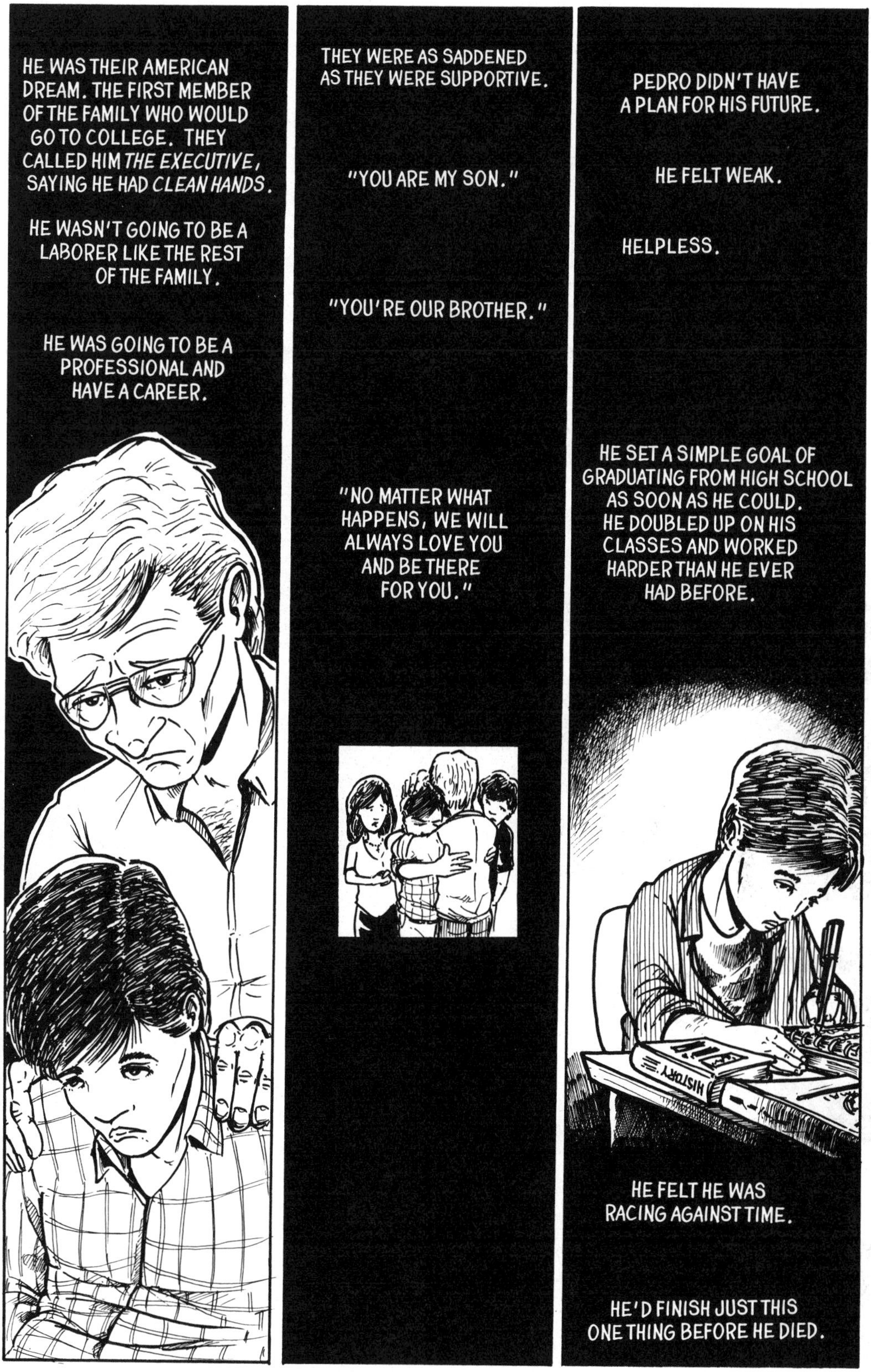
HE WAS THEIR AMERICAN DREAM. THE FIRST MEMBER OF THE FAMILY WHO WOULD GO TO COLLEGE. THEY CALLED HIM *THE EXECUTIVE*, SAYING HE HAD *CLEAN HANDS*.
HE WASN'T GOING TO BE A LABORER LIKE THE REST OF THE FAMILY.
HE WAS GOING TO BE A PROFESSIONAL AND HAVE A CAREER.
THEY WERE AS SADDENED AS THEY WERE SUPPORTIVE.
"YOU ARE MY SON."
"YOU'RE OUR BROTHER."
"NO MATTER WHAT HAPPENS, WE WILL ALWAYS LOVE YOU AND BE THERE FOR YOU."
PEDRO DIDN'T HAVE A PLAN FOR HIS FUTURE.
HE FELT WEAK.
HELPLESS.
HE SET A SIMPLE GOAL OF GRADUATING FROM HIGH SCHOOL AS SOON AS HE COULD. HE DOUBLED UP ON HIS CLASSES AND WORKED HARDER THAN HE EVER HAD BEFORE.
HISTORY
HE FELT HE WAS RACING AGAINST TIME.
HE'D FINISH JUST THIS ONE THING BEFORE HE DIED.

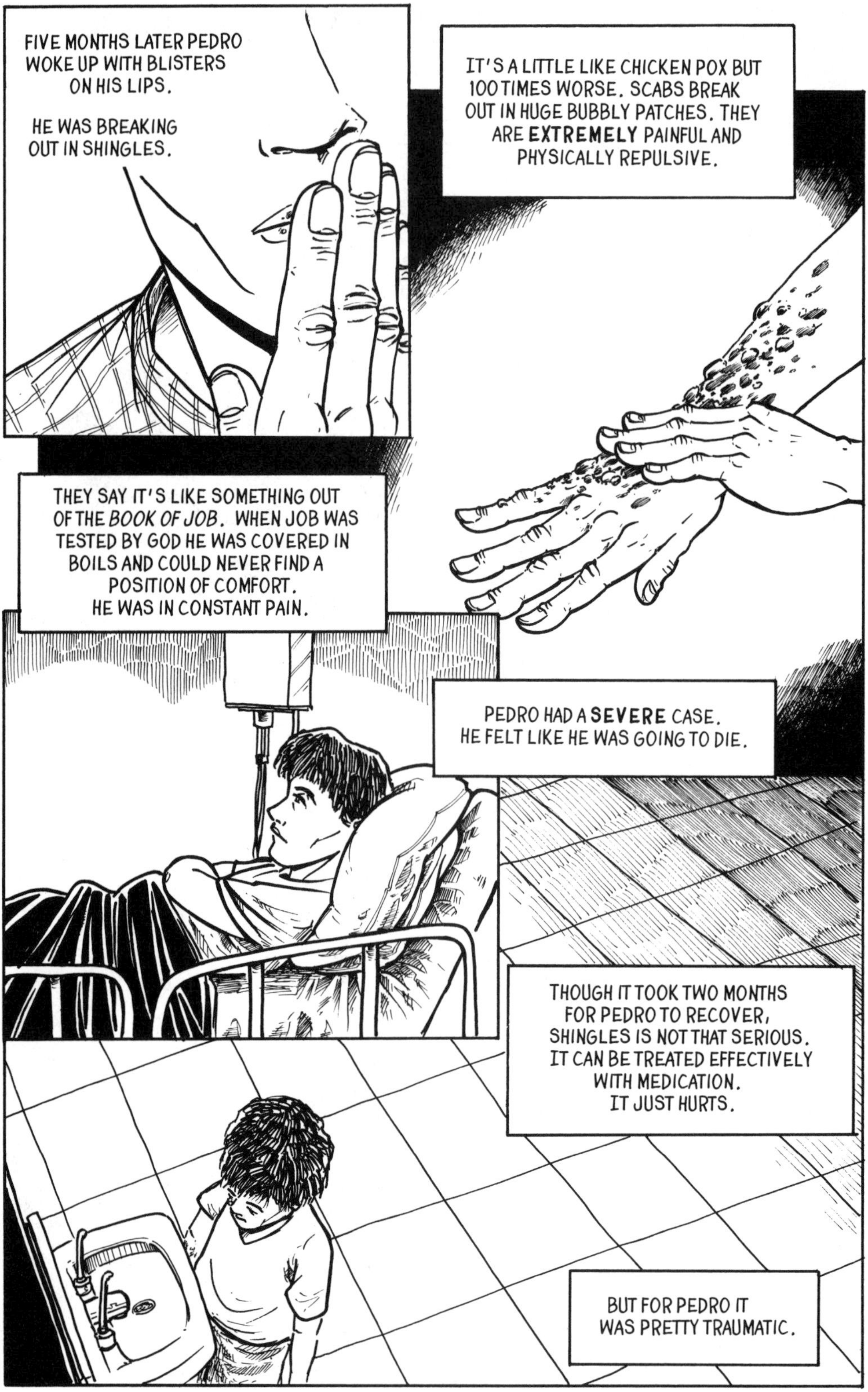

FIVE MONTHS LATER PEDRO WOKE UP WITH BLISTERS ON HIS LIPS.
HE WAS BREAKING OUT IN SHINGLES.
IT'S A LITTLE LIKE CHICKEN POX BUT 100 TIMES WORSE. SCABS BREAK OUT IN HUGE BUBBLY PATCHES. THEY ARE **EXTREMELY** PAINFUL AND PHYSICALLY REPULSIVE.
THEY SAY IT'S LIKE SOMETHING OUT OF THE *BOOK OF JOB*. WHEN JOB WAS TESTED BY GOD HE WAS COVERED IN BOILS AND COULD NEVER FIND A POSITION OF COMFORT. HE WAS IN CONSTANT PAIN.
PEDRO HAD A **SEVERE** CASE. HE FELT LIKE HE WAS GOING TO DIE.
THOUGH IT TOOK TWO MONTHS FOR PEDRO TO RECOVER, SHINGLES IS NOT THAT SERIOUS. IT CAN BE TREATED EFFECTIVELY WITH MEDICATION. IT JUST HURTS.
BUT FOR PEDRO IT WAS PRETTY TRAUMATIC.

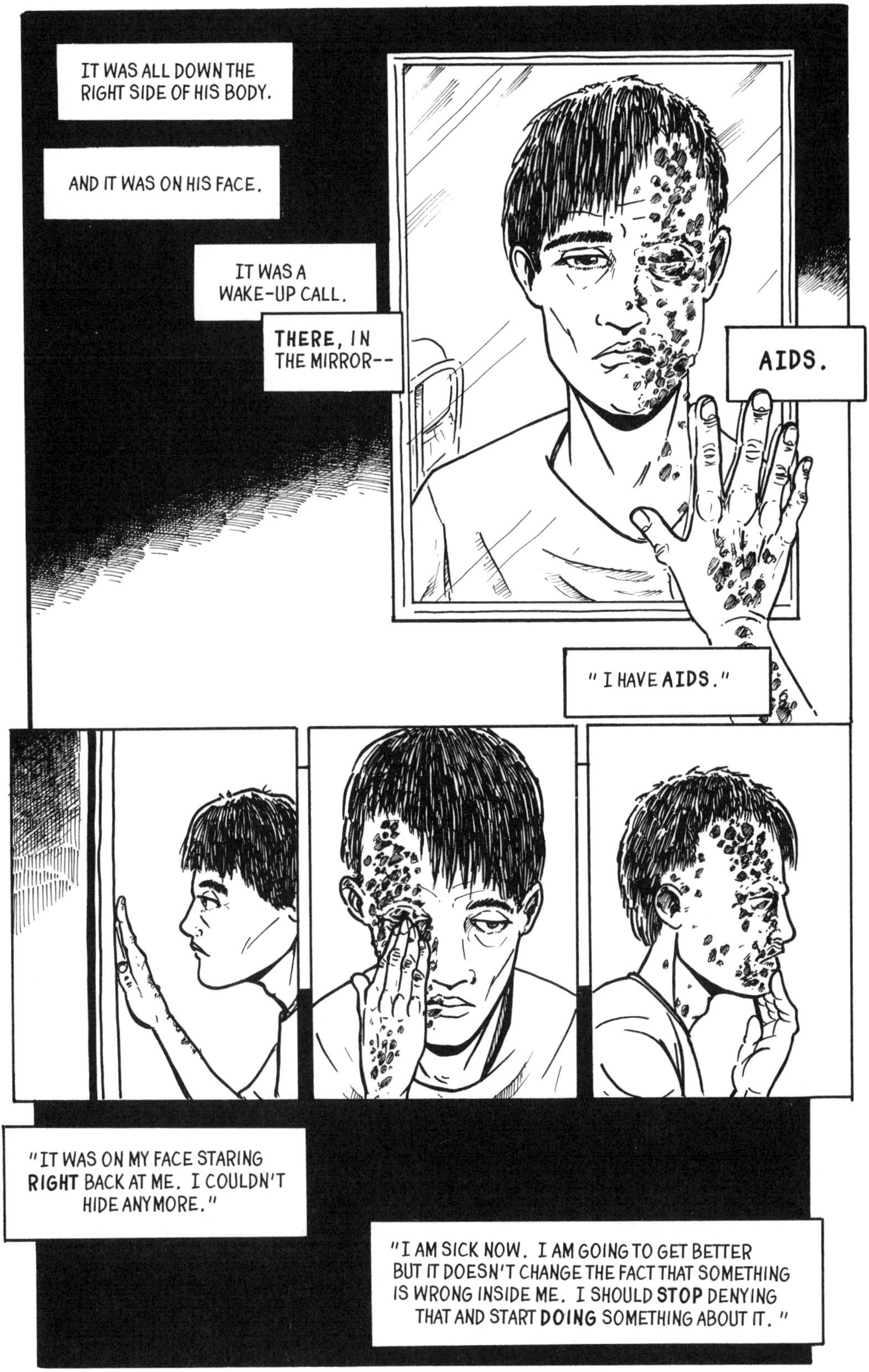
IT WAS ALL DOWN THE RIGHT SIDE OF HIS BODY.
AND IT WAS ON HIS FACE.
IT WAS A WAKE-UP CALL.
THERE, IN THE MIRROR--
AIDS.
"I HAVE AIDS."
"IT WAS ON MY FACE STARING RIGHT BACK AT ME. I COULDN'T HIDE ANYMORE."
"I AM SICK NOW. I AM GOING TO GET BETTER BUT IT DOESN'T CHANGE THE FACT THAT SOMETHING IS WRONG INSIDE ME. I SHOULD STOP DENYING THAT AND START DOING SOMETHING ABOUT IT."

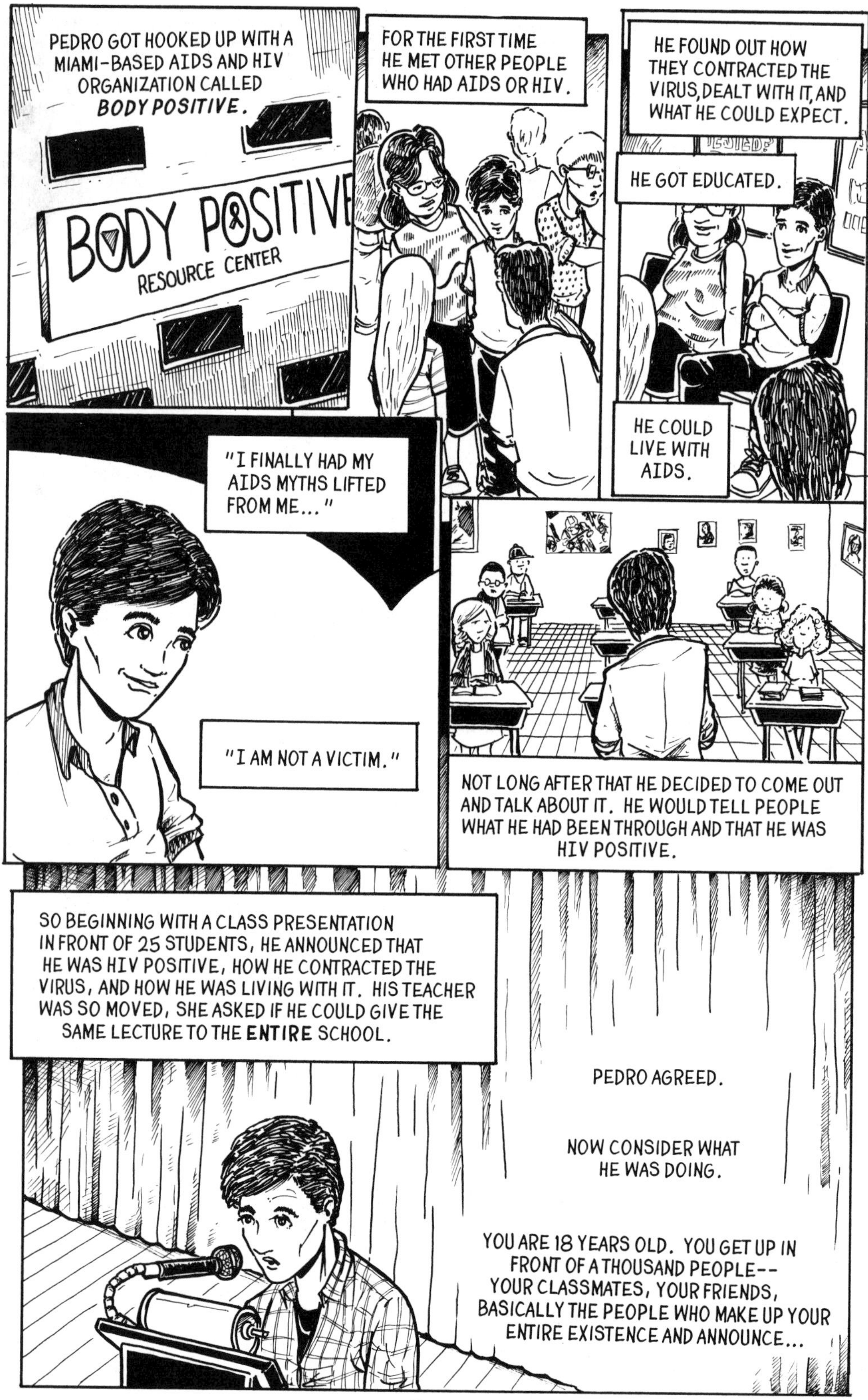
PEDRO GOT HOOKED UP WITH A MIAMI-BASED AIDS AND HIV ORGANIZATION CALLED BODY POSITIVE.
BODY POSITIVE RESOURCE CENTER
FOR THE FIRST TIME HE MET OTHER PEOPLE WHO HAD AIDS OR HIV.
HE FOUND OUT HOW THEY CONTRACTED THE VIRUS, DEALT WITH IT, AND WHAT HE COULD EXPECT.
HE GOT EDUCATED.
HE COULD LIVE WITH AIDS.
"I FINALLY HAD MY AIDS MYTHS LIFTED FROM ME..."
"I AM NOT A VICTIM."
NOT LONG AFTER THAT HE DECIDED TO COME OUT AND TALK ABOUT IT. HE WOULD TELL PEOPLE WHAT HE HAD BEEN THROUGH AND THAT HE WAS HIV POSITIVE.
SO BEGINNING WITH A CLASS PRESENTATION IN FRONT OF 25 STUDENTS, HE ANNOUNCED THAT HE WAS HIV POSITIVE, HOW HE CONTRACTED THE VIRUS, AND HOW HE WAS LIVING WITH IT. HIS TEACHER WAS SO MOVED, SHE ASKED IF HE COULD GIVE THE SAME LECTURE TO THE ENTIRE SCHOOL.
PEDRO AGREED.
NOW CONSIDER WHAT HE WAS DOING.
YOU ARE 18 YEARS OLD. YOU GET UP IN FRONT OF A THOUSAND PEOPLE-- YOUR CLASSMATES, YOUR FRIENDS, BASICALLY THE PEOPLE WHO MAKE UP YOUR ENTIRE EXISTENCE AND ANNOUNCE...

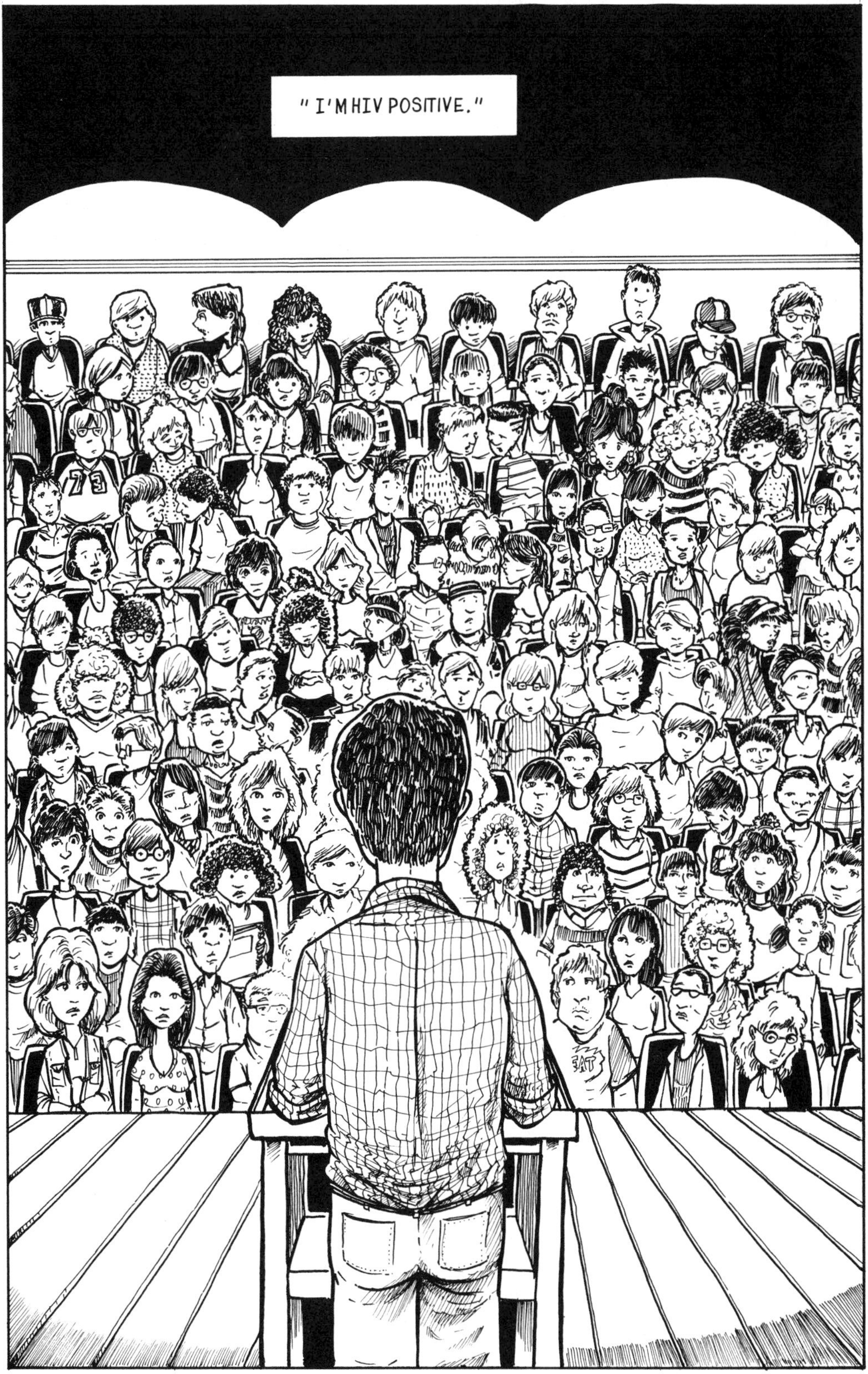
"I'M HIV POSITIVE."

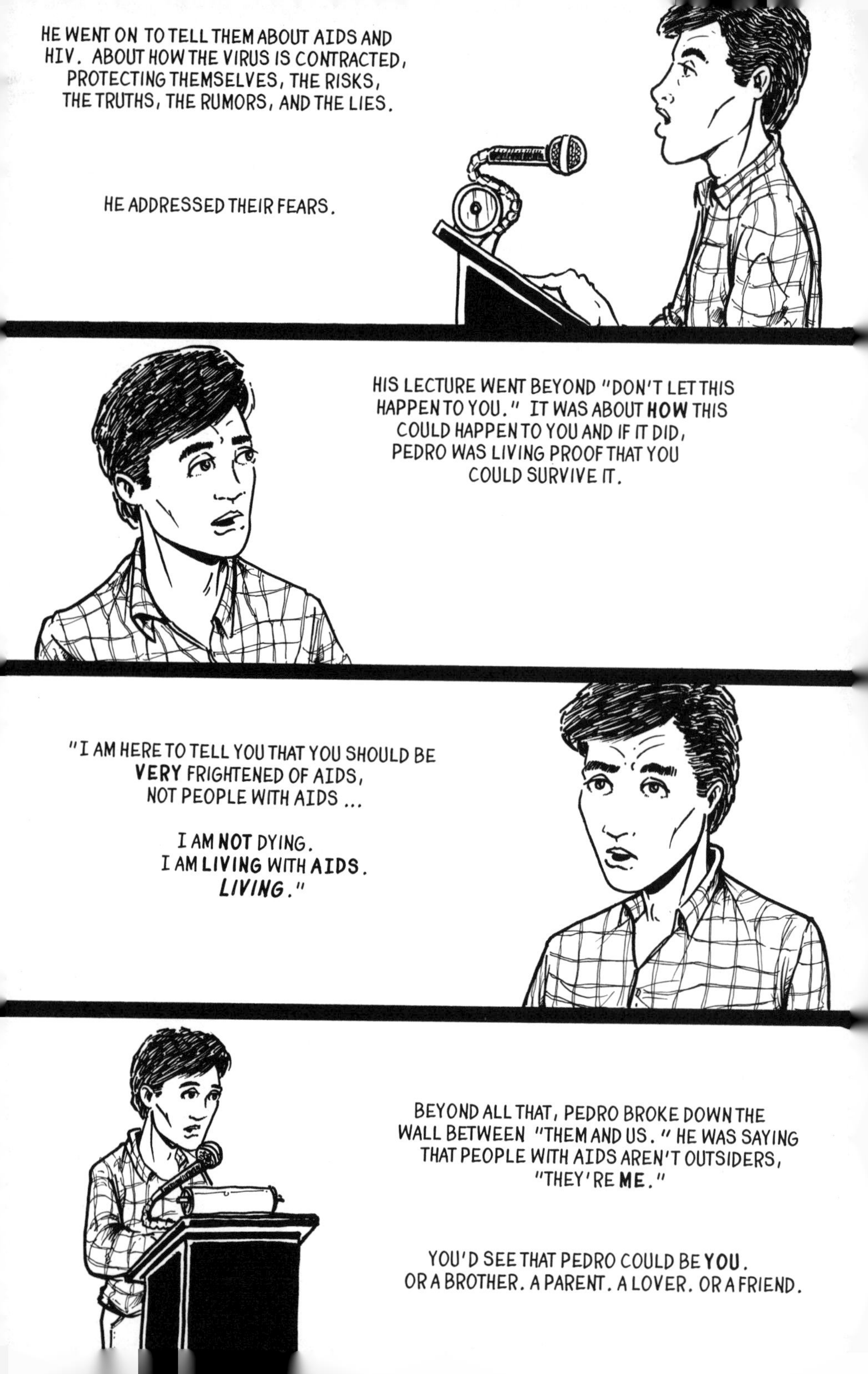
HE WENT ON TO TELL THEM ABOUT AIDS AND HIV. ABOUT HOW THE VIRUS IS CONTRACTED, PROTECTING THEMSELVES, THE RISKS, THE TRUTHS, THE RUMORS, AND THE LIES.
HE ADDRESSED THEIR FEARS.
HIS LECTURE WENT BEYOND "DON'T LET THIS HAPPEN TO YOU." IT WAS ABOUT **HOW** THIS COULD HAPPEN TO YOU AND IF IT DID, PEDRO WAS LIVING PROOF THAT YOU COULD SURVIVE IT.
"I AM HERE TO TELL YOU THAT YOU SHOULD BE **VERY** FRIGHTENED OF AIDS, NOT PEOPLE WITH AIDS ...
I AM **NOT** DYING.
I AM **LIVING** WITH **AIDS**.
LIVING."
BEYOND ALL THAT, PEDRO BROKE DOWN THE WALL BETWEEN "THEM AND US." HE WAS SAYING THAT PEOPLE WITH AIDS AREN'T OUTSIDERS, "THEY'RE **ME**."
YOU'D SEE THAT PEDRO COULD BE **YOU**. OR A BROTHER. A PARENT. A LOVER. OR A FRIEND.

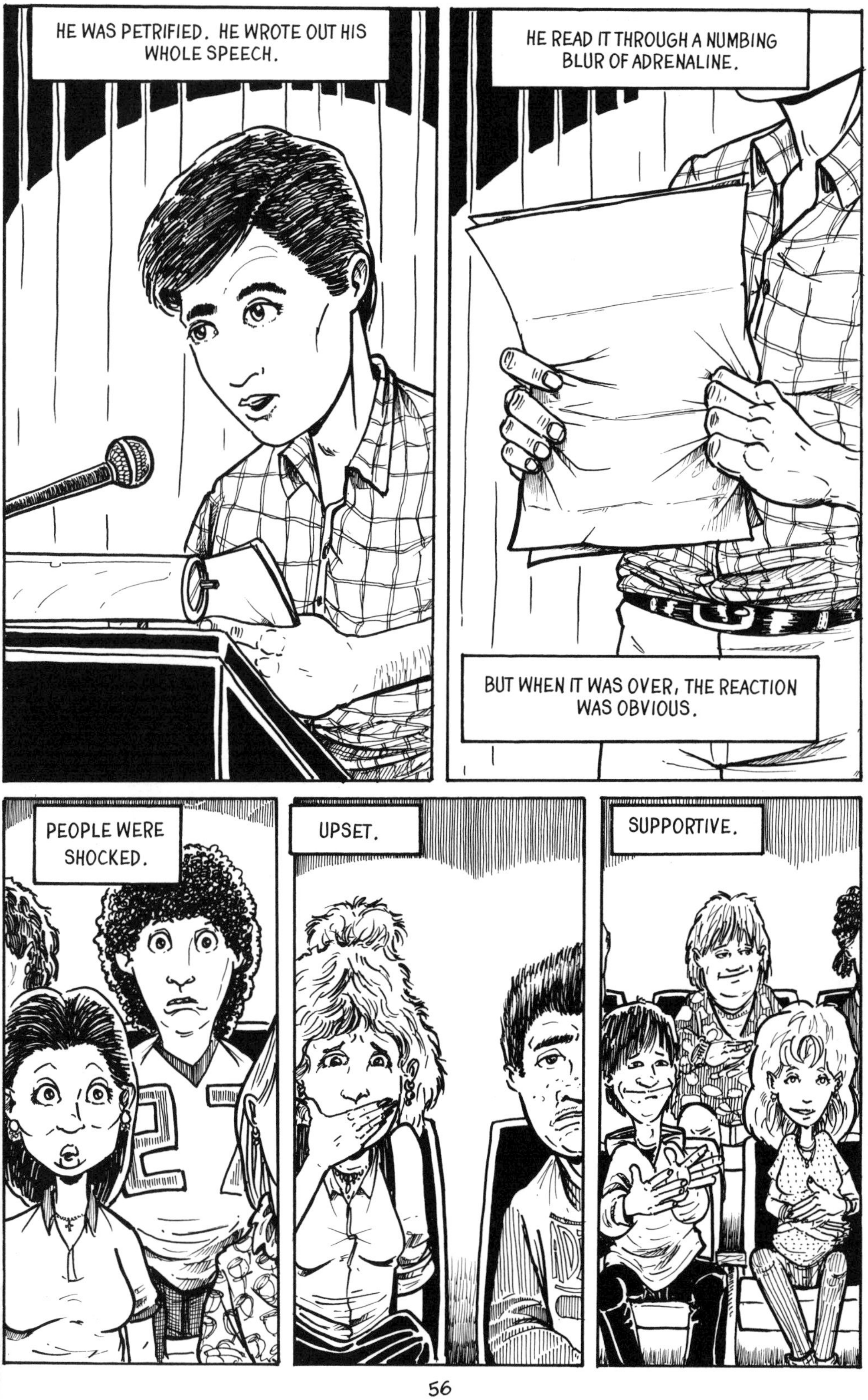
HE WAS PETRIFIED. HE WROTE OUT HIS WHOLE SPEECH.
HE READ IT THROUGH A NUMBING BLUR OF ADRENALINE.
BUT WHEN IT WAS OVER, THE REACTION WAS OBVIOUS.
PEOPLE WERE SHOCKED.
UPSET.
SUPPORTIVE.

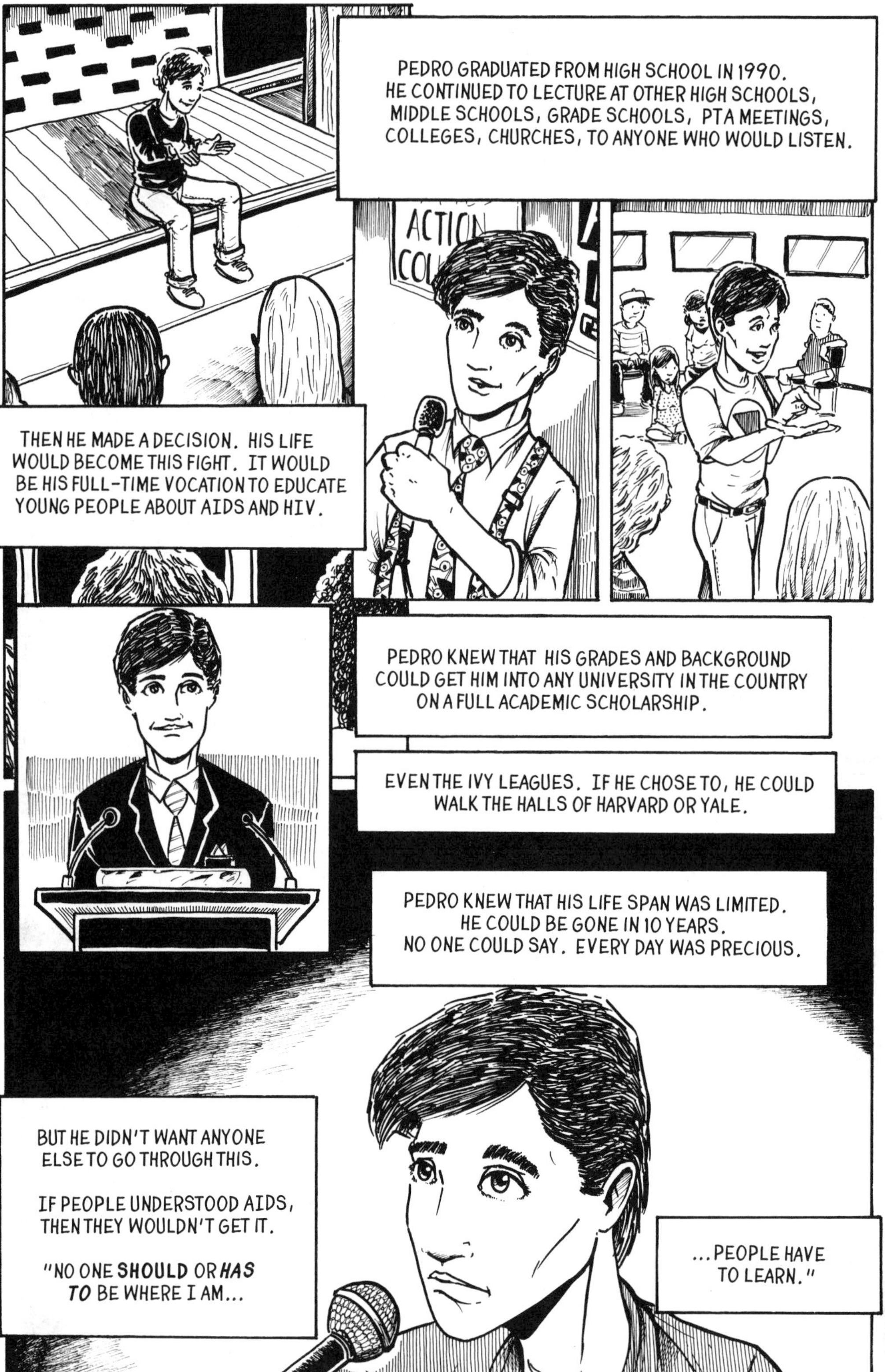
PEDRO GRADUATED FROM HIGH SCHOOL IN 1990. HE CONTINUED TO LECTURE AT OTHER HIGH SCHOOLS, MIDDLE SCHOOLS, GRADE SCHOOLS, PTA MEETINGS, COLLEGES, CHURCHES, TO ANYONE WHO WOULD LISTEN.
ACTION
THEN HE MADE A DECISION. HIS LIFE WOULD BECOME THIS FIGHT. IT WOULD BE HIS FULL-TIME VOCATION TO EDUCATE YOUNG PEOPLE ABOUT AIDS AND HIV.
PEDRO KNEW THAT HIS GRADES AND BACKGROUND COULD GET HIM INTO ANY UNIVERSITY IN THE COUNTRY ON A FULL ACADEMIC SCHOLARSHIP.
EVEN THE IVY LEAGUES. IF HE CHOSE TO, HE COULD WALK THE HALLS OF HARVARD OR YALE.
PEDRO KNEW THAT HIS LIFE SPAN WAS LIMITED. HE COULD BE GONE IN 10 YEARS. NO ONE COULD SAY. EVERY DAY WAS PRECIOUS.
BUT HE DIDN'T WANT ANYONE ELSE TO GO THROUGH THIS.
IF PEOPLE UNDERSTOOD AIDS, THEN THEY WOULDN'T GET IT.
"NO ONE **SHOULD** OR ***HAS TO*** BE WHERE I AM...
...PEOPLE HAVE TO LEARN."

1993: PEDRO

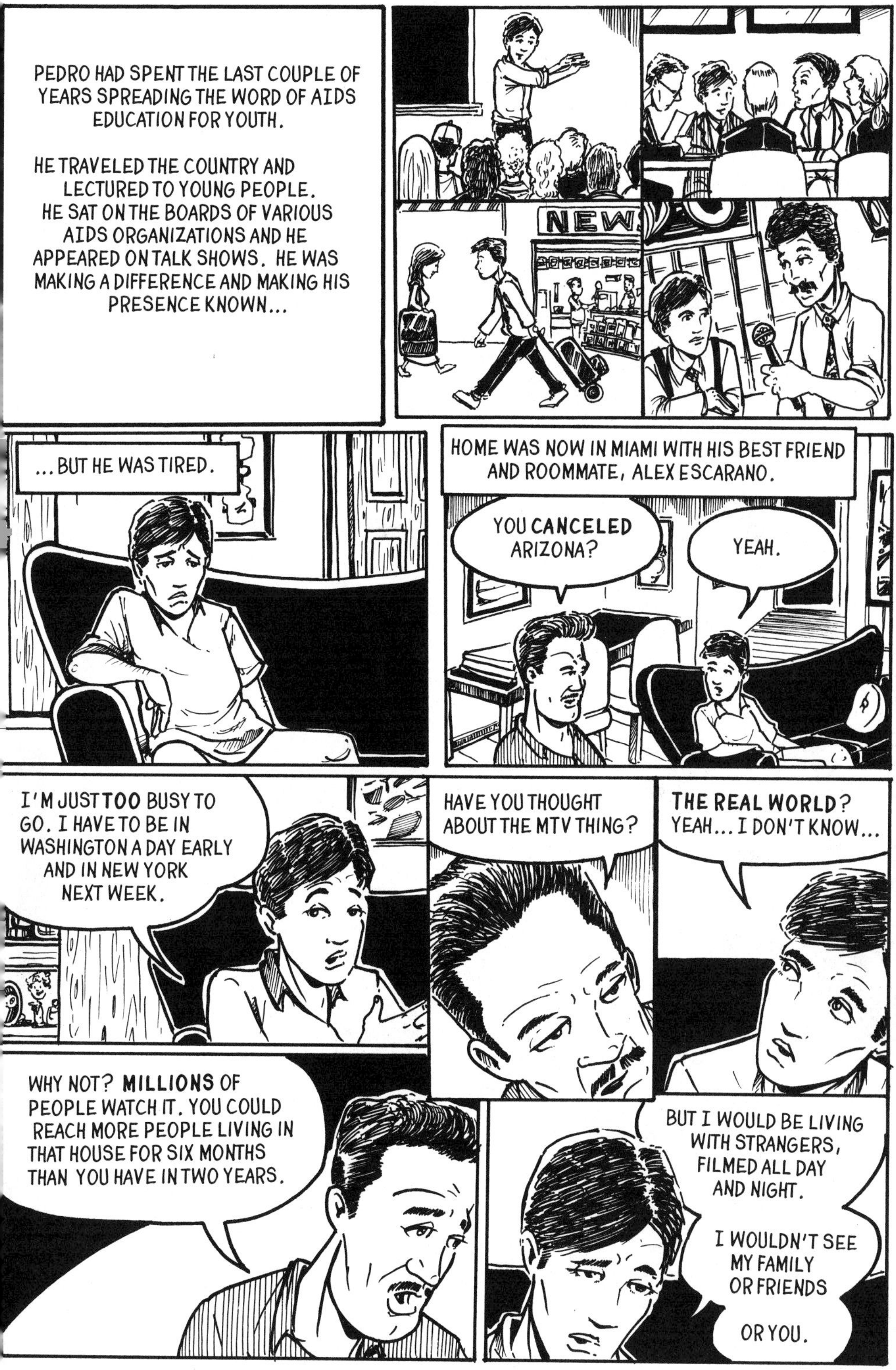
PEDRO HAD SPENT THE LAST COUPLE OF YEARS SPREADING THE WORD OF AIDS EDUCATION FOR YOUTH.
HE TRAVELED THE COUNTRY AND LECTURED TO YOUNG PEOPLE. HE SAT ON THE BOARDS OF VARIOUS AIDS ORGANIZATIONS AND HE APPEARED ON TALK SHOWS. HE WAS MAKING A DIFFERENCE AND MAKING HIS PRESENCE KNOWN...
NEWS
...BUT HE WAS TIRED.
HOME WAS NOW IN MIAMI WITH HIS BEST FRIEND AND ROOMMATE, ALEX ESCARANO.
YOU CANCELED ARIZONA?
YEAH.
I'M JUST TOO BUSY TO GO. I HAVE TO BE IN WASHINGTON A DAY EARLY AND IN NEW YORK NEXT WEEK.
HAVE YOU THOUGHT ABOUT THE MTV THING?
THE REAL WORLD? YEAH... I DON'T KNOW...
WHY NOT? MILLIONS OF PEOPLE WATCH IT. YOU COULD REACH MORE PEOPLE LIVING IN THAT HOUSE FOR SIX MONTHS THAN YOU HAVE IN TWO YEARS.
BUT I WOULD BE LIVING WITH STRANGERS, FILMED ALL DAY AND NIGHT.
I WOULDN'T SEE MY FAMILY OR FRIENDS
OR YOU.

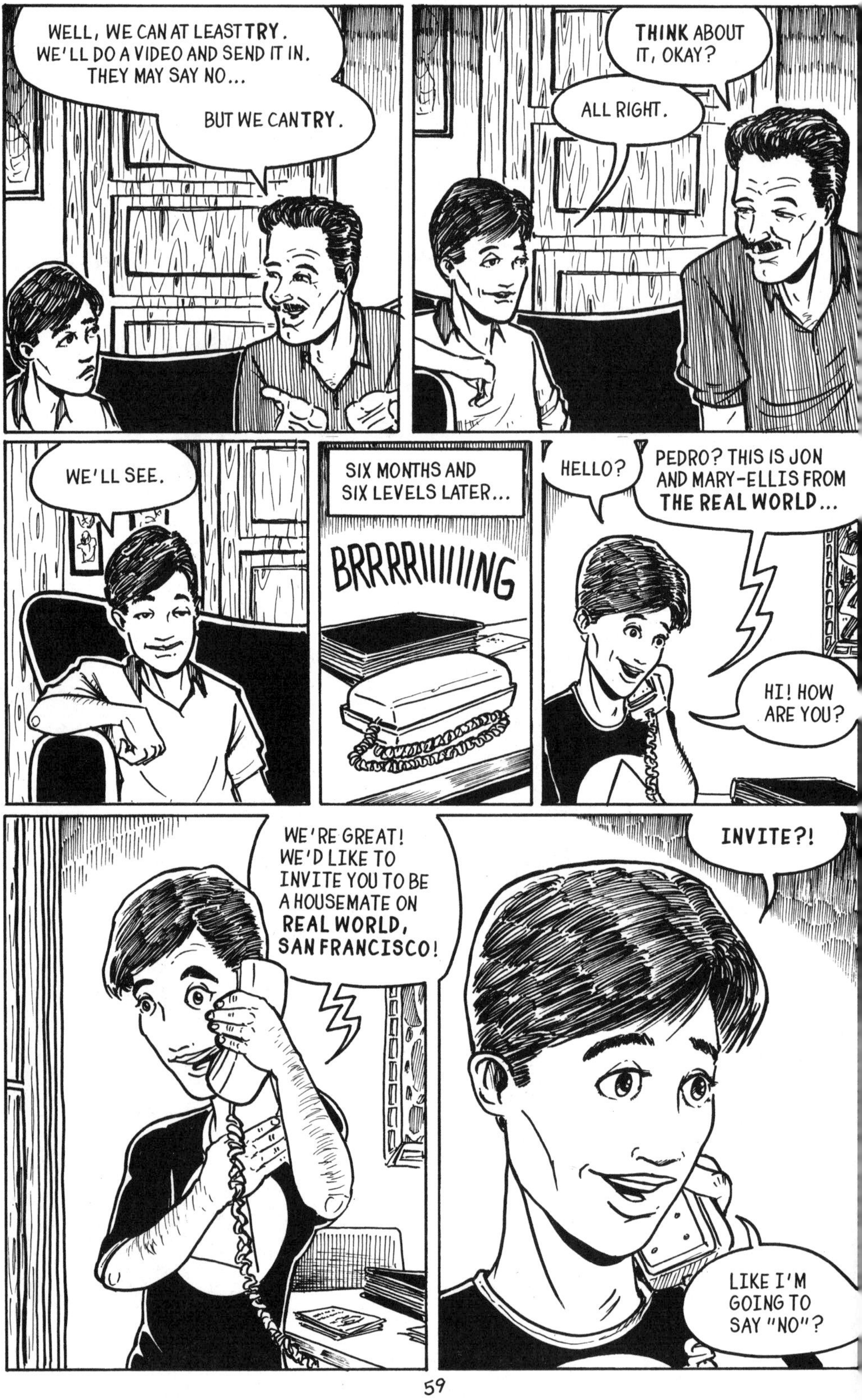
WELL, WE CAN AT LEAST TRY. WE'LL DO A VIDEO AND SEND IT IN. THEY MAY SAY NO...
BUT WE CAN TRY.
THINK ABOUT IT, OKAY?
ALL RIGHT.
WE'LL SEE.
SIX MONTHS AND SIX LEVELS LATER...
BRRRRIIIIIING
HELLO?
PEDRO? THIS IS JON AND MARY-ELLIS FROM THE REAL WORLD...
HI! HOW ARE YOU?
WE'RE GREAT! WE'D LIKE TO INVITE YOU TO BE A HOUSEMATE ON REAL WORLD, SAN FRANCISCO!
INVITE?!
LIKE I'M GOING TO SAY "NO"?

CHAPTER FOUR

SIX MONTHS BELOW
THE CROOKEDEST STREET
IN THE WORLD

MOVING DAY

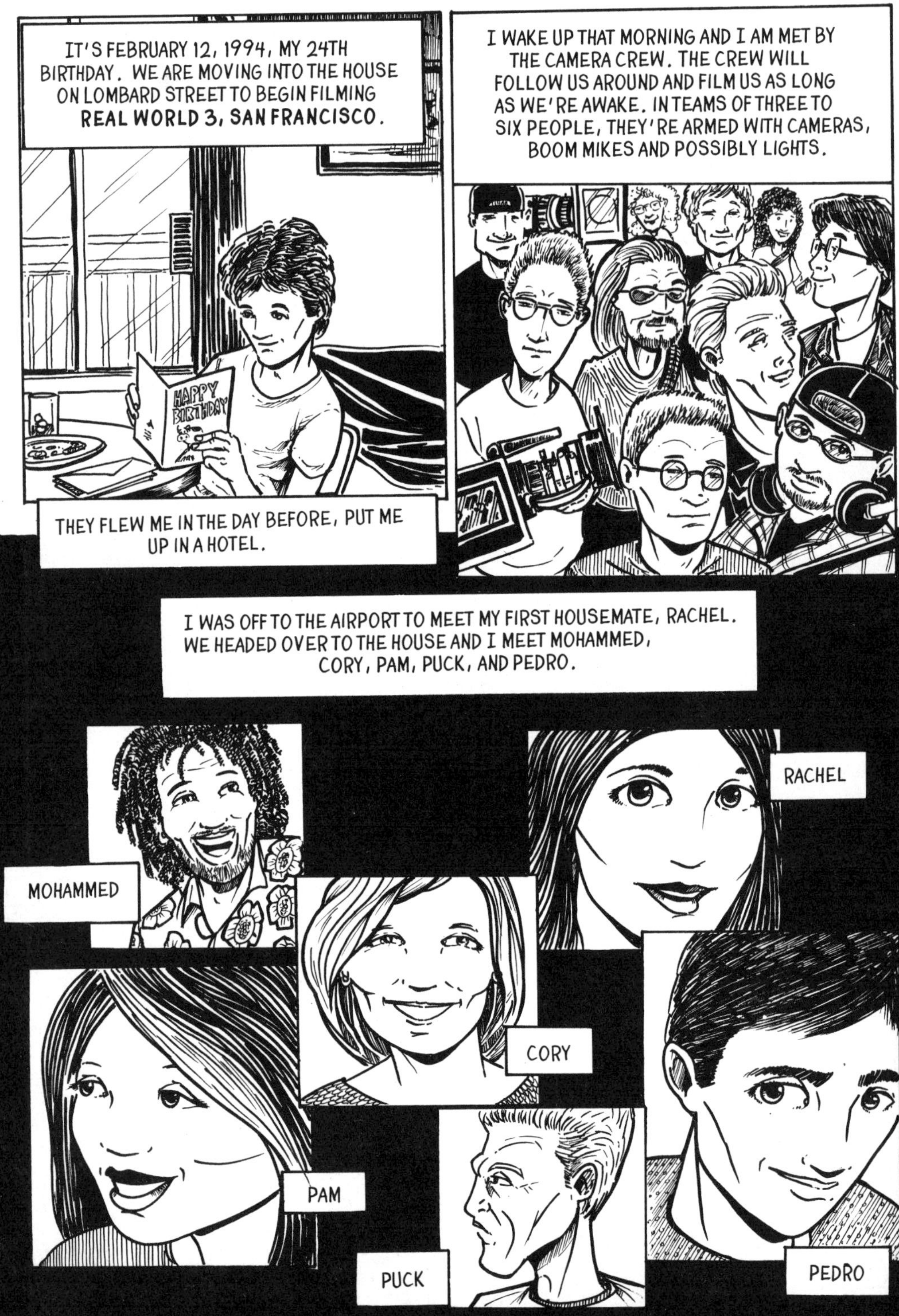
IT'S FEBRUARY 12, 1994, MY 24TH BIRTHDAY. WE ARE MOVING INTO THE HOUSE ON LOMBARD STREET TO BEGIN FILMING REAL WORLD 3, SAN FRANCISCO.
HAPPY BIRTHDAY
THEY FLEW ME IN THE DAY BEFORE, PUT ME UP IN A HOTEL.
I WAKE UP THAT MORNING AND I AM MET BY THE CAMERA CREW. THE CREW WILL FOLLOW US AROUND AND FILM US AS LONG AS WE'RE AWAKE. IN TEAMS OF THREE TO SIX PEOPLE, THEY'RE ARMED WITH CAMERAS, BOOM MIKES AND POSSIBLY LIGHTS.
I WAS OFF TO THE AIRPORT TO MEET MY FIRST HOUSEMATE, RACHEL. WE HEADED OVER TO THE HOUSE AND I MEET MOHAMMED, CORY, PAM, PUCK, AND PEDRO.
MOHAMMED
RACHEL
CORY
PAM
PUCK
PEDRO

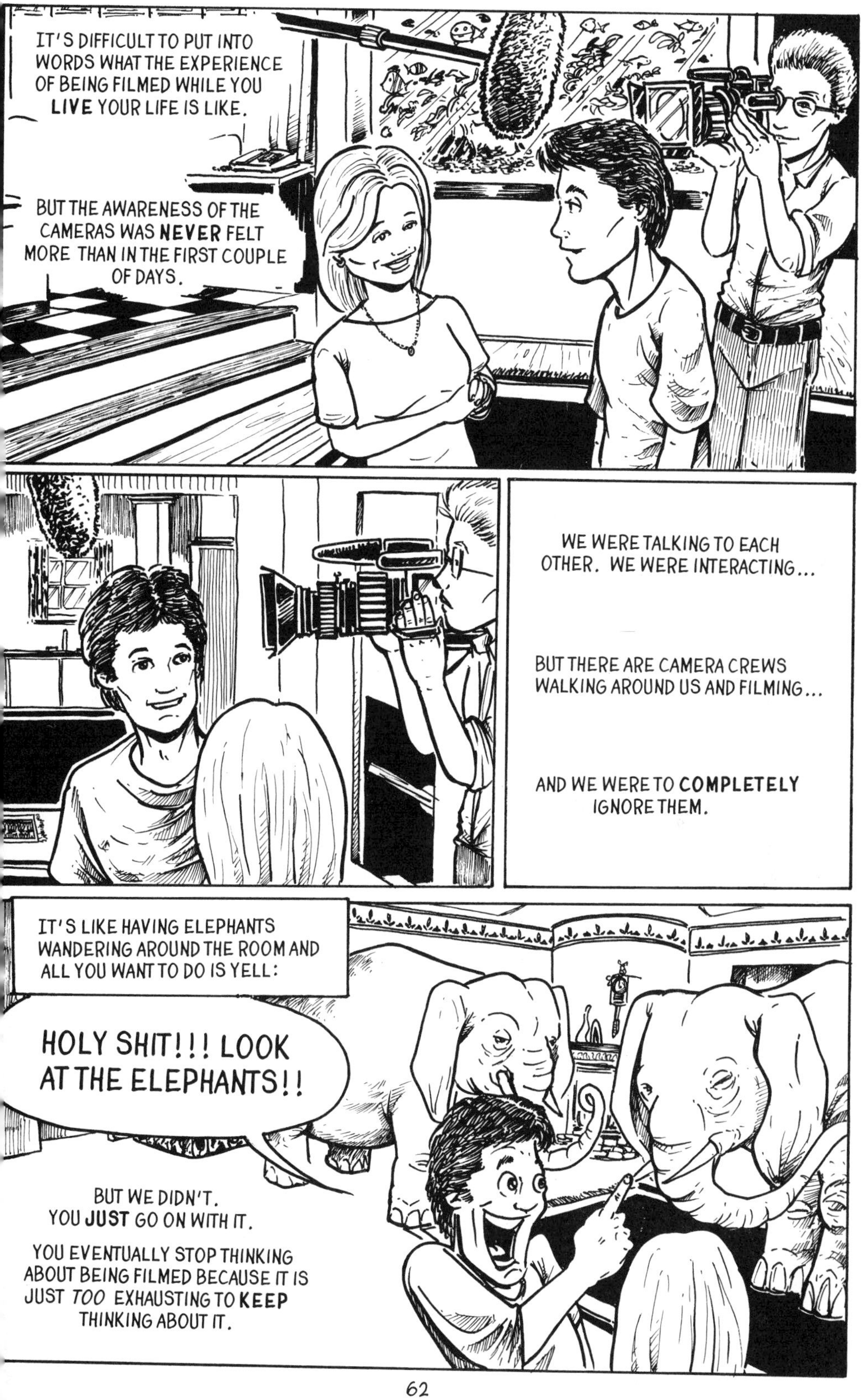
IT'S DIFFICULT TO PUT INTO WORDS WHAT THE EXPERIENCE OF BEING FILMED WHILE YOU **LIVE** YOUR LIFE IS LIKE.
BUT THE AWARENESS OF THE CAMERAS WAS **NEVER** FELT MORE THAN IN THE FIRST COUPLE OF DAYS.
WE WERE TALKING TO EACH OTHER. WE WERE INTERACTING...
BUT THERE ARE CAMERA CREWS WALKING AROUND US AND FILMING...
AND WE WERE TO **COMPLETELY** IGNORE THEM.
IT'S LIKE HAVING ELEPHANTS WANDERING AROUND THE ROOM AND ALL YOU WANT TO DO IS YELL:
HOLY SHIT!!! LOOK AT THE ELEPHANTS!!
BUT WE DIDN'T. YOU **JUST** GO ON WITH IT.
YOU EVENTUALLY STOP THINKING ABOUT BEING FILMED BECAUSE IT IS JUST *TOO* EXHAUSTING TO **KEEP** THINKING ABOUT IT.

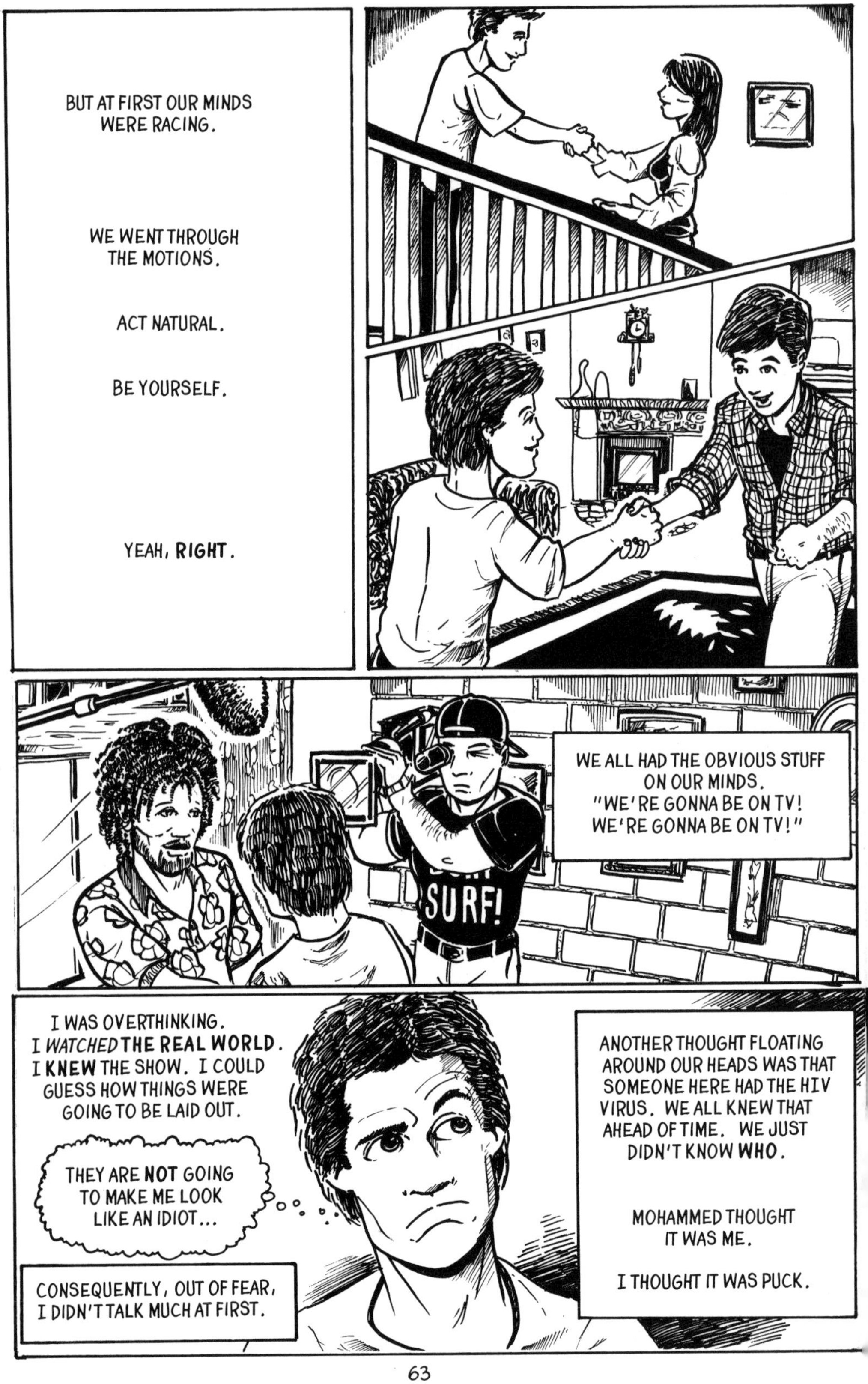
BUT AT FIRST OUR MINDS WERE RACING.
WE WENT THROUGH THE MOTIONS.
ACT NATURAL.
BE YOURSELF.
YEAH, **RIGHT**.
SURF!
WE ALL HAD THE OBVIOUS STUFF ON OUR MINDS. "WE'RE GONNA BE ON TV! WE'RE GONNA BE ON TV!"
I WAS OVERTHINKING. I *WATCHED* **THE REAL WORLD**. I **KNEW** THE SHOW. I COULD GUESS HOW THINGS WERE GOING TO BE LAID OUT.
THEY ARE **NOT** GOING TO MAKE ME LOOK LIKE AN IDIOT...
CONSEQUENTLY, OUT OF FEAR, I DIDN'T TALK MUCH AT FIRST.
ANOTHER THOUGHT FLOATING AROUND OUR HEADS WAS THAT SOMEONE HERE HAD THE HIV VIRUS. WE ALL KNEW THAT AHEAD OF TIME. WE JUST DIDN'T KNOW **WHO**.
MOHAMMED THOUGHT IT WAS ME.
I THOUGHT IT WAS PUCK.

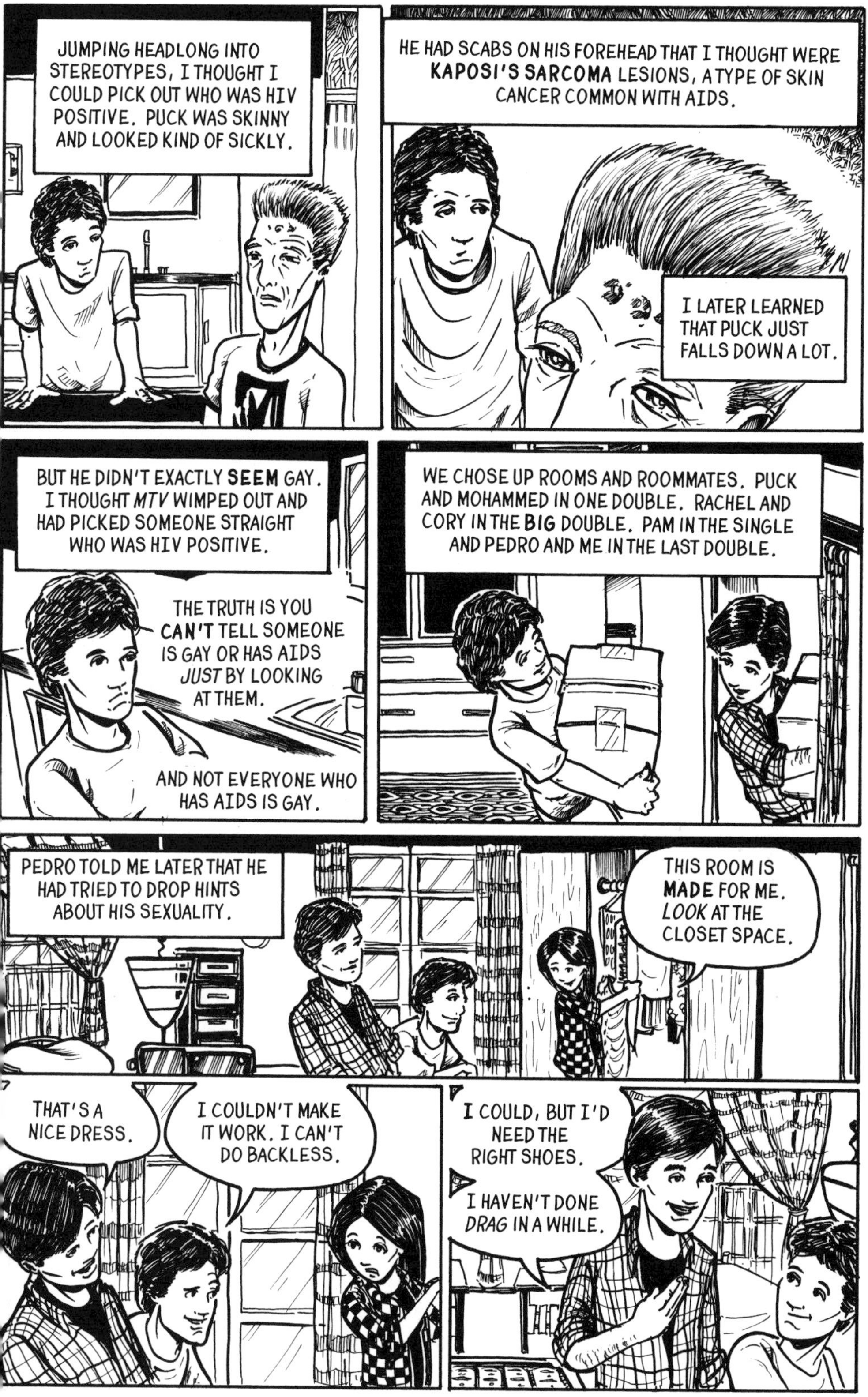
JUMPING HEADLONG INTO STEREOTYPES, I THOUGHT I COULD PICK OUT WHO WAS HIV POSITIVE. PUCK WAS SKINNY AND LOOKED KIND OF SICKLY.
HE HAD SCABS ON HIS FOREHEAD THAT I THOUGHT WERE **KAPOSI'S SARCOMA** LESIONS, A TYPE OF SKIN CANCER COMMON WITH AIDS.
I LATER LEARNED THAT PUCK JUST FALLS DOWN A LOT.
BUT HE DIDN'T EXACTLY **SEEM** GAY. I THOUGHT *MTV* WIMPED OUT AND HAD PICKED SOMEONE STRAIGHT WHO WAS HIV POSITIVE.
THE TRUTH IS YOU **CAN'T** TELL SOMEONE IS GAY OR HAS AIDS *JUST* BY LOOKING AT THEM.
AND NOT EVERYONE WHO HAS AIDS IS GAY.
WE CHOSE UP ROOMS AND ROOMMATES. PUCK AND MOHAMMED IN ONE DOUBLE. RACHEL AND CORY IN THE **BIG** DOUBLE. PAM IN THE SINGLE AND PEDRO AND ME IN THE LAST DOUBLE.
PEDRO TOLD ME LATER THAT HE HAD TRIED TO DROP HINTS ABOUT HIS SEXUALITY.
THIS ROOM IS **MADE** FOR ME. *LOOK* AT THE CLOSET SPACE.
THAT'S A NICE DRESS.
I COULDN'T MAKE IT WORK. I CAN'T DO BACKLESS.
I COULD, BUT I'D NEED THE RIGHT SHOES.
I HAVEN'T DONE *DRAG* IN A WHILE.

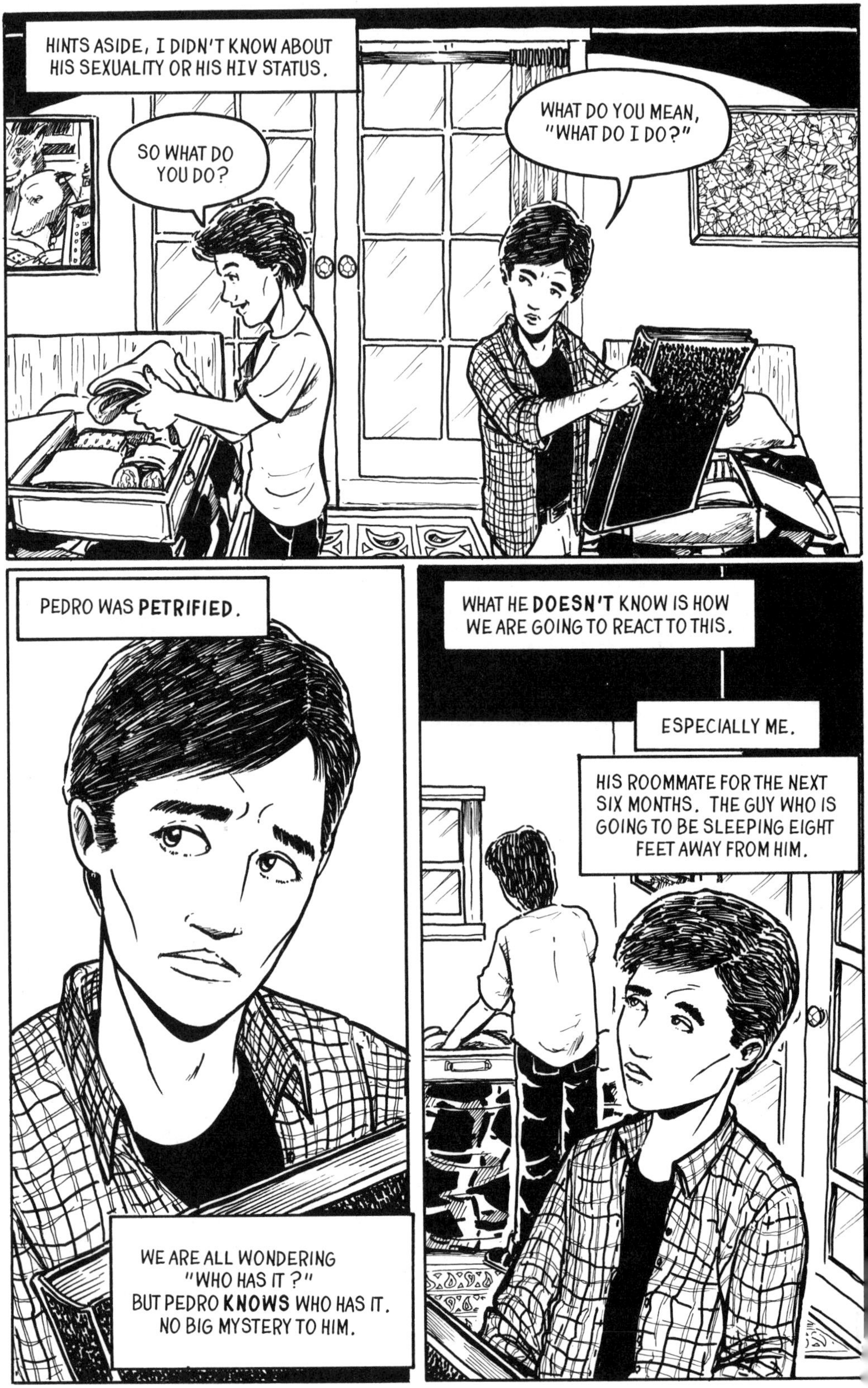
HINTS ASIDE, I DIDN'T KNOW ABOUT HIS SEXUALITY OR HIS HIV STATUS.
SO WHAT DO YOU DO?
WHAT DO YOU MEAN, "WHAT DO I DO?"
PEDRO WAS **PETRIFIED**.
WE ARE ALL WONDERING "WHO HAS IT?" BUT PEDRO **KNOWS** WHO HAS IT. NO BIG MYSTERY TO HIM.
WHAT HE **DOESN'T** KNOW IS HOW WE ARE GOING TO REACT TO THIS.
ESPECIALLY ME.
HIS ROOMMATE FOR THE NEXT SIX MONTHS. THE GUY WHO IS GOING TO BE SLEEPING EIGHT FEET AWAY FROM HIM.

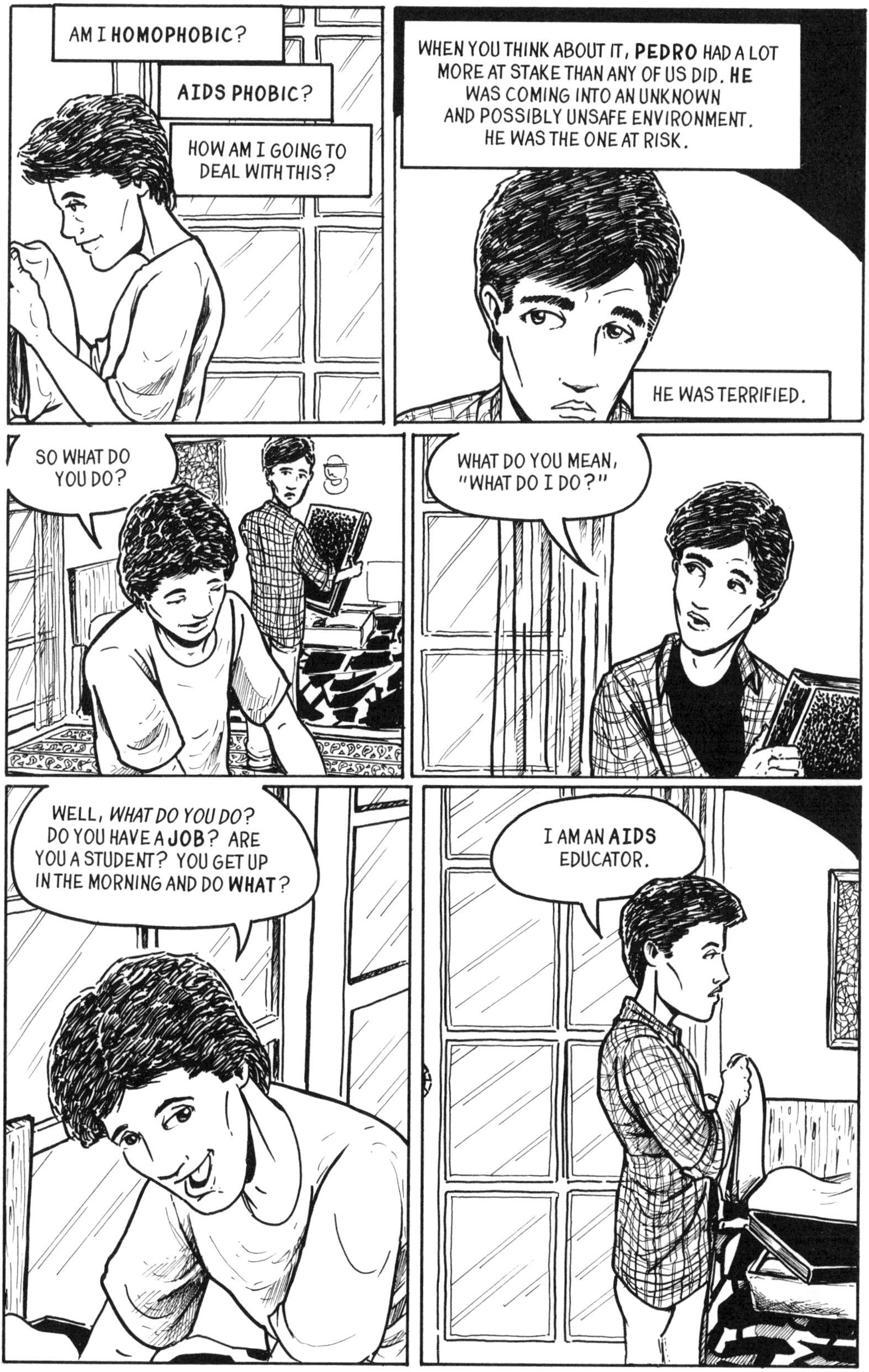
AM I **HOMOPHOBIC**?
AIDS PHOBIC?
HOW AM I GOING TO DEAL WITH THIS?
WHEN YOU THINK ABOUT IT, **PEDRO** HAD A LOT MORE AT STAKE THAN ANY OF US DID. **HE** WAS COMING INTO AN UNKNOWN AND POSSIBLY UNSAFE ENVIRONMENT. HE WAS THE ONE AT RISK.
HE WAS TERRIFIED.
SO WHAT DO YOU DO?
WHAT DO YOU MEAN, "WHAT DO I DO?"
WELL, *WHAT DO YOU DO?* DO YOU HAVE A **JOB**? ARE YOU A STUDENT? YOU GET UP IN THE MORNING AND DO **WHAT**?
I AM AN **AIDS** EDUCATOR.

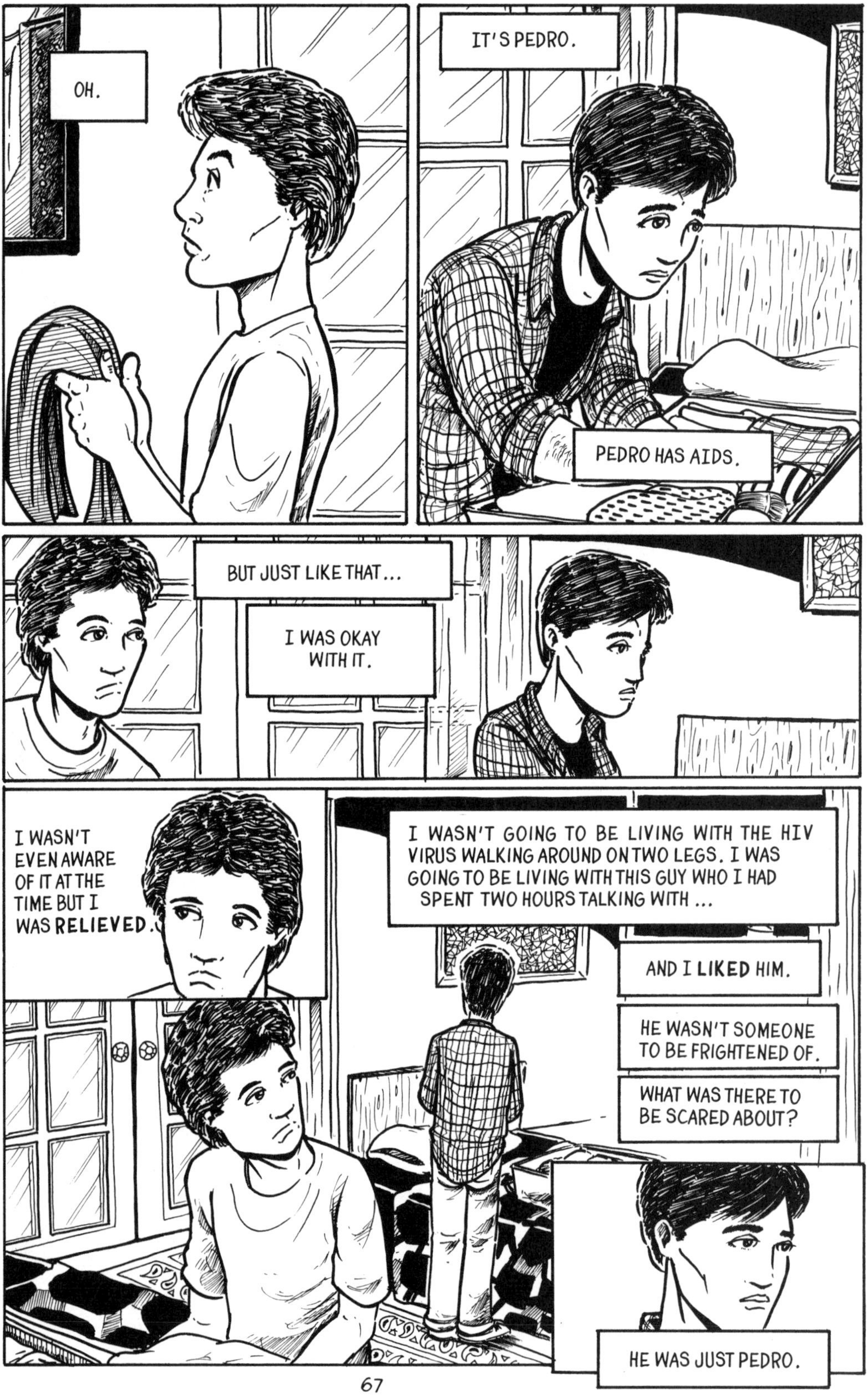
OH.
IT'S PEDRO.
PEDRO HAS AIDS.
BUT JUST LIKE THAT...
I WAS OKAY WITH IT.
I WASN'T EVEN AWARE OF IT AT THE TIME BUT I WAS RELIEVED.
I WASN'T GOING TO BE LIVING WITH THE HIV VIRUS WALKING AROUND ON TWO LEGS. I WAS GOING TO BE LIVING WITH THIS GUY WHO I HAD SPENT TWO HOURS TALKING WITH ...
AND I LIKED HIM.
HE WASN'T SOMEONE TO BE FRIGHTENED OF.
WHAT WAS THERE TO BE SCARED ABOUT?
HE WAS JUST PEDRO.

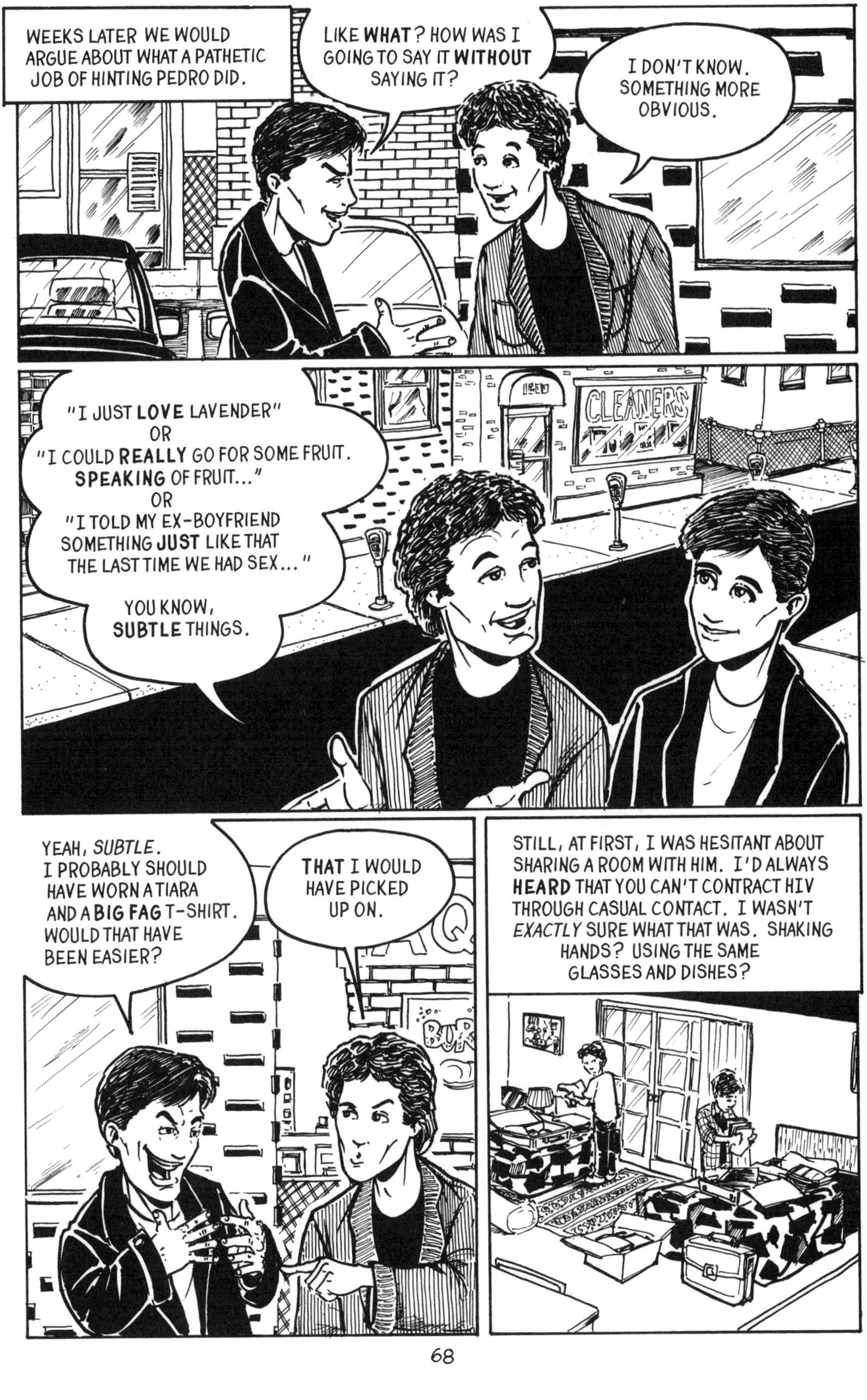
WEEKS LATER WE WOULD ARGUE ABOUT WHAT A PATHETIC JOB OF HINTING PEDRO DID.
LIKE **WHAT**? HOW WAS I GOING TO SAY IT **WITHOUT** SAYING IT?
I DON'T KNOW. SOMETHING MORE OBVIOUS.
"I JUST **LOVE** LAVENDER" OR "I COULD **REALLY** GO FOR SOME FRUIT. **SPEAKING** OF FRUIT..." OR "I TOLD MY EX-BOYFRIEND SOMETHING **JUST** LIKE THAT THE LAST TIME WE HAD SEX..." YOU KNOW, **SUBTLE** THINGS.
CLEANERS
YEAH, *SUBTLE*. I PROBABLY SHOULD HAVE WORN A TIARA AND A **BIG FAG** T-SHIRT. WOULD THAT HAVE BEEN EASIER?
THAT I WOULD HAVE PICKED UP ON.
STILL, AT FIRST, I WAS HESITANT ABOUT SHARING A ROOM WITH HIM. I'D ALWAYS **HEARD** THAT YOU CAN'T CONTRACT HIV THROUGH CASUAL CONTACT. I WASN'T *EXACTLY* SURE WHAT THAT WAS. SHAKING HANDS? USING THE SAME GLASSES AND DISHES?

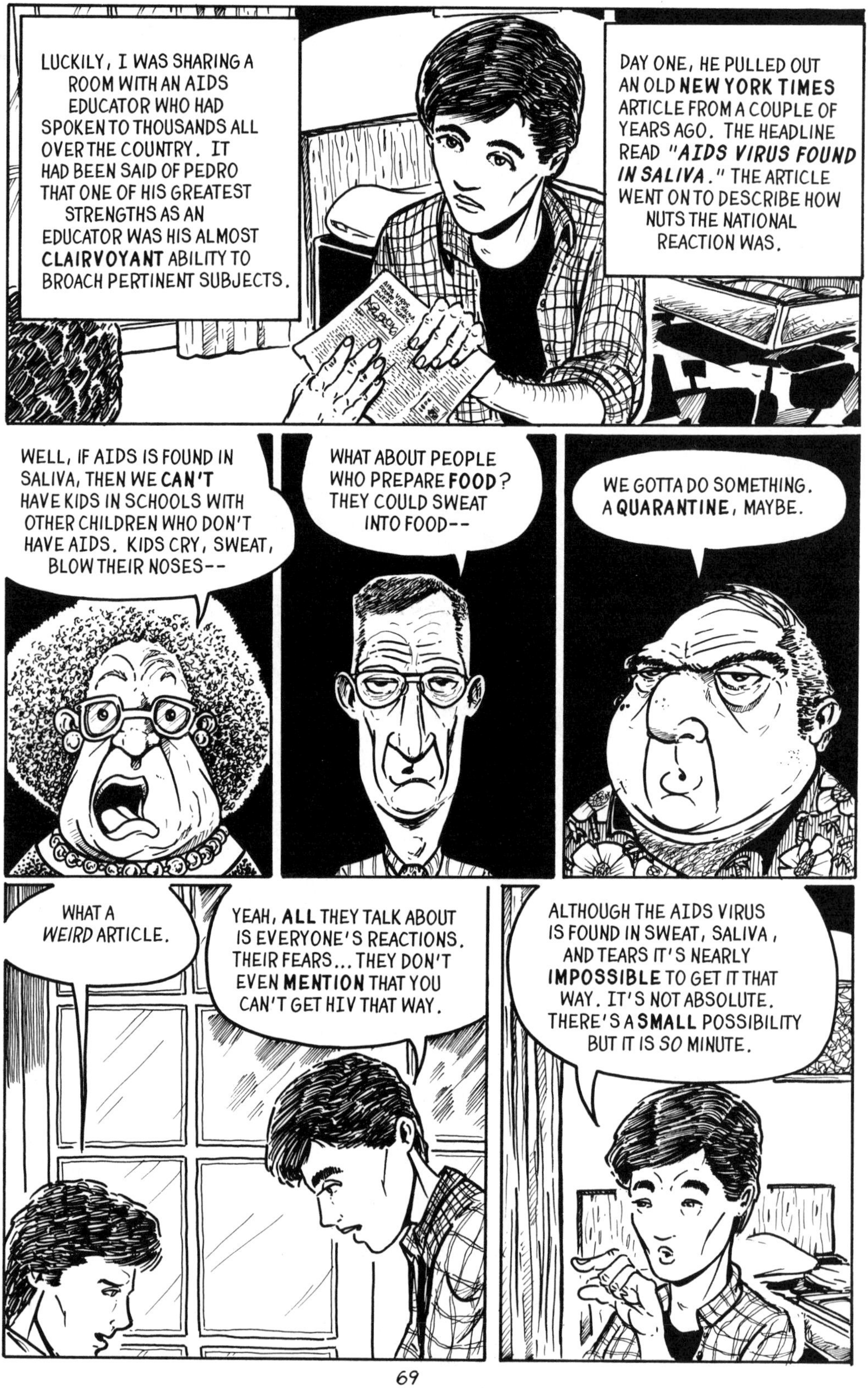
LUCKILY, I WAS SHARING A ROOM WITH AN AIDS EDUCATOR WHO HAD SPOKEN TO THOUSANDS ALL OVER THE COUNTRY. IT HAD BEEN SAID OF PEDRO THAT ONE OF HIS GREATEST STRENGTHS AS AN EDUCATOR WAS HIS ALMOST **CLAIRVOYANT** ABILITY TO BROACH PERTINENT SUBJECTS.
DAY ONE, HE PULLED OUT AN OLD **NEW YORK TIMES** ARTICLE FROM A COUPLE OF YEARS AGO. THE HEADLINE READ ***"AIDS VIRUS FOUND IN SALIVA."*** THE ARTICLE WENT ON TO DESCRIBE HOW NUTS THE NATIONAL REACTION WAS.
WELL, IF AIDS IS FOUND IN SALIVA, THEN WE **CAN'T** HAVE KIDS IN SCHOOLS WITH OTHER CHILDREN WHO DON'T HAVE AIDS. KIDS CRY, SWEAT, BLOW THEIR NOSES--
WHAT ABOUT PEOPLE WHO PREPARE **FOOD**? THEY COULD SWEAT INTO FOOD--
WE GOTTA DO SOMETHING. A **QUARANTINE**, MAYBE.
WHAT A *WEIRD* ARTICLE.
YEAH, **ALL** THEY TALK ABOUT IS EVERYONE'S REACTIONS. THEIR FEARS... THEY DON'T EVEN **MENTION** THAT YOU CAN'T GET HIV THAT WAY.
ALTHOUGH THE AIDS VIRUS IS FOUND IN SWEAT, SALIVA, AND TEARS IT'S NEARLY **IMPOSSIBLE** TO GET IT THAT WAY. IT'S NOT ABSOLUTE. THERE'S A **SMALL** POSSIBILITY BUT IT IS *SO* MINUTE.

PRETTY SNEAKY, SIS. HE WAS GIVING ME MY FIRST AIDS EDUCATION LESSON AND HE WAS TELLING ME *JUST* THE SORT OF INFORMATION SOMEONE HE IS SHARING A ROOM WITH SHOULD HAVE. THIS WAS "YOU-ARE-NOT-GOING-TO-GET-AIDS-BY-LIVING-WITH-ME" 101. I WASN'T EVEN AWARE HE WAS DOING IT.

YOU CAN'T GET AIDS FROM KISSING, CAN YOU?

WELL, THEORETICALLY YES, BUT NO ONE HAS EVER CONTRACTED HIV THAT WAY. THERE HAS NEVER BEEN A **SINGLE** CASE REPORTED OF SOMEONE GETTING AIDS THROUGH JUST KISSING.

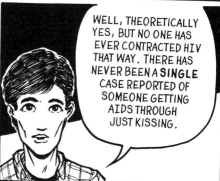

BUT THEORETICALLY **YES**.

WELL, YES.

LET'S SAY I HAVE AIDS, WHICH I DO...

AND I AM KISSING SOMEONE WHO DOESN'T. LET'S SAY **YOU**.

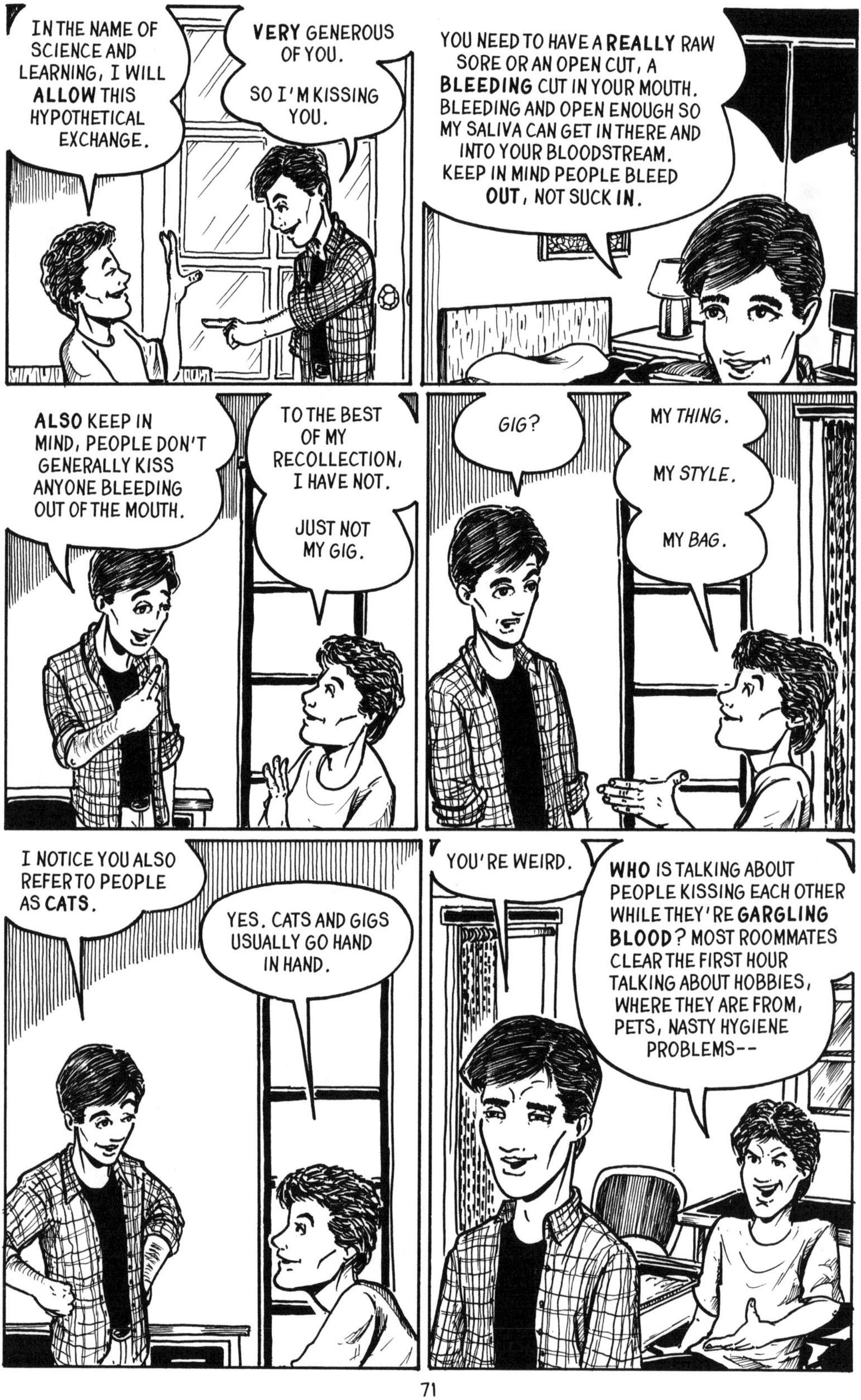
IN THE NAME OF SCIENCE AND LEARNING, I WILL **ALLOW** THIS HYPOTHETICAL EXCHANGE.
VERY GENEROUS OF YOU.
SO I'M KISSING YOU.
YOU NEED TO HAVE A **REALLY** RAW SORE OR AN OPEN CUT, A **BLEEDING** CUT IN YOUR MOUTH. BLEEDING AND OPEN ENOUGH SO MY SALIVA CAN GET IN THERE AND INTO YOUR BLOODSTREAM. KEEP IN MIND PEOPLE BLEED **OUT**, NOT SUCK **IN**.
ALSO KEEP IN MIND, PEOPLE DON'T GENERALLY KISS ANYONE BLEEDING OUT OF THE MOUTH.
TO THE BEST OF MY RECOLLECTION, I HAVE NOT.
JUST NOT MY GIG.
GIG?
MY *THING*.
MY *STYLE*.
MY *BAG*.
I NOTICE YOU ALSO REFER TO PEOPLE AS **CATS**.
YES. CATS AND GIGS USUALLY GO HAND IN HAND.
YOU'RE WEIRD.
WHO IS TALKING ABOUT PEOPLE KISSING EACH OTHER WHILE THEY'RE **GARGLING BLOOD**? MOST ROOMMATES CLEAR THE FIRST HOUR TALKING ABOUT HOBBIES, WHERE THEY ARE FROM, PETS, NASTY HYGIENE PROBLEMS--

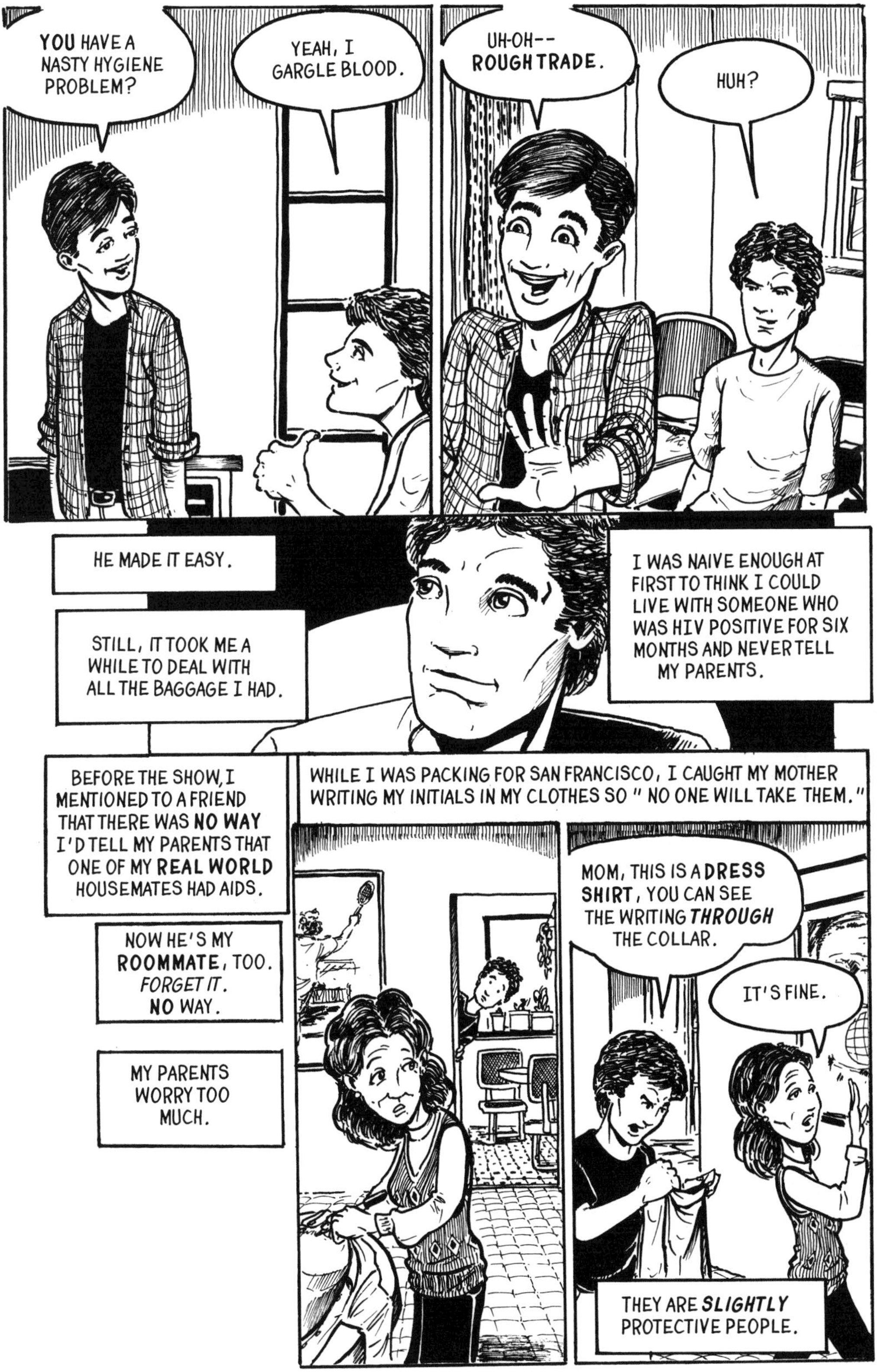
YOU HAVE A NASTY HYGIENE PROBLEM?
YEAH, I GARGLE BLOOD.
UH-OH-- ROUGH TRADE.
HUH?
HE MADE IT EASY.
STILL, IT TOOK ME A WHILE TO DEAL WITH ALL THE BAGGAGE I HAD.
I WAS NAIVE ENOUGH AT FIRST TO THINK I COULD LIVE WITH SOMEONE WHO WAS HIV POSITIVE FOR SIX MONTHS AND NEVER TELL MY PARENTS.
BEFORE THE SHOW, I MENTIONED TO A FRIEND THAT THERE WAS NO WAY I'D TELL MY PARENTS THAT ONE OF MY REAL WORLD HOUSEMATES HAD AIDS.
NOW HE'S MY ROOMMATE, TOO. FORGET IT. NO WAY.
MY PARENTS WORRY TOO MUCH.
WHILE I WAS PACKING FOR SAN FRANCISCO, I CAUGHT MY MOTHER WRITING MY INITIALS IN MY CLOTHES SO " NO ONE WILL TAKE THEM."
MOM, THIS IS A DRESS SHIRT, YOU CAN SEE THE WRITING THROUGH THE COLLAR.
IT'S FINE.
THEY ARE SLIGHTLY PROTECTIVE PEOPLE.

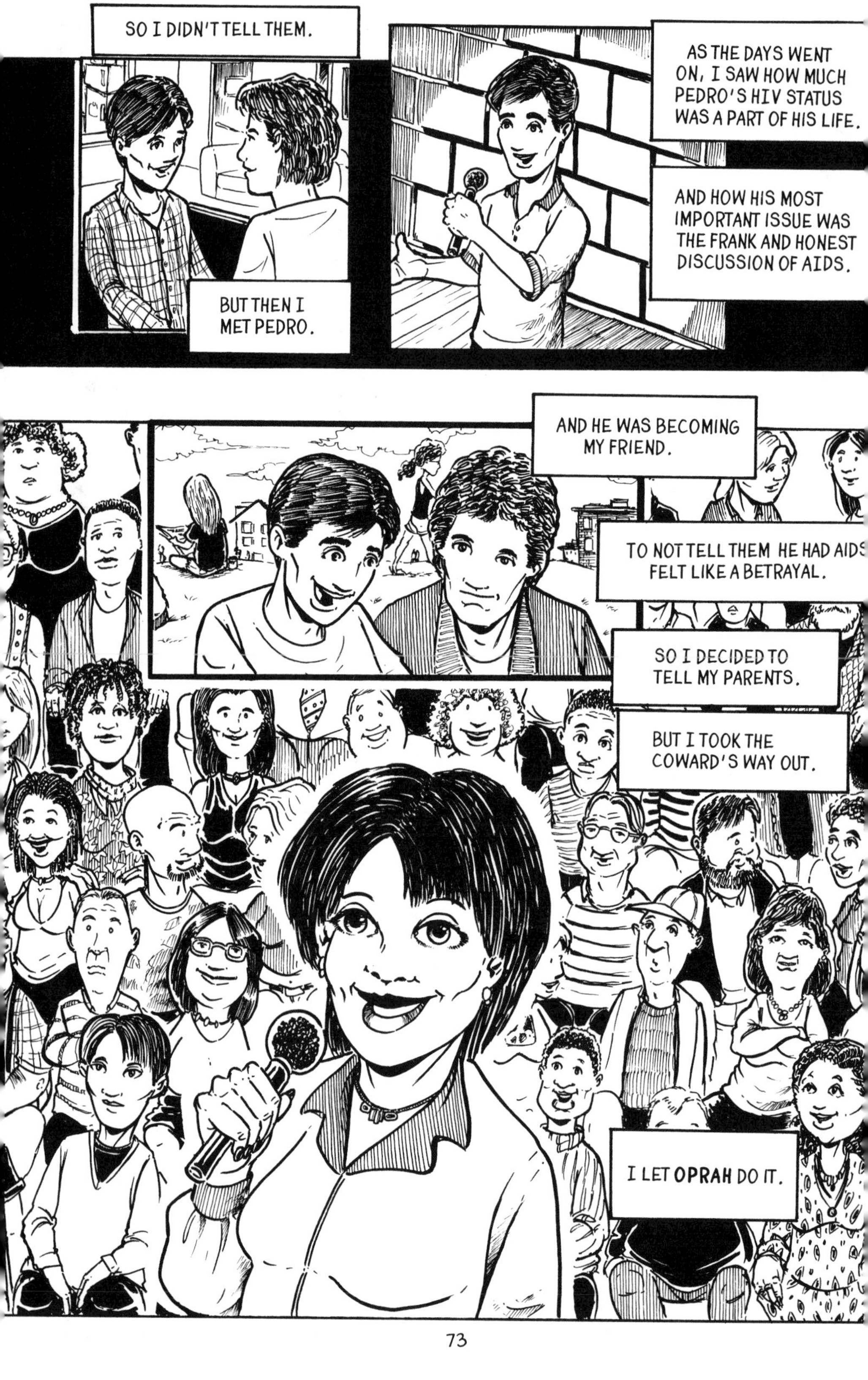
SO I DIDN'T TELL THEM.
BUT THEN I MET PEDRO.
AS THE DAYS WENT ON, I SAW HOW MUCH PEDRO'S HIV STATUS WAS A PART OF HIS LIFE.
AND HOW HIS MOST IMPORTANT ISSUE WAS THE FRANK AND HONEST DISCUSSION OF AIDS.
AND HE WAS BECOMING MY FRIEND.
TO NOT TELL THEM HE HAD AIDS FELT LIKE A BETRAYAL.
SO I DECIDED TO TELL MY PARENTS.
BUT I TOOK THE COWARD'S WAY OUT.
I LET **OPRAH** DO IT.

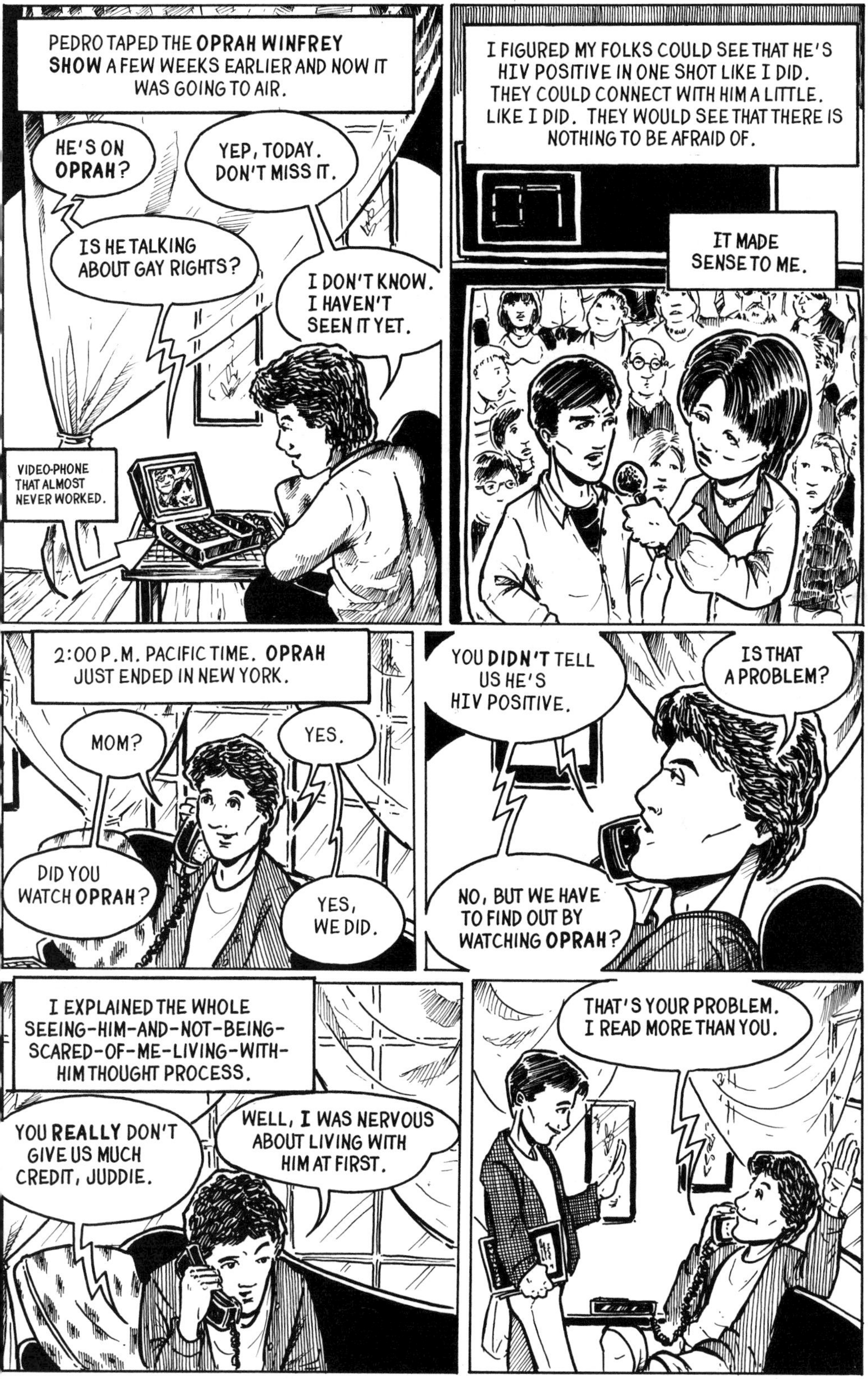
PEDRO TAPED THE OPRAH WINFREY SHOW A FEW WEEKS EARLIER AND NOW IT WAS GOING TO AIR.
HE'S ON OPRAH?
YEP, TODAY. DON'T MISS IT.
IS HE TALKING ABOUT GAY RIGHTS?
I DON'T KNOW. I HAVEN'T SEEN IT YET.
VIDEO-PHONE THAT ALMOST NEVER WORKED.
I FIGURED MY FOLKS COULD SEE THAT HE'S HIV POSITIVE IN ONE SHOT LIKE I DID. THEY COULD CONNECT WITH HIM A LITTLE. LIKE I DID. THEY WOULD SEE THAT THERE IS NOTHING TO BE AFRAID OF.
IT MADE SENSE TO ME.
2:00 P.M. PACIFIC TIME. OPRAH JUST ENDED IN NEW YORK.
MOM?
YES.
DID YOU WATCH OPRAH?
YES, WE DID.
YOU DIDN'T TELL US HE'S HIV POSITIVE.
IS THAT A PROBLEM?
NO, BUT WE HAVE TO FIND OUT BY WATCHING OPRAH?
I EXPLAINED THE WHOLE SEEING-HIM-AND-NOT-BEING-SCARED-OF-ME-LIVING-WITH-HIM THOUGHT PROCESS.
YOU REALLY DON'T GIVE US MUCH CREDIT, JUDDIE.
WELL, I WAS NERVOUS ABOUT LIVING WITH HIM AT FIRST.
THAT'S YOUR PROBLEM. I READ MORE THAN YOU.

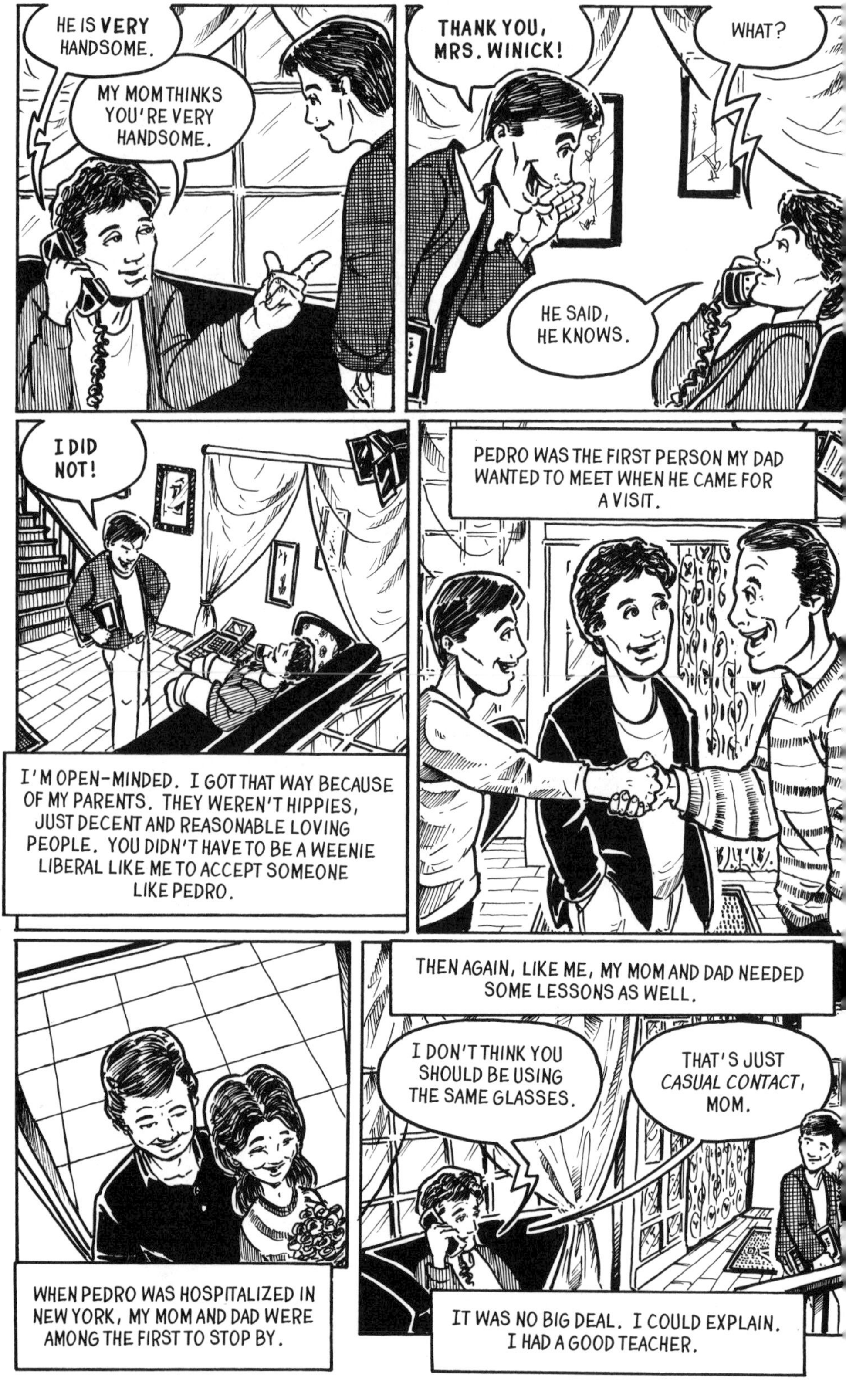

HE IS VERY HANDSOME.
MY MOM THINKS YOU'RE VERY HANDSOME.
THANK YOU, MRS. WINICK!
WHAT?
HE SAID, HE KNOWS.
I DID NOT!
I'M OPEN-MINDED. I GOT THAT WAY BECAUSE OF MY PARENTS. THEY WEREN'T HIPPIES, JUST DECENT AND REASONABLE LOVING PEOPLE. YOU DIDN'T HAVE TO BE A WEENIE LIBERAL LIKE ME TO ACCEPT SOMEONE LIKE PEDRO.
PEDRO WAS THE FIRST PERSON MY DAD WANTED TO MEET WHEN HE CAME FOR A VISIT.
WHEN PEDRO WAS HOSPITALIZED IN NEW YORK, MY MOM AND DAD WERE AMONG THE FIRST TO STOP BY.
THEN AGAIN, LIKE ME, MY MOM AND DAD NEEDED SOME LESSONS AS WELL.
I DON'T THINK YOU SHOULD BE USING THE SAME GLASSES.
THAT'S JUST CASUAL CONTACT, MOM.
IT WAS NO BIG DEAL. I COULD EXPLAIN. I HAD A GOOD TEACHER.

THE LITTLE THINGS

WATCHING *STAR TREK*, HAIRY FEET, AND GREETING CARDS

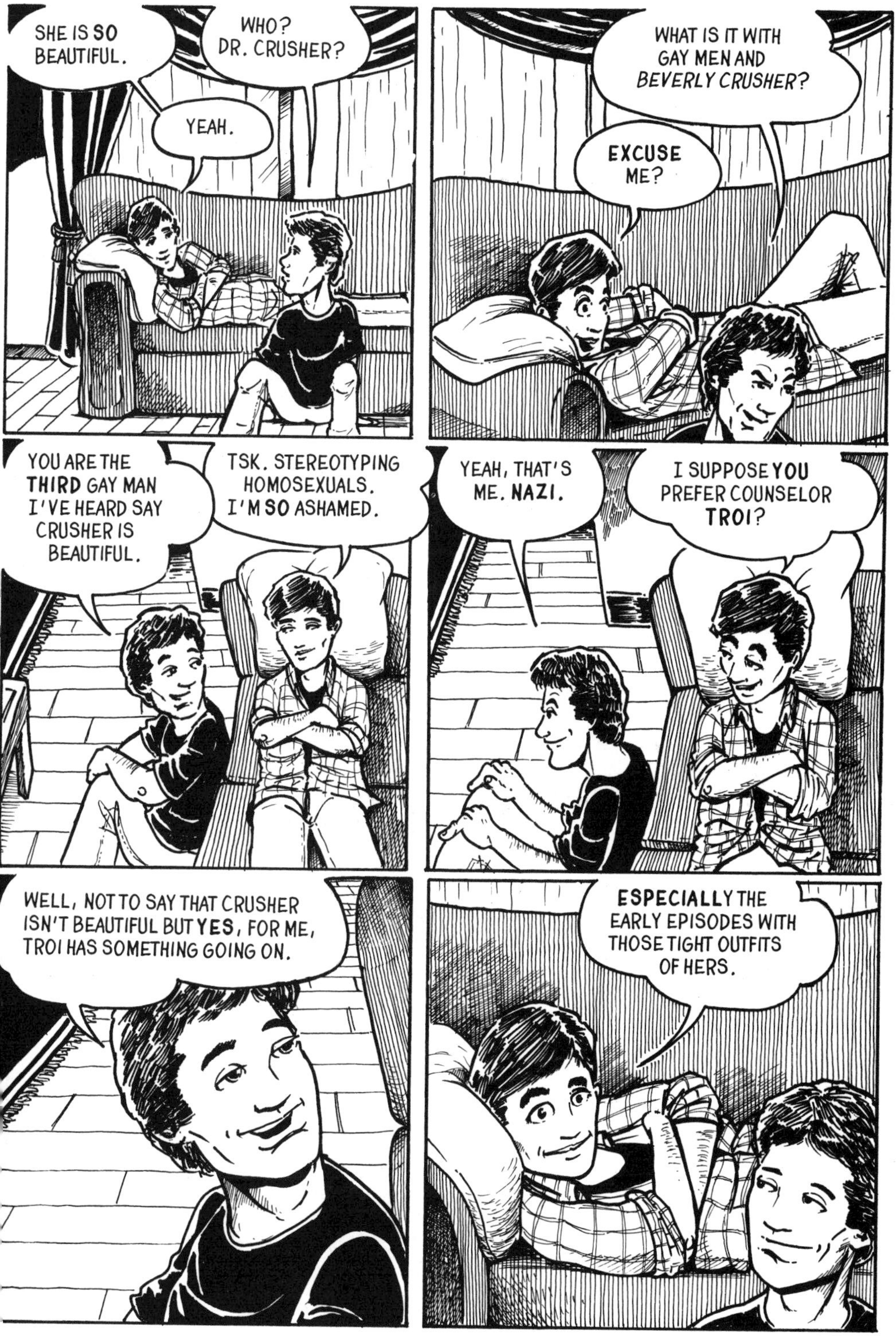
SHE IS SO BEAUTIFUL.
WHO? DR. CRUSHER?
YEAH.
WHAT IS IT WITH GAY MEN AND BEVERLY CRUSHER?
EXCUSE ME?
YOU ARE THE THIRD GAY MAN I'VE HEARD SAY CRUSHER IS BEAUTIFUL.
TSK. STEREOTYPING HOMOSEXUALS. I'M SO ASHAMED.
YEAH, THAT'S ME. NAZI.
I SUPPOSE YOU PREFER COUNSELOR TROI?
WELL, NOT TO SAY THAT CRUSHER ISN'T BEAUTIFUL BUT YES, FOR ME, TROI HAS SOMETHING GOING ON.
ESPECIALLY THE EARLY EPISODES WITH THOSE TIGHT OUTFITS OF HERS.

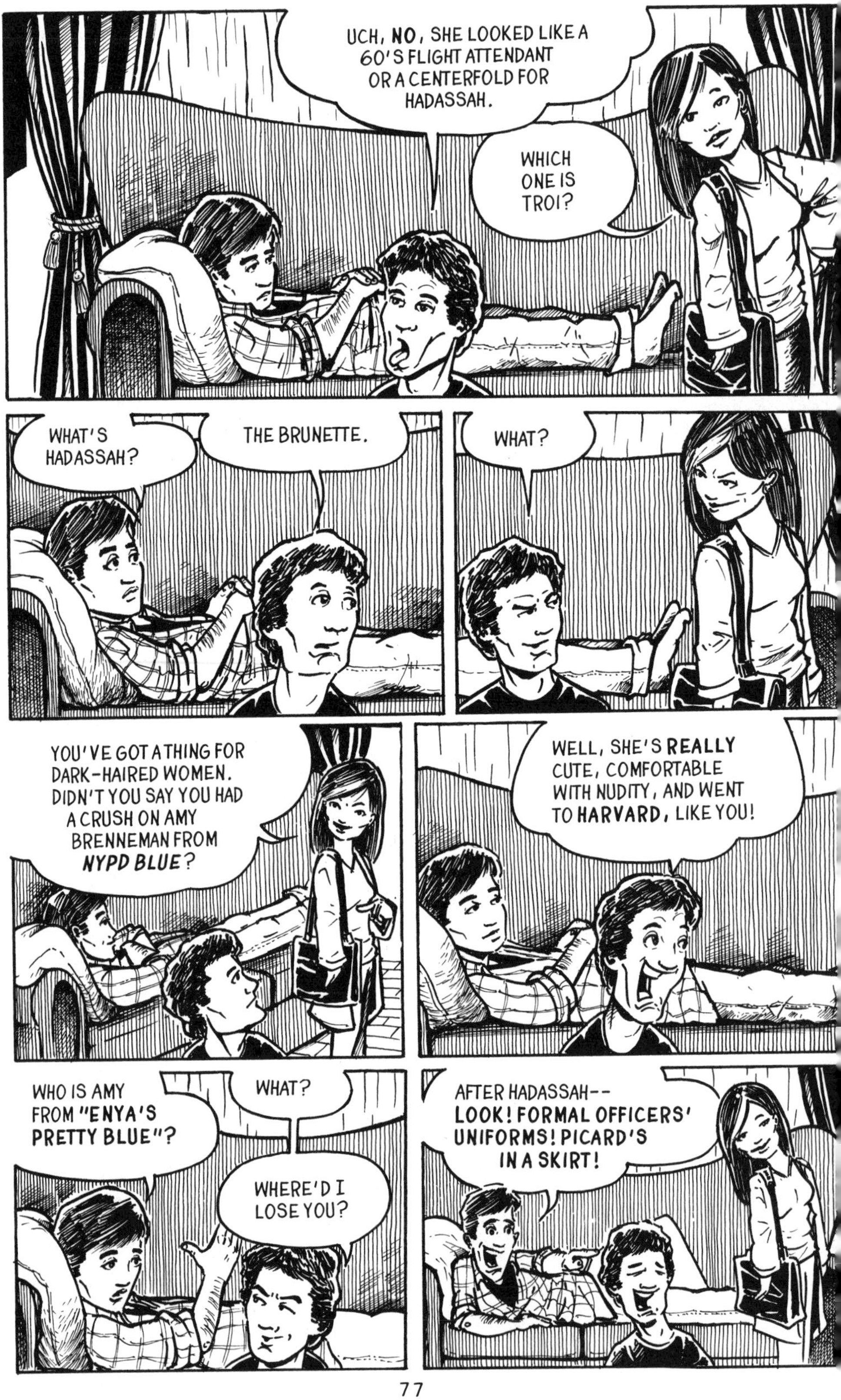
UCH, NO, SHE LOOKED LIKE A 60'S FLIGHT ATTENDANT OR A CENTERFOLD FOR HADASSAH.
WHICH ONE IS TROI?
WHAT'S HADASSAH?
THE BRUNETTE.
WHAT?
YOU'VE GOT A THING FOR DARK-HAIRED WOMEN. DIDN'T YOU SAY YOU HAD A CRUSH ON AMY BRENNEMAN FROM NYPD BLUE?
WELL, SHE'S REALLY CUTE, COMFORTABLE WITH NUDITY, AND WENT TO HARVARD, LIKE YOU!
WHO IS AMY FROM "ENYA'S PRETTY BLUE"?
WHAT?
WHERE'D I LOSE YOU?
AFTER HADASSAH-- LOOK! FORMAL OFFICERS' UNIFORMS! PICARD'S IN A SKIRT!

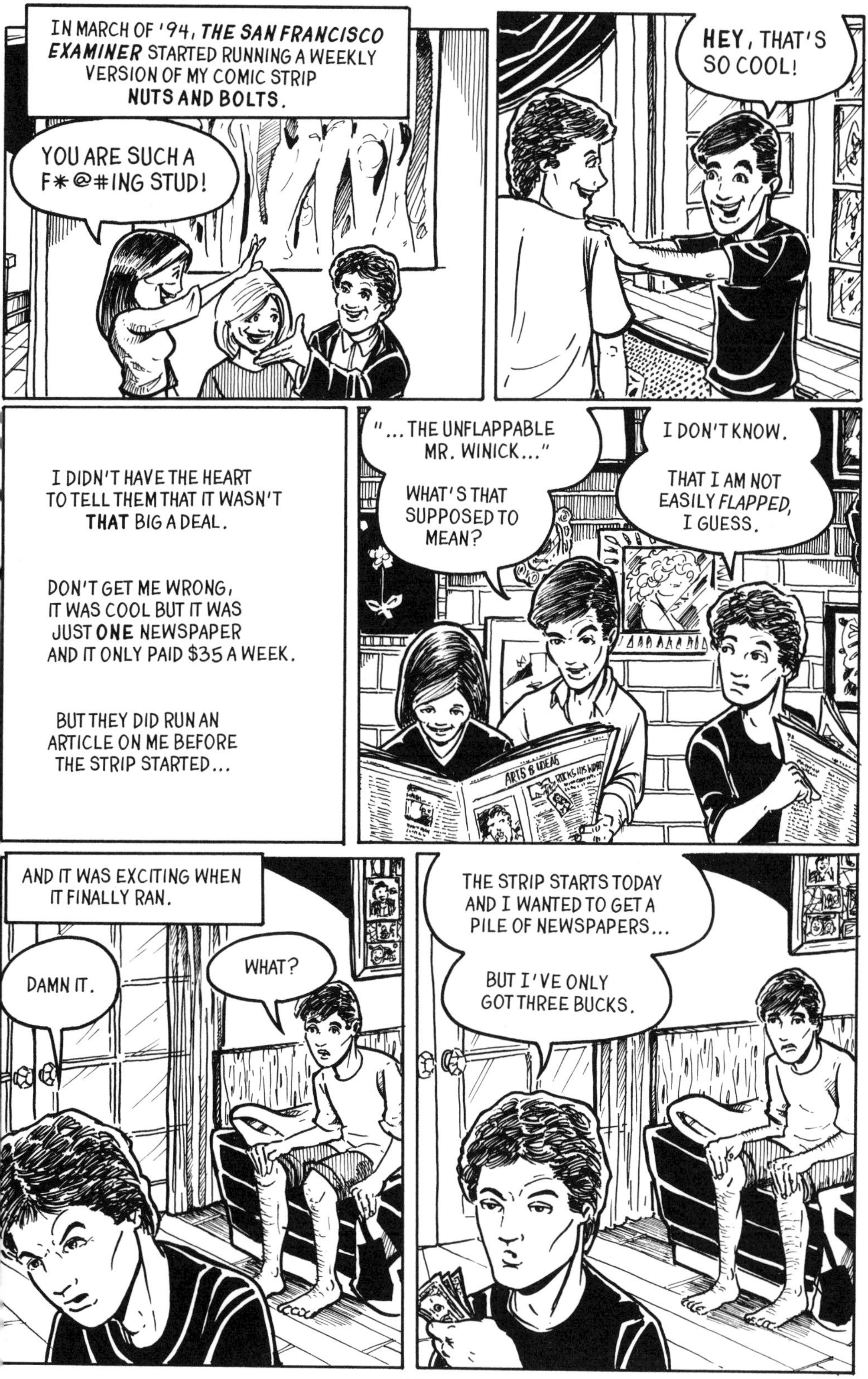
IN MARCH OF '94, THE SAN FRANCISCO EXAMINER STARTED RUNNING A WEEKLY VERSION OF MY COMIC STRIP NUTS AND BOLTS.
YOU ARE SUCH A F*@#ING STUD!
HEY, THAT'S SO COOL!
I DIDN'T HAVE THE HEART TO TELL THEM THAT IT WASN'T THAT BIG A DEAL.
DON'T GET ME WRONG, IT WAS COOL BUT IT WAS JUST ONE NEWSPAPER AND IT ONLY PAID $35 A WEEK.
BUT THEY DID RUN AN ARTICLE ON ME BEFORE THE STRIP STARTED...
"...THE UNFLAPPABLE MR. WINICK..." WHAT'S THAT SUPPOSED TO MEAN?
I DON'T KNOW. THAT I AM NOT EASILY FLAPPED, I GUESS.
ARTS & IDEAS
AND IT WAS EXCITING WHEN IT FINALLY RAN.
DAMN IT.
WHAT?
THE STRIP STARTS TODAY AND I WANTED TO GET A PILE OF NEWSPAPERS...
BUT I'VE ONLY GOT THREE BUCKS.

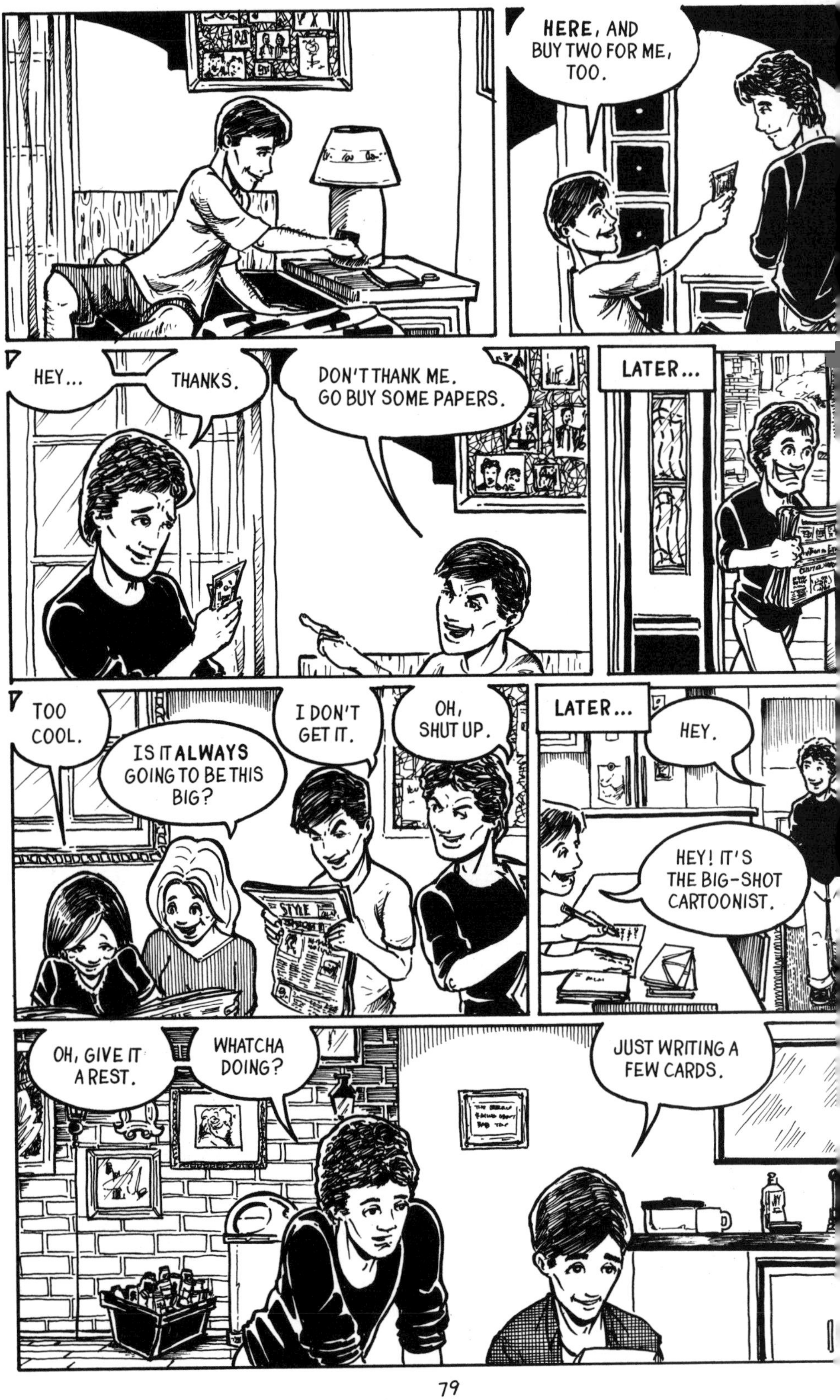

HERE, AND BUY TWO FOR ME, TOO.
HEY...
THANKS.
DON'T THANK ME. GO BUY SOME PAPERS.
LATER...
TOO COOL.
IS IT ALWAYS GOING TO BE THIS BIG?
I DON'T GET IT.
OH, SHUT UP.
LATER...
HEY.
HEY! IT'S THE BIG-SHOT CARTOONIST.
OH, GIVE IT A REST.
WHATCHA DOING?
JUST WRITING A FEW CARDS.

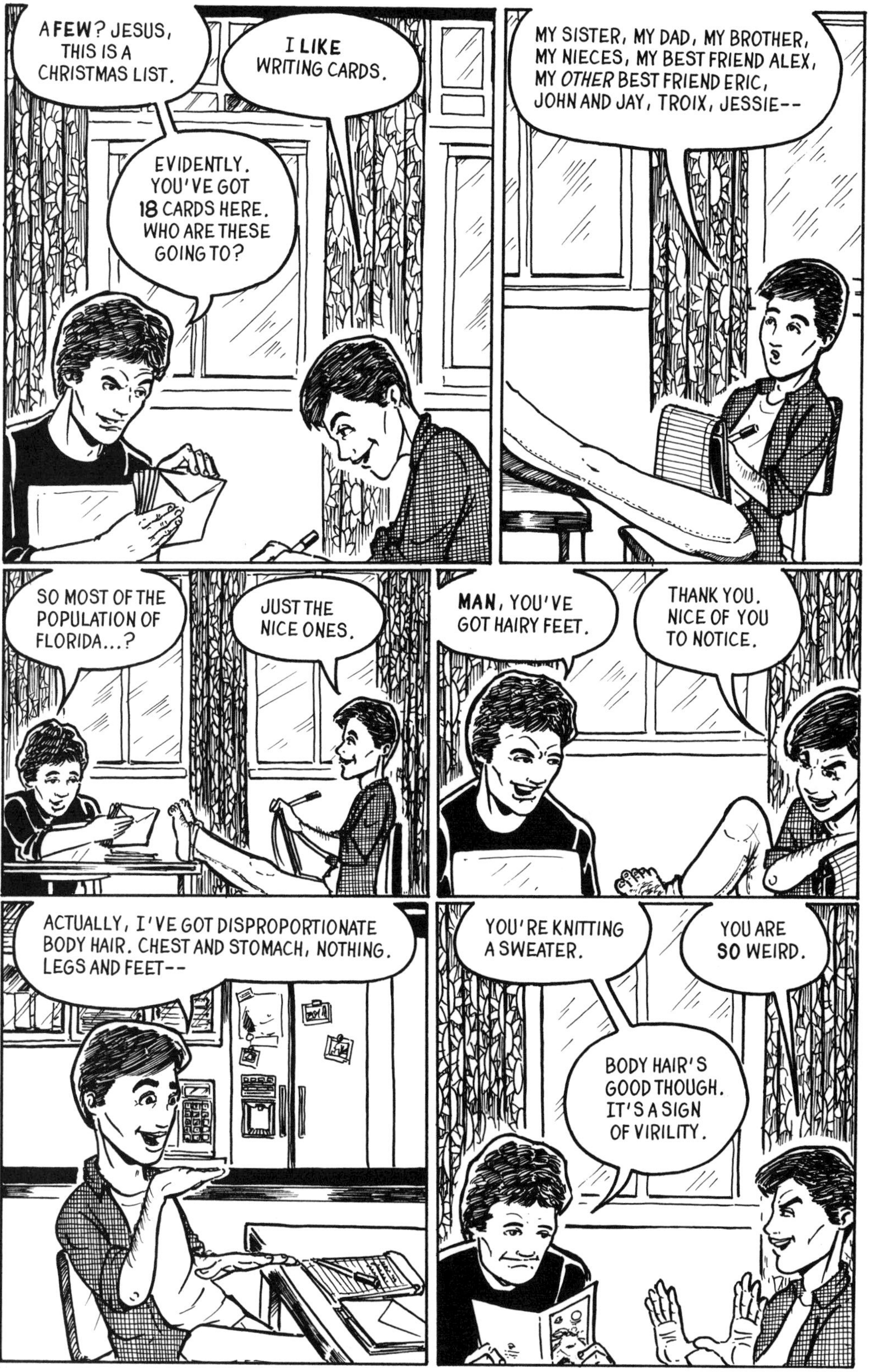
A FEW? JESUS, THIS IS A CHRISTMAS LIST.
I LIKE WRITING CARDS.
EVIDENTLY. YOU'VE GOT 18 CARDS HERE. WHO ARE THESE GOING TO?
MY SISTER, MY DAD, MY BROTHER, MY NIECES, MY BEST FRIEND ALEX, MY OTHER BEST FRIEND ERIC, JOHN AND JAY, TROIX, JESSIE--
SO MOST OF THE POPULATION OF FLORIDA...?
JUST THE NICE ONES.
MAN, YOU'VE GOT HAIRY FEET.
THANK YOU. NICE OF YOU TO NOTICE.
ACTUALLY, I'VE GOT DISPROPORTIONATE BODY HAIR. CHEST AND STOMACH, NOTHING. LEGS AND FEET--
YOU'RE KNITTING A SWEATER.
YOU ARE SO WEIRD.
BODY HAIR'S GOOD THOUGH. IT'S A SIGN OF VIRILITY.

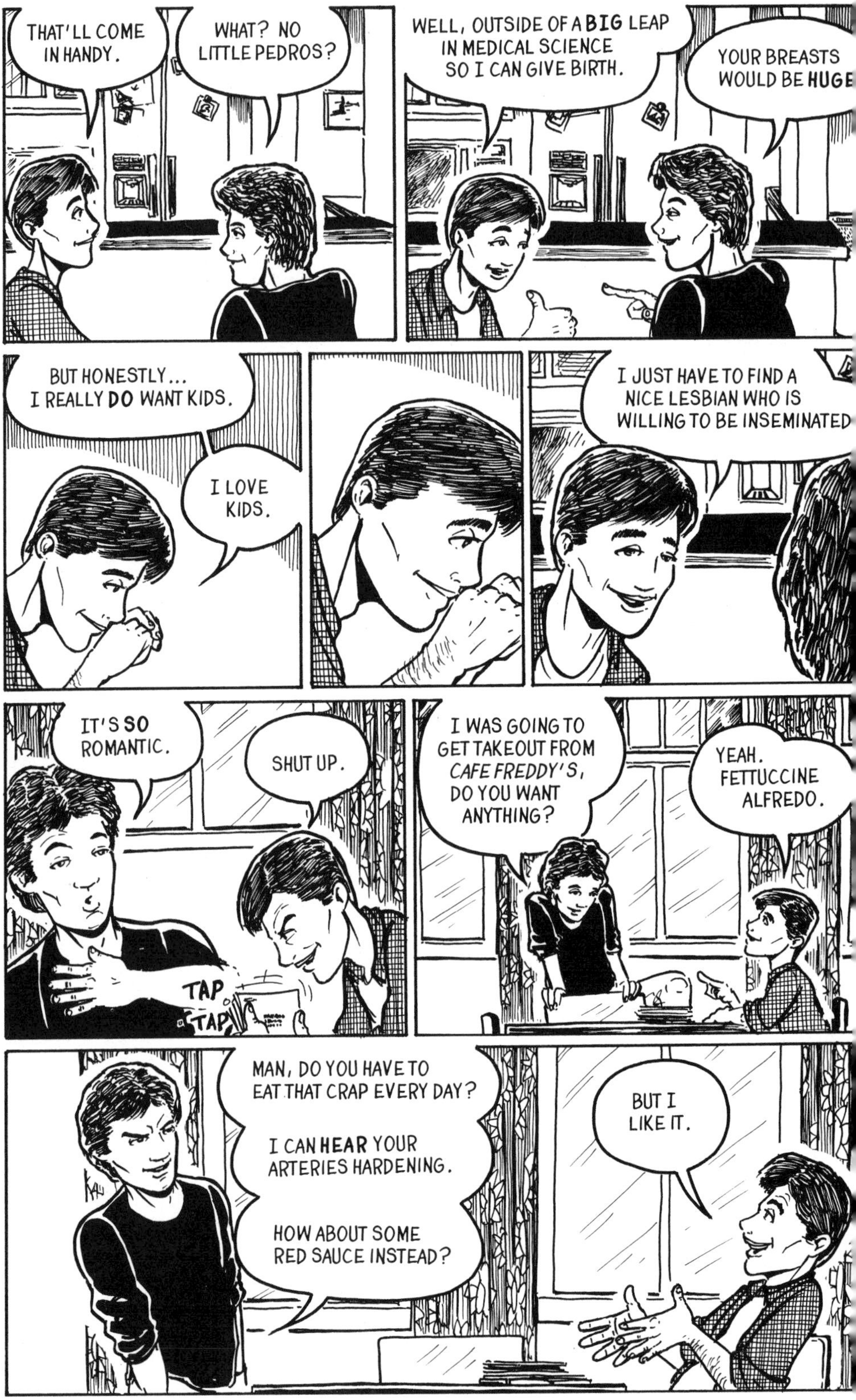
THAT'LL COME IN HANDY.
WHAT? NO LITTLE PEDROS?
WELL, OUTSIDE OF A BIG LEAP IN MEDICAL SCIENCE SO I CAN GIVE BIRTH.
YOUR BREASTS WOULD BE HUGE
BUT HONESTLY... I REALLY DO WANT KIDS.
I LOVE KIDS.
I JUST HAVE TO FIND A NICE LESBIAN WHO IS WILLING TO BE INSEMINATED
IT'S SO ROMANTIC.
SHUT UP.
TAP TAP
I WAS GOING TO GET TAKEOUT FROM CAFE FREDDY'S, DO YOU WANT ANYTHING?
YEAH. FETTUCCINE ALFREDO.
MAN, DO YOU HAVE TO EAT THAT CRAP EVERY DAY?
I CAN HEAR YOUR ARTERIES HARDENING.
HOW ABOUT SOME RED SAUCE INSTEAD?
BUT I LIKE IT.

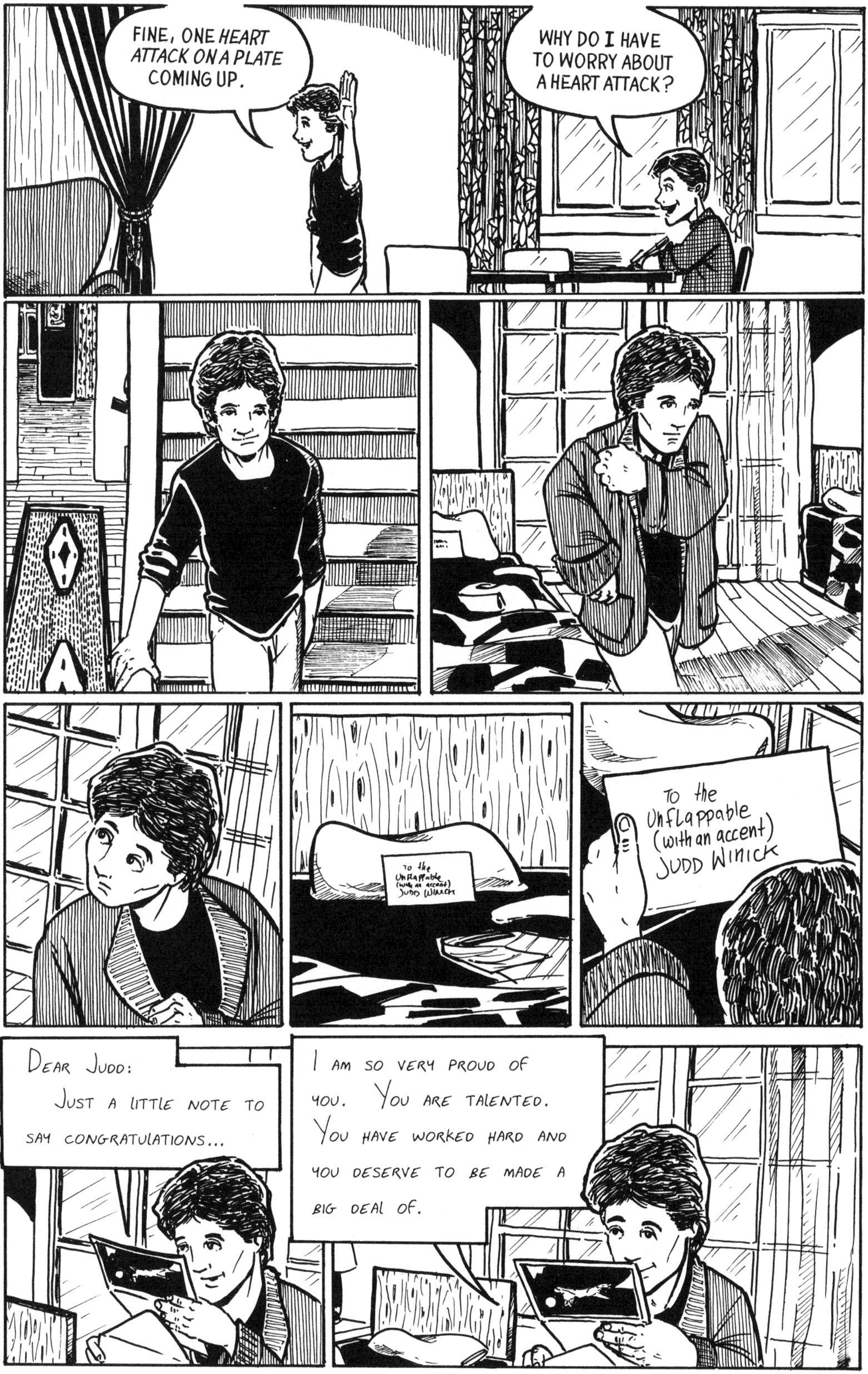
FINE, ONE HEART ATTACK ON A PLATE COMING UP.
WHY DO I HAVE TO WORRY ABOUT A HEART ATTACK?
To the Unflappable (with an accent) JUDD WINICK
To the Unflappable (with an accent) JUDD WINICK
DEAR JUDD: JUST A LITTLE NOTE TO SAY CONGRATULATIONS...
I AM SO VERY PROUD OF YOU. YOU ARE TALENTED. YOU HAVE WORKED HARD AND YOU DESERVE TO BE MADE A BIG DEAL OF.

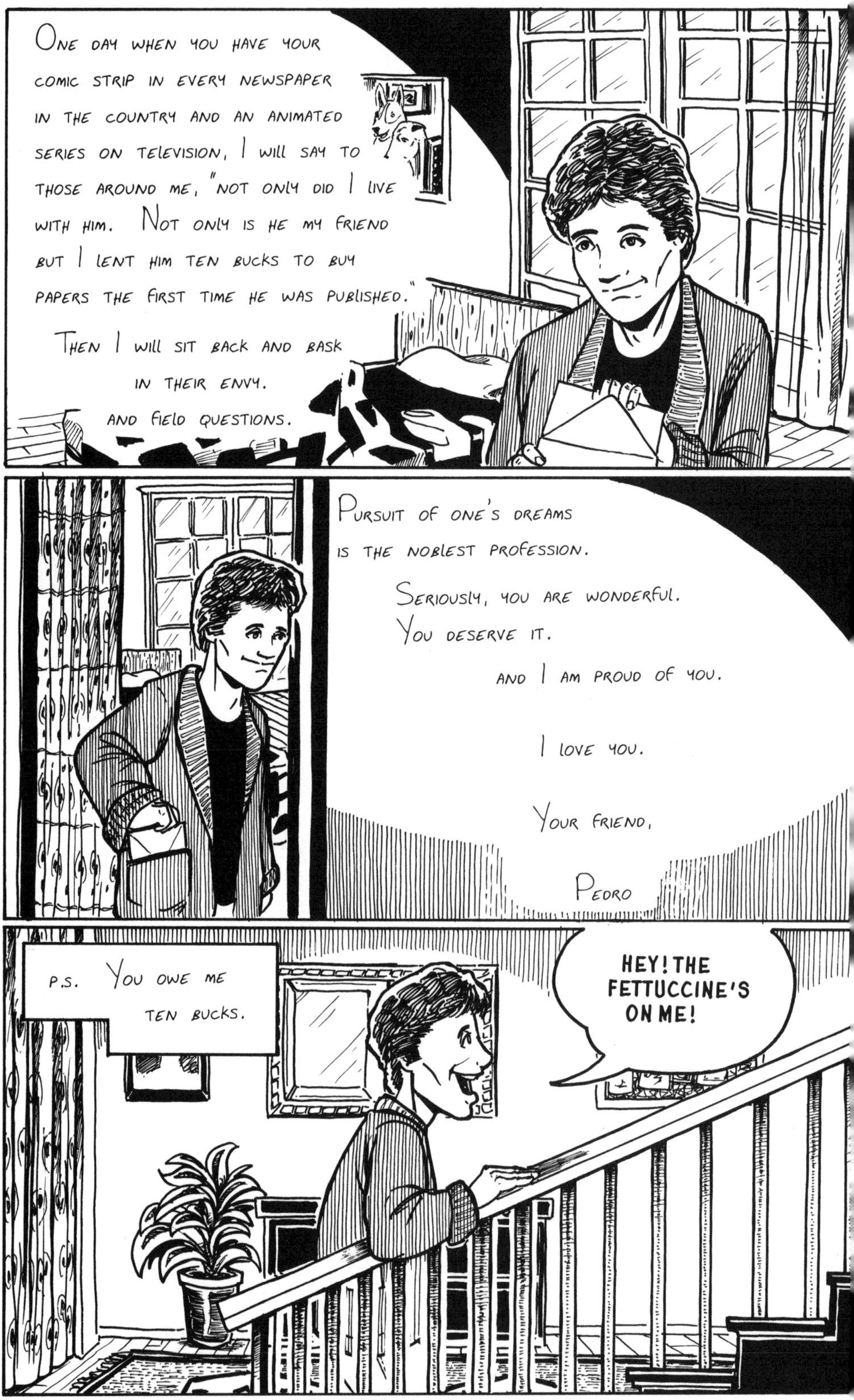
One day when you have your comic strip in every newspaper in the country and an animated series on television, I will say to those around me, "Not only did I live with him. Not only is he my friend but I lent him ten bucks to buy papers the first time he was published."
Then I will sit back and bask in their envy.
And field questions.
Pursuit of one's dreams is the noblest profession.
Seriously, you are wonderful. You deserve it.
And I am proud of you.
I love you.
Your friend,
Pedro
P.S. You owe me ten bucks.
HEY! THE FETTUCCINE'S ON ME!

PAM

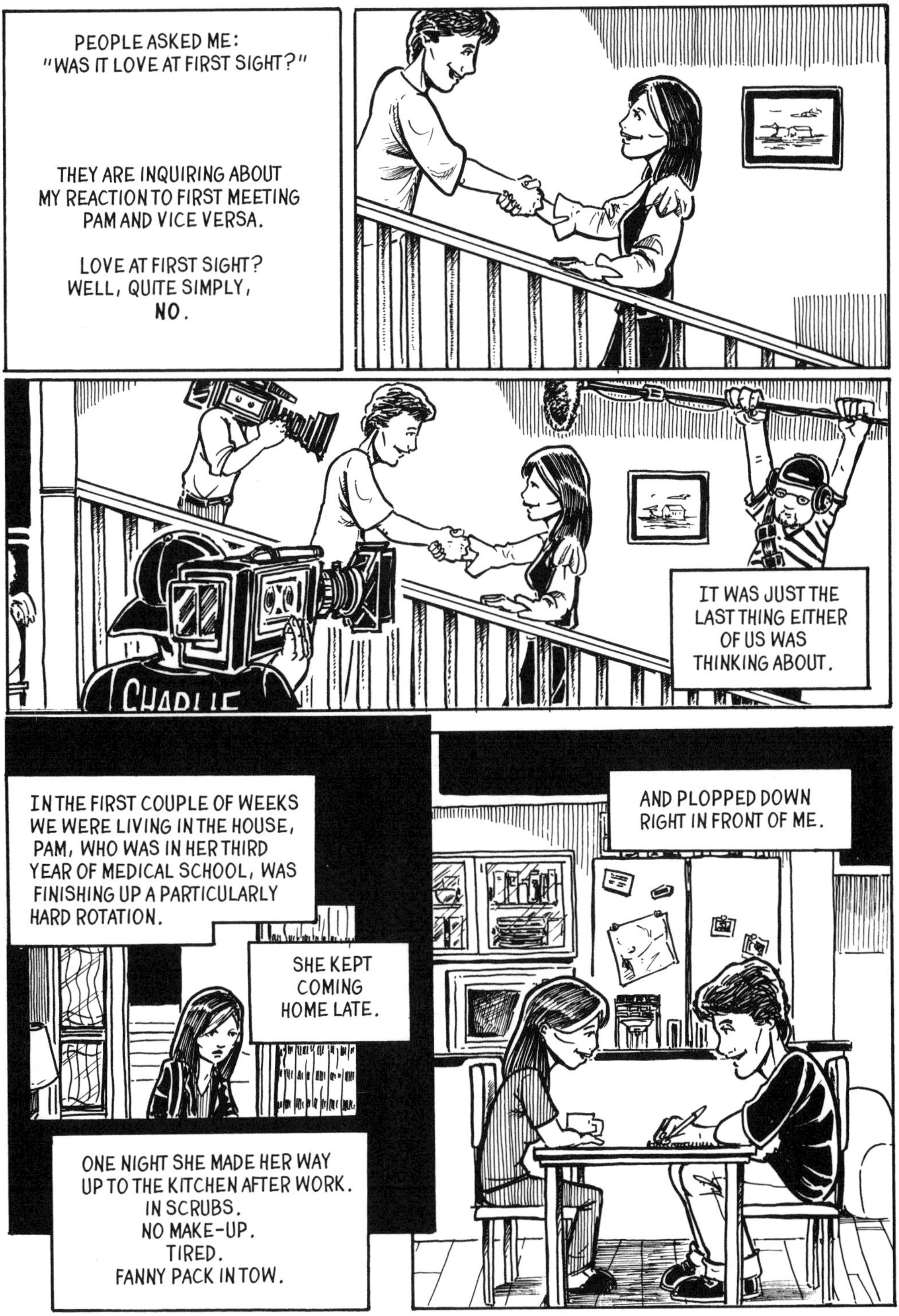
PEOPLE ASKED ME: "WAS IT LOVE AT FIRST SIGHT?"
THEY ARE INQUIRING ABOUT MY REACTION TO FIRST MEETING PAM AND VICE VERSA.
LOVE AT FIRST SIGHT? WELL, QUITE SIMPLY, NO.
IT WAS JUST THE LAST THING EITHER OF US WAS THINKING ABOUT.
IN THE FIRST COUPLE OF WEEKS WE WERE LIVING IN THE HOUSE, PAM, WHO WAS IN HER THIRD YEAR OF MEDICAL SCHOOL, WAS FINISHING UP A PARTICULARLY HARD ROTATION.
SHE KEPT COMING HOME LATE.
ONE NIGHT SHE MADE HER WAY UP TO THE KITCHEN AFTER WORK. IN SCRUBS. NO MAKE-UP. TIRED. FANNY PACK IN TOW.
AND PLOPPED DOWN RIGHT IN FRONT OF ME.

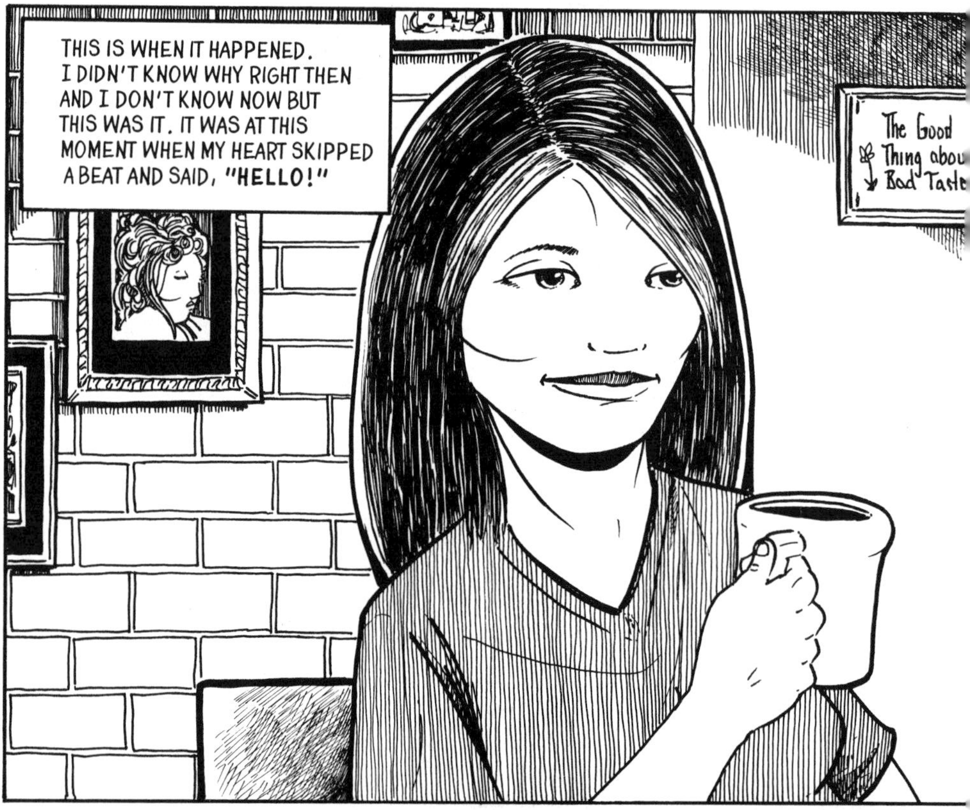
THIS IS WHEN IT HAPPENED. I DIDN'T KNOW WHY RIGHT THEN AND I DON'T KNOW NOW BUT THIS WAS IT. IT WAS AT THIS MOMENT WHEN MY HEART SKIPPED A BEAT AND SAID, "HELLO!"
The Good Thing about Bad Taste

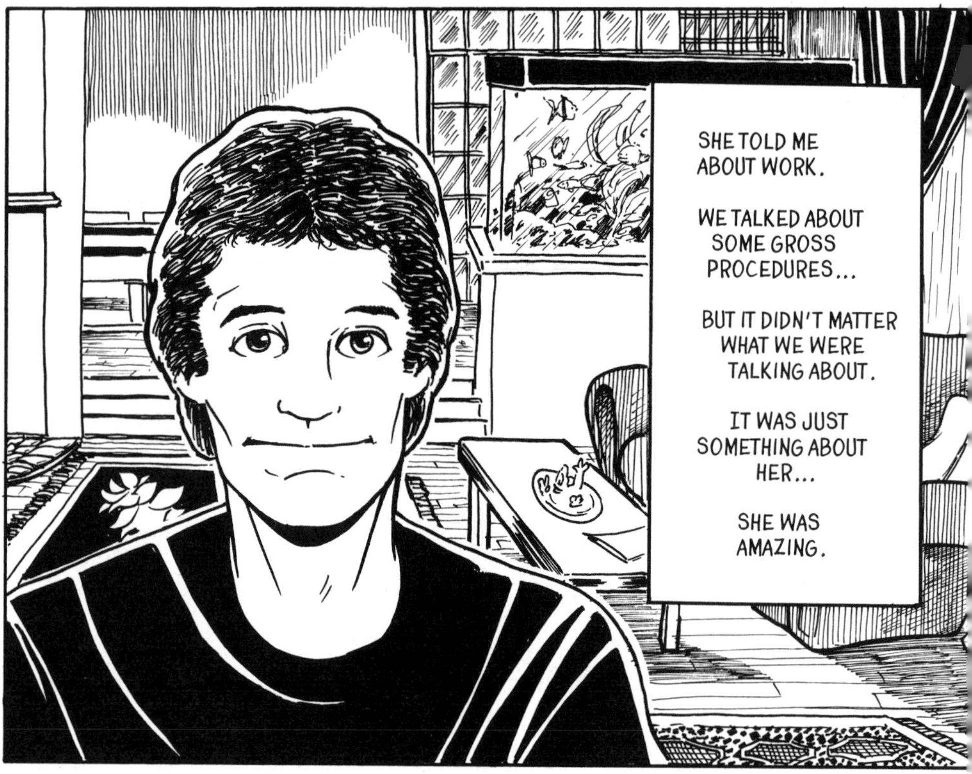
SHE TOLD ME ABOUT WORK.
WE TALKED ABOUT SOME GROSS PROCEDURES...
BUT IT DIDN'T MATTER WHAT WE WERE TALKING ABOUT.
IT WAS JUST SOMETHING ABOUT HER...
SHE WAS AMAZING.

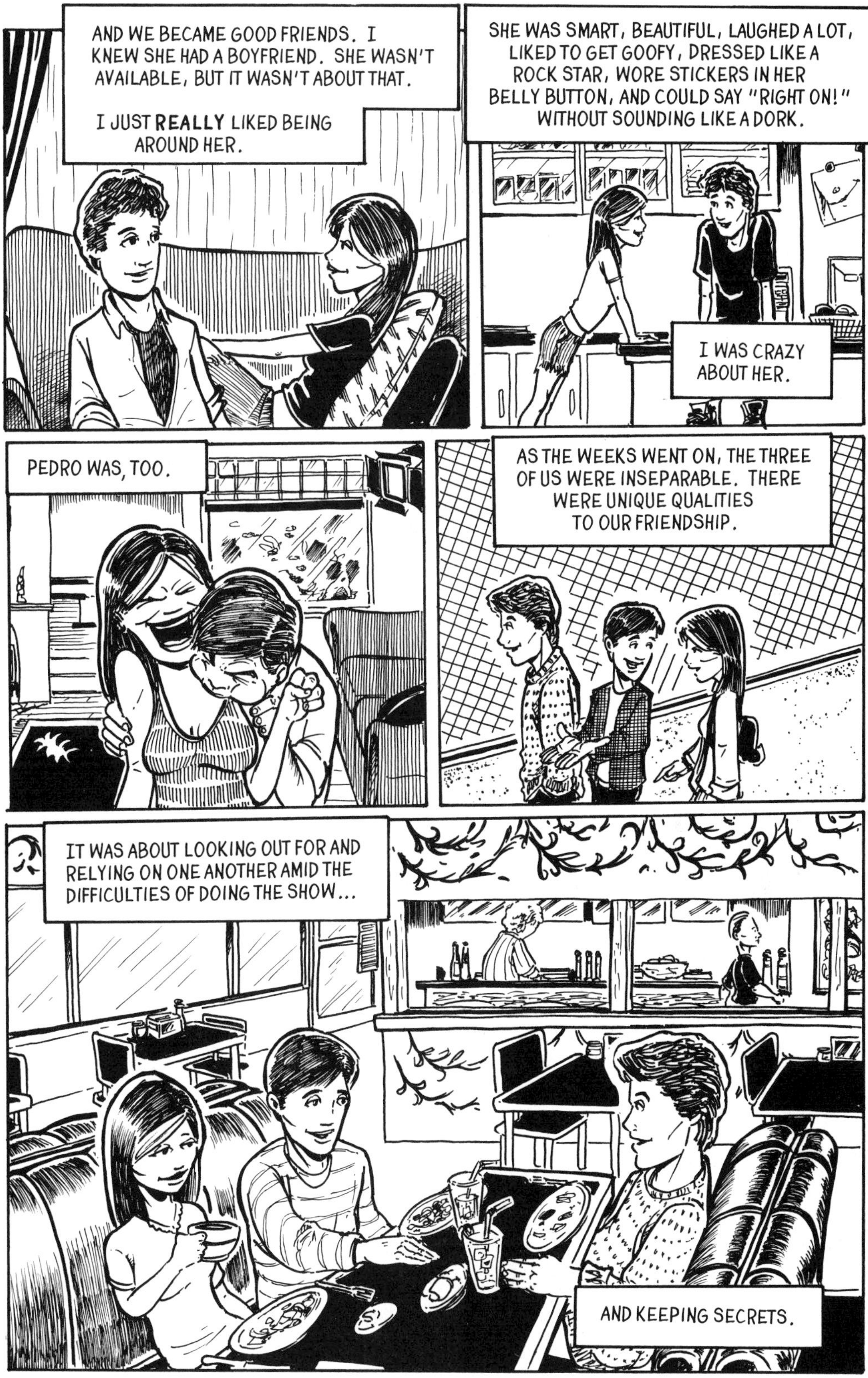
AND WE BECAME GOOD FRIENDS. I KNEW SHE HAD A BOYFRIEND. SHE WASN'T AVAILABLE, BUT IT WASN'T ABOUT THAT.
I JUST **REALLY** LIKED BEING AROUND HER.
SHE WAS SMART, BEAUTIFUL, LAUGHED A LOT, LIKED TO GET GOOFY, DRESSED LIKE A ROCK STAR, WORE STICKERS IN HER BELLY BUTTON, AND COULD SAY "RIGHT ON!" WITHOUT SOUNDING LIKE A DORK.
I WAS CRAZY ABOUT HER.
PEDRO WAS, TOO.
AS THE WEEKS WENT ON, THE THREE OF US WERE INSEPARABLE. THERE WERE UNIQUE QUALITIES TO OUR FRIENDSHIP.
IT WAS ABOUT LOOKING OUT FOR AND RELYING ON ONE ANOTHER AMID THE DIFFICULTIES OF DOING THE SHOW...
AND KEEPING SECRETS.

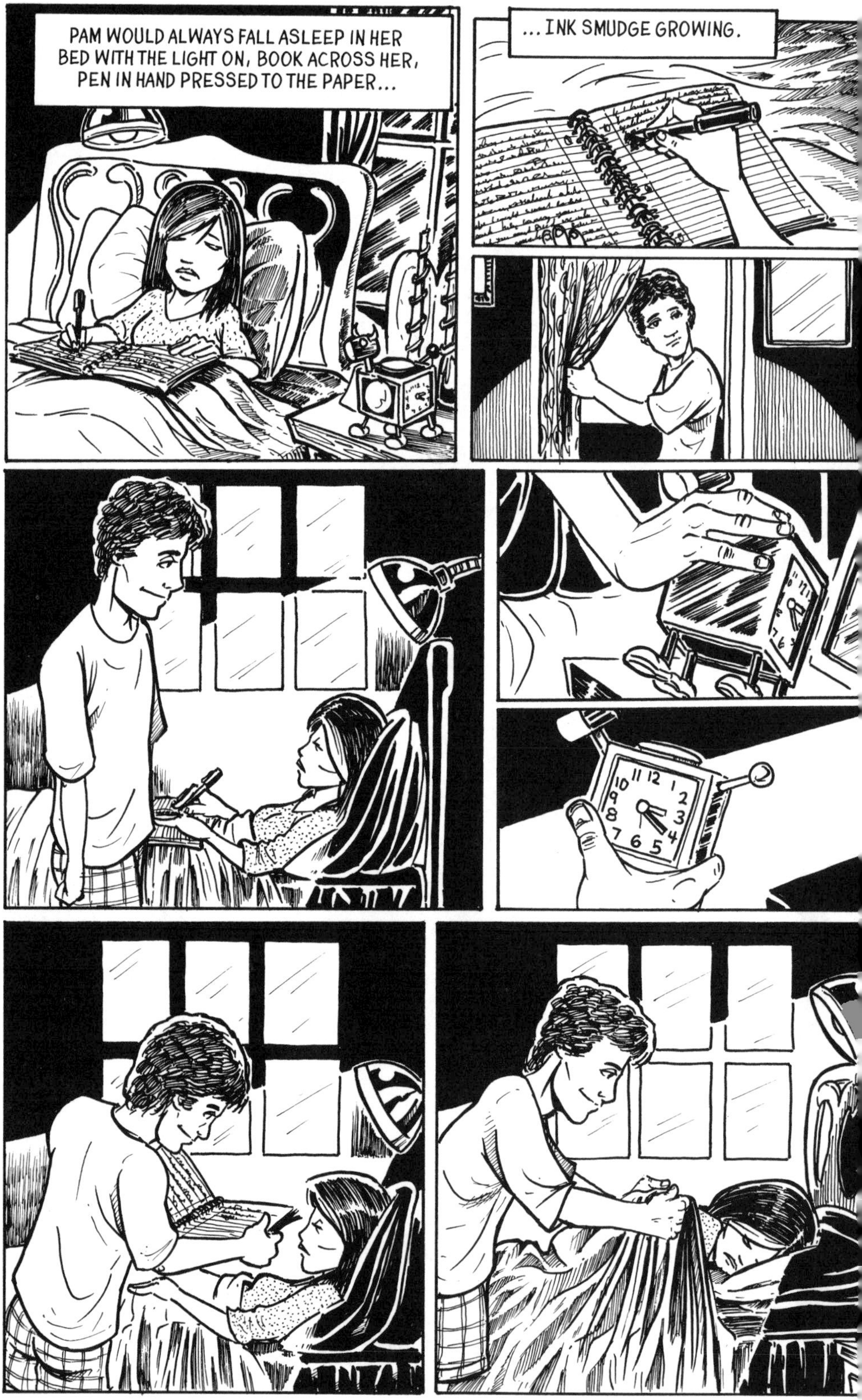
PAM WOULD ALWAYS FALL ASLEEP IN HER BED WITH THE LIGHT ON, BOOK ACROSS HER, PEN IN HAND PRESSED TO THE PAPER...
...INK SMUDGE GROWING.

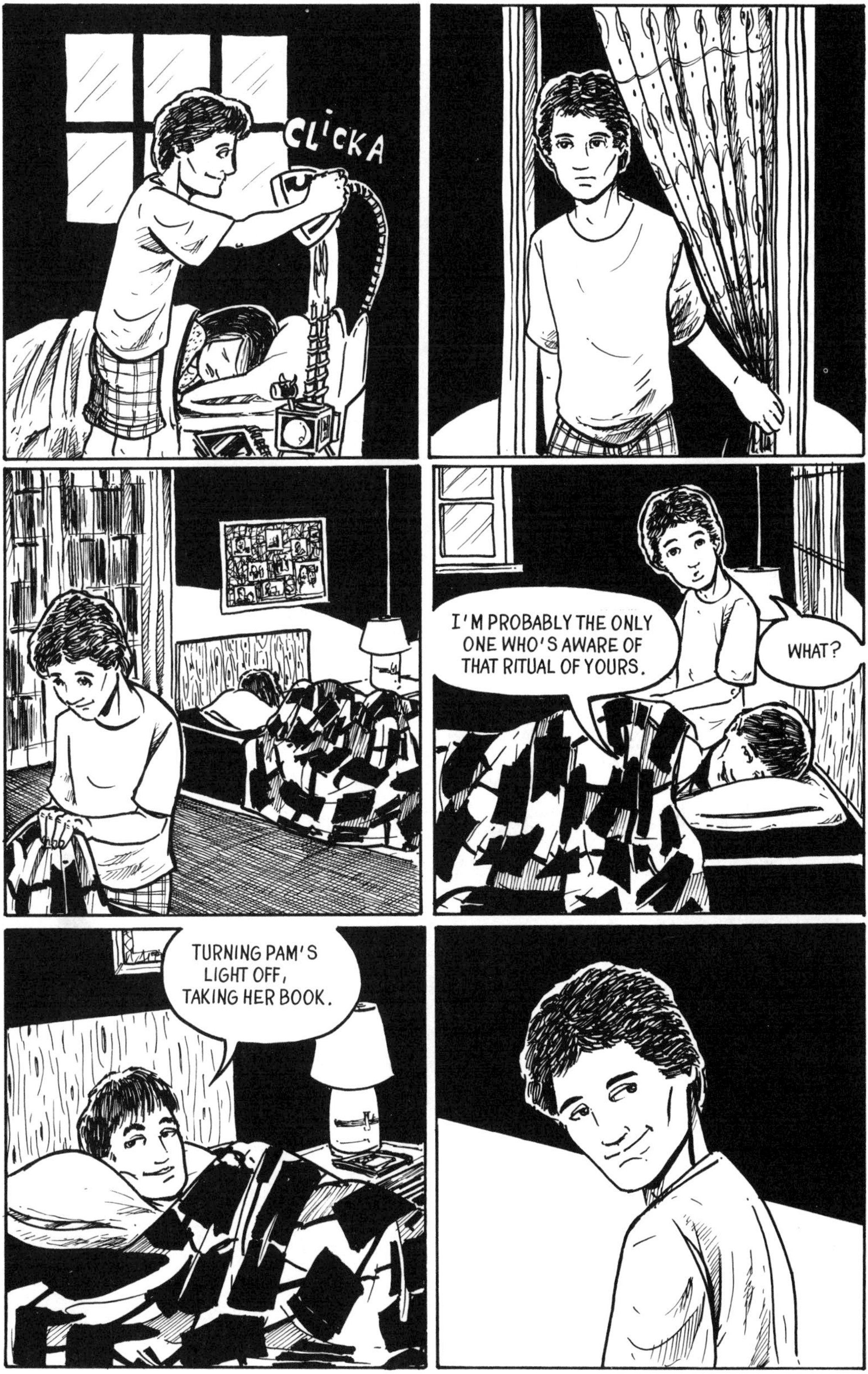
CLICKA
I'M PROBABLY THE ONLY ONE WHO'S AWARE OF THAT RITUAL OF YOURS.
WHAT?
TURNING PAM'S LIGHT OFF, TAKING HER BOOK.

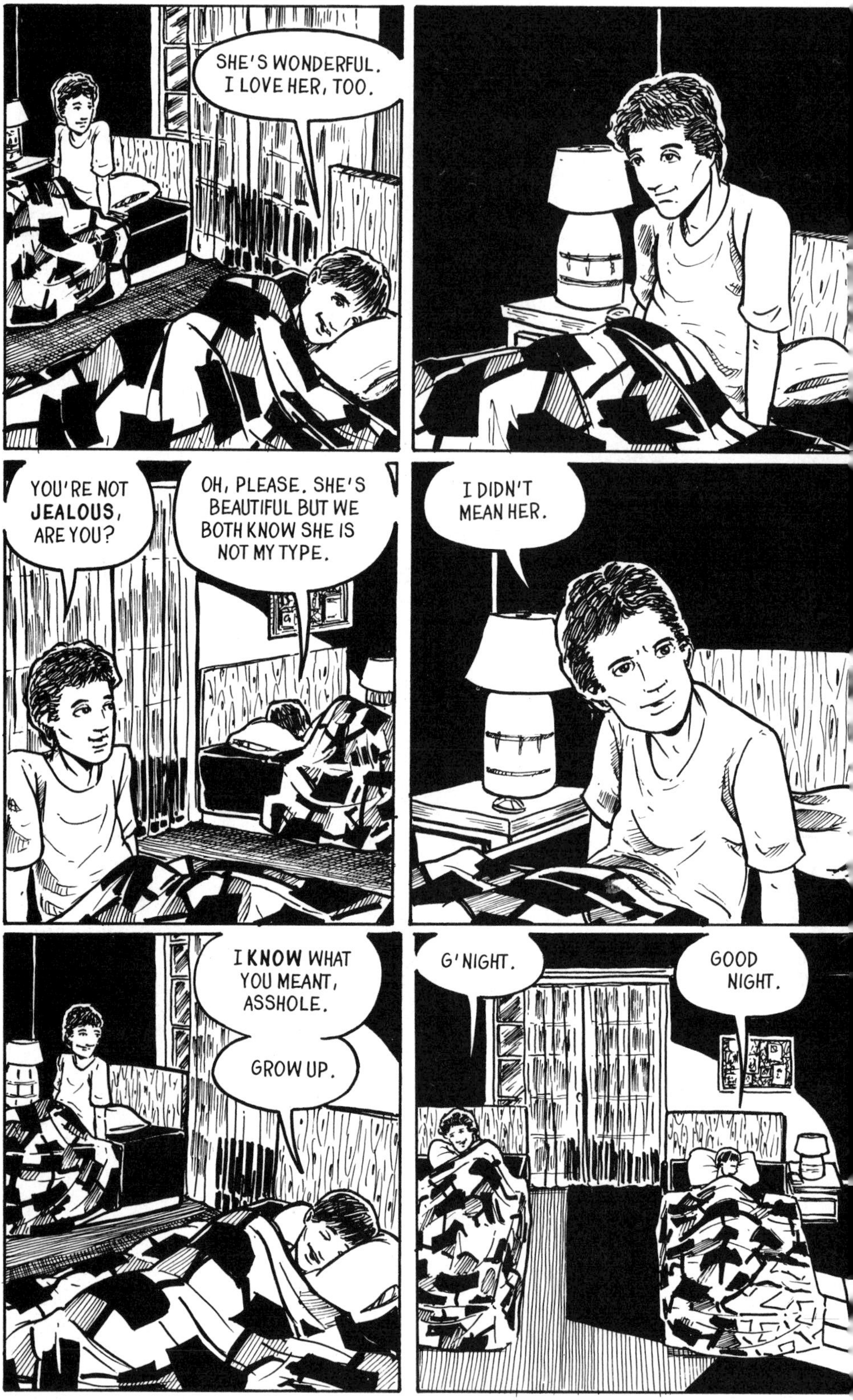
SHE'S WONDERFUL. I LOVE HER, TOO.
YOU'RE NOT JEALOUS, ARE YOU?
OH, PLEASE. SHE'S BEAUTIFUL BUT WE BOTH KNOW SHE IS NOT MY TYPE.
I DIDN'T MEAN HER.
I KNOW WHAT YOU MEANT, ASSHOLE.
GROW UP.
G'NIGHT.
GOOD NIGHT.

SMALL PROBLEMS
LITTLE SECRETS

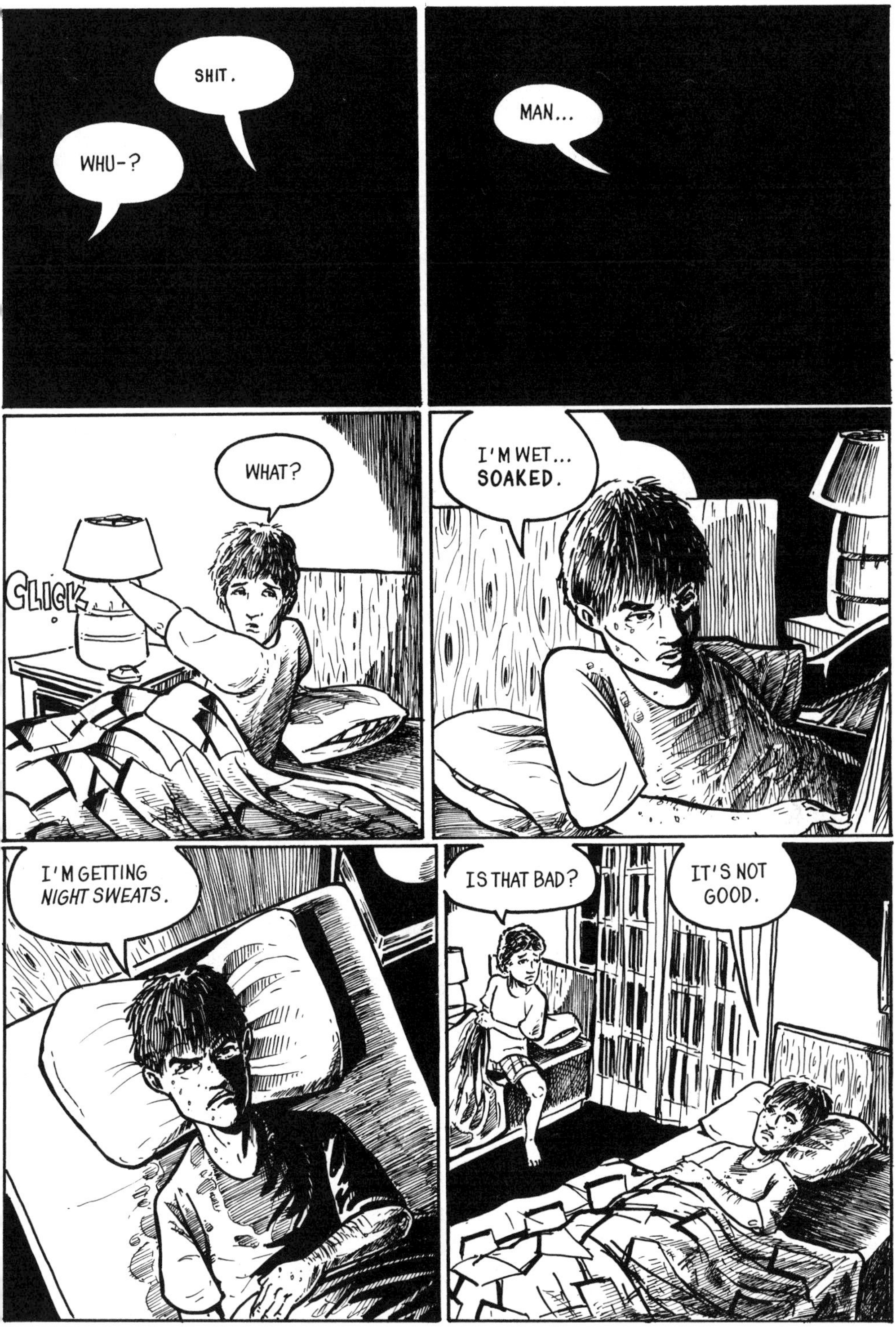
SHIT.
WHU-?
MAN...
WHAT?
CLICK
I'M WET... SOAKED.
I'M GETTING *NIGHT SWEATS*.
IS THAT BAD?
IT'S NOT GOOD.

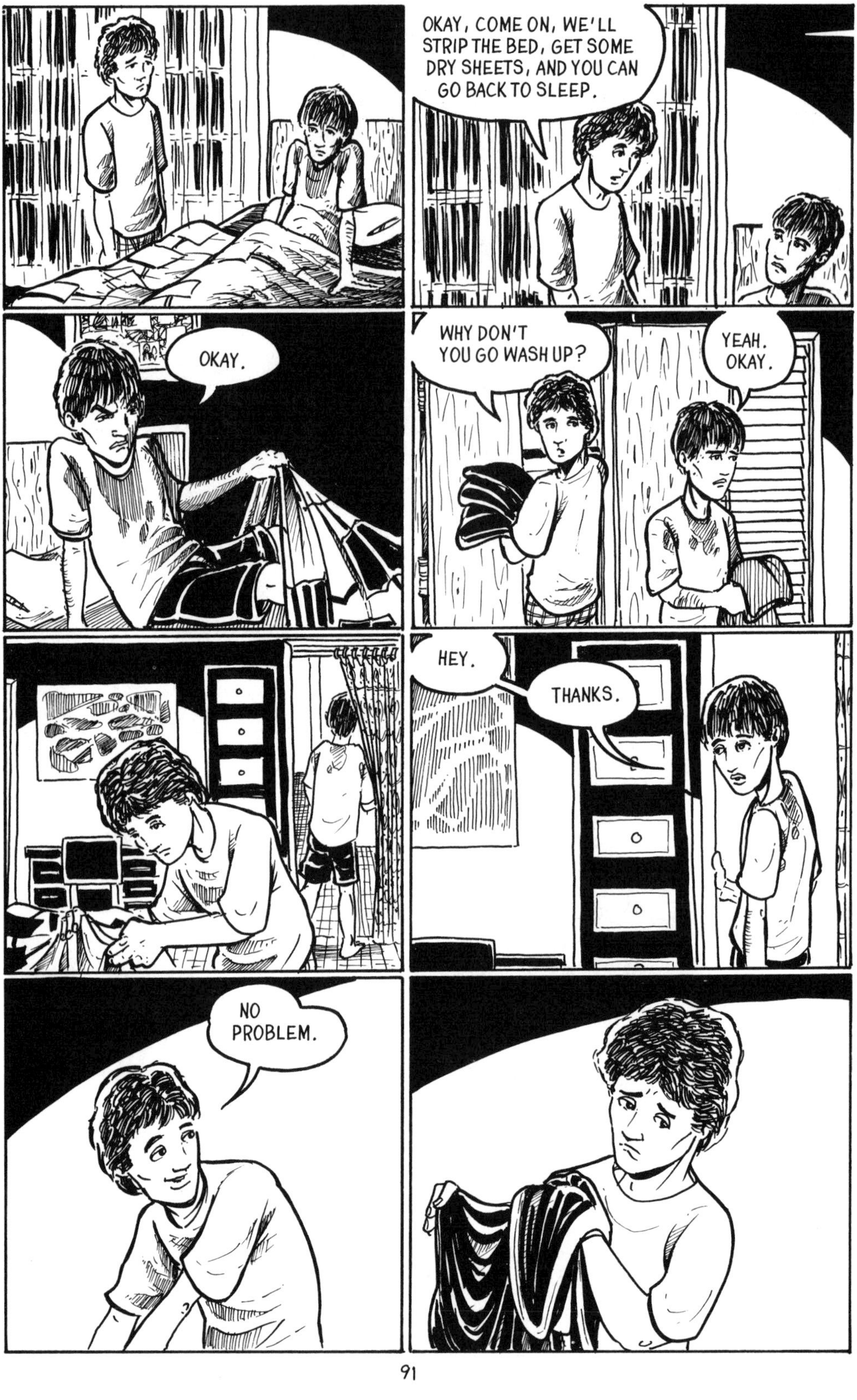
OKAY, COME ON, WE'LL STRIP THE BED, GET SOME DRY SHEETS, AND YOU CAN GO BACK TO SLEEP.
OKAY.
WHY DON'T YOU GO WASH UP?
YEAH. OKAY.
HEY.
THANKS.
NO PROBLEM.

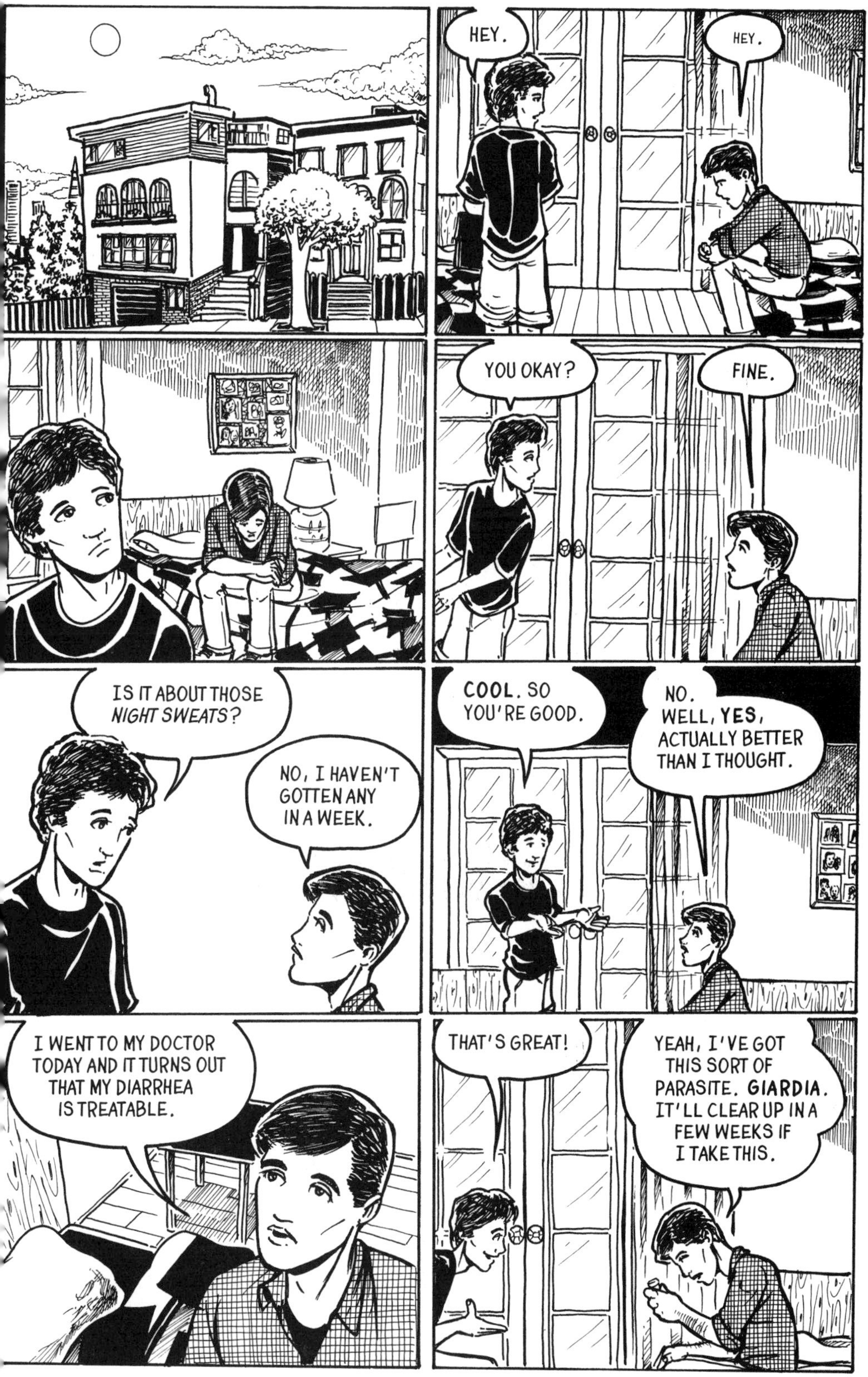
HEY.
HEY.
YOU OKAY?
FINE.
IS IT ABOUT THOSE *NIGHT SWEATS*?
NO, I HAVEN'T GOTTEN ANY IN A WEEK.
COOL. SO YOU'RE GOOD.
NO. WELL, **YES**, ACTUALLY BETTER THAN I THOUGHT.
I WENT TO MY DOCTOR TODAY AND IT TURNS OUT THAT MY DIARRHEA IS TREATABLE.
THAT'S GREAT!
YEAH, I'VE GOT THIS SORT OF PARASITE. **GIARDIA**. IT'LL CLEAR UP IN A FEW WEEKS IF I TAKE THIS.

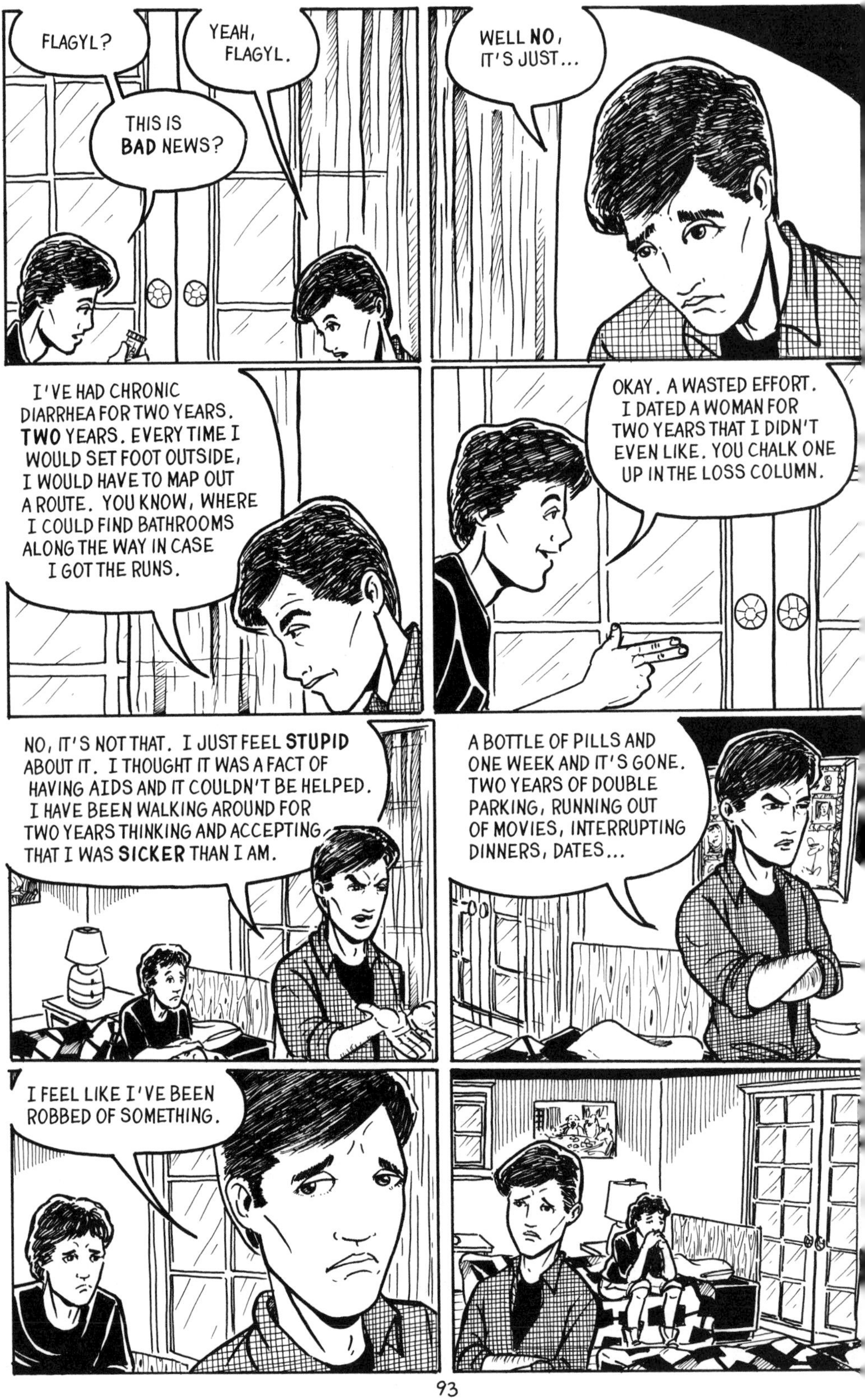
FLAGYL?
YEAH, FLAGYL.
THIS IS BAD NEWS?
WELL NO, IT'S JUST...
I'VE HAD CHRONIC DIARRHEA FOR TWO YEARS. TWO YEARS. EVERY TIME I WOULD SET FOOT OUTSIDE, I WOULD HAVE TO MAP OUT A ROUTE. YOU KNOW, WHERE I COULD FIND BATHROOMS ALONG THE WAY IN CASE I GOT THE RUNS.
OKAY. A WASTED EFFORT. I DATED A WOMAN FOR TWO YEARS THAT I DIDN'T EVEN LIKE. YOU CHALK ONE UP IN THE LOSS COLUMN.
NO, IT'S NOT THAT. I JUST FEEL STUPID ABOUT IT. I THOUGHT IT WAS A FACT OF HAVING AIDS AND IT COULDN'T BE HELPED. I HAVE BEEN WALKING AROUND FOR TWO YEARS THINKING AND ACCEPTING THAT I WAS SICKER THAN I AM.
A BOTTLE OF PILLS AND ONE WEEK AND IT'S GONE. TWO YEARS OF DOUBLE PARKING, RUNNING OUT OF MOVIES, INTERRUPTING DINNERS, DATES...
I FEEL LIKE I'VE BEEN ROBBED OF SOMETHING.

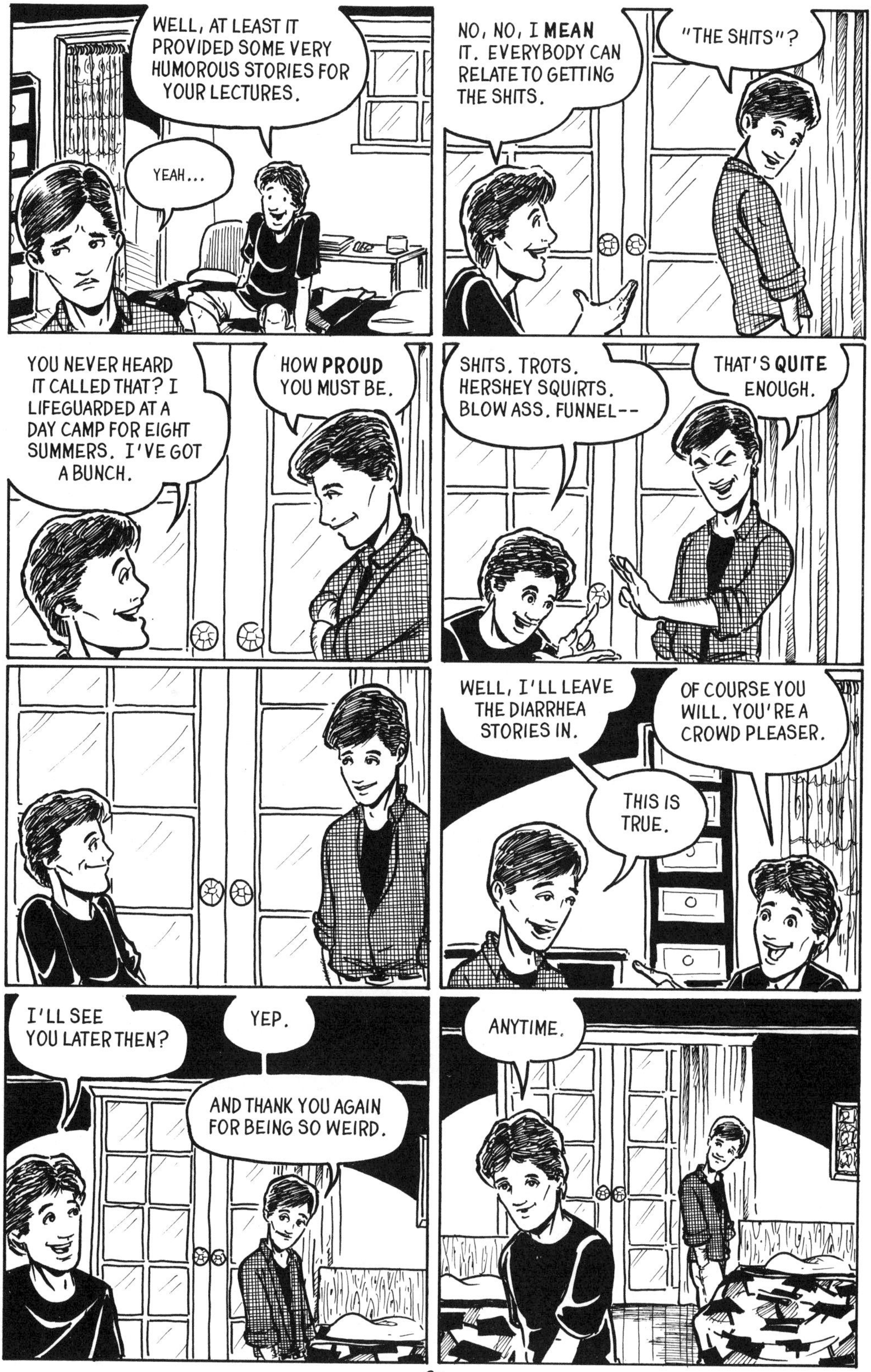
WELL, AT LEAST IT PROVIDED SOME VERY HUMOROUS STORIES FOR YOUR LECTURES.
YEAH...
NO, NO, I **MEAN** IT. EVERYBODY CAN RELATE TO GETTING THE SHITS.
"THE SHITS"?
YOU NEVER HEARD IT CALLED THAT? I LIFEGUARDED AT A DAY CAMP FOR EIGHT SUMMERS. I'VE GOT A BUNCH.
HOW **PROUD** YOU MUST BE.
SHITS. TROTS. HERSHEY SQUIRTS. BLOW ASS. FUNNEL--
THAT'S **QUITE** ENOUGH.
WELL, I'LL LEAVE THE DIARRHEA STORIES IN.
OF COURSE YOU WILL. YOU'RE A CROWD PLEASER.
THIS IS TRUE.
I'LL SEE YOU LATER THEN?
YEP.
AND THANK YOU AGAIN FOR BEING SO WEIRD.
ANYTIME.

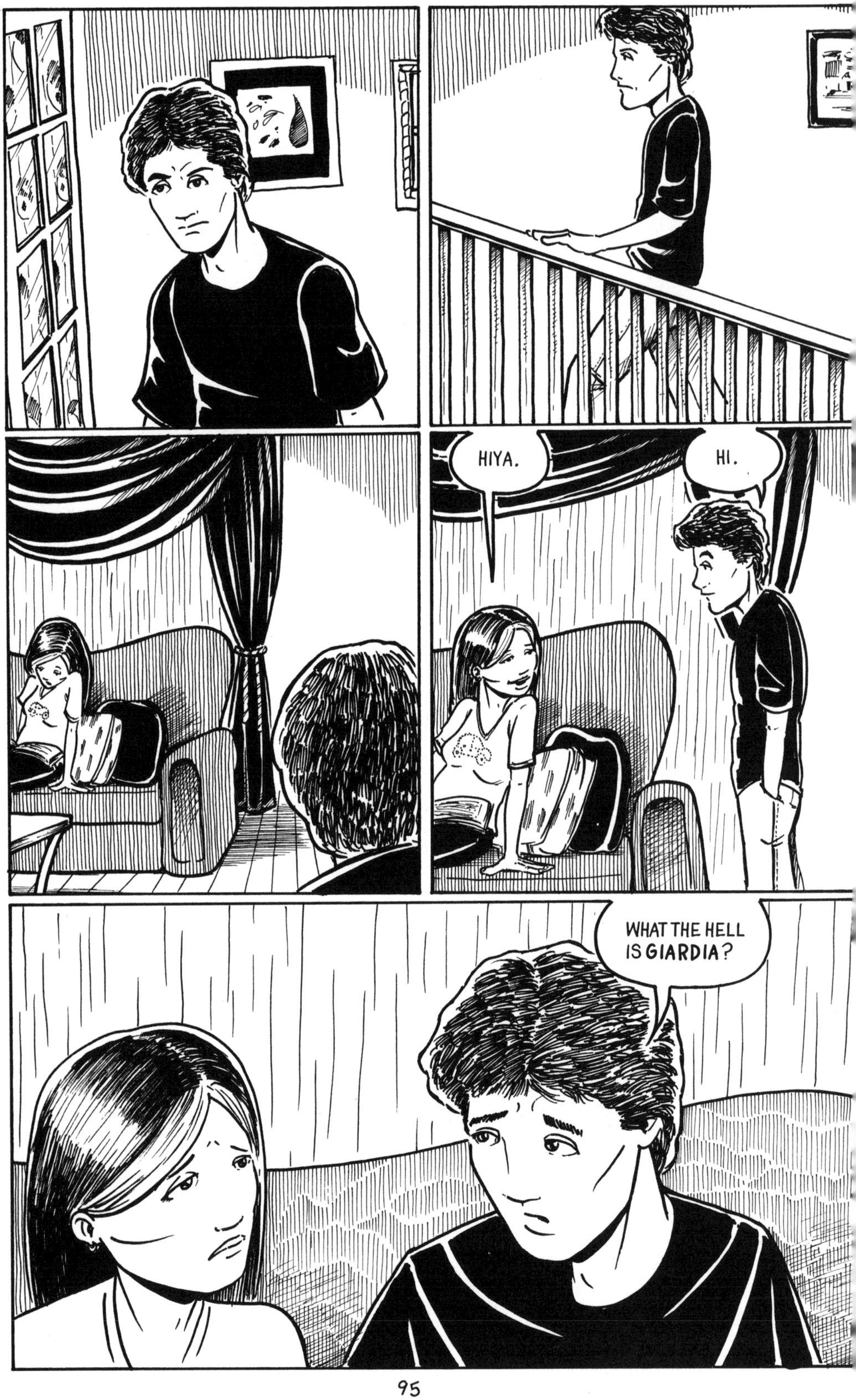
HIYA.
HI.
WHAT THE HELL IS GIARDIA?

PEDRO TALKING THE TALK

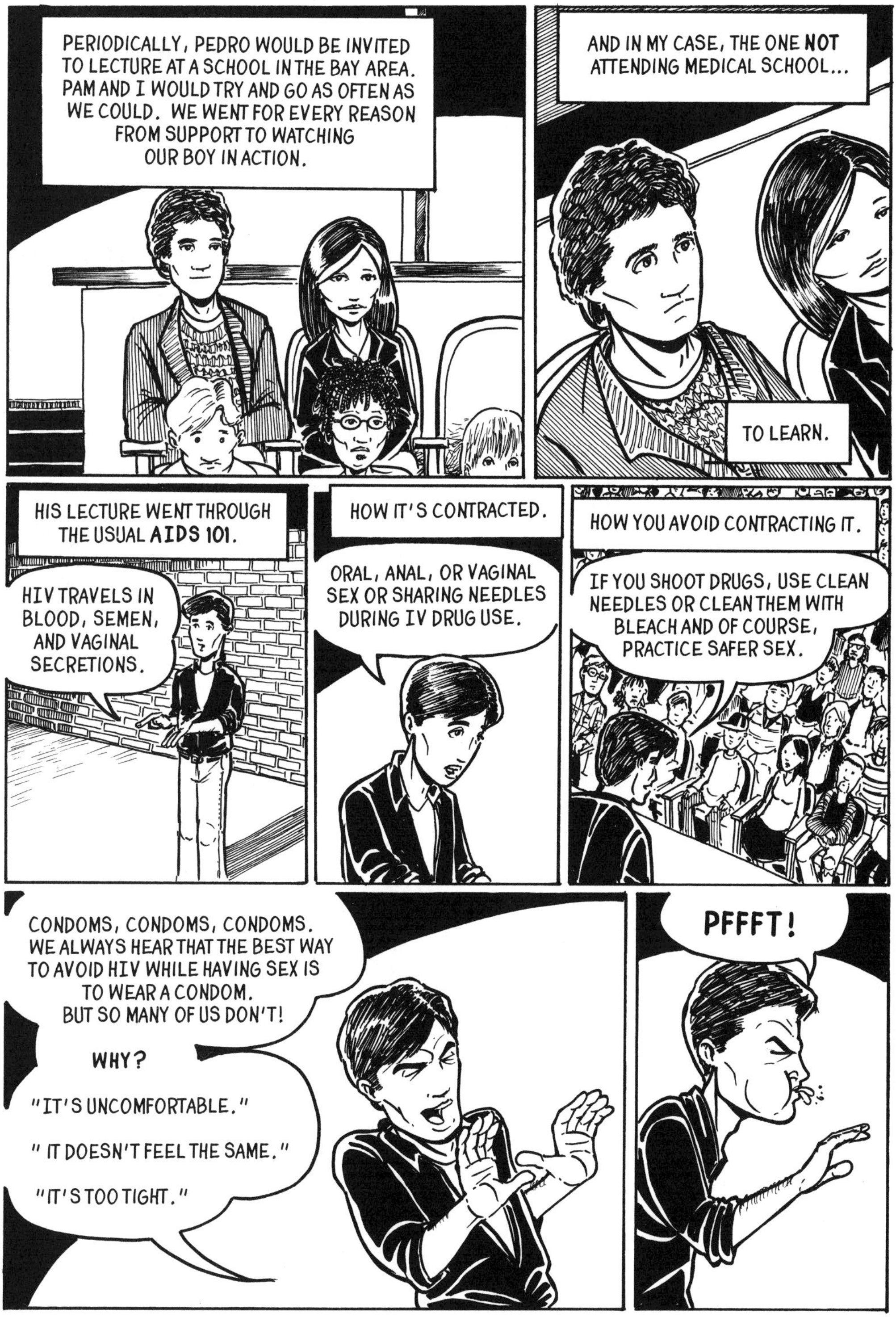
PERIODICALLY, PEDRO WOULD BE INVITED TO LECTURE AT A SCHOOL IN THE BAY AREA. PAM AND I WOULD TRY AND GO AS OFTEN AS WE COULD. WE WENT FOR EVERY REASON FROM SUPPORT TO WATCHING OUR BOY IN ACTION.
AND IN MY CASE, THE ONE NOT ATTENDING MEDICAL SCHOOL...
TO LEARN.
HIS LECTURE WENT THROUGH THE USUAL AIDS 101.
HIV TRAVELS IN BLOOD, SEMEN, AND VAGINAL SECRETIONS.
HOW IT'S CONTRACTED.
ORAL, ANAL, OR VAGINAL SEX OR SHARING NEEDLES DURING IV DRUG USE.
HOW YOU AVOID CONTRACTING IT.
IF YOU SHOOT DRUGS, USE CLEAN NEEDLES OR CLEAN THEM WITH BLEACH AND OF COURSE, PRACTICE SAFER SEX.
CONDOMS, CONDOMS, CONDOMS. WE ALWAYS HEAR THAT THE BEST WAY TO AVOID HIV WHILE HAVING SEX IS TO WEAR A CONDOM. BUT SO MANY OF US DON'T!
WHY?
"IT'S UNCOMFORTABLE."
" IT DOESN'T FEEL THE SAME."
"IT'S TOO TIGHT."
PFFFT!

IF ANYTHING, A CONDOM CAN **INCREASE** PLEASURE BY PREVENTING YOU FROM EJACULATING TOO SOON.

AND *TOO TIGHT*?

IF YOUR PARTNER TELLS YOU A CONDOM IS TOO TIGHT...

Snap

Snap

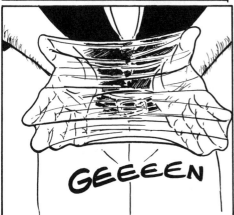

GEEEEN

IF YOUR PARTNER SAYS A CONDOM IS TOO TIGHT-- TELL THEM TO SEE A DOCTOR.

HA HA HA HA HA HA HA HA HA HA HA HA HA HA HA HA

AND IF THEY SEE A DOCTOR AND IT'S **STILL** TOO TIGHT-- HAVE THEM SEE **ME**.

HA HA HA HA HA HA

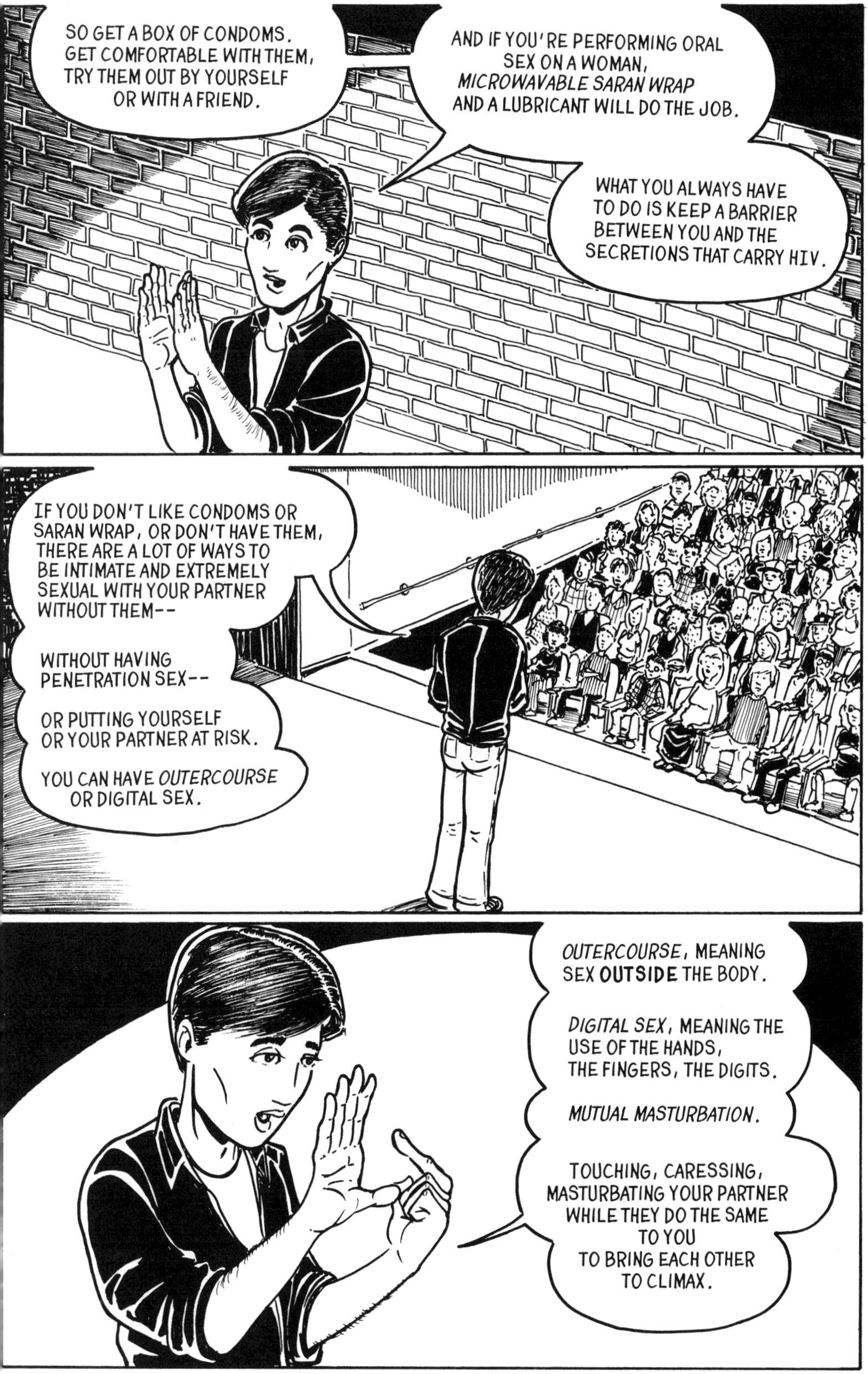
SO GET A BOX OF CONDOMS. GET COMFORTABLE WITH THEM, TRY THEM OUT BY YOURSELF OR WITH A FRIEND.
AND IF YOU'RE PERFORMING ORAL SEX ON A WOMAN, *MICROWAVABLE SARAN WRAP* AND A LUBRICANT WILL DO THE JOB.
WHAT YOU ALWAYS HAVE TO DO IS KEEP A BARRIER BETWEEN YOU AND THE SECRETIONS THAT CARRY HIV.
IF YOU DON'T LIKE CONDOMS OR SARAN WRAP, OR DON'T HAVE THEM, THERE ARE A LOT OF WAYS TO BE INTIMATE AND EXTREMELY SEXUAL WITH YOUR PARTNER WITHOUT THEM--
WITHOUT HAVING PENETRATION SEX--
OR PUTTING YOURSELF OR YOUR PARTNER AT RISK.
YOU CAN HAVE *OUTERCOURSE* OR DIGITAL SEX.
OUTERCOURSE, MEANING SEX **OUTSIDE** THE BODY.
DIGITAL SEX, MEANING THE USE OF THE HANDS, THE FINGERS, THE DIGITS.
MUTUAL MASTURBATION.
TOUCHING, CARESSING, MASTURBATING YOUR PARTNER WHILE THEY DO THE SAME TO YOU TO BRING EACH OTHER TO CLIMAX.

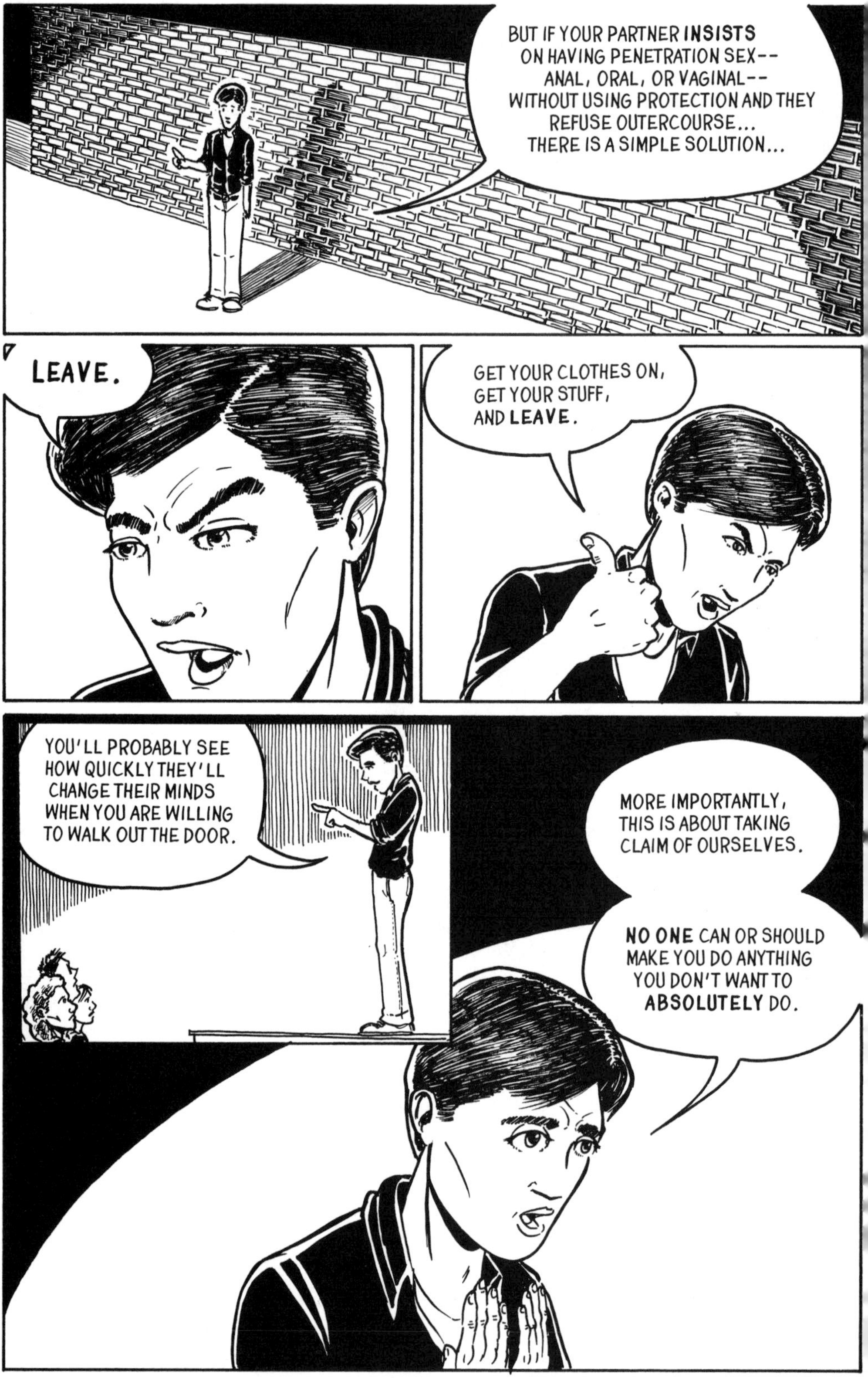
BUT IF YOUR PARTNER **INSISTS** ON HAVING PENETRATION SEX-- ANAL, ORAL, OR VAGINAL-- WITHOUT USING PROTECTION AND THEY REFUSE OUTERCOURSE... THERE IS A SIMPLE SOLUTION...
LEAVE.
GET YOUR CLOTHES ON, GET YOUR STUFF, AND **LEAVE.**
YOU'LL PROBABLY SEE HOW QUICKLY THEY'LL CHANGE THEIR MINDS WHEN YOU ARE WILLING TO WALK OUT THE DOOR.
MORE IMPORTANTLY, THIS IS ABOUT TAKING CLAIM OF OURSELVES.
NO ONE CAN OR SHOULD MAKE YOU DO ANYTHING YOU DON'T WANT TO **ABSOLUTELY** DO.

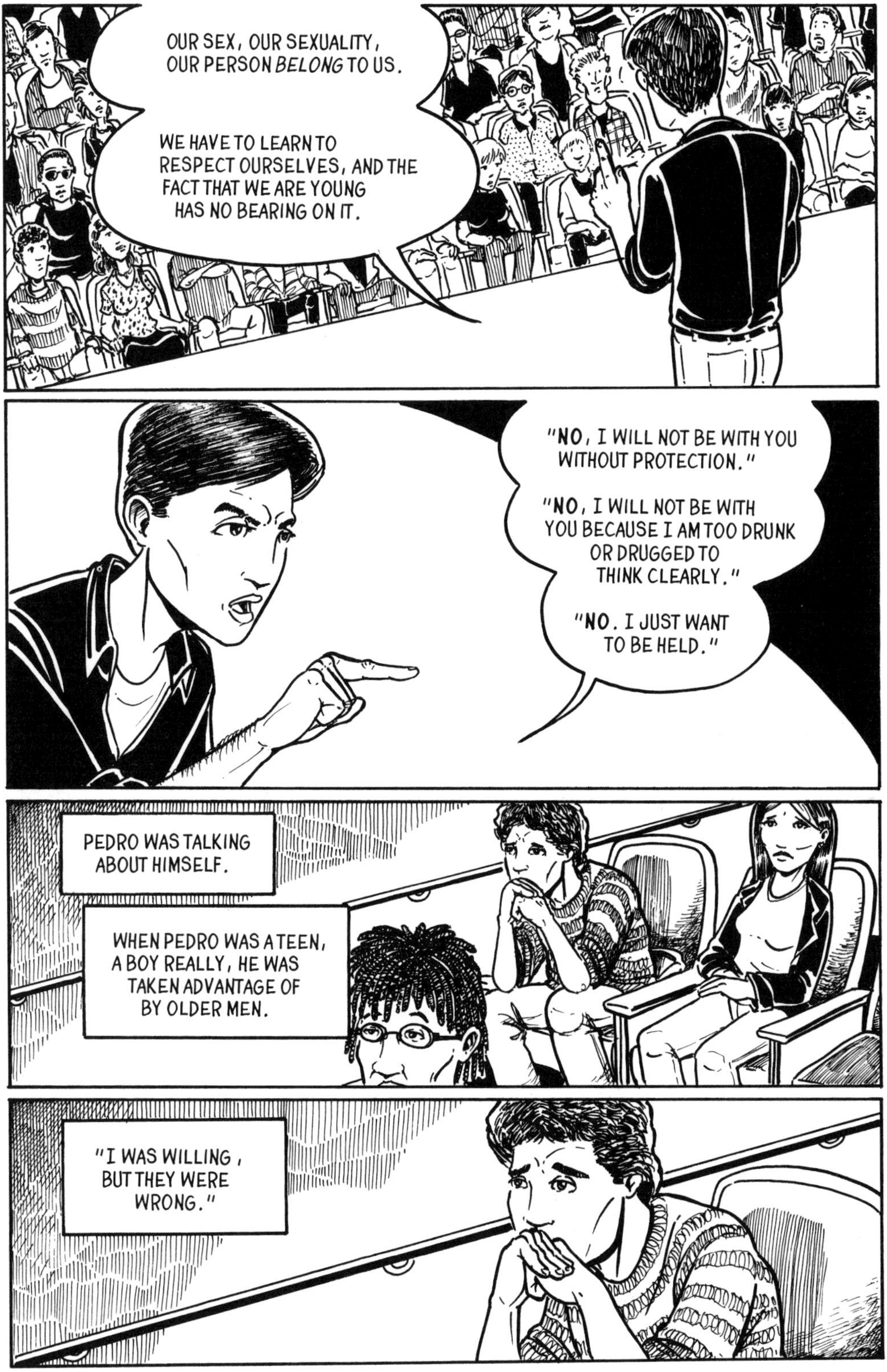
OUR SEX, OUR SEXUALITY, OUR PERSON *BELONG* TO US.
WE HAVE TO LEARN TO RESPECT OURSELVES, AND THE FACT THAT WE ARE YOUNG HAS NO BEARING ON IT.
"**NO**, I WILL NOT BE WITH YOU WITHOUT PROTECTION."
"**NO**, I WILL NOT BE WITH YOU BECAUSE I AM TOO DRUNK OR DRUGGED TO THINK CLEARLY."
"**NO**. I JUST WANT TO BE HELD."
PEDRO WAS TALKING ABOUT HIMSELF.
WHEN PEDRO WAS A TEEN, A BOY REALLY, HE WAS TAKEN ADVANTAGE OF BY OLDER MEN.
"I WAS WILLING, BUT THEY WERE WRONG."

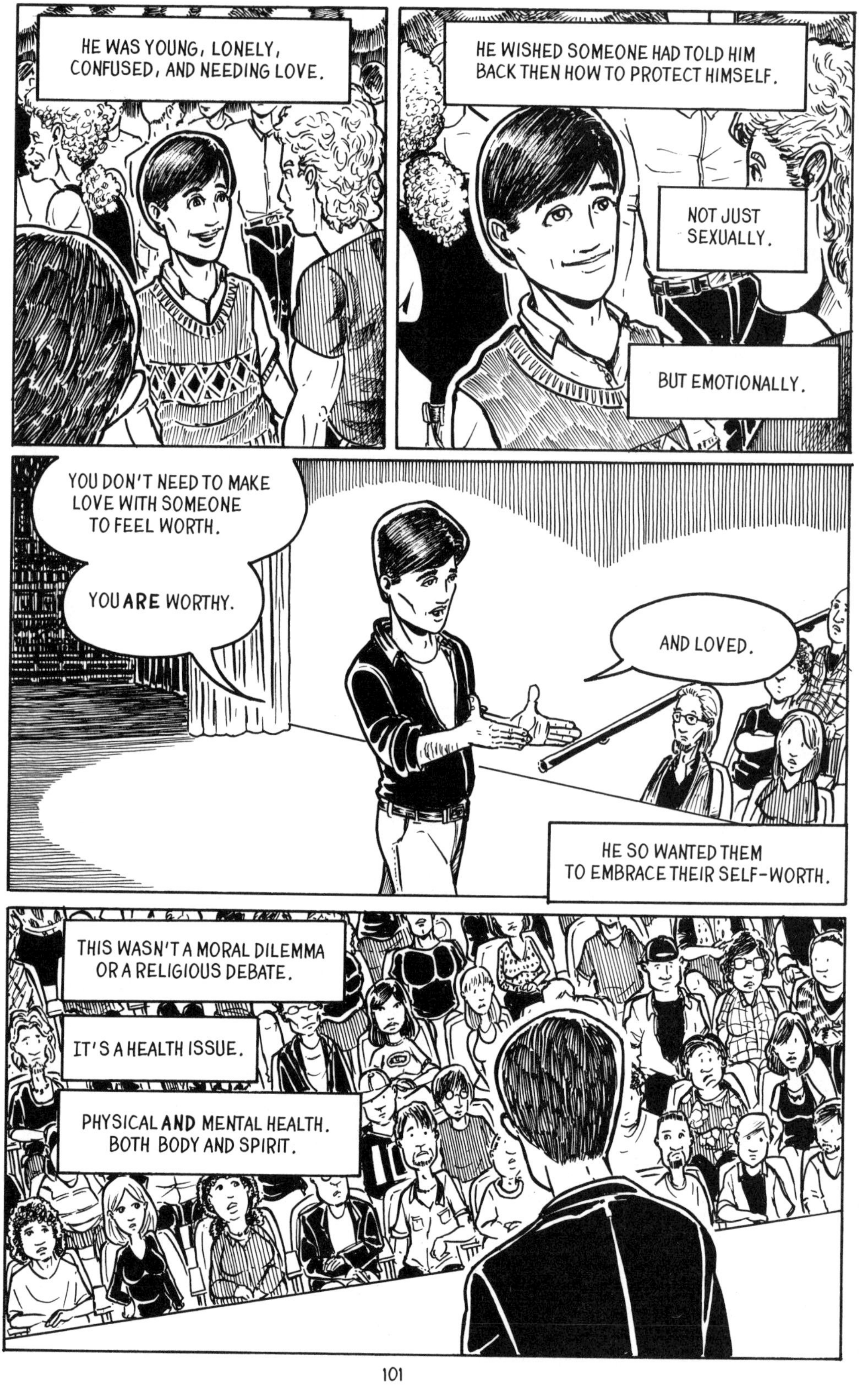
HE WAS YOUNG, LONELY, CONFUSED, AND NEEDING LOVE.
HE WISHED SOMEONE HAD TOLD HIM BACK THEN HOW TO PROTECT HIMSELF.
NOT JUST SEXUALLY.
BUT EMOTIONALLY.
YOU DON'T NEED TO MAKE LOVE WITH SOMEONE TO FEEL WORTH.
YOU **ARE** WORTHY.
AND LOVED.
HE SO WANTED THEM TO EMBRACE THEIR SELF-WORTH.
THIS WASN'T A MORAL DILEMMA OR A RELIGIOUS DEBATE.
IT'S A HEALTH ISSUE.
PHYSICAL **AND** MENTAL HEALTH. BOTH BODY AND SPIRIT.

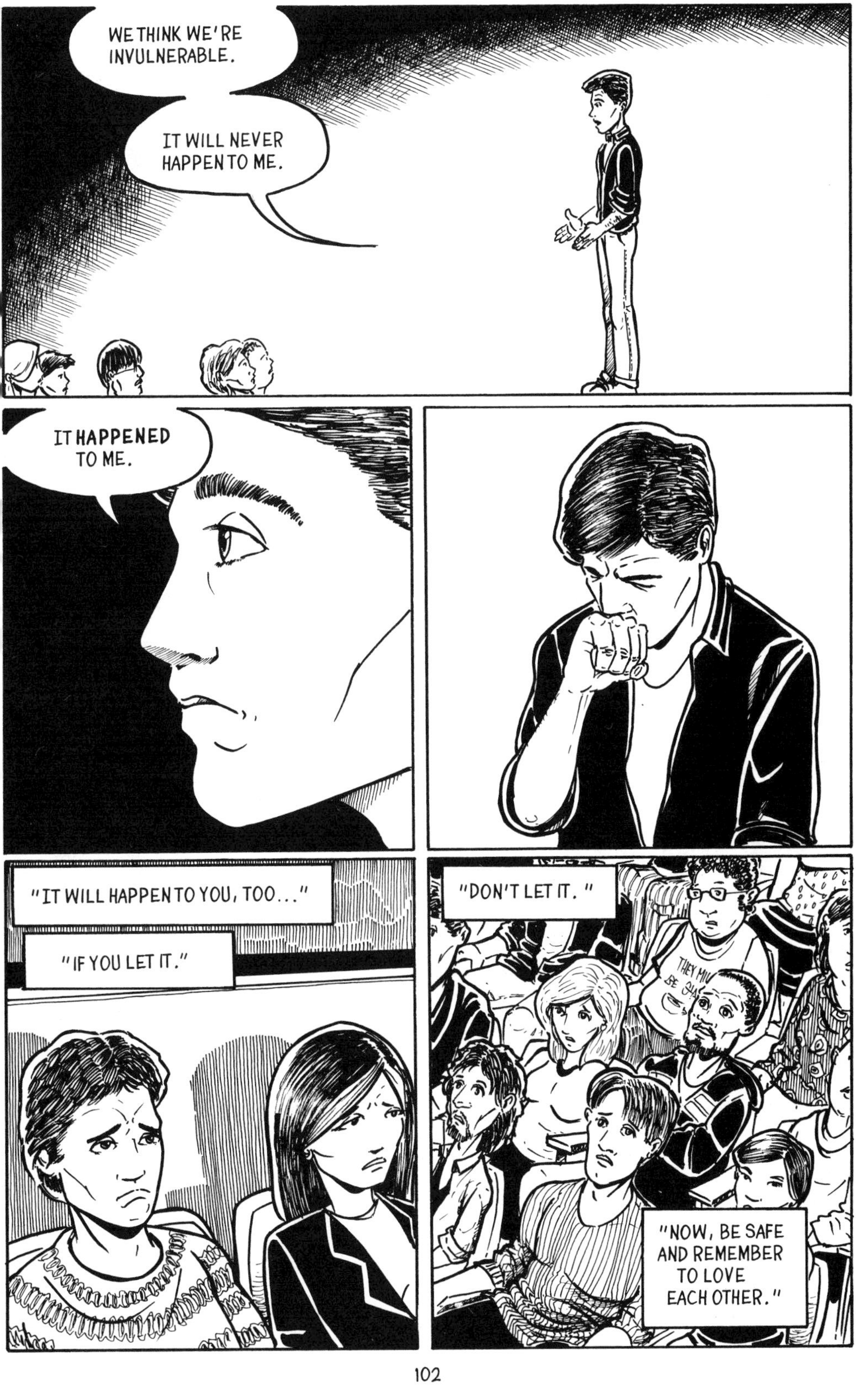
WE THINK WE'RE INVULNERABLE.
IT WILL NEVER HAPPEN TO ME.
IT HAPPENED TO ME.
"IT WILL HAPPEN TO YOU, TOO..."
"IF YOU LET IT."
"DON'T LET IT."
"NOW, BE SAFE AND REMEMBER TO LOVE EACH OTHER."

SEAN

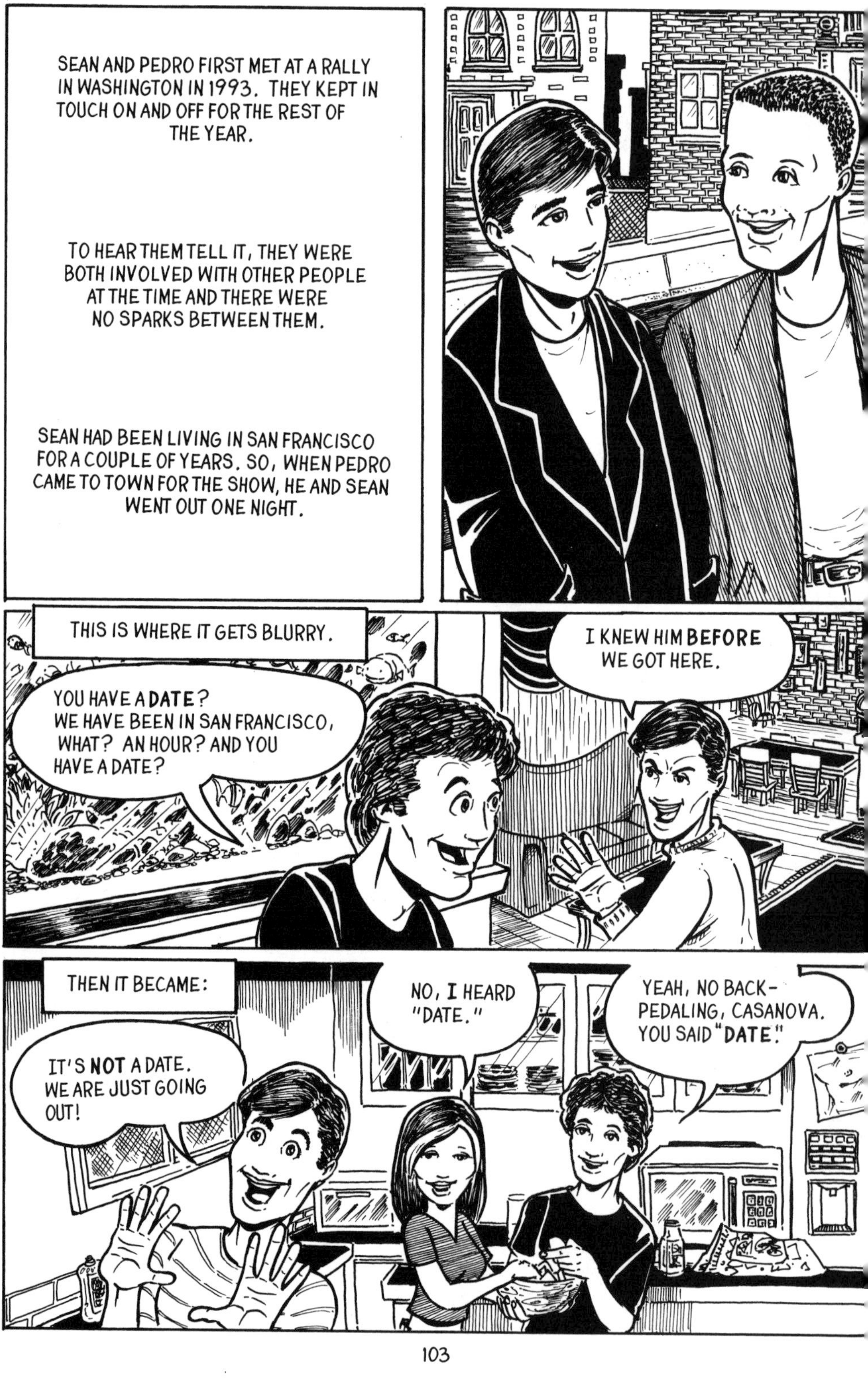
SEAN AND PEDRO FIRST MET AT A RALLY IN WASHINGTON IN 1993. THEY KEPT IN TOUCH ON AND OFF FOR THE REST OF THE YEAR.
TO HEAR THEM TELL IT, THEY WERE BOTH INVOLVED WITH OTHER PEOPLE AT THE TIME AND THERE WERE NO SPARKS BETWEEN THEM.
SEAN HAD BEEN LIVING IN SAN FRANCISCO FOR A COUPLE OF YEARS. SO, WHEN PEDRO CAME TO TOWN FOR THE SHOW, HE AND SEAN WENT OUT ONE NIGHT.
THIS IS WHERE IT GETS BLURRY.
YOU HAVE A **DATE**? WE HAVE BEEN IN SAN FRANCISCO, WHAT? AN HOUR? AND YOU HAVE A DATE?
I KNEW HIM **BEFORE** WE GOT HERE.
THEN IT BECAME:
IT'S **NOT** A DATE. WE ARE JUST GOING OUT!
NO, **I** HEARD "DATE."
YEAH, NO BACK-PEDALING, CASANOVA. YOU SAID "**DATE**."

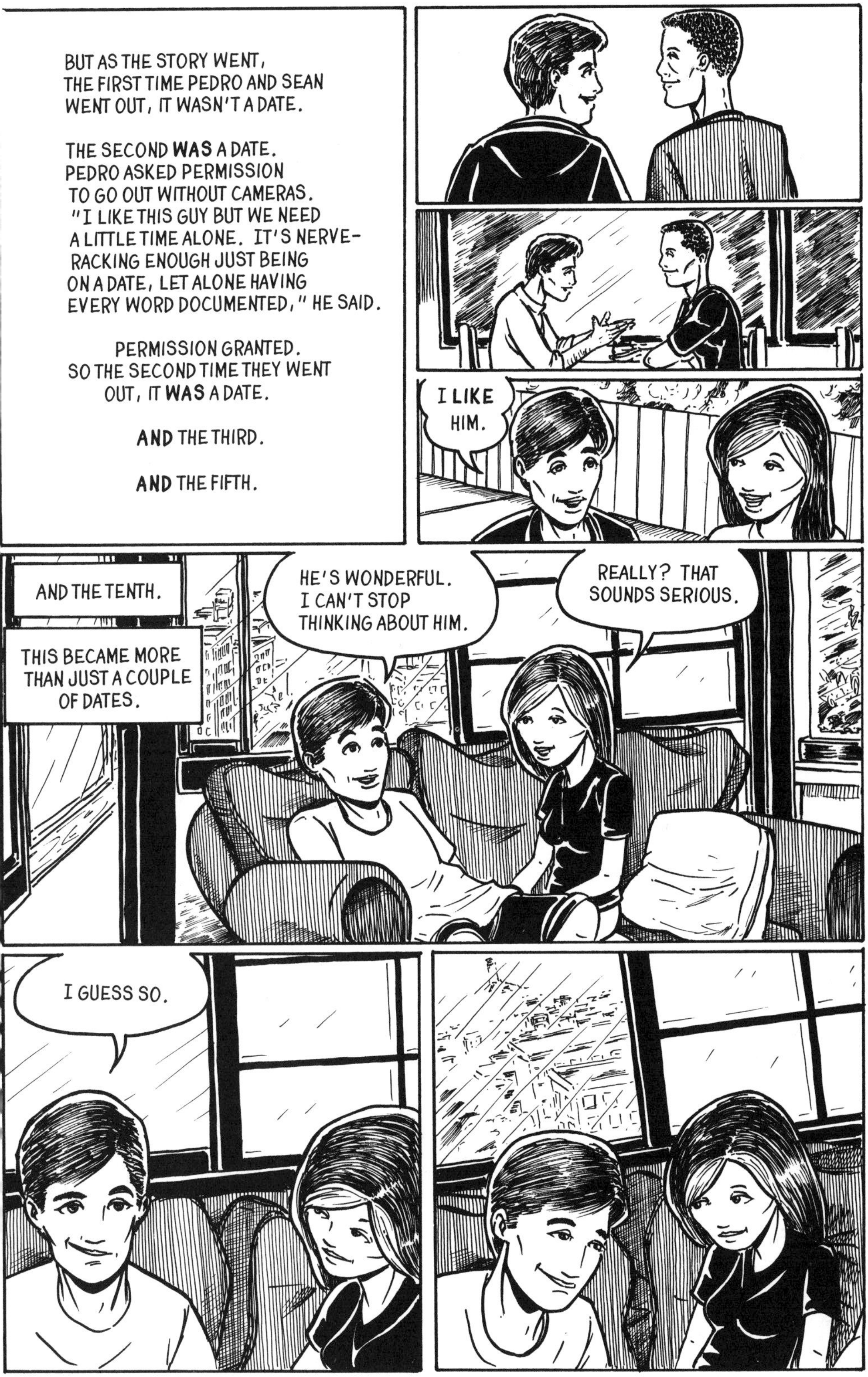
BUT AS THE STORY WENT, THE FIRST TIME PEDRO AND SEAN WENT OUT, IT WASN'T A DATE.
THE SECOND **WAS** A DATE. PEDRO ASKED PERMISSION TO GO OUT WITHOUT CAMERAS. "I LIKE THIS GUY BUT WE NEED A LITTLE TIME ALONE. IT'S NERVE-RACKING ENOUGH JUST BEING ON A DATE, LET ALONE HAVING EVERY WORD DOCUMENTED," HE SAID.
PERMISSION GRANTED. SO THE SECOND TIME THEY WENT OUT, IT **WAS** A DATE.
AND THE THIRD.
AND THE FIFTH.
I **LIKE** HIM.
AND THE TENTH.
THIS BECAME MORE THAN JUST A COUPLE OF DATES.
HE'S WONDERFUL. I CAN'T STOP THINKING ABOUT HIM.
REALLY? THAT SOUNDS SERIOUS.
I GUESS SO.

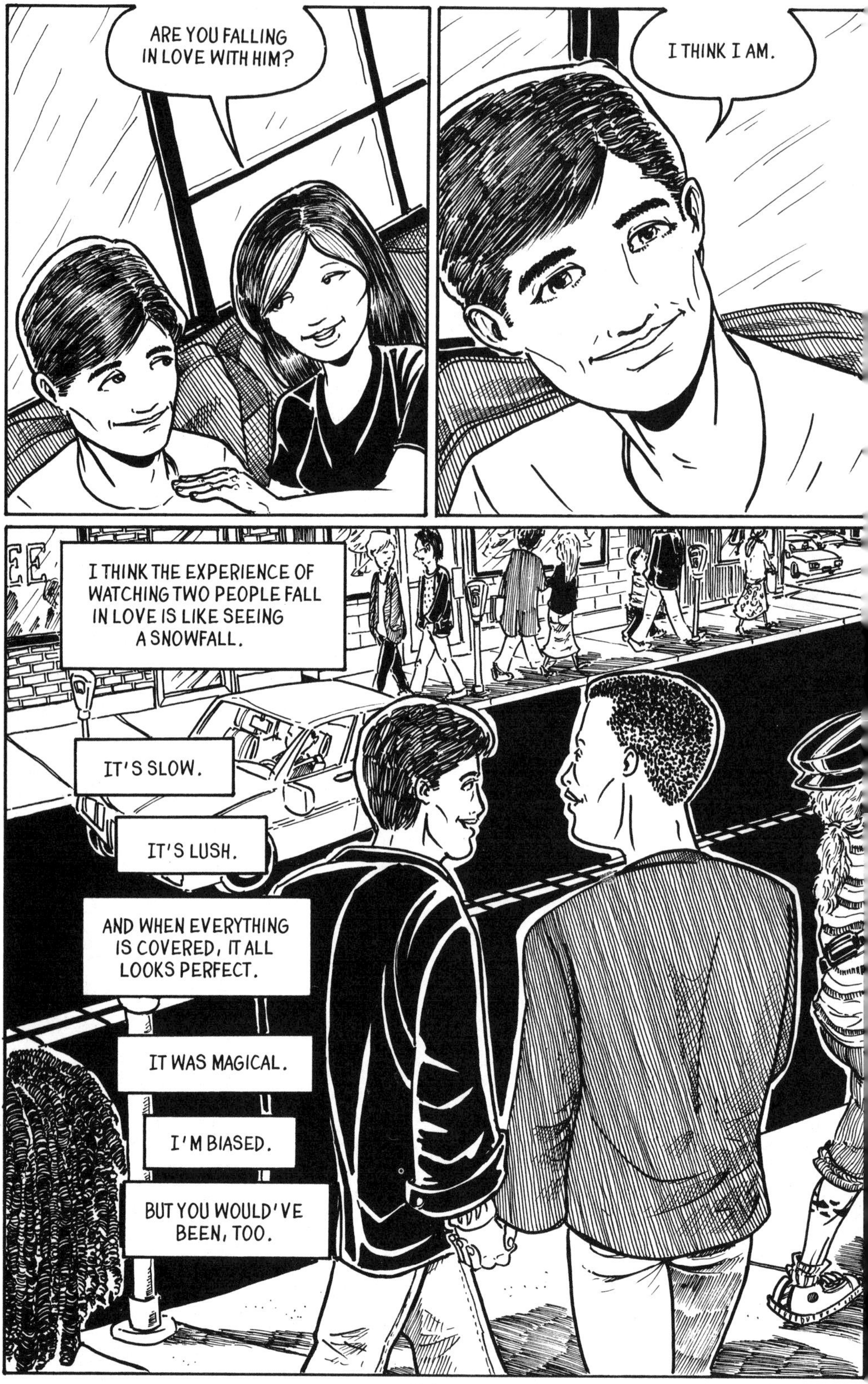
ARE YOU FALLING IN LOVE WITH HIM?
I THINK I AM.
I THINK THE EXPERIENCE OF WATCHING TWO PEOPLE FALL IN LOVE IS LIKE SEEING A SNOWFALL.
IT'S SLOW.
IT'S LUSH.
AND WHEN EVERYTHING IS COVERED, IT ALL LOOKS PERFECT.
IT WAS MAGICAL.
I'M BIASED.
BUT YOU WOULD'VE BEEN, TOO.

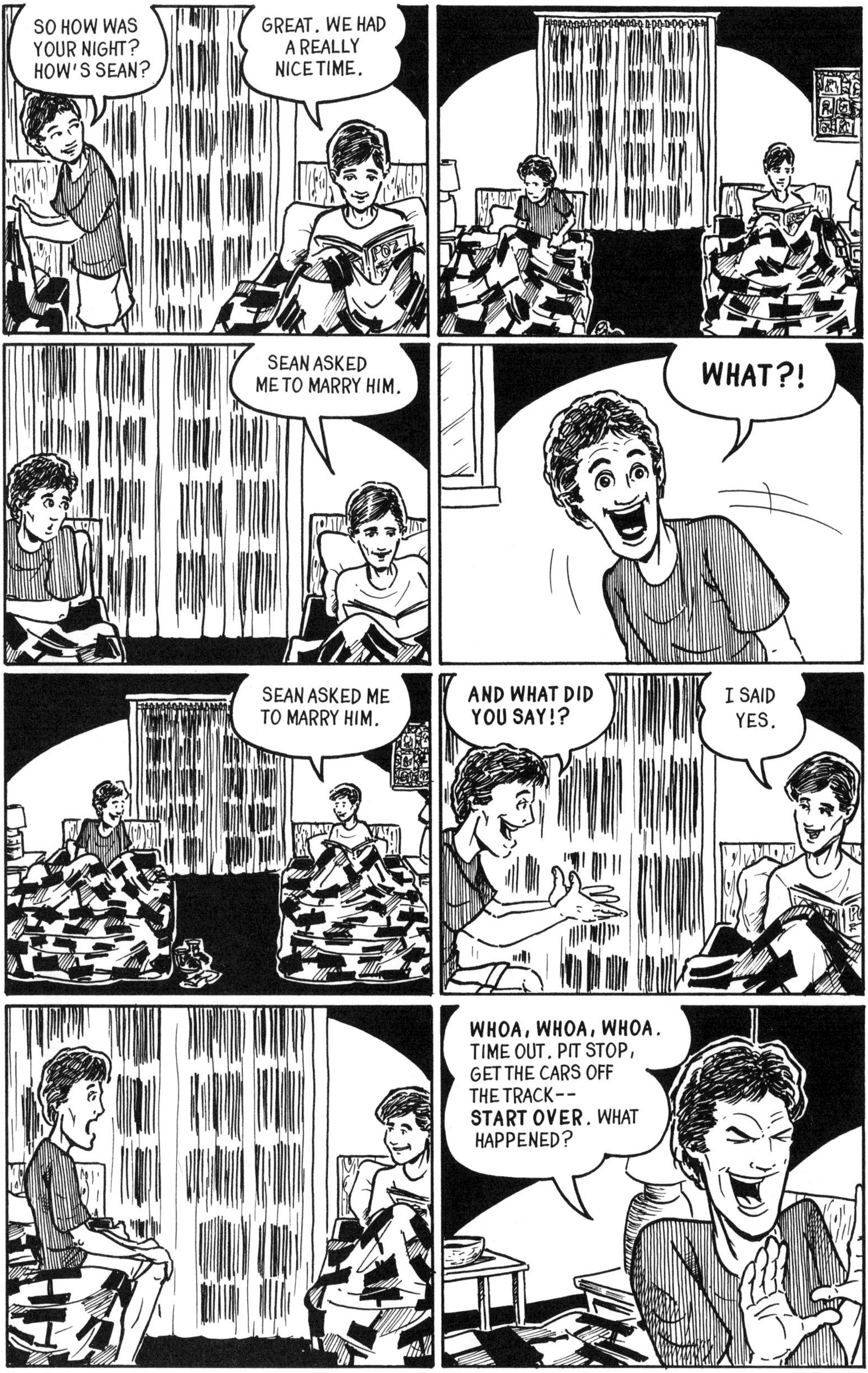
SO HOW WAS YOUR NIGHT? HOW'S SEAN?
GREAT. WE HAD A REALLY NICE TIME.
POZ
SEAN ASKED ME TO MARRY HIM.
WHAT?!
SEAN ASKED ME TO MARRY HIM.
AND WHAT DID YOU SAY!?
I SAID YES.
WHOA, WHOA, WHOA. TIME OUT. PIT STOP, GET THE CARS OFF THE TRACK-- START OVER. WHAT HAPPENED?

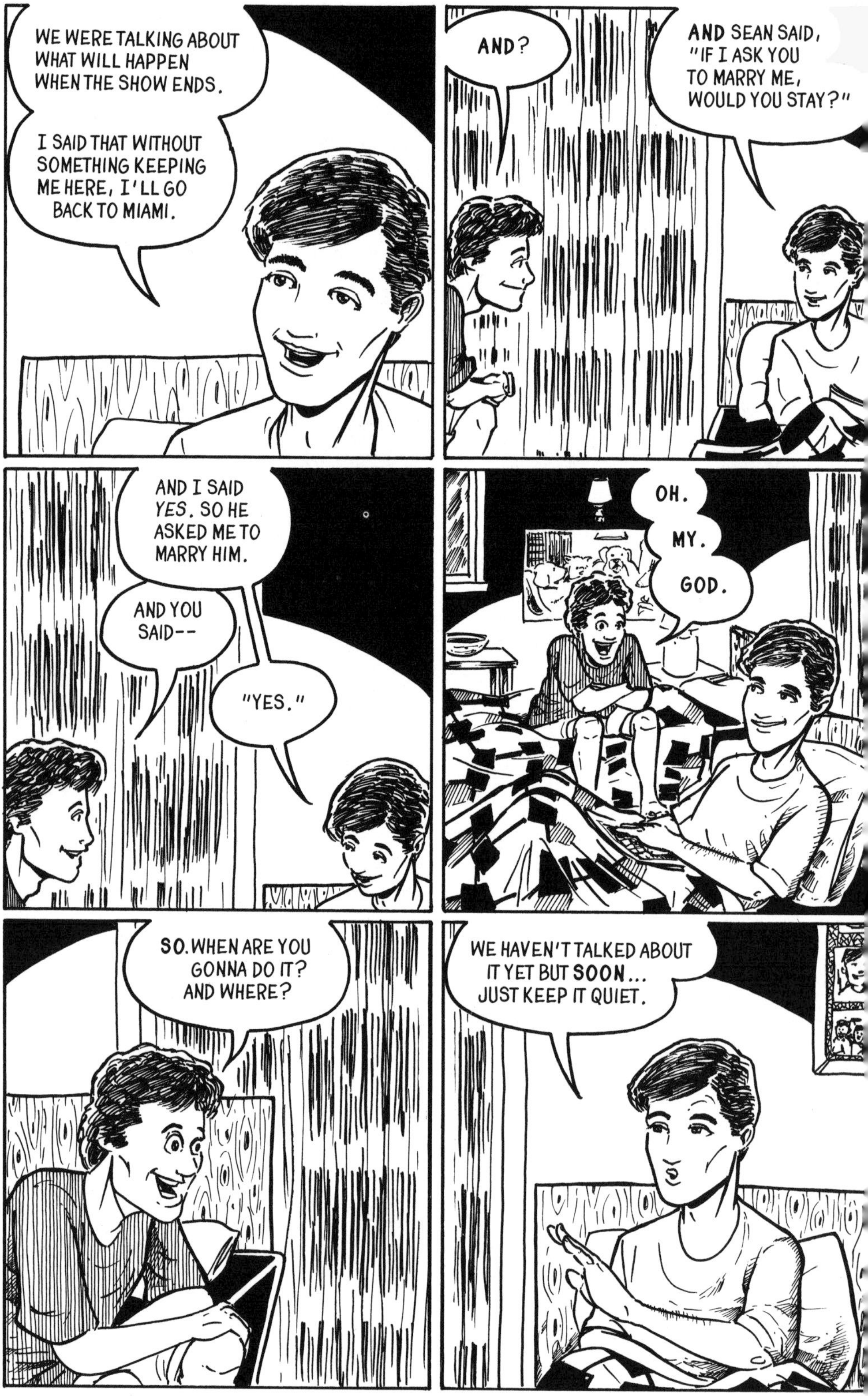
WE WERE TALKING ABOUT WHAT WILL HAPPEN WHEN THE SHOW ENDS.
I SAID THAT WITHOUT SOMETHING KEEPING ME HERE, I'LL GO BACK TO MIAMI.
AND?
AND SEAN SAID, "IF I ASK YOU TO MARRY ME, WOULD YOU STAY?"
AND I SAID *YES*. SO HE ASKED ME TO MARRY HIM.
AND YOU SAID--
"YES."
OH.
MY.
GOD.
SO. WHEN ARE YOU GONNA DO IT? AND WHERE?
WE HAVEN'T TALKED ABOUT IT YET BUT **SOON**... JUST KEEP IT QUIET.

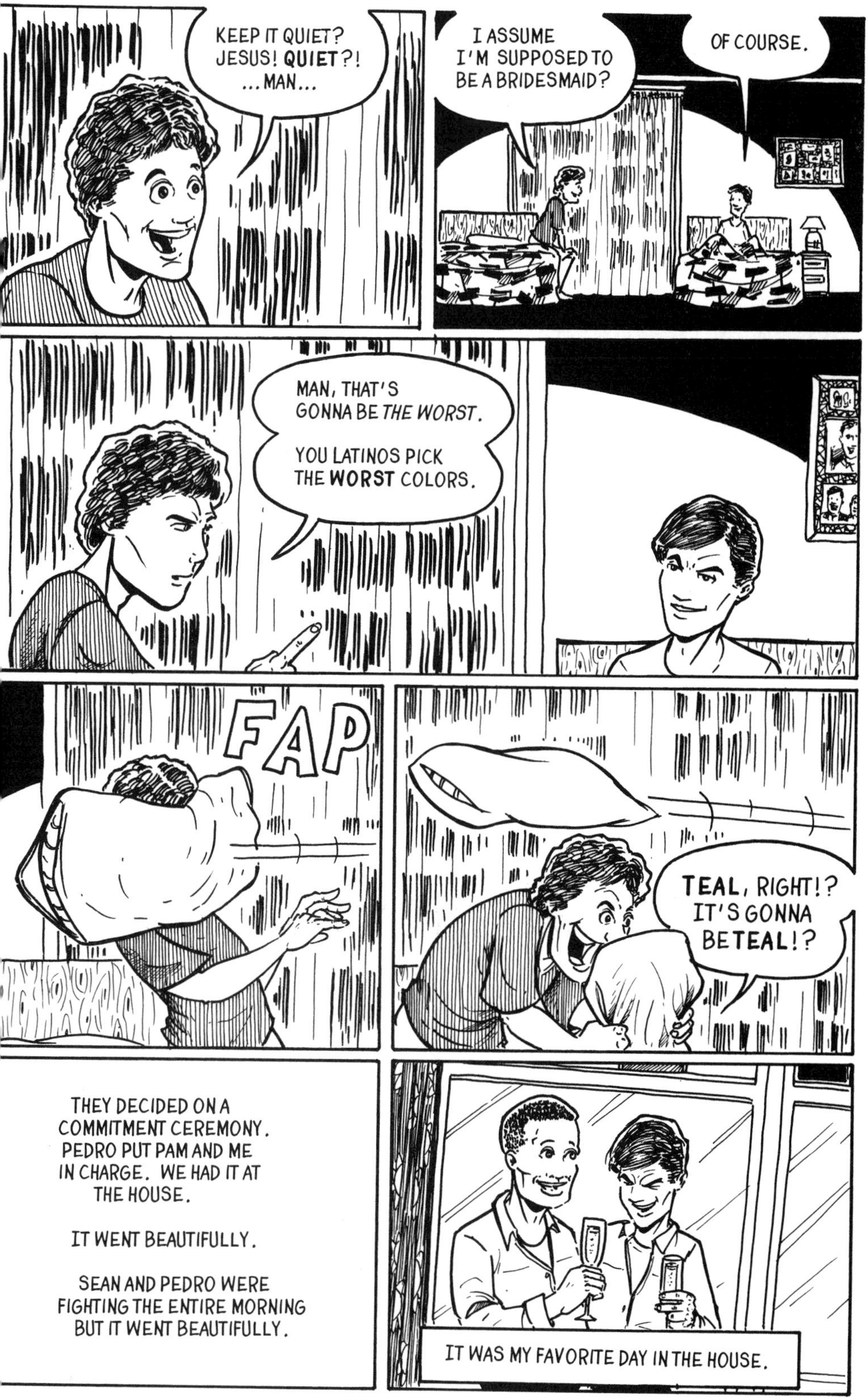
KEEP IT QUIET? JESUS! QUIET?! ...MAN...
I ASSUME I'M SUPPOSED TO BE A BRIDESMAID?
OF COURSE.
MAN, THAT'S GONNA BE THE WORST.
YOU LATINOS PICK THE WORST COLORS.
FAP
TEAL, RIGHT!? IT'S GONNA BE TEAL!?
THEY DECIDED ON A COMMITMENT CEREMONY. PEDRO PUT PAM AND ME IN CHARGE. WE HAD IT AT THE HOUSE.
IT WENT BEAUTIFULLY.
SEAN AND PEDRO WERE FIGHTING THE ENTIRE MORNING BUT IT WENT BEAUTIFULLY.
IT WAS MY FAVORITE DAY IN THE HOUSE.

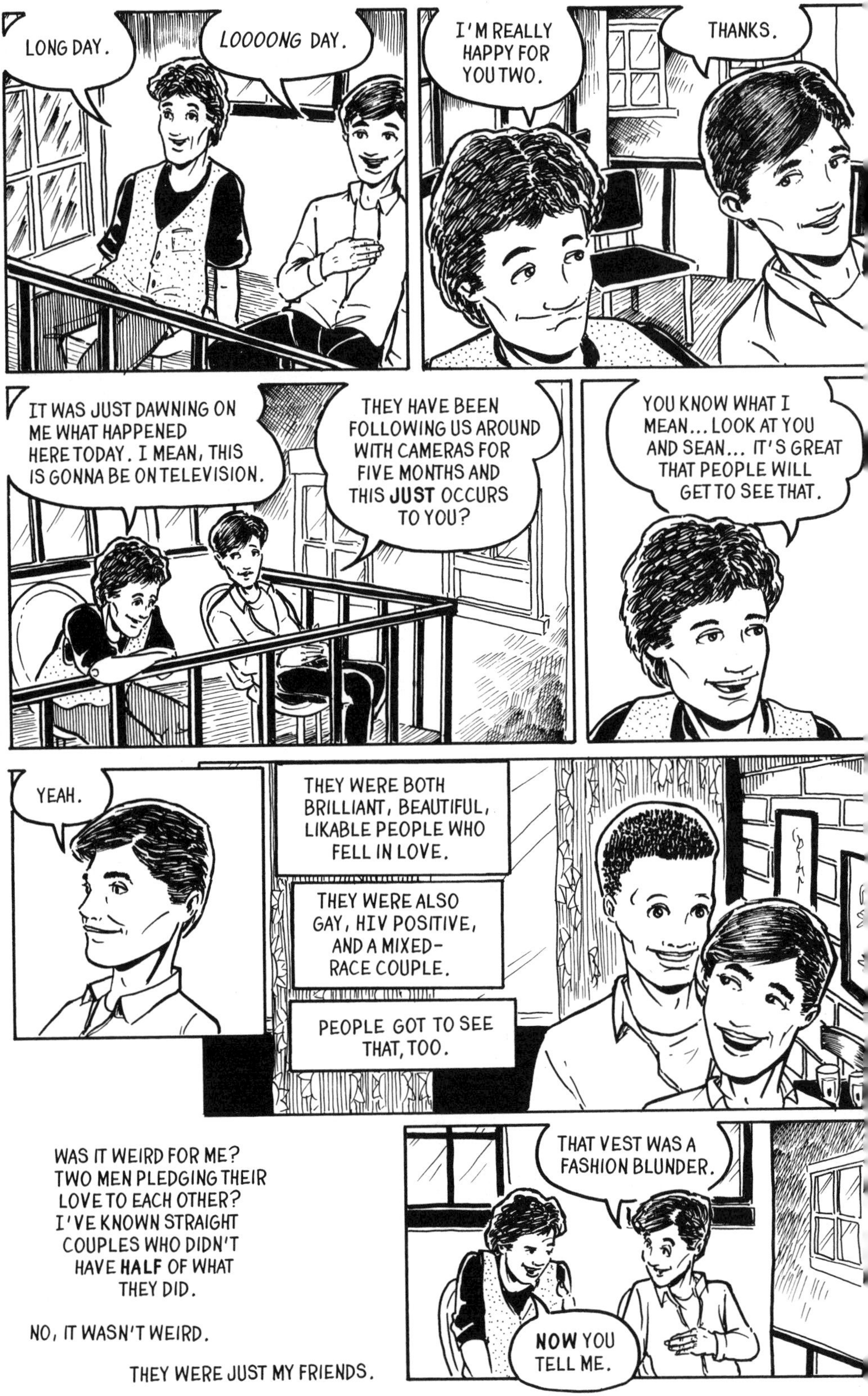
LONG DAY.
LOOOONG DAY.
I'M REALLY HAPPY FOR YOU TWO.
THANKS.
IT WAS JUST DAWNING ON ME WHAT HAPPENED HERE TODAY. I MEAN, THIS IS GONNA BE ON TELEVISION.
THEY HAVE BEEN FOLLOWING US AROUND WITH CAMERAS FOR FIVE MONTHS AND THIS **JUST** OCCURS TO YOU?
YOU KNOW WHAT I MEAN... LOOK AT YOU AND SEAN... IT'S GREAT THAT PEOPLE WILL GET TO SEE THAT.
YEAH.
THEY WERE BOTH BRILLIANT, BEAUTIFUL, LIKABLE PEOPLE WHO FELL IN LOVE.
THEY WERE ALSO GAY, HIV POSITIVE, AND A MIXED-RACE COUPLE.
PEOPLE GOT TO SEE THAT, TOO.
WAS IT WEIRD FOR ME? TWO MEN PLEDGING THEIR LOVE TO EACH OTHER? I'VE KNOWN STRAIGHT COUPLES WHO DIDN'T HAVE **HALF** OF WHAT THEY DID.
NO, IT WASN'T WEIRD.
THEY WERE JUST MY FRIENDS.
THAT VEST WAS A FASHION BLUNDER.
NOW YOU TELL ME.

LOOKING FORWARD, LOOKING BACK

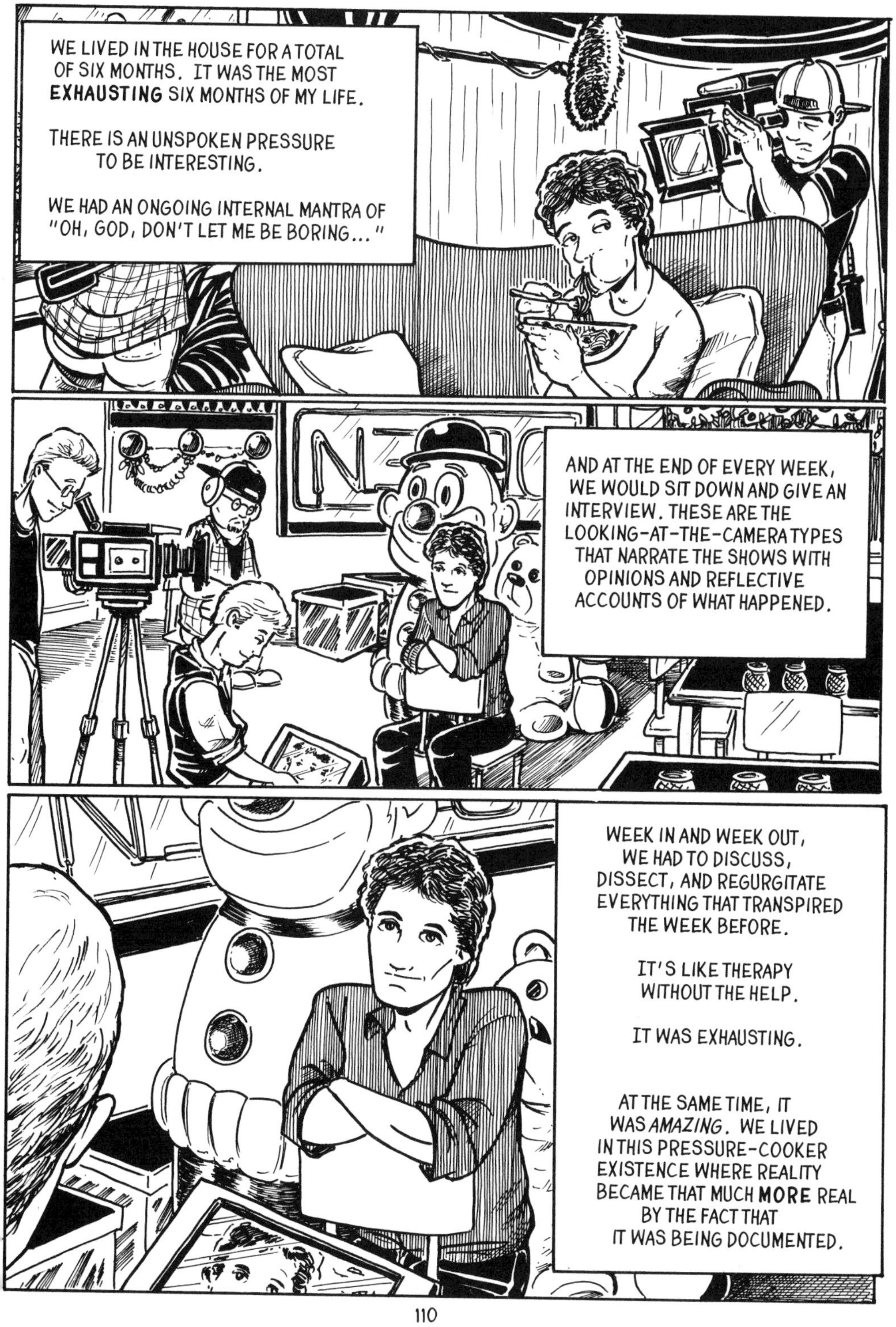
WE LIVED IN THE HOUSE FOR A TOTAL OF SIX MONTHS. IT WAS THE MOST **EXHAUSTING** SIX MONTHS OF MY LIFE.
THERE IS AN UNSPOKEN PRESSURE TO BE INTERESTING.
WE HAD AN ONGOING INTERNAL MANTRA OF "OH, GOD, DON'T LET ME BE BORING..."
AND AT THE END OF EVERY WEEK, WE WOULD SIT DOWN AND GIVE AN INTERVIEW. THESE ARE THE LOOKING-AT-THE-CAMERA TYPES THAT NARRATE THE SHOWS WITH OPINIONS AND REFLECTIVE ACCOUNTS OF WHAT HAPPENED.
WEEK IN AND WEEK OUT, WE HAD TO DISCUSS, DISSECT, AND REGURGITATE EVERYTHING THAT TRANSPIRED THE WEEK BEFORE.
IT'S LIKE THERAPY WITHOUT THE HELP.
IT WAS EXHAUSTING.
AT THE SAME TIME, IT WAS *AMAZING*. WE LIVED IN THIS PRESSURE-COOKER EXISTENCE WHERE REALITY BECAME THAT MUCH **MORE** REAL BY THE FACT THAT IT WAS BEING DOCUMENTED.

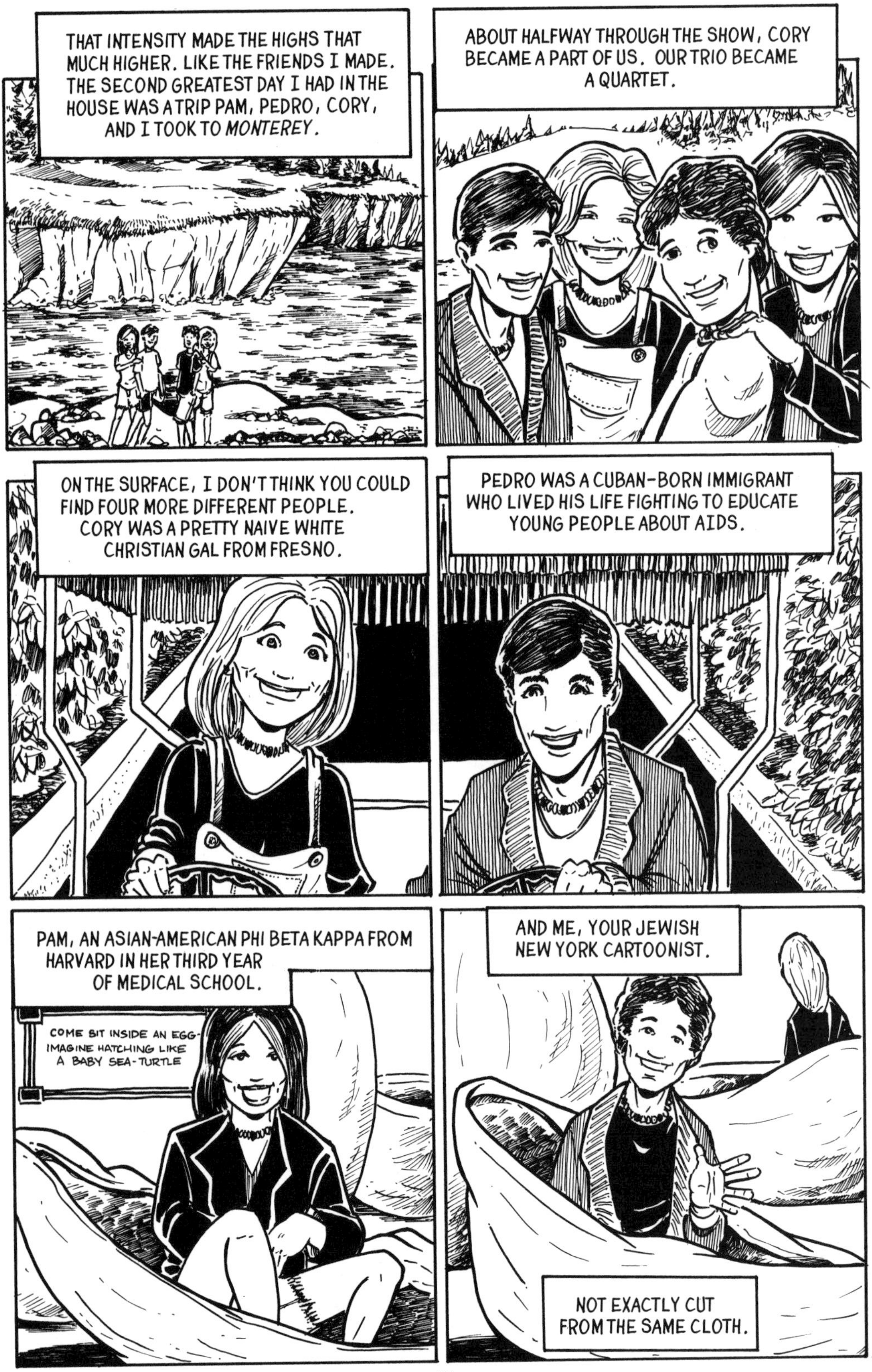
THAT INTENSITY MADE THE HIGHS THAT MUCH HIGHER. LIKE THE FRIENDS I MADE. THE SECOND GREATEST DAY I HAD IN THE HOUSE WAS A TRIP PAM, PEDRO, CORY, AND I TOOK TO *MONTEREY*.
ABOUT HALFWAY THROUGH THE SHOW, CORY BECAME A PART OF US. OUR TRIO BECAME A QUARTET.
ON THE SURFACE, I DON'T THINK YOU COULD FIND FOUR MORE DIFFERENT PEOPLE. CORY WAS A PRETTY NAIVE WHITE CHRISTIAN GAL FROM FRESNO.
PEDRO WAS A CUBAN-BORN IMMIGRANT WHO LIVED HIS LIFE FIGHTING TO EDUCATE YOUNG PEOPLE ABOUT AIDS.
PAM, AN ASIAN-AMERICAN PHI BETA KAPPA FROM HARVARD IN HER THIRD YEAR OF MEDICAL SCHOOL.
COME SIT INSIDE AN EGG- IMAGINE HATCHING LIKE A BABY SEA-TURTLE
AND ME, YOUR JEWISH NEW YORK CARTOONIST.
NOT EXACTLY CUT FROM THE SAME CLOTH.

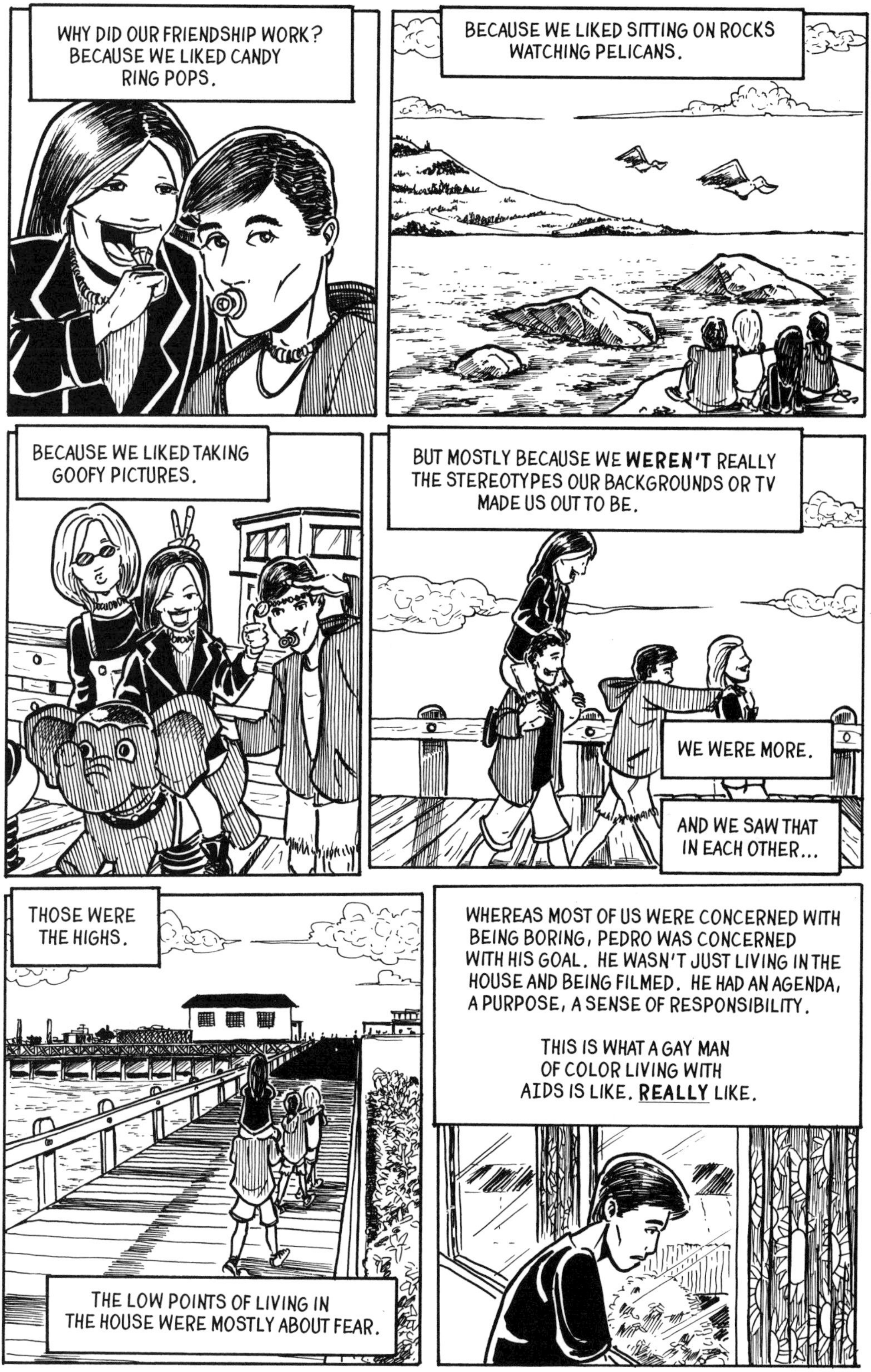
WHY DID OUR FRIENDSHIP WORK? BECAUSE WE LIKED CANDY RING POPS.
BECAUSE WE LIKED SITTING ON ROCKS WATCHING PELICANS.
BECAUSE WE LIKED TAKING GOOFY PICTURES.
BUT MOSTLY BECAUSE WE **WEREN'T** REALLY THE STEREOTYPES OUR BACKGROUNDS OR TV MADE US OUT TO BE.
WE WERE MORE.
AND WE SAW THAT IN EACH OTHER...
THOSE WERE THE HIGHS.
THE LOW POINTS OF LIVING IN THE HOUSE WERE MOSTLY ABOUT FEAR.
WHEREAS MOST OF US WERE CONCERNED WITH BEING BORING, PEDRO WAS CONCERNED WITH HIS GOAL. HE WASN'T JUST LIVING IN THE HOUSE AND BEING FILMED. HE HAD AN AGENDA, A PURPOSE, A SENSE OF RESPONSIBILITY.
THIS IS WHAT A GAY MAN OF COLOR LIVING WITH AIDS IS LIKE. REALLY LIKE.

HE WAS LIVING WITH AIDS.

HE WASN'T SICK.

HE COULD HOLD A JOB.

HE COULD FALL IN LOVE.

BE IN A RELATIONSHIP.

DO EVERYTHING AND ANYTHING
ANYONE ELSE COULD DO.

HE WASN'T GOING TO
BE THE "SICKLY AIDS BOY"
FROM *MTV*.

HE WAS GOING TO SHOW THEM
THAT YOU COULD SUCCEED AND
LIVE WITH AIDS AND HIV.

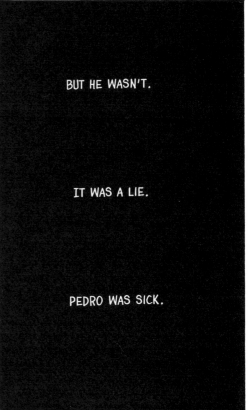

BUT HE WASN'T.

IT WAS A LIE.

PEDRO WAS SICK.

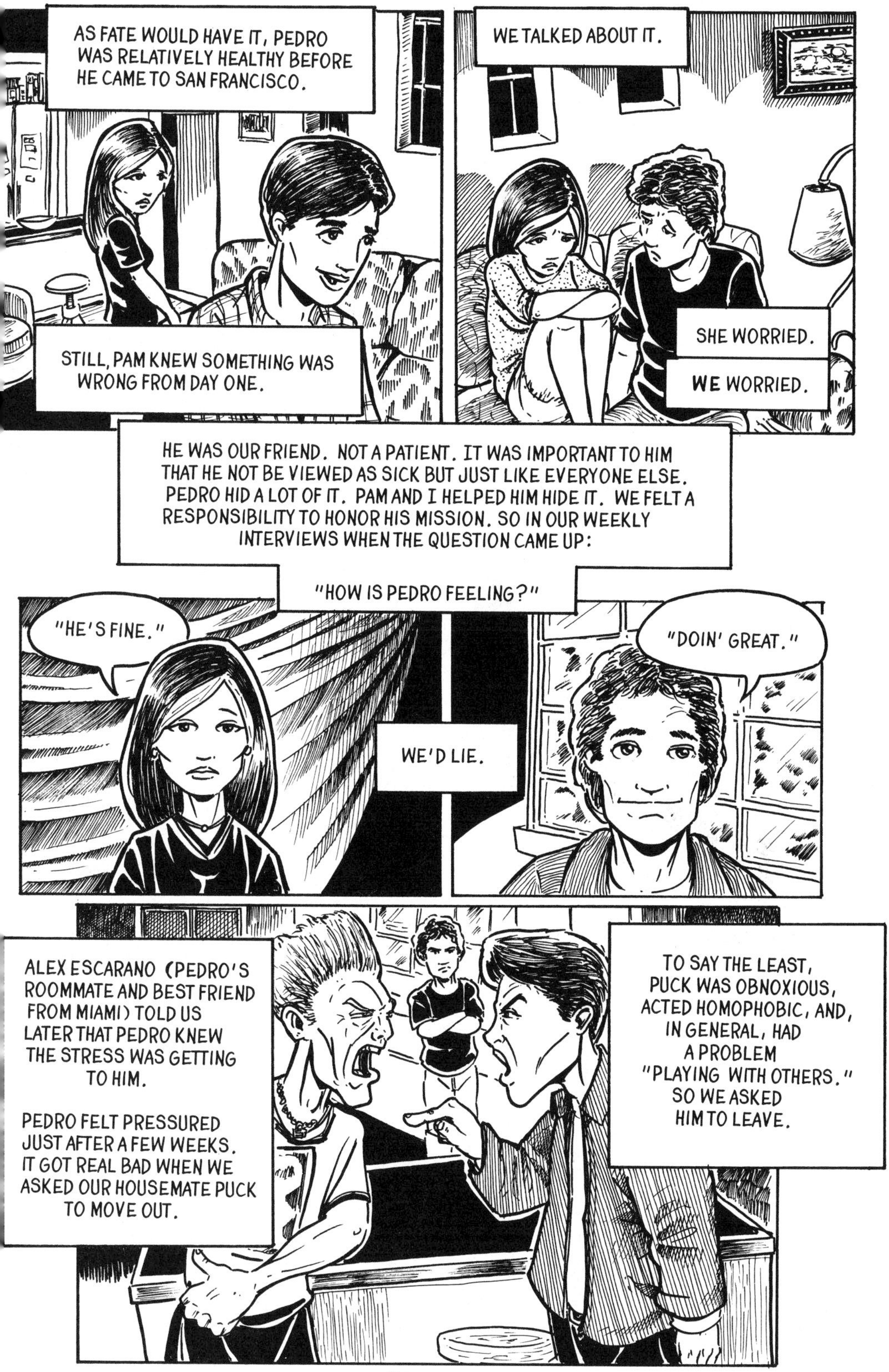
AS FATE WOULD HAVE IT, PEDRO WAS RELATIVELY HEALTHY BEFORE HE CAME TO SAN FRANCISCO.
STILL, PAM KNEW SOMETHING WAS WRONG FROM DAY ONE.
WE TALKED ABOUT IT.
SHE WORRIED.
WE WORRIED.
HE WAS OUR FRIEND. NOT A PATIENT. IT WAS IMPORTANT TO HIM THAT HE NOT BE VIEWED AS SICK BUT JUST LIKE EVERYONE ELSE. PEDRO HID A LOT OF IT. PAM AND I HELPED HIM HIDE IT. WE FELT A RESPONSIBILITY TO HONOR HIS MISSION. SO IN OUR WEEKLY INTERVIEWS WHEN THE QUESTION CAME UP:
"HOW IS PEDRO FEELING?"
"HE'S FINE."
WE'D LIE.
"DOIN' GREAT."
ALEX ESCARANO (PEDRO'S ROOMMATE AND BEST FRIEND FROM MIAMI) TOLD US LATER THAT PEDRO KNEW THE STRESS WAS GETTING TO HIM.
PEDRO FELT PRESSURED JUST AFTER A FEW WEEKS. IT GOT REAL BAD WHEN WE ASKED OUR HOUSEMATE PUCK TO MOVE OUT.
TO SAY THE LEAST, PUCK WAS OBNOXIOUS, ACTED HOMOPHOBIC, AND, IN GENERAL, HAD A PROBLEM "PLAYING WITH OTHERS." SO WE ASKED HIM TO LEAVE.

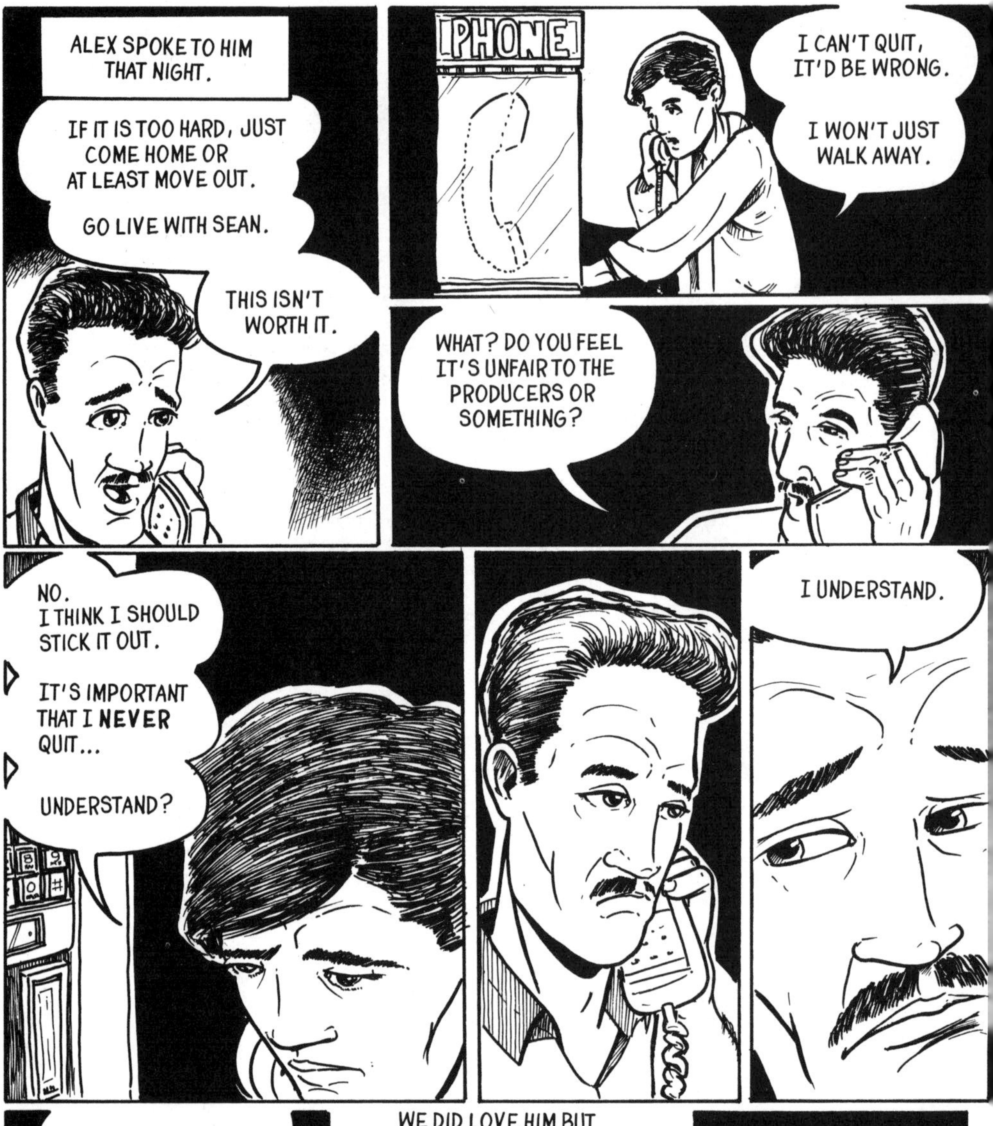
ALEX SPOKE TO HIM THAT NIGHT.
IF IT IS TOO HARD, JUST COME HOME OR AT LEAST MOVE OUT.
GO LIVE WITH SEAN.
THIS ISN'T WORTH IT.
PHONE
I CAN'T QUIT, IT'D BE WRONG.
I WON'T JUST WALK AWAY.
WHAT? DO YOU FEEL IT'S UNFAIR TO THE PRODUCERS OR SOMETHING?
NO. I THINK I SHOULD STICK IT OUT.
IT'S IMPORTANT THAT I **NEVER** QUIT...
UNDERSTAND?
I UNDERSTAND.

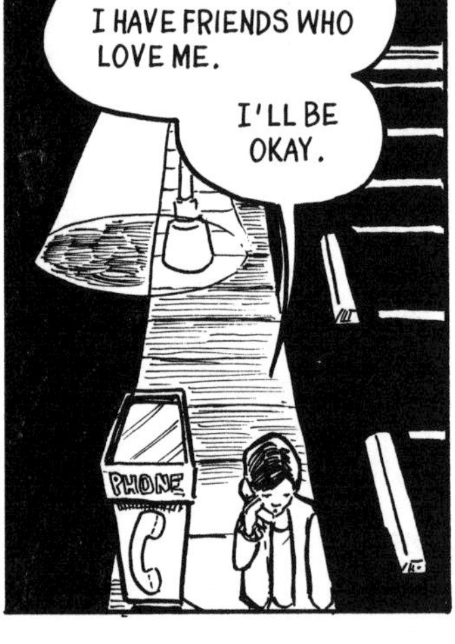
I HAVE FRIENDS WHO LOVE ME.
I'LL BE OKAY.
PHONE

WE DID LOVE HIM BUT HE WASN'T OKAY.

HE HAD NIGHT SWEATS, WEIGHT LOSS, HE WAS SLEEPING MORE AND MORE.

HE THEN CAUGHT PCP. PNEUMOCYSTIS CARINII PNEUMONIA.

HE RECOVERED QUICKLY BUT NEITHER PAM NOR I GOT OVER IT.

WE NEVER VERBALIZED IT, BUT WE SAW HIM DIFFERENTLY.

WE SAW HIM AS SICK.

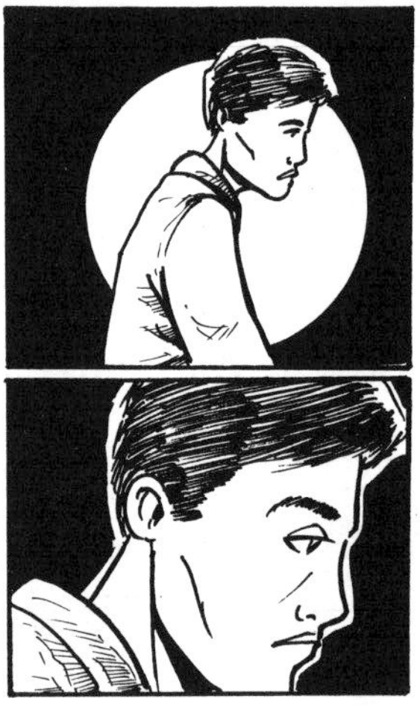

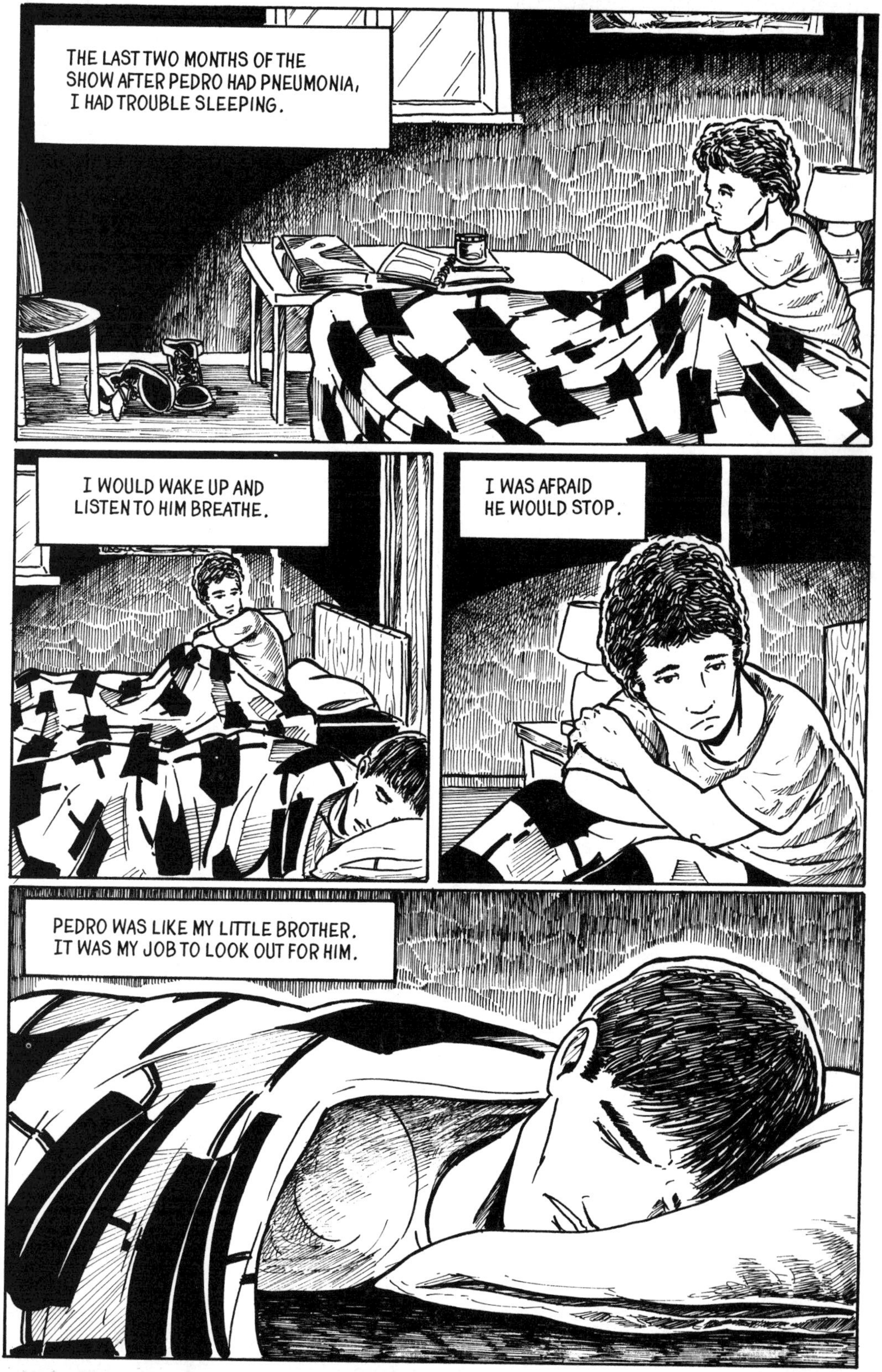
THE LAST TWO MONTHS OF THE SHOW AFTER PEDRO HAD PNEUMONIA, I HAD TROUBLE SLEEPING.
I WOULD WAKE UP AND LISTEN TO HIM BREATHE.
I WAS AFRAID HE WOULD STOP.
PEDRO WAS LIKE MY LITTLE BROTHER. IT WAS MY JOB TO LOOK OUT FOR HIM.

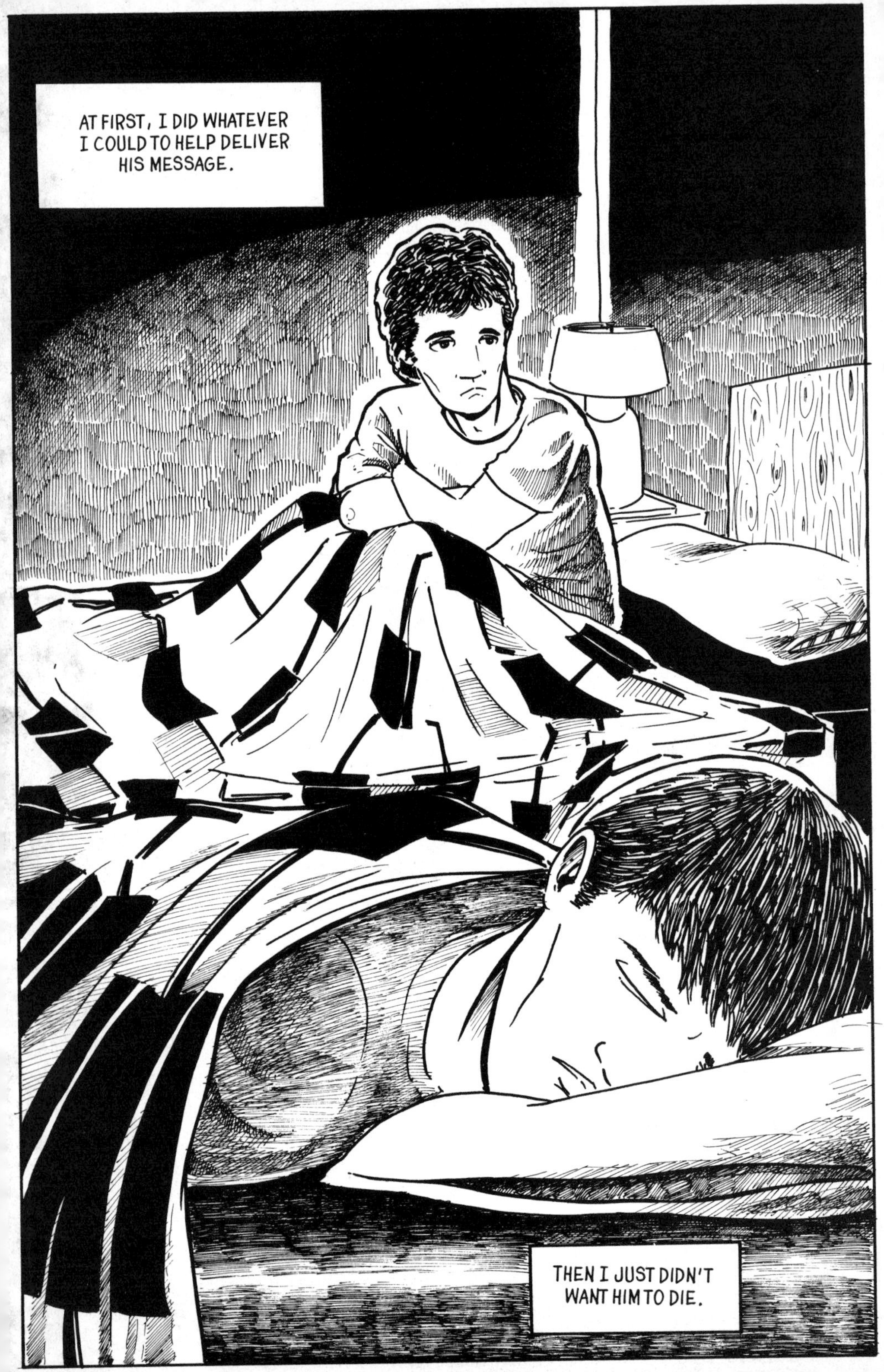
AT FIRST, I DID WHATEVER I COULD TO HELP DELIVER HIS MESSAGE.
THEN I JUST DIDN'T WANT HIM TO DIE.

CHAPTER FIVE

GOOD-BYES

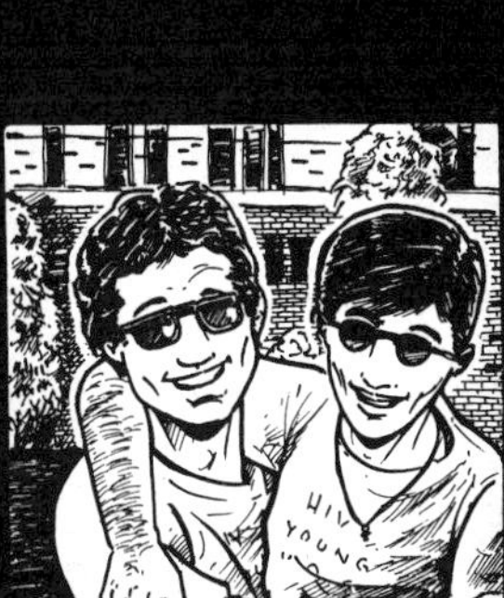
HIV
YOUNG

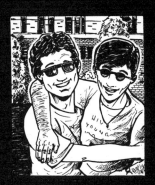

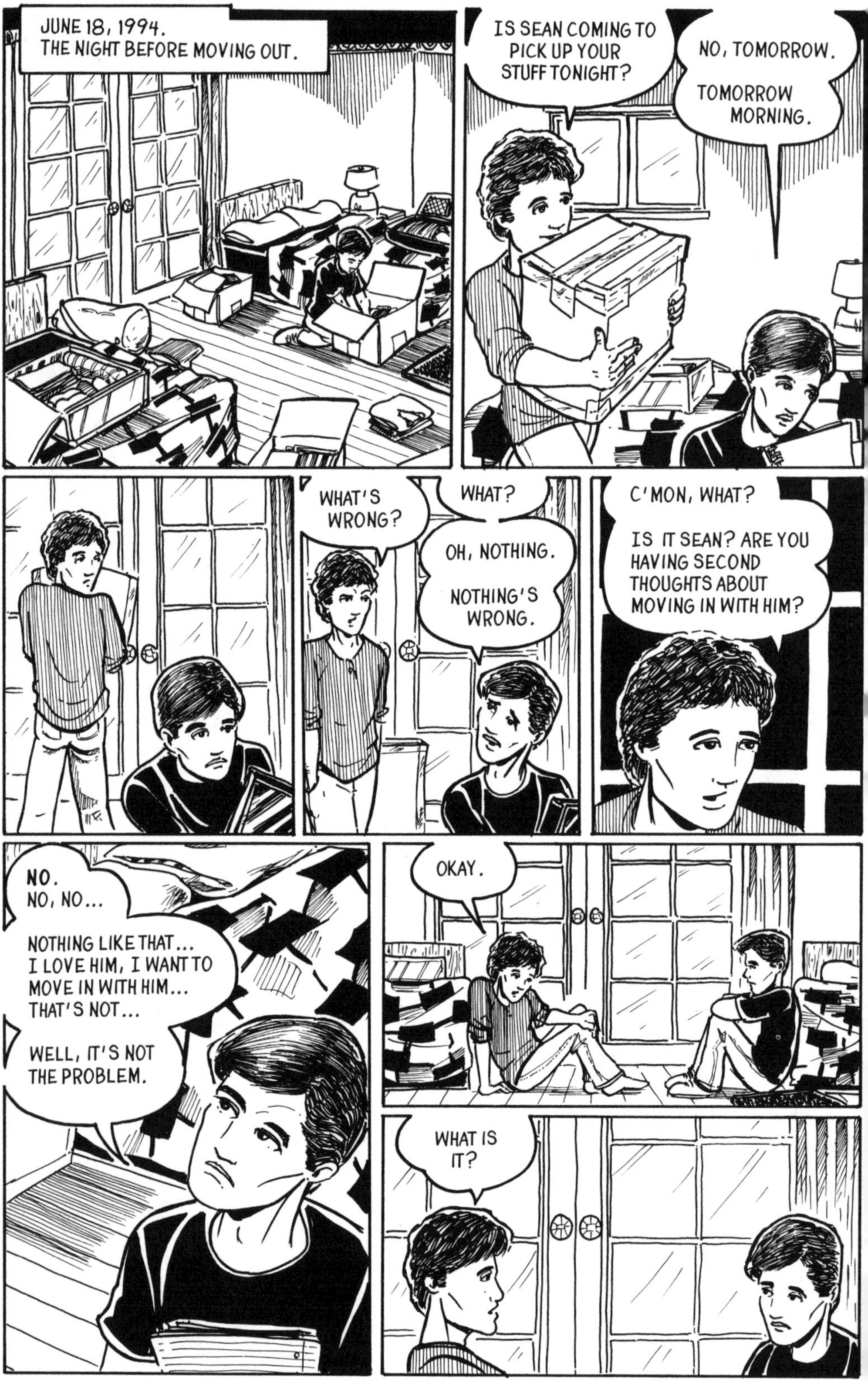
JUNE 18, 1994.
THE NIGHT BEFORE MOVING OUT.
IS SEAN COMING TO PICK UP YOUR STUFF TONIGHT?
NO, TOMORROW.
TOMORROW MORNING.
WHAT'S WRONG?
WHAT?
OH, NOTHING.
NOTHING'S WRONG.
C'MON, WHAT?
IS IT SEAN? ARE YOU HAVING SECOND THOUGHTS ABOUT MOVING IN WITH HIM?
NO.
NO, NO...
NOTHING LIKE THAT... I LOVE HIM, I WANT TO MOVE IN WITH HIM... THAT'S NOT...
WELL, IT'S NOT THE PROBLEM.
OKAY.
WHAT IS IT?

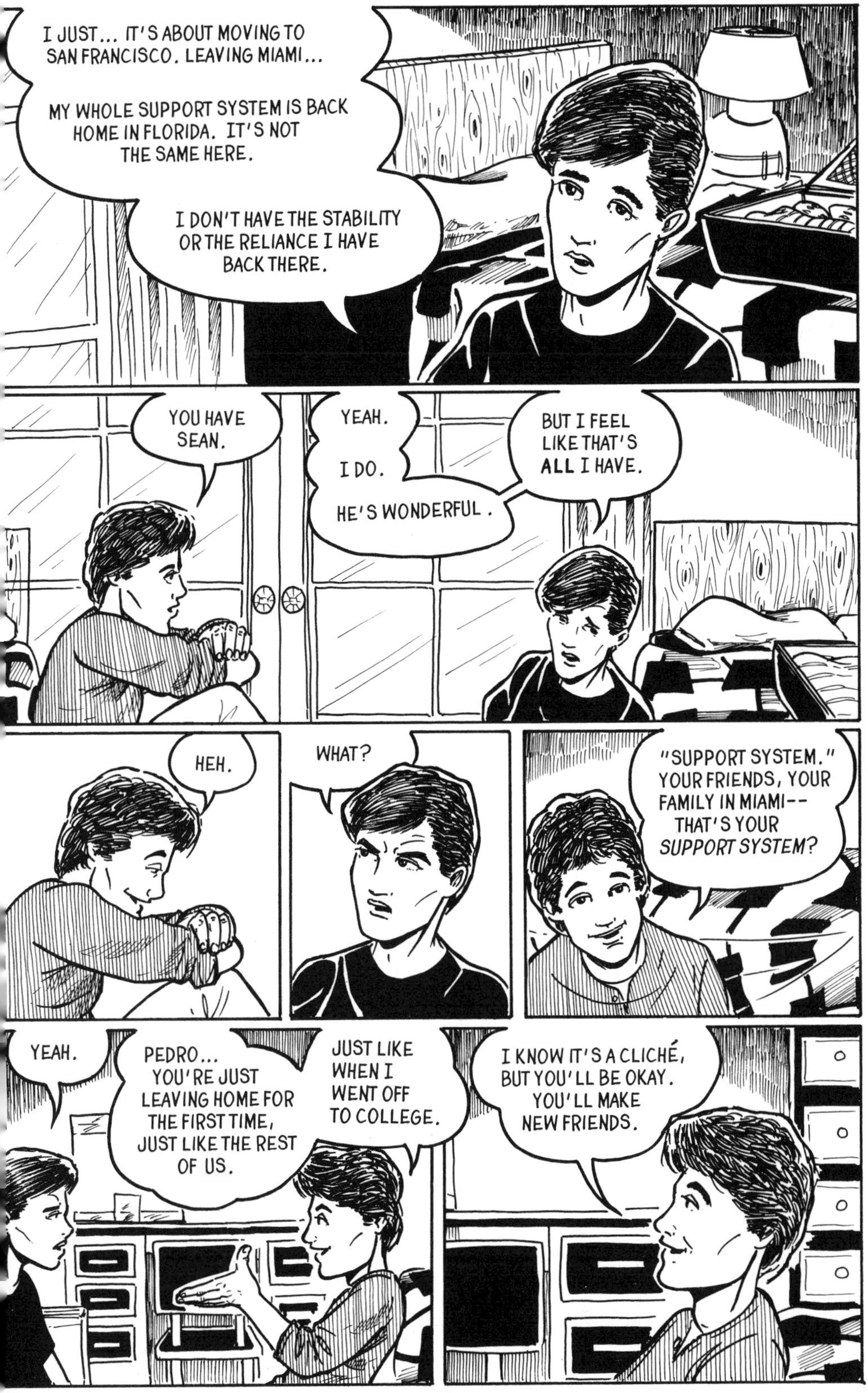
I JUST... IT'S ABOUT MOVING TO SAN FRANCISCO. LEAVING MIAMI...
MY WHOLE SUPPORT SYSTEM IS BACK HOME IN FLORIDA. IT'S NOT THE SAME HERE.
I DON'T HAVE THE STABILITY OR THE RELIANCE I HAVE BACK THERE.
YOU HAVE SEAN.
YEAH.
I DO.
HE'S WONDERFUL.
BUT I FEEL LIKE THAT'S **ALL** I HAVE.
HEH.
WHAT?
"SUPPORT SYSTEM." YOUR FRIENDS, YOUR FAMILY IN MIAMI-- THAT'S YOUR *SUPPORT SYSTEM*?
YEAH.
PEDRO... YOU'RE JUST LEAVING HOME FOR THE FIRST TIME, JUST LIKE THE REST OF US.
JUST LIKE WHEN I WENT OFF TO COLLEGE.
I KNOW IT'S A CLICHÉ, BUT YOU'LL BE OKAY. YOU'LL MAKE NEW FRIENDS.

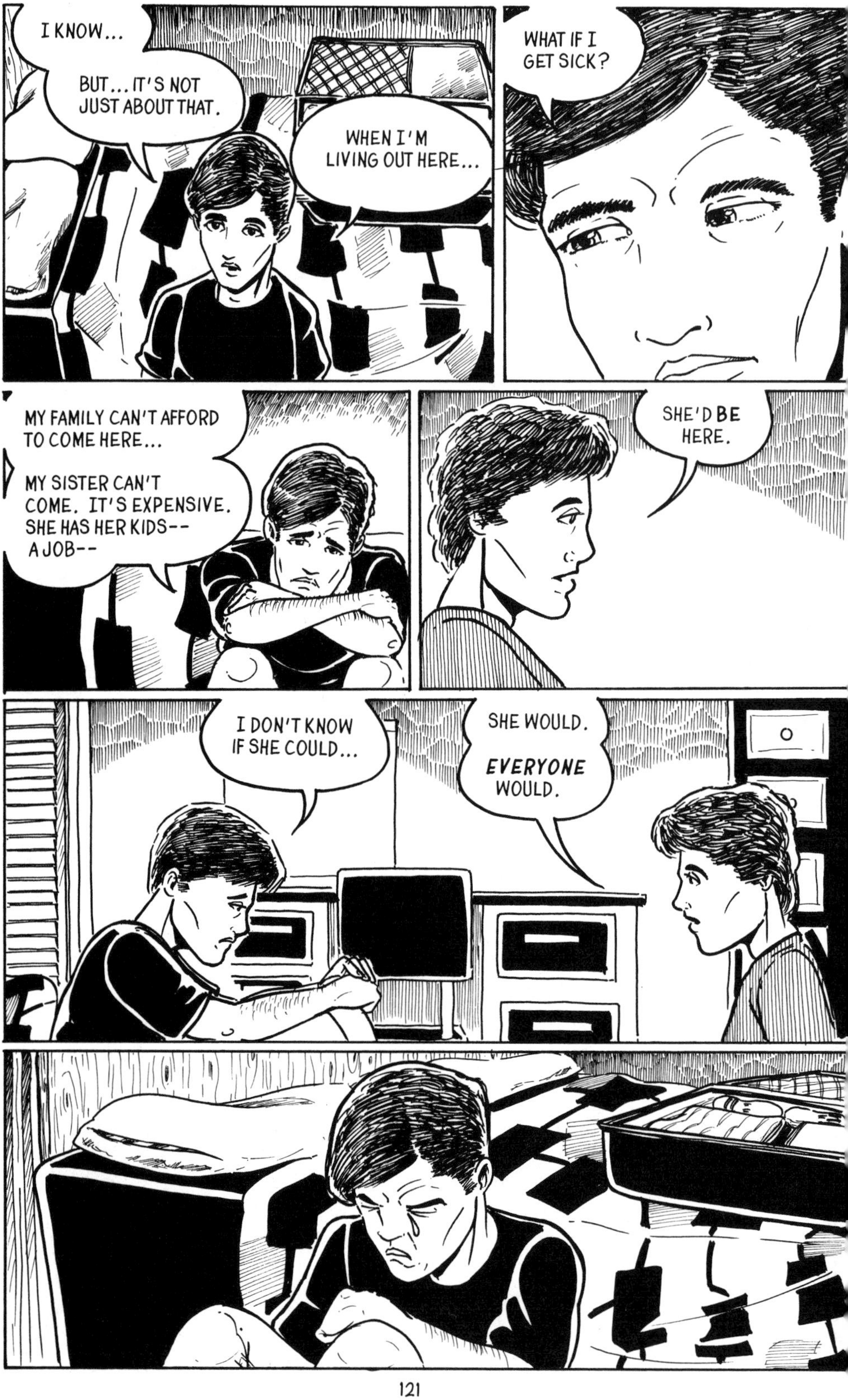
I KNOW...
BUT... IT'S NOT JUST ABOUT THAT.
WHEN I'M LIVING OUT HERE...
WHAT IF I GET SICK?
MY FAMILY CAN'T AFFORD TO COME HERE...
MY SISTER CAN'T COME. IT'S EXPENSIVE. SHE HAS HER KIDS-- A JOB--
SHE'D **BE** HERE.
I DON'T KNOW IF SHE COULD...
SHE WOULD.
EVERYONE WOULD.

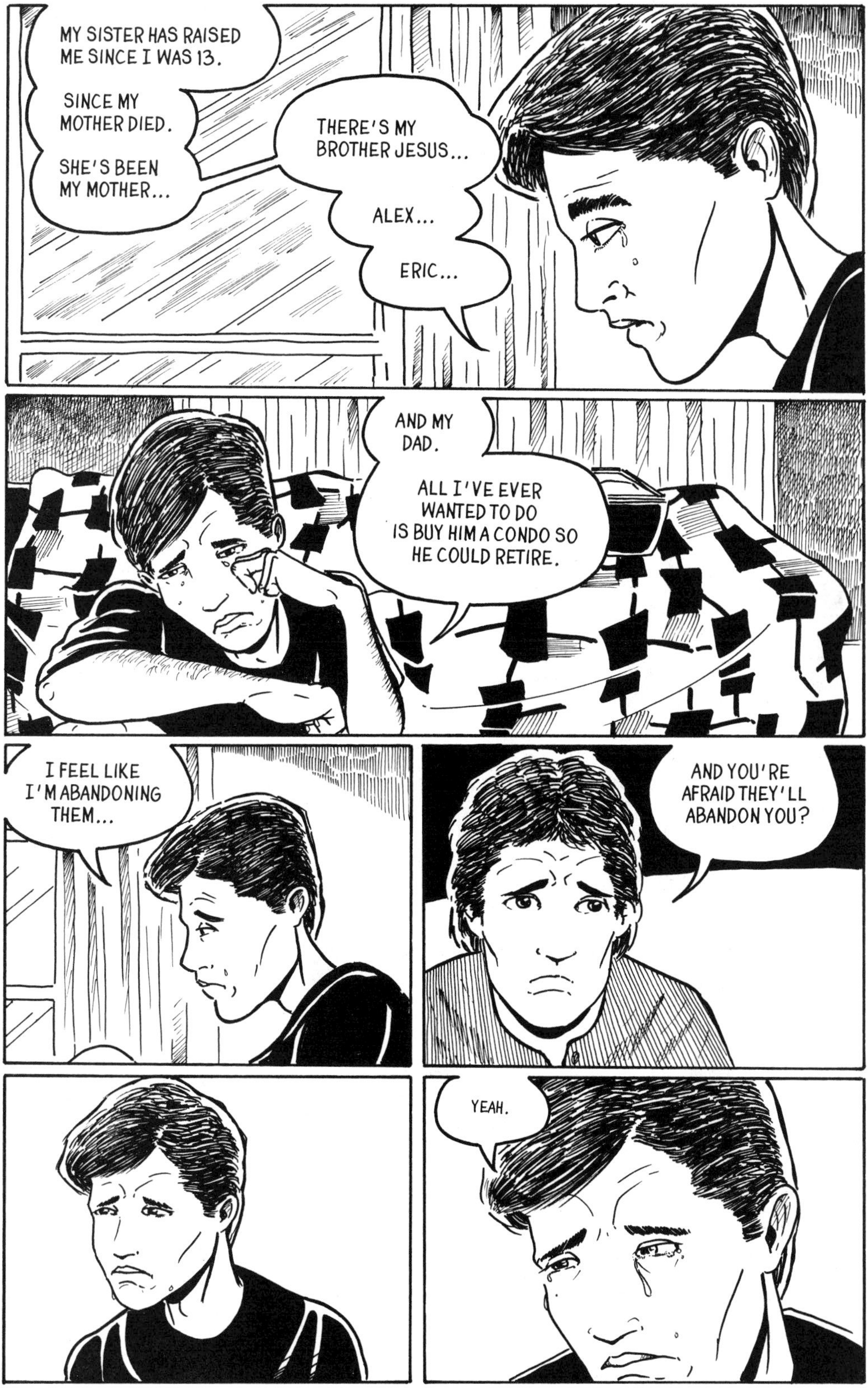
MY SISTER HAS RAISED ME SINCE I WAS 13.
SINCE MY MOTHER DIED.
SHE'S BEEN MY MOTHER...
THERE'S MY BROTHER JESUS...
ALEX...
ERIC...
AND MY DAD.
ALL I'VE EVER WANTED TO DO IS BUY HIM A CONDO SO HE COULD RETIRE.
I FEEL LIKE I'M ABANDONING THEM...
AND YOU'RE AFRAID THEY'LL ABANDON YOU?
YEAH.

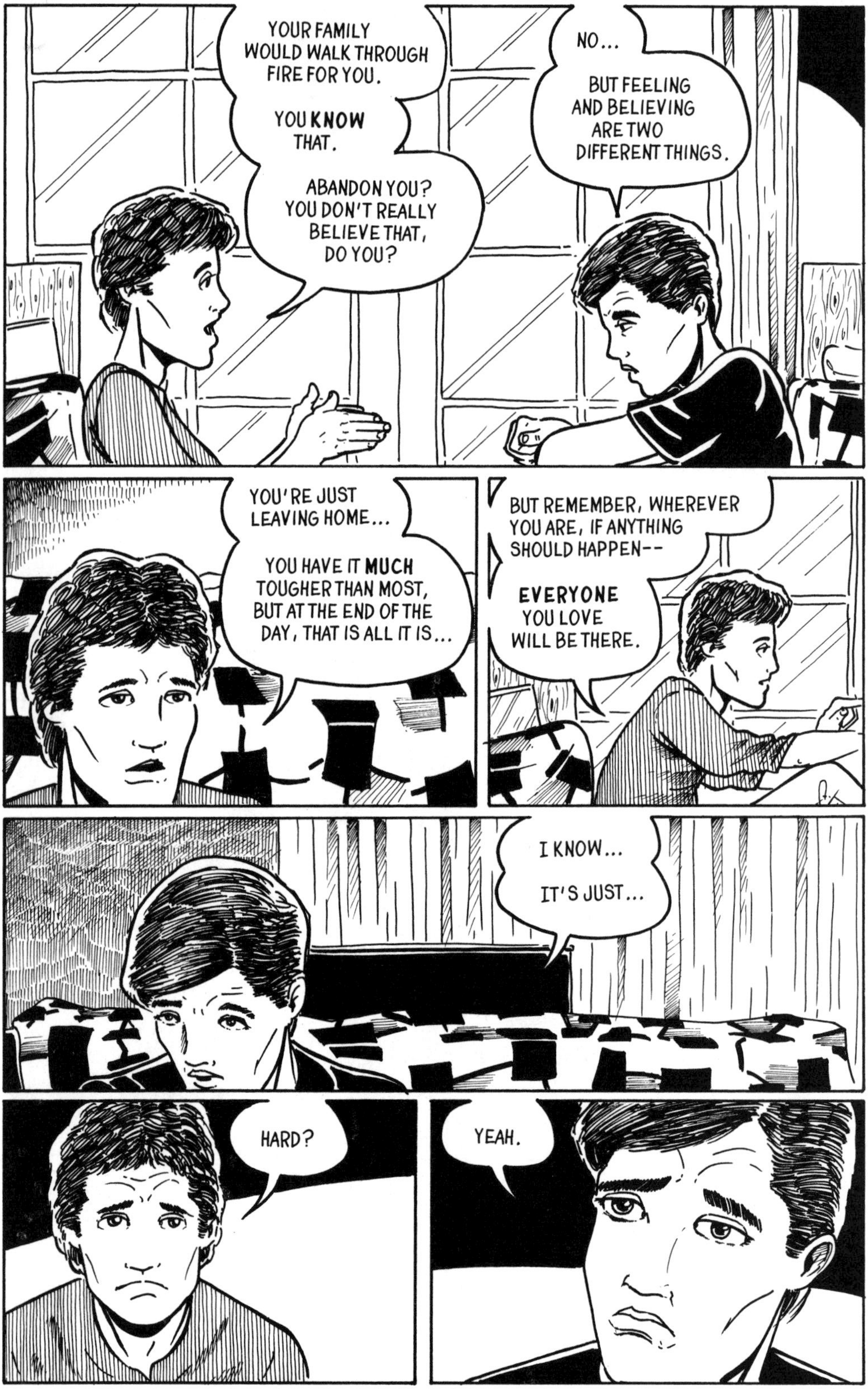
YOUR FAMILY WOULD WALK THROUGH FIRE FOR YOU.
YOU **KNOW** THAT.
ABANDON YOU? YOU DON'T REALLY BELIEVE THAT, DO YOU?
NO...
BUT FEELING AND BELIEVING ARE TWO DIFFERENT THINGS.
YOU'RE JUST LEAVING HOME...
YOU HAVE IT **MUCH** TOUGHER THAN MOST, BUT AT THE END OF THE DAY, THAT IS ALL IT IS...
BUT REMEMBER, WHEREVER YOU ARE, IF ANYTHING SHOULD HAPPEN--
EVERYONE YOU LOVE WILL BE THERE.
I KNOW...
IT'S JUST...
HARD?
YEAH.

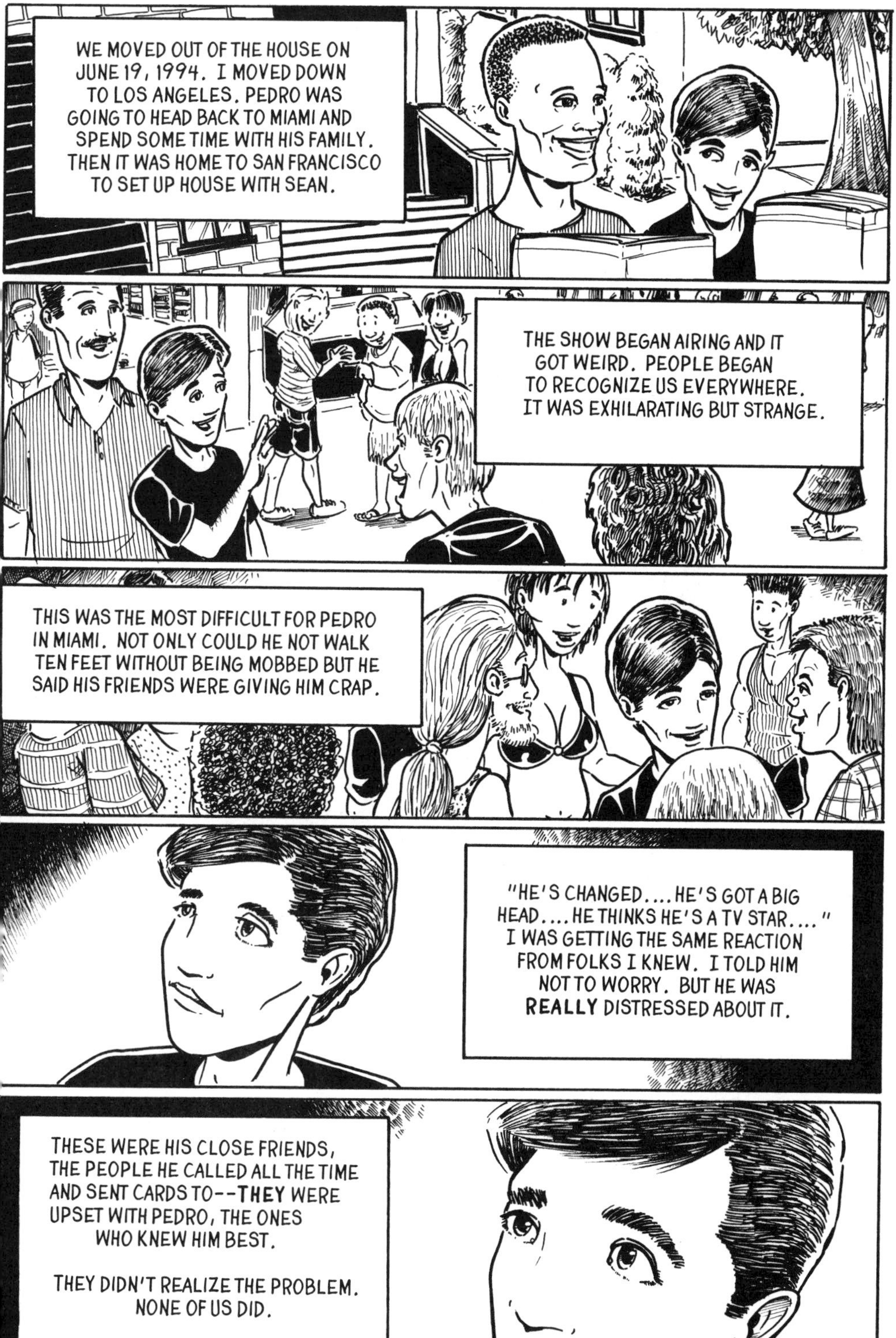
WE MOVED OUT OF THE HOUSE ON JUNE 19, 1994. I MOVED DOWN TO LOS ANGELES. PEDRO WAS GOING TO HEAD BACK TO MIAMI AND SPEND SOME TIME WITH HIS FAMILY. THEN IT WAS HOME TO SAN FRANCISCO TO SET UP HOUSE WITH SEAN.
THE SHOW BEGAN AIRING AND IT GOT WEIRD. PEOPLE BEGAN TO RECOGNIZE US EVERYWHERE. IT WAS EXHILARATING BUT STRANGE.
THIS WAS THE MOST DIFFICULT FOR PEDRO IN MIAMI. NOT ONLY COULD HE NOT WALK TEN FEET WITHOUT BEING MOBBED BUT HE SAID HIS FRIENDS WERE GIVING HIM CRAP.
"HE'S CHANGED.... HE'S GOT A BIG HEAD.... HE THINKS HE'S A TV STAR...." I WAS GETTING THE SAME REACTION FROM FOLKS I KNEW. I TOLD HIM NOT TO WORRY. BUT HE WAS **REALLY** DISTRESSED ABOUT IT.
THESE WERE HIS CLOSE FRIENDS, THE PEOPLE HE CALLED ALL THE TIME AND SENT CARDS TO--**THEY** WERE UPSET WITH PEDRO, THE ONES WHO KNEW HIM BEST.
THEY DIDN'T REALIZE THE PROBLEM. NONE OF US DID.
PEDRO'S MIND WAS CLOUDED.

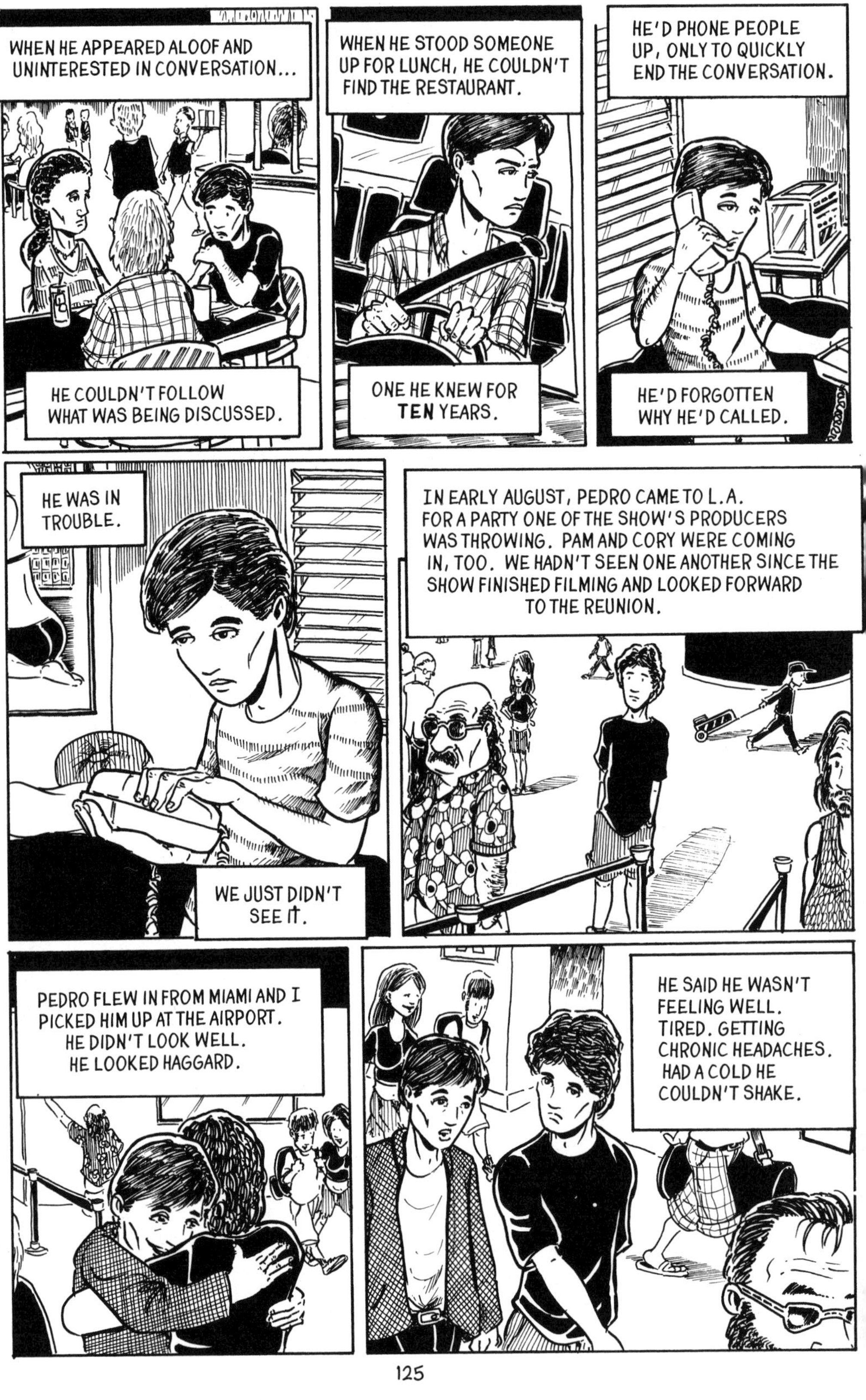
WHEN HE APPEARED ALOOF AND UNINTERESTED IN CONVERSATION...
HE COULDN'T FOLLOW WHAT WAS BEING DISCUSSED.
WHEN HE STOOD SOMEONE UP FOR LUNCH, HE COULDN'T FIND THE RESTAURANT.
ONE HE KNEW FOR **TEN** YEARS.
HE'D PHONE PEOPLE UP, ONLY TO QUICKLY END THE CONVERSATION.
HE'D FORGOTTEN WHY HE'D CALLED.
HE WAS IN TROUBLE.
WE JUST DIDN'T SEE IT.
IN EARLY AUGUST, PEDRO CAME TO L.A. FOR A PARTY ONE OF THE SHOW'S PRODUCERS WAS THROWING. PAM AND CORY WERE COMING IN, TOO. WE HADN'T SEEN ONE ANOTHER SINCE THE SHOW FINISHED FILMING AND LOOKED FORWARD TO THE REUNION.
PEDRO FLEW IN FROM MIAMI AND I PICKED HIM UP AT THE AIRPORT. HE DIDN'T LOOK WELL. HE LOOKED HAGGARD.
HE SAID HE WASN'T FEELING WELL. TIRED. GETTING CHRONIC HEADACHES. HAD A COLD HE COULDN'T SHAKE.

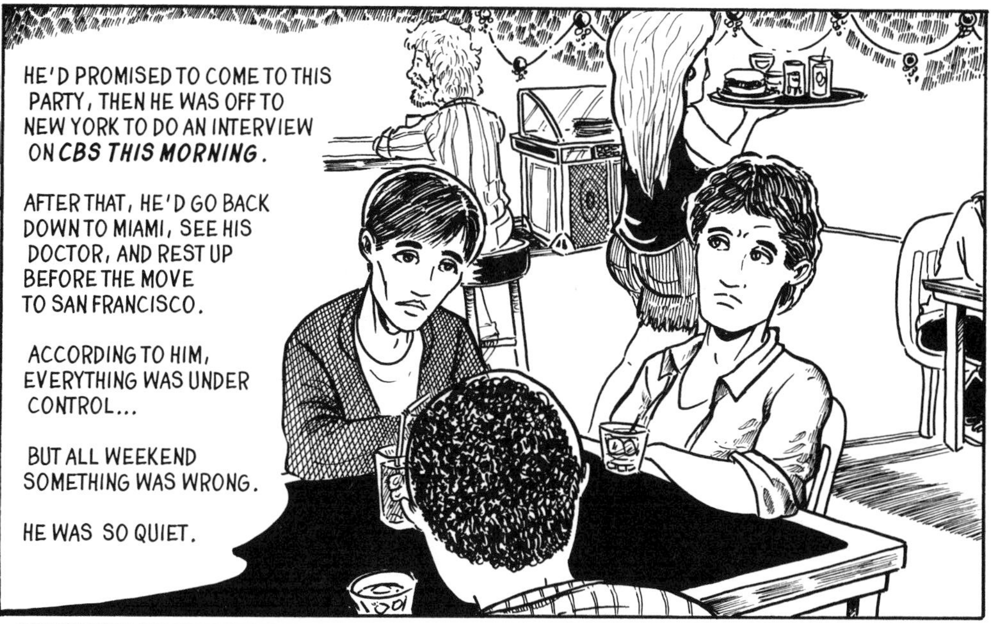
HE'D PROMISED TO COME TO THIS PARTY, THEN HE WAS OFF TO NEW YORK TO DO AN INTERVIEW ON ***CBS THIS MORNING***.
AFTER THAT, HE'D GO BACK DOWN TO MIAMI, SEE HIS DOCTOR, AND REST UP BEFORE THE MOVE TO SAN FRANCISCO.
ACCORDING TO HIM, EVERYTHING WAS UNDER CONTROL...
BUT ALL WEEKEND SOMETHING WAS WRONG.
HE WAS SO QUIET.

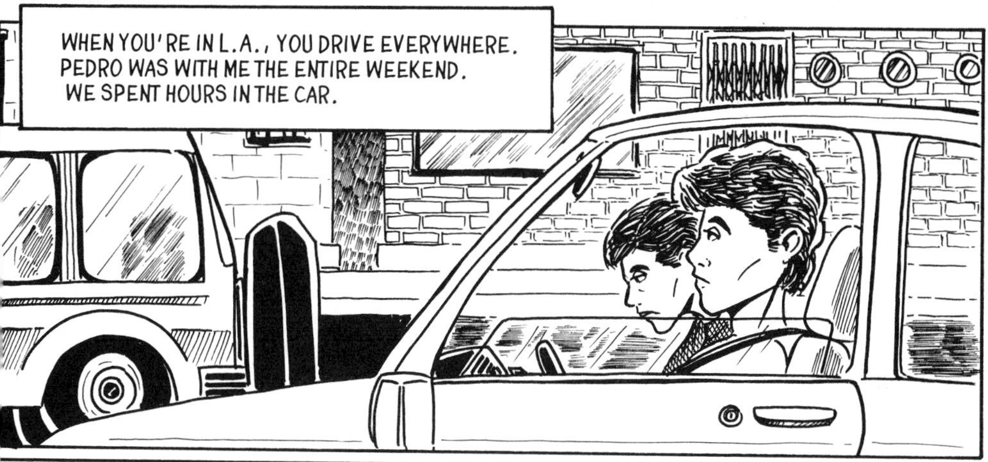
WHEN YOU'RE IN L.A., YOU DRIVE EVERYWHERE. PEDRO WAS WITH ME THE ENTIRE WEEKEND. WE SPENT HOURS IN THE CAR.

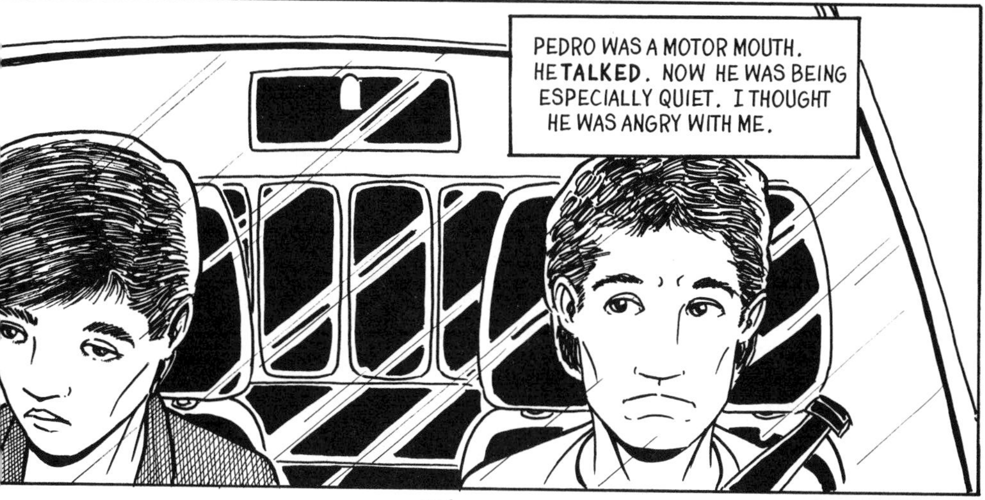
PEDRO WAS A MOTOR MOUTH. HE **TALKED**. NOW HE WAS BEING ESPECIALLY QUIET. I THOUGHT HE WAS ANGRY WITH ME.

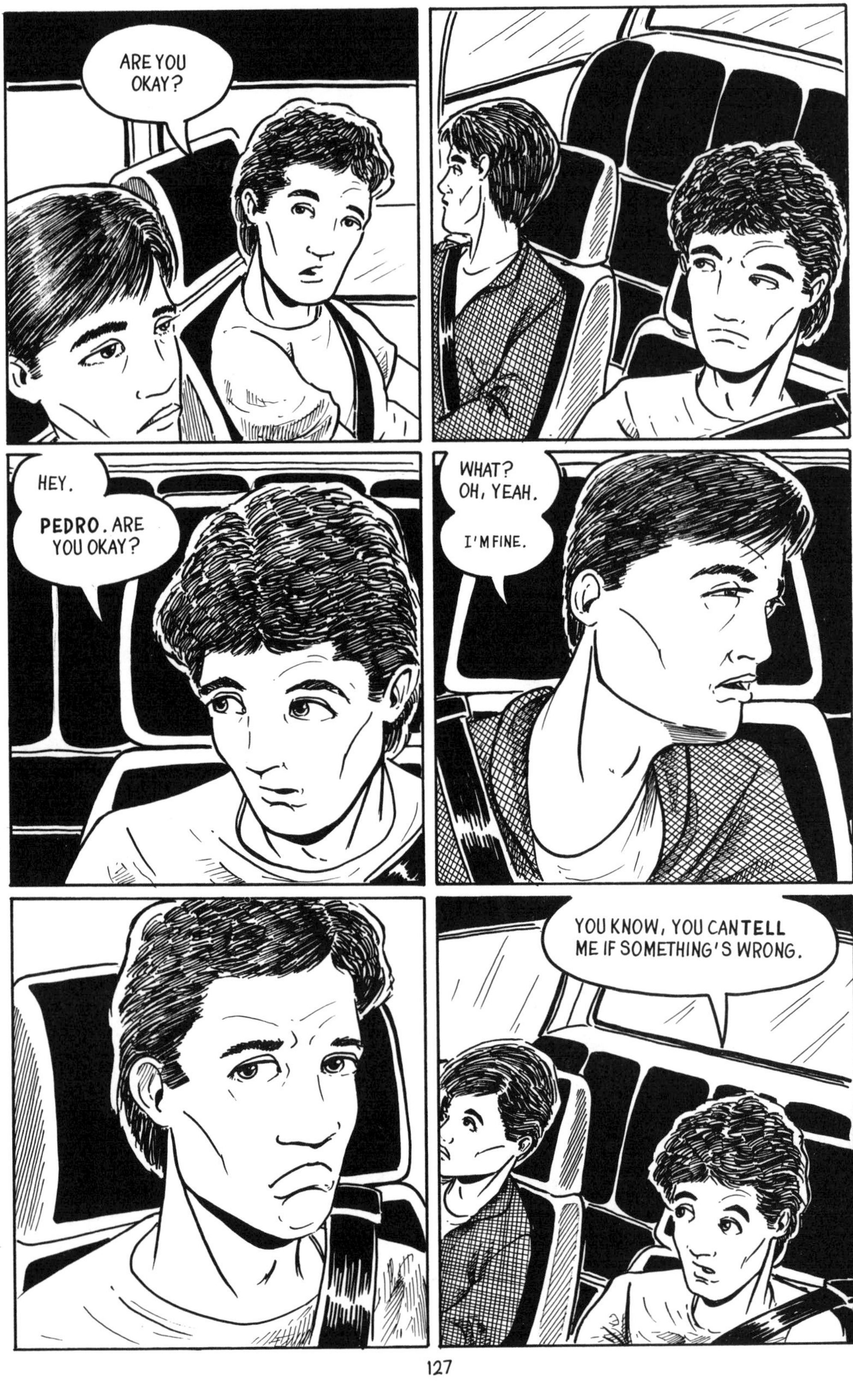
ARE YOU OKAY?
HEY.
PEDRO. ARE YOU OKAY?
WHAT? OH, YEAH.
I'M FINE.
YOU KNOW, YOU CAN TELL ME IF SOMETHING'S WRONG.

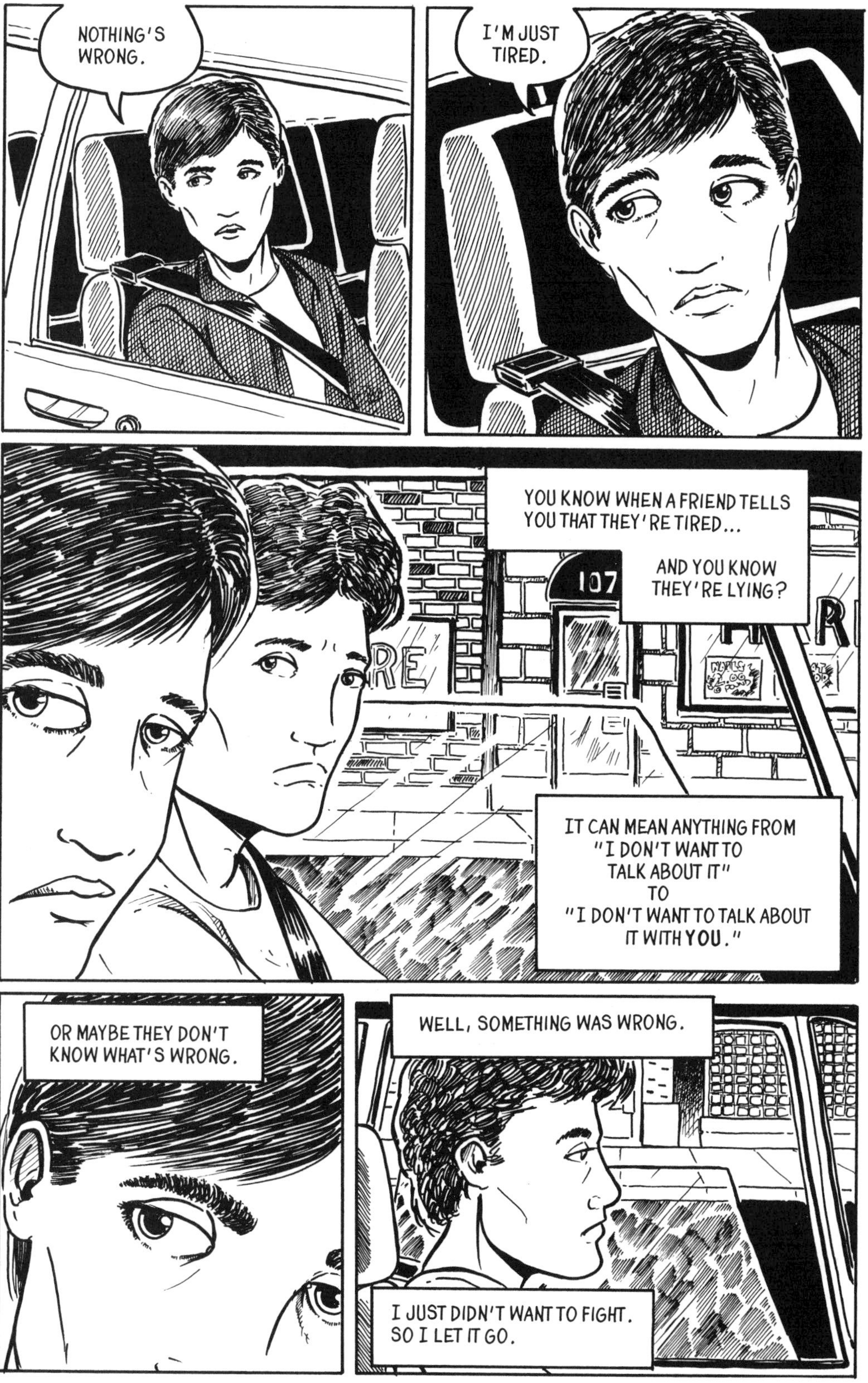
NOTHING'S WRONG.
I'M JUST TIRED.
YOU KNOW WHEN A FRIEND TELLS YOU THAT THEY'RE TIRED...
AND YOU KNOW THEY'RE LYING?
107
IT CAN MEAN ANYTHING FROM "I DON'T WANT TO TALK ABOUT IT" TO "I DON'T WANT TO TALK ABOUT IT WITH **YOU**."
OR MAYBE THEY DON'T KNOW WHAT'S WRONG.
WELL, SOMETHING WAS WRONG.
I JUST DIDN'T WANT TO FIGHT. SO I LET IT GO.

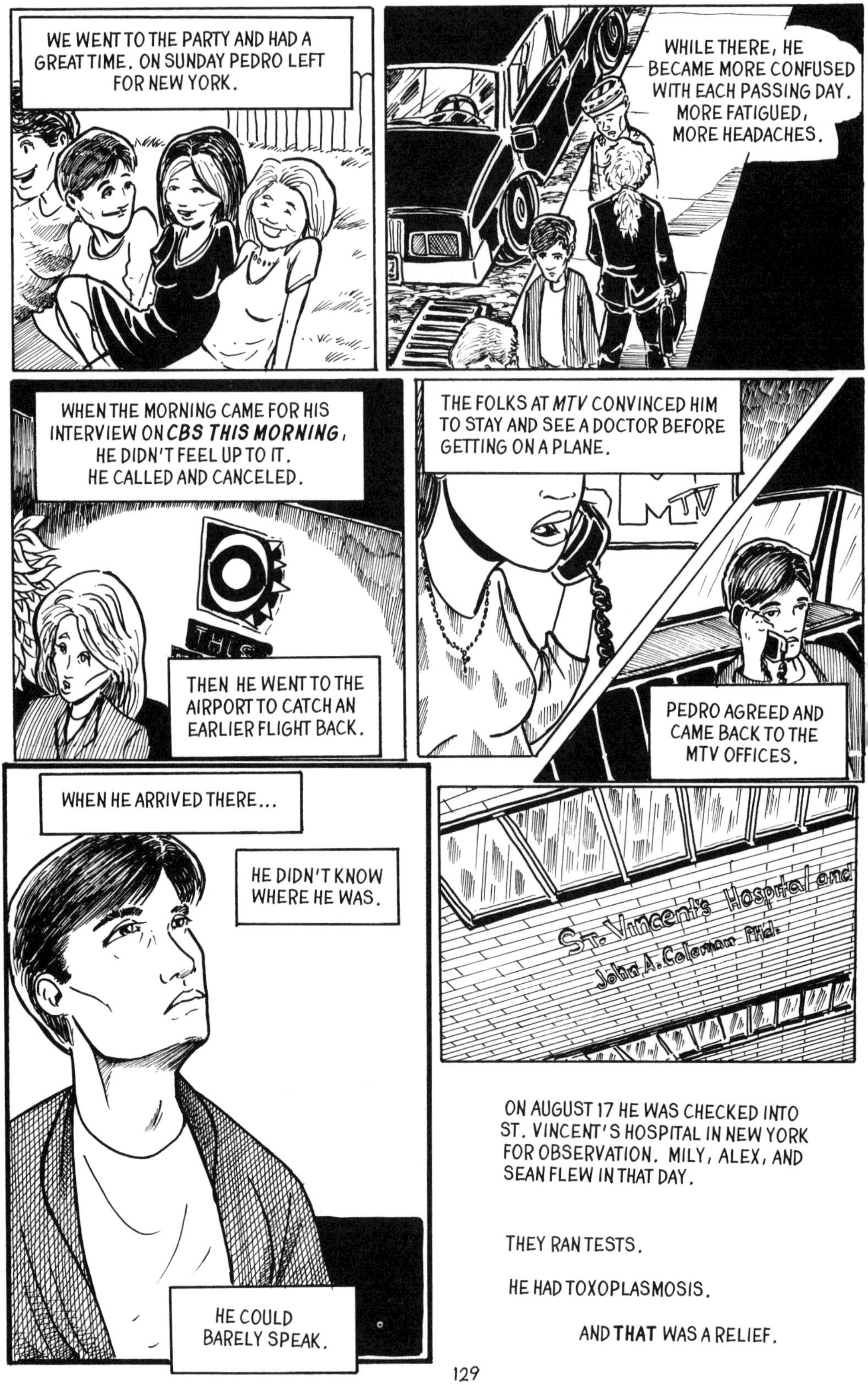
WE WENT TO THE PARTY AND HAD A GREAT TIME. ON SUNDAY PEDRO LEFT FOR NEW YORK.
WHILE THERE, HE BECAME MORE CONFUSED WITH EACH PASSING DAY. MORE FATIGUED, MORE HEADACHES.
WHEN THE MORNING CAME FOR HIS INTERVIEW ON CBS THIS MORNING, HE DIDN'T FEEL UP TO IT. HE CALLED AND CANCELED.
THEN HE WENT TO THE AIRPORT TO CATCH AN EARLIER FLIGHT BACK.
THE FOLKS AT MTV CONVINCED HIM TO STAY AND SEE A DOCTOR BEFORE GETTING ON A PLANE.
MTV
PEDRO AGREED AND CAME BACK TO THE MTV OFFICES.
WHEN HE ARRIVED THERE...
HE DIDN'T KNOW WHERE HE WAS.
HE COULD BARELY SPEAK.
St. Vincent's Hospital and
John A. Coleman PHd.

ON AUGUST 17 HE WAS CHECKED INTO ST. VINCENT'S HOSPITAL IN NEW YORK FOR OBSERVATION. MILY, ALEX, AND SEAN FLEW IN THAT DAY.

THEY RAN TESTS.

HE HAD TOXOPLASMOSIS.

AND **THAT** WAS A RELIEF.

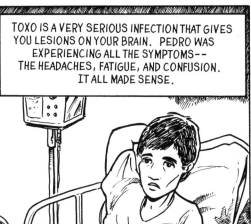

TOXO IS A VERY SERIOUS INFECTION THAT GIVES YOU LESIONS ON YOUR BRAIN. PEDRO WAS EXPERIENCING ALL THE SYMPTOMS-- THE HEADACHES, FATIGUE, AND CONFUSION. IT ALL MADE SENSE.

IT'S TREATABLE WITH MEDICATION SO IT'S SOMETHING PEDRO COULD BEAT.

HE'D BE BACK AT A HUNDRED PERCENT IN A MONTH OR SO.

IT WAS A RELIEF.

IMMEDIATELY PUT ON MEDICATION, HE IMPROVED.

BUT IN A WEEK HE BEGAN TO SLIP AGAIN.

HIS DOCTORS FELT PEDRO SHOULD BE MAKING BETTER PROGRESS. THEY RAN MORE TESTS AND ANOTHER MRI.

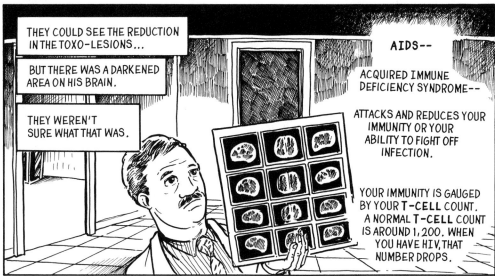

THEY COULD SEE THE REDUCTION IN THE TOXO-LESIONS...

BUT THERE WAS A DARKENED AREA ON HIS BRAIN.

THEY WEREN'T SURE WHAT THAT WAS.

AIDS--

ACQUIRED IMMUNE DEFICIENCY SYNDROME--

ATTACKS AND REDUCES YOUR IMMUNITY OR YOUR ABILITY TO FIGHT OFF INFECTION.

YOUR IMMUNITY IS GAUGED BY YOUR T-CELL COUNT. A NORMAL T-CELL COUNT IS AROUND 1,200. WHEN YOU HAVE HIV, THAT NUMBER DROPS.

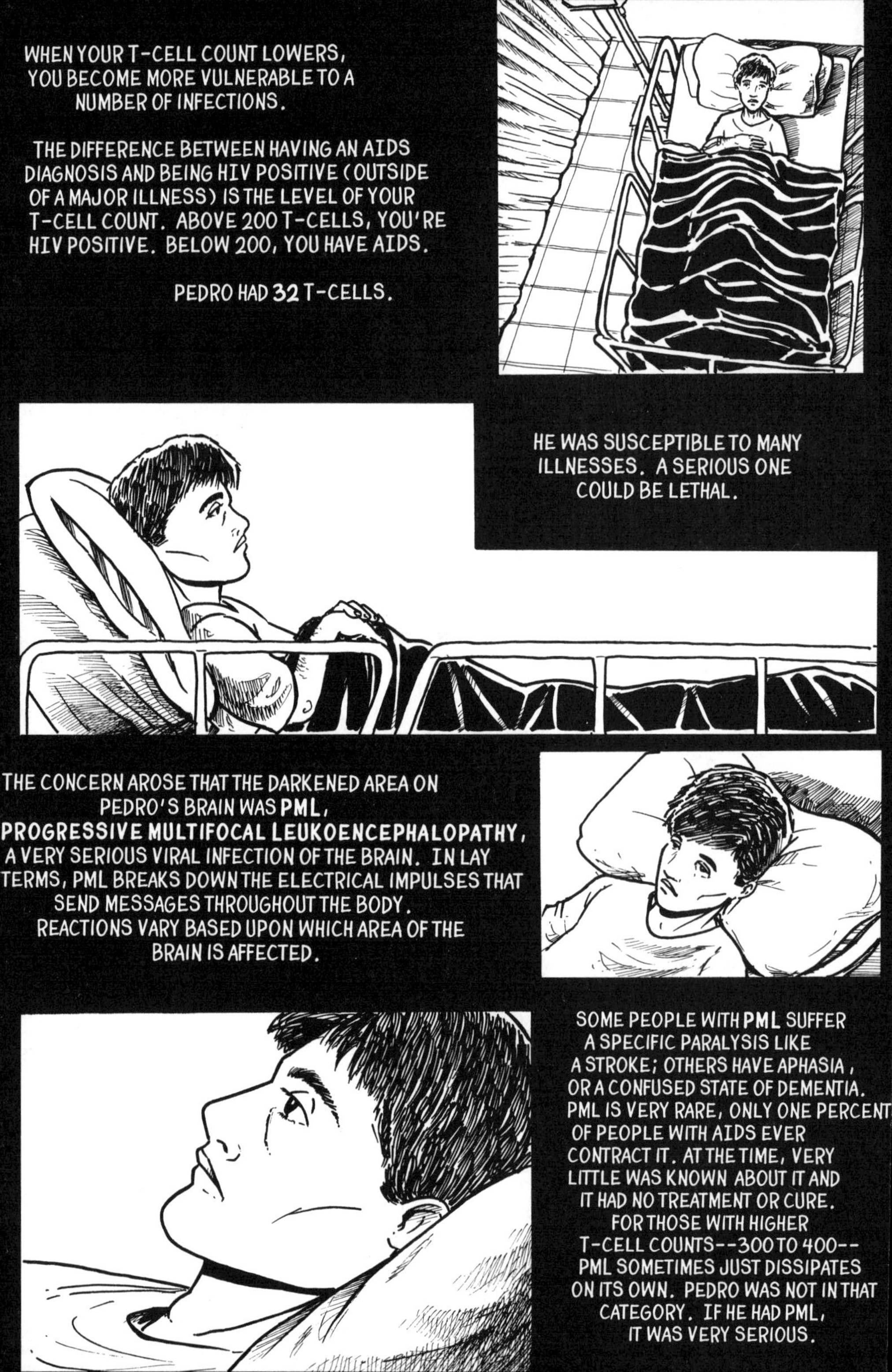
WHEN YOUR T-CELL COUNT LOWERS, YOU BECOME MORE VULNERABLE TO A NUMBER OF INFECTIONS.
THE DIFFERENCE BETWEEN HAVING AN AIDS DIAGNOSIS AND BEING HIV POSITIVE (OUTSIDE OF A MAJOR ILLNESS) IS THE LEVEL OF YOUR T-CELL COUNT. ABOVE 200 T-CELLS, YOU'RE HIV POSITIVE. BELOW 200, YOU HAVE AIDS.
PEDRO HAD **32** T-CELLS.
HE WAS SUSCEPTIBLE TO MANY ILLNESSES. A SERIOUS ONE COULD BE LETHAL.
THE CONCERN AROSE THAT THE DARKENED AREA ON PEDRO'S BRAIN WAS **PML**, **PROGRESSIVE MULTIFOCAL LEUKOENCEPHALOPATHY**, A VERY SERIOUS VIRAL INFECTION OF THE BRAIN. IN LAY TERMS, PML BREAKS DOWN THE ELECTRICAL IMPULSES THAT SEND MESSAGES THROUGHOUT THE BODY. REACTIONS VARY BASED UPON WHICH AREA OF THE BRAIN IS AFFECTED.
SOME PEOPLE WITH **PML** SUFFER A SPECIFIC PARALYSIS LIKE A STROKE; OTHERS HAVE APHASIA, OR A CONFUSED STATE OF DEMENTIA. PML IS VERY RARE, ONLY ONE PERCENT OF PEOPLE WITH AIDS EVER CONTRACT IT. AT THE TIME, VERY LITTLE WAS KNOWN ABOUT IT AND IT HAD NO TREATMENT OR CURE. FOR THOSE WITH HIGHER T-CELL COUNTS--300 TO 400--PML SOMETIMES JUST DISSIPATES ON ITS OWN. PEDRO WAS NOT IN THAT CATEGORY. IF HE HAD PML, IT WAS VERY SERIOUS.

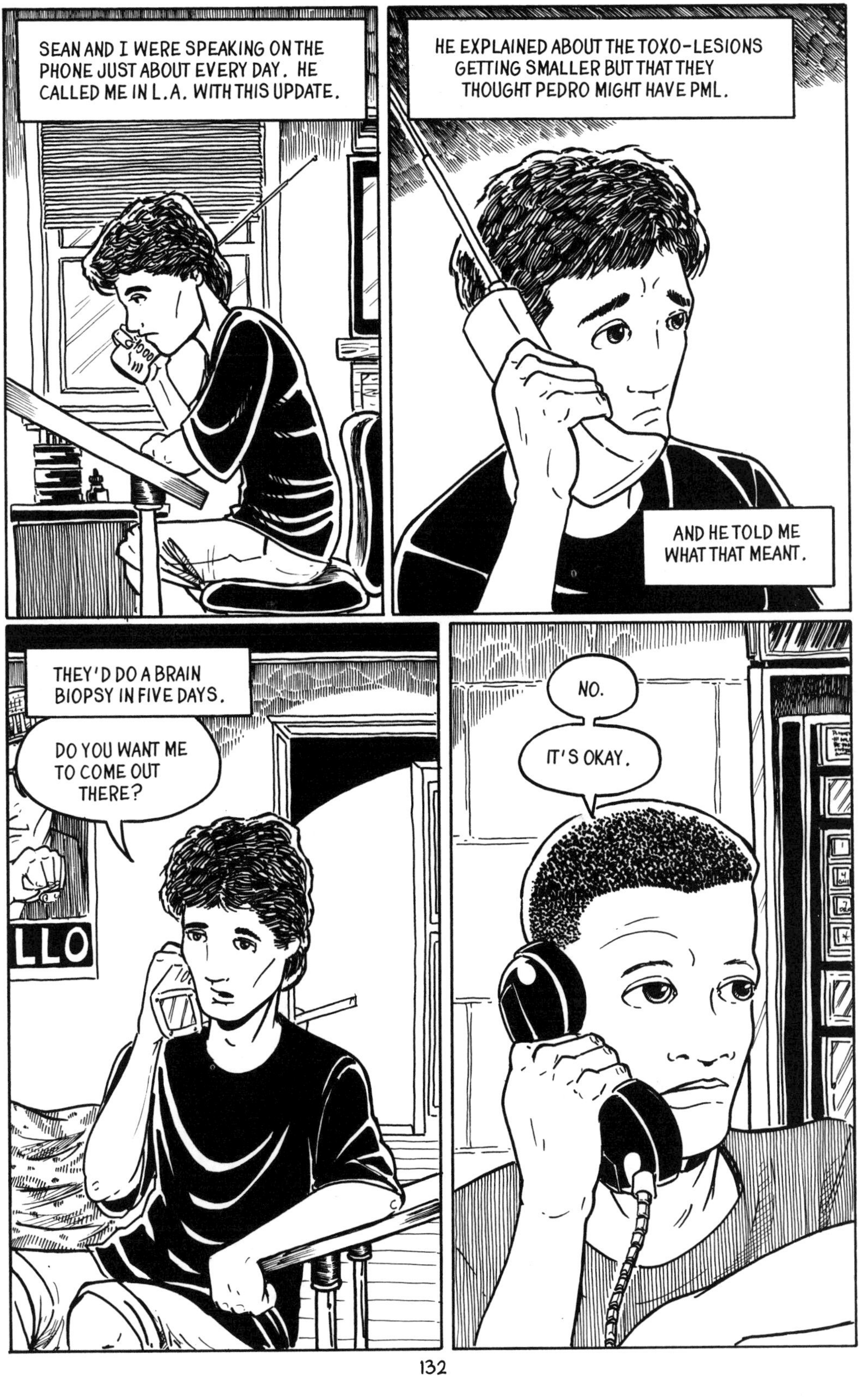
SEAN AND I WERE SPEAKING ON THE PHONE JUST ABOUT EVERY DAY. HE CALLED ME IN L.A. WITH THIS UPDATE.
HE EXPLAINED ABOUT THE TOXO-LESIONS GETTING SMALLER BUT THAT THEY THOUGHT PEDRO MIGHT HAVE PML.
AND HE TOLD ME WHAT THAT MEANT.
THEY'D DO A BRAIN BIOPSY IN FIVE DAYS.
DO YOU WANT ME TO COME OUT THERE?
NO.
IT'S OKAY.
LLO

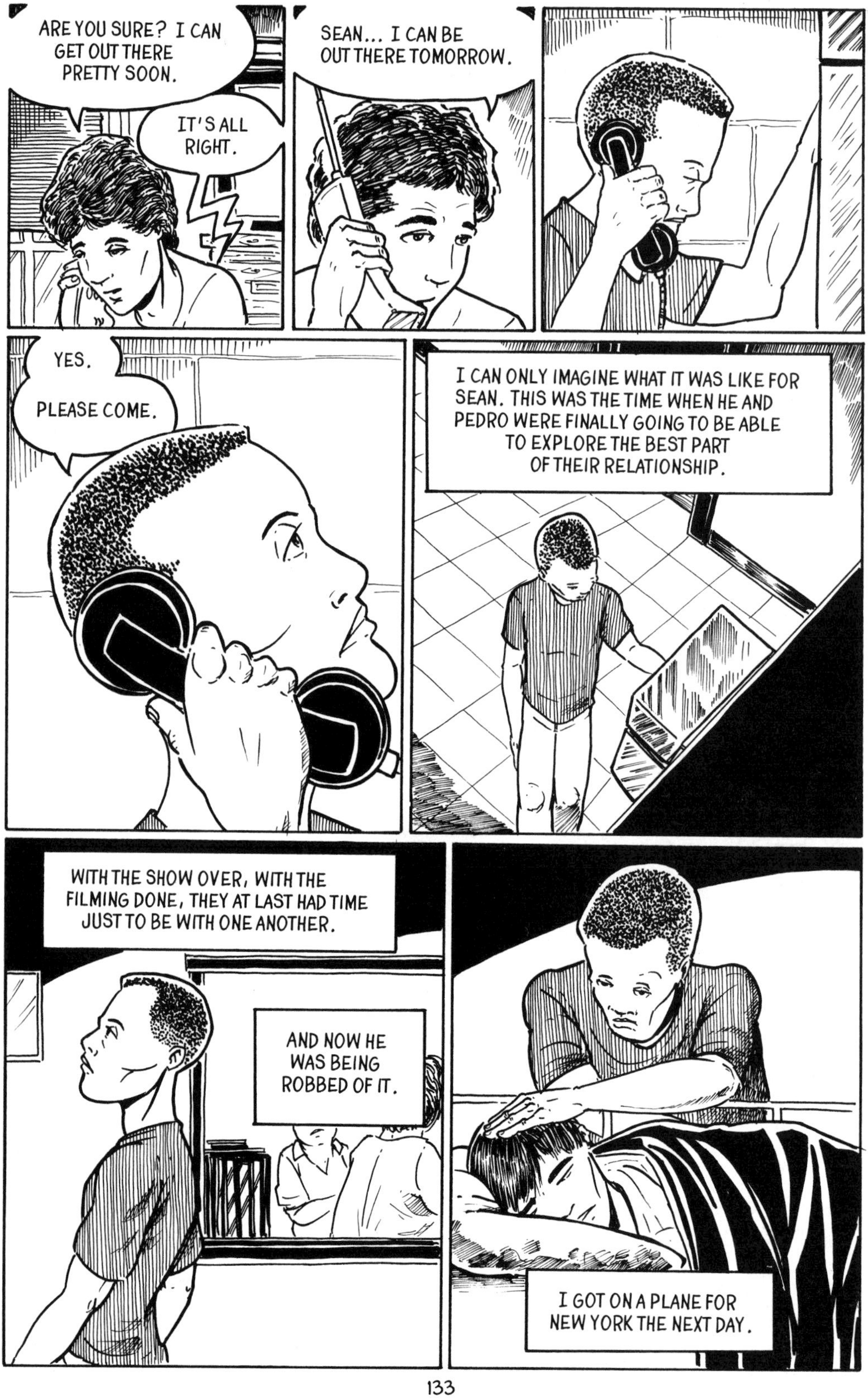
ARE YOU SURE? I CAN GET OUT THERE PRETTY SOON.
IT'S ALL RIGHT.
SEAN... I CAN BE OUT THERE TOMORROW.
YES.
PLEASE COME.
I CAN ONLY IMAGINE WHAT IT WAS LIKE FOR SEAN. THIS WAS THE TIME WHEN HE AND PEDRO WERE FINALLY GOING TO BE ABLE TO EXPLORE THE BEST PART OF THEIR RELATIONSHIP.
WITH THE SHOW OVER, WITH THE FILMING DONE, THEY AT LAST HAD TIME JUST TO BE WITH ONE ANOTHER.
AND NOW HE WAS BEING ROBBED OF IT.
I GOT ON A PLANE FOR NEW YORK THE NEXT DAY.

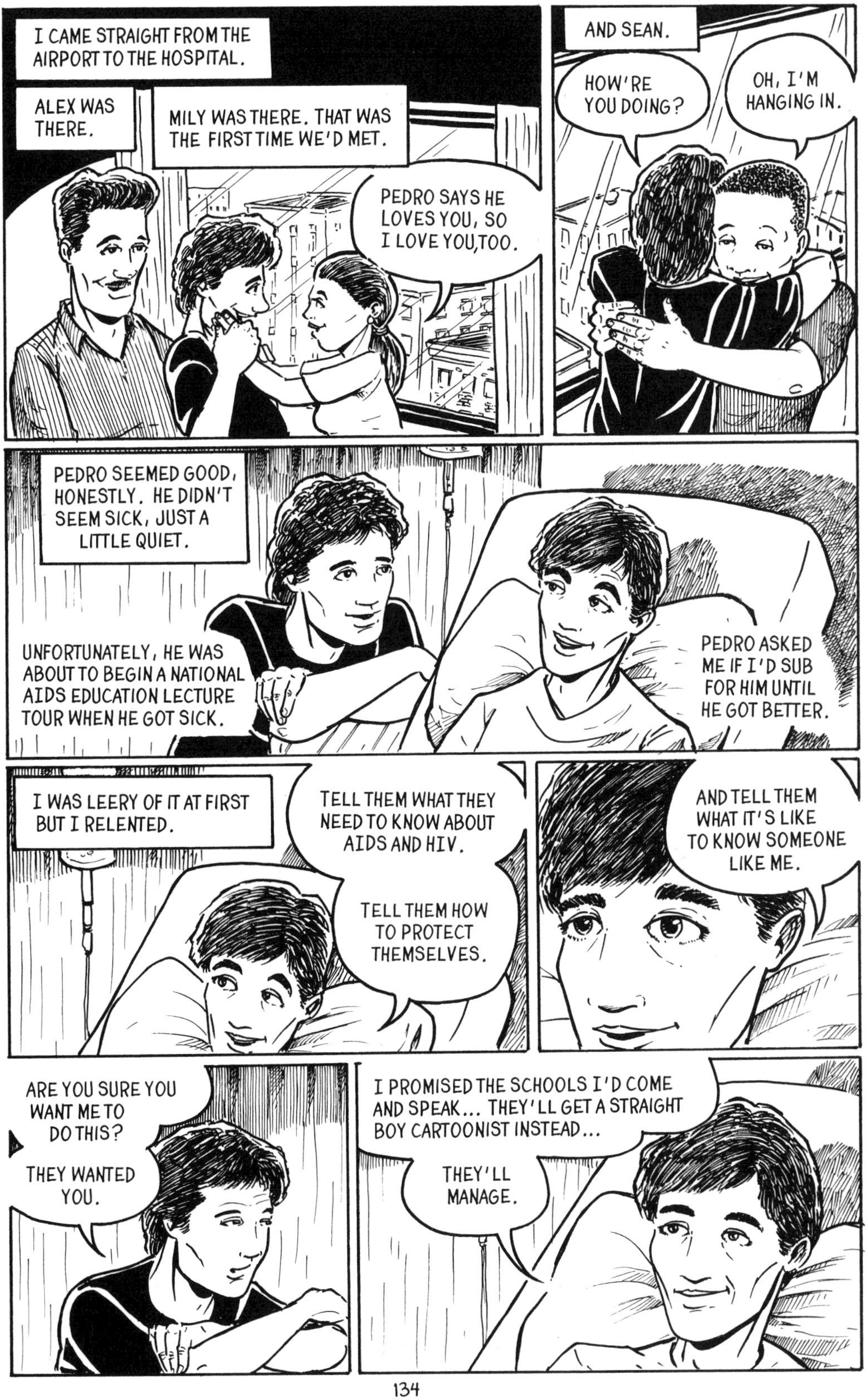
I CAME STRAIGHT FROM THE AIRPORT TO THE HOSPITAL.
ALEX WAS THERE.
MILY WAS THERE. THAT WAS THE FIRST TIME WE'D MET.
PEDRO SAYS HE LOVES YOU, SO I LOVE YOU,TOO.
AND SEAN.
HOW'RE YOU DOING?
OH, I'M HANGING IN.
PEDRO SEEMED GOOD, HONESTLY. HE DIDN'T SEEM SICK, JUST A LITTLE QUIET.
UNFORTUNATELY, HE WAS ABOUT TO BEGIN A NATIONAL AIDS EDUCATION LECTURE TOUR WHEN HE GOT SICK.
PEDRO ASKED ME IF I'D SUB FOR HIM UNTIL HE GOT BETTER.
I WAS LEERY OF IT AT FIRST BUT I RELENTED.
TELL THEM WHAT THEY NEED TO KNOW ABOUT AIDS AND HIV.
TELL THEM HOW TO PROTECT THEMSELVES.
AND TELL THEM WHAT IT'S LIKE TO KNOW SOMEONE LIKE ME.
ARE YOU SURE YOU WANT ME TO DO THIS?
THEY WANTED YOU.
I PROMISED THE SCHOOLS I'D COME AND SPEAK... THEY'LL GET A STRAIGHT BOY CARTOONIST INSTEAD...
THEY'LL MANAGE.

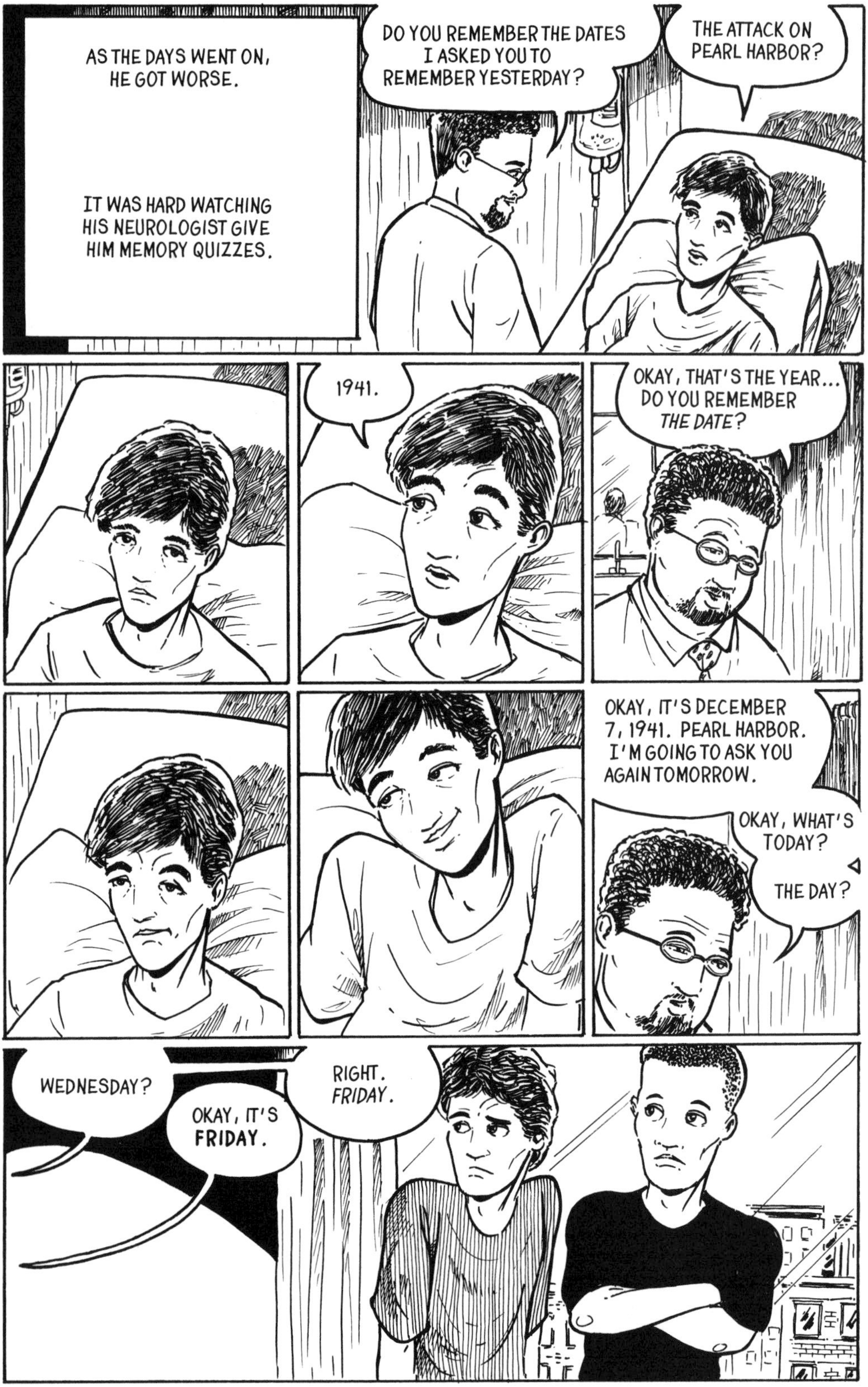
AS THE DAYS WENT ON, HE GOT WORSE.
IT WAS HARD WATCHING HIS NEUROLOGIST GIVE HIM MEMORY QUIZZES.
DO YOU REMEMBER THE DATES I ASKED YOU TO REMEMBER YESTERDAY?
THE ATTACK ON PEARL HARBOR?
1941.
OKAY, THAT'S THE YEAR... DO YOU REMEMBER *THE DATE*?
OKAY, IT'S DECEMBER 7, 1941. PEARL HARBOR. I'M GOING TO ASK YOU AGAIN TOMORROW.
OKAY, WHAT'S TODAY?
THE DAY?
WEDNESDAY?
OKAY, IT'S **FRIDAY**.
RIGHT. *FRIDAY*.

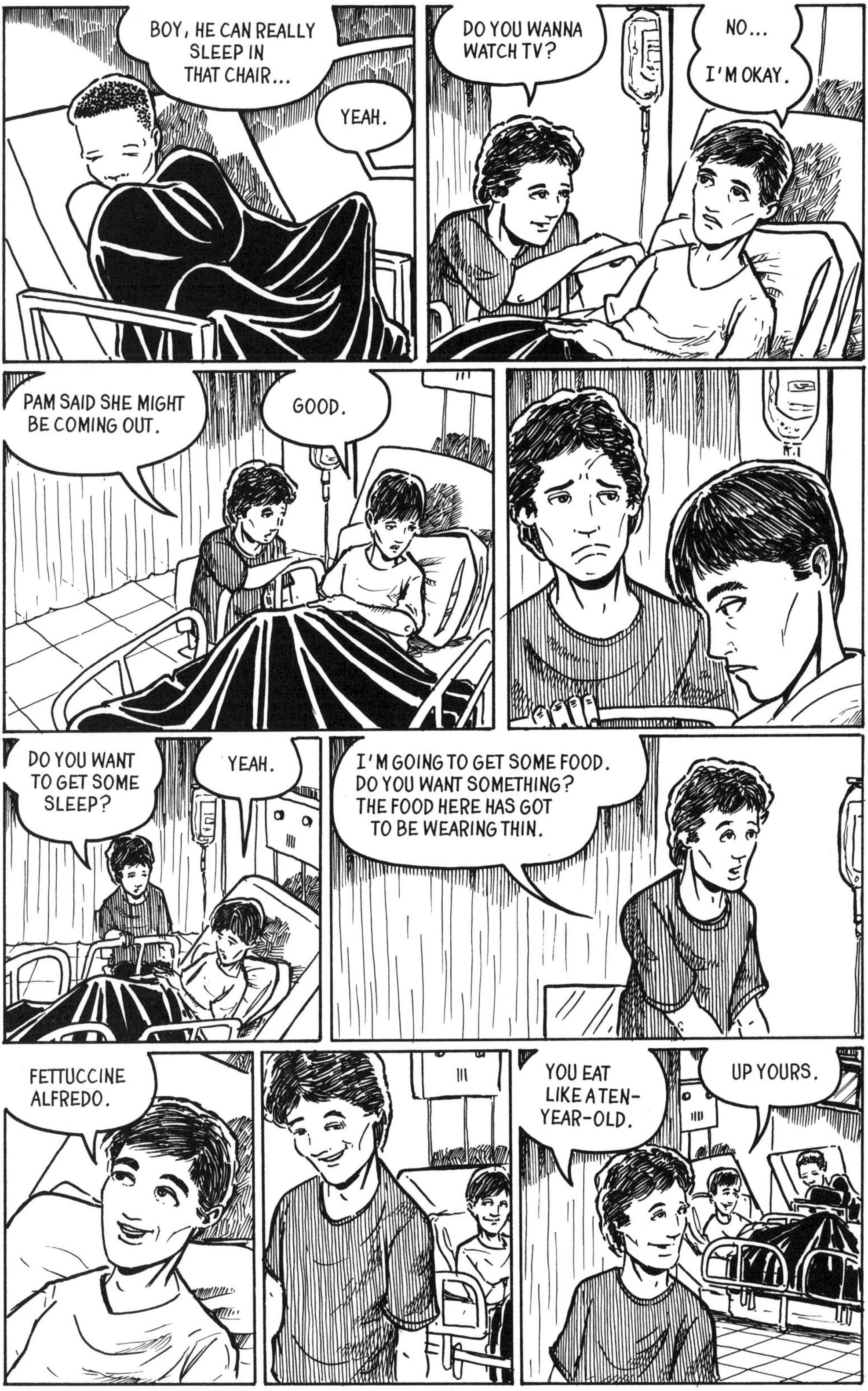
BOY, HE CAN REALLY SLEEP IN THAT CHAIR...
YEAH.
DO YOU WANNA WATCH TV?
NO...
I'M OKAY.
PAM SAID SHE MIGHT BE COMING OUT.
GOOD.
DO YOU WANT TO GET SOME SLEEP?
YEAH.
I'M GOING TO GET SOME FOOD. DO YOU WANT SOMETHING? THE FOOD HERE HAS GOT TO BE WEARING THIN.
FETTUCCINE ALFREDO.
YOU EAT LIKE A TEN-YEAR-OLD.
UP YOURS.

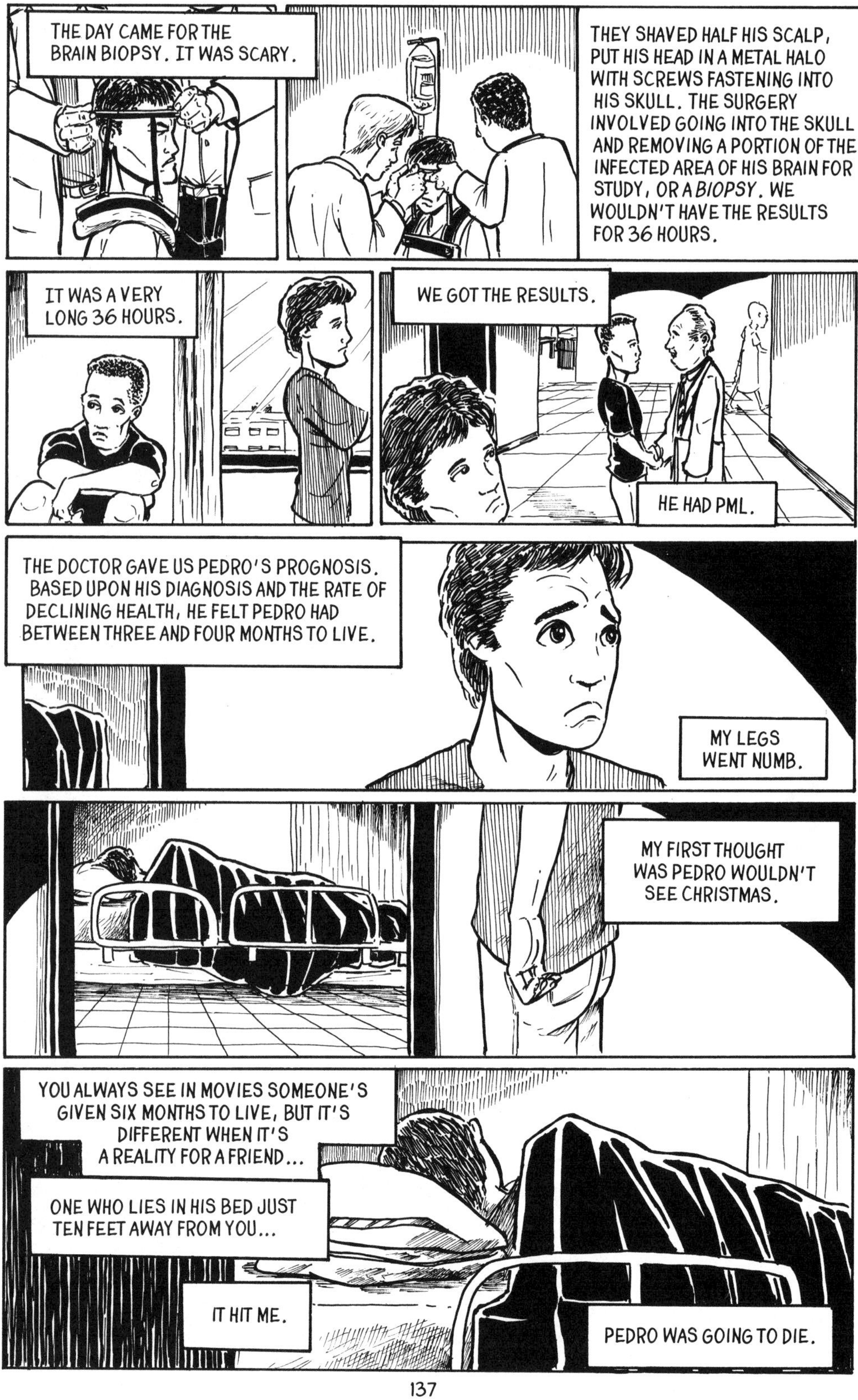
THE DAY CAME FOR THE BRAIN BIOPSY. IT WAS SCARY.
THEY SHAVED HALF HIS SCALP, PUT HIS HEAD IN A METAL HALO WITH SCREWS FASTENING INTO HIS SKULL. THE SURGERY INVOLVED GOING INTO THE SKULL AND REMOVING A PORTION OF THE INFECTED AREA OF HIS BRAIN FOR STUDY, OR A *BIOPSY*. WE WOULDN'T HAVE THE RESULTS FOR 36 HOURS.
IT WAS A VERY LONG 36 HOURS.
WE GOT THE RESULTS.
HE HAD PML.
THE DOCTOR GAVE US PEDRO'S PROGNOSIS. BASED UPON HIS DIAGNOSIS AND THE RATE OF DECLINING HEALTH, HE FELT PEDRO HAD BETWEEN THREE AND FOUR MONTHS TO LIVE.
MY LEGS WENT NUMB.
MY FIRST THOUGHT WAS PEDRO WOULDN'T SEE CHRISTMAS.
YOU ALWAYS SEE IN MOVIES SOMEONE'S GIVEN SIX MONTHS TO LIVE, BUT IT'S DIFFERENT WHEN IT'S A REALITY FOR A FRIEND...
ONE WHO LIES IN HIS BED JUST TEN FEET AWAY FROM YOU...
IT HIT ME.
PEDRO WAS GOING TO DIE.

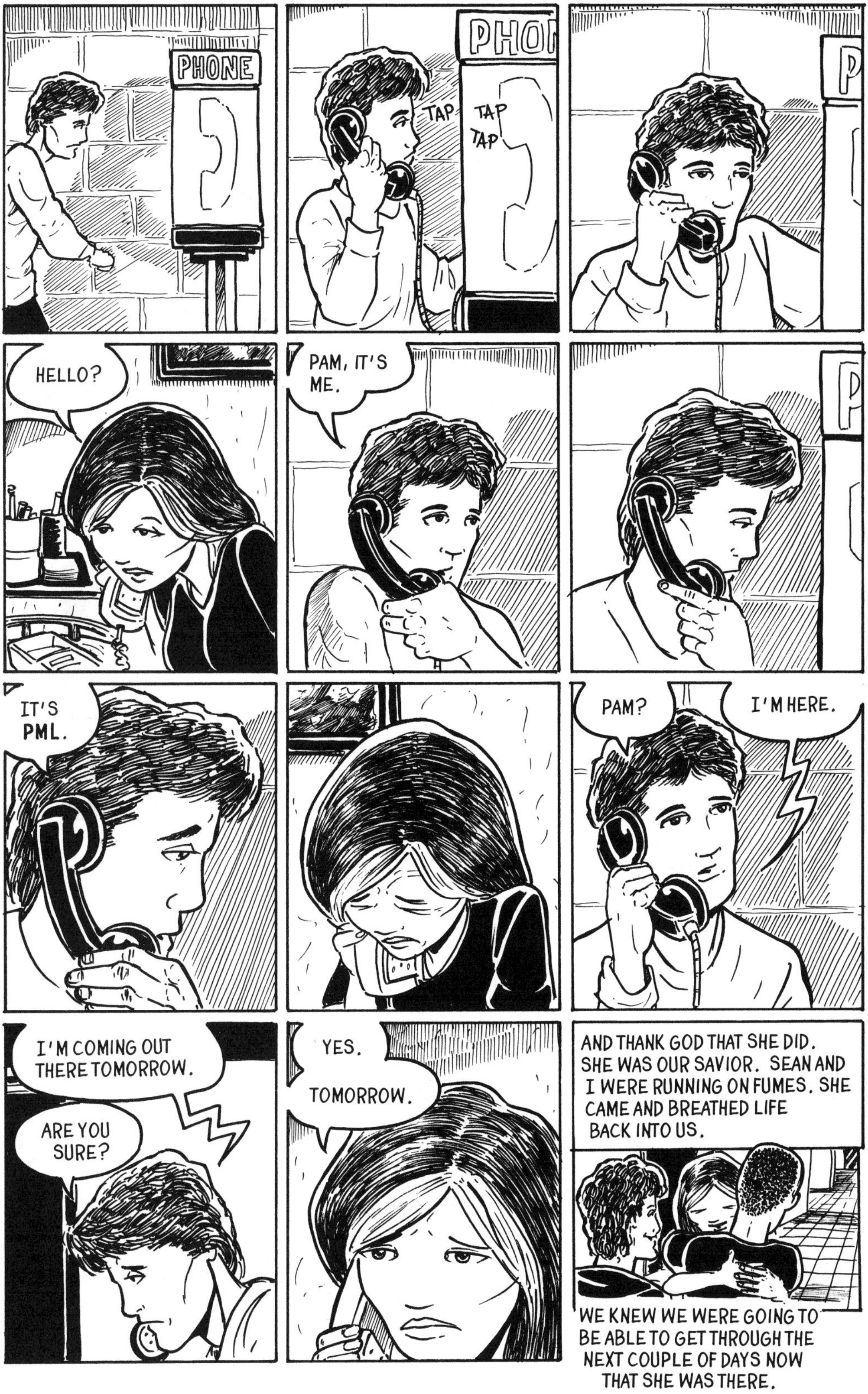
PHONE
PHO
TAP TAP TAP
P
HELLO?
PAM, IT'S ME.
P
IT'S PML.
PAM?
I'M HERE.
I'M COMING OUT THERE TOMORROW.
ARE YOU SURE?
YES.
TOMORROW.
AND THANK GOD THAT SHE DID. SHE WAS OUR SAVIOR. SEAN AND I WERE RUNNING ON FUMES. SHE CAME AND BREATHED LIFE BACK INTO US.
WE KNEW WE WERE GOING TO BE ABLE TO GET THROUGH THE NEXT COUPLE OF DAYS NOW THAT SHE WAS THERE.

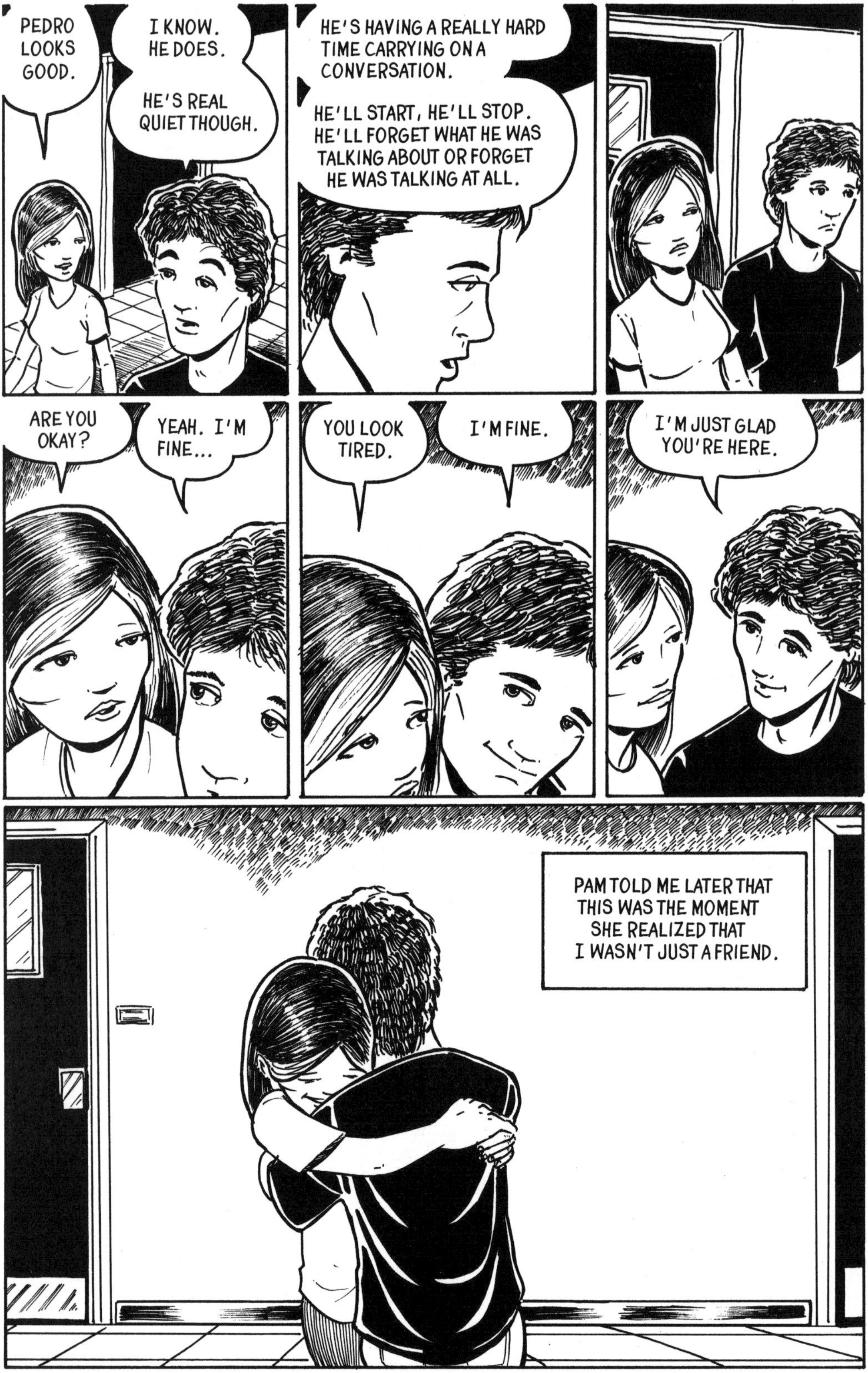
PEDRO LOOKS GOOD.
I KNOW. HE DOES.
HE'S REAL QUIET THOUGH.
HE'S HAVING A REALLY HARD TIME CARRYING ON A CONVERSATION.
HE'LL START, HE'LL STOP. HE'LL FORGET WHAT HE WAS TALKING ABOUT OR FORGET HE WAS TALKING AT ALL.
ARE YOU OKAY?
YEAH. I'M FINE...
YOU LOOK TIRED.
I'M FINE.
I'M JUST GLAD YOU'RE HERE.
PAM TOLD ME LATER THAT THIS WAS THE MOMENT SHE REALIZED THAT I WASN'T JUST A FRIEND.

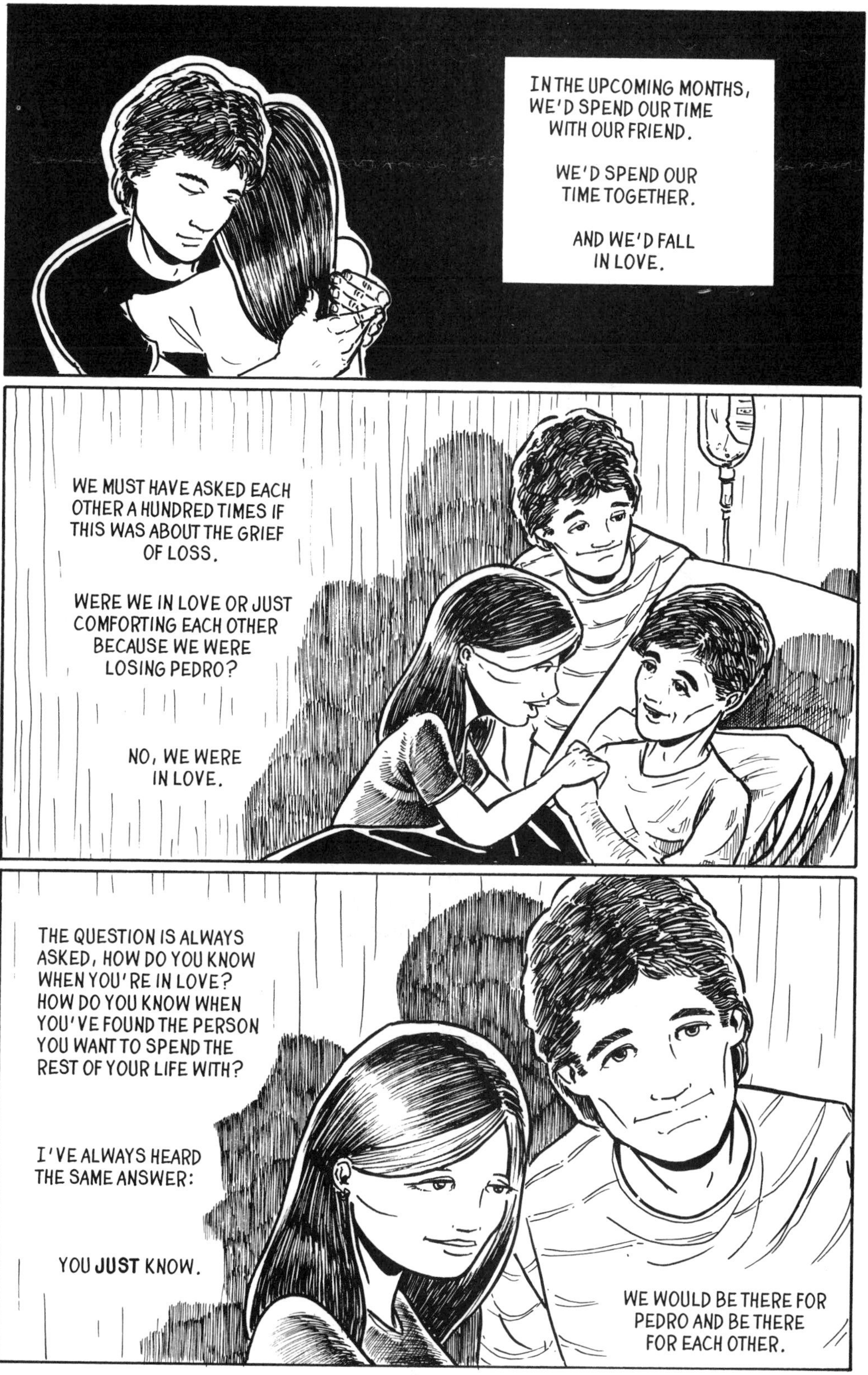
IN THE UPCOMING MONTHS, WE'D SPEND OUR TIME WITH OUR FRIEND.
WE'D SPEND OUR TIME TOGETHER.
AND WE'D FALL IN LOVE.
WE MUST HAVE ASKED EACH OTHER A HUNDRED TIMES IF THIS WAS ABOUT THE GRIEF OF LOSS.
WERE WE IN LOVE OR JUST COMFORTING EACH OTHER BECAUSE WE WERE LOSING PEDRO?
NO, WE WERE IN LOVE.
THE QUESTION IS ALWAYS ASKED, HOW DO YOU KNOW WHEN YOU'RE IN LOVE? HOW DO YOU KNOW WHEN YOU'VE FOUND THE PERSON YOU WANT TO SPEND THE REST OF YOUR LIFE WITH?
I'VE ALWAYS HEARD THE SAME ANSWER:
YOU **JUST** KNOW.
WE WOULD BE THERE FOR PEDRO AND BE THERE FOR EACH OTHER.

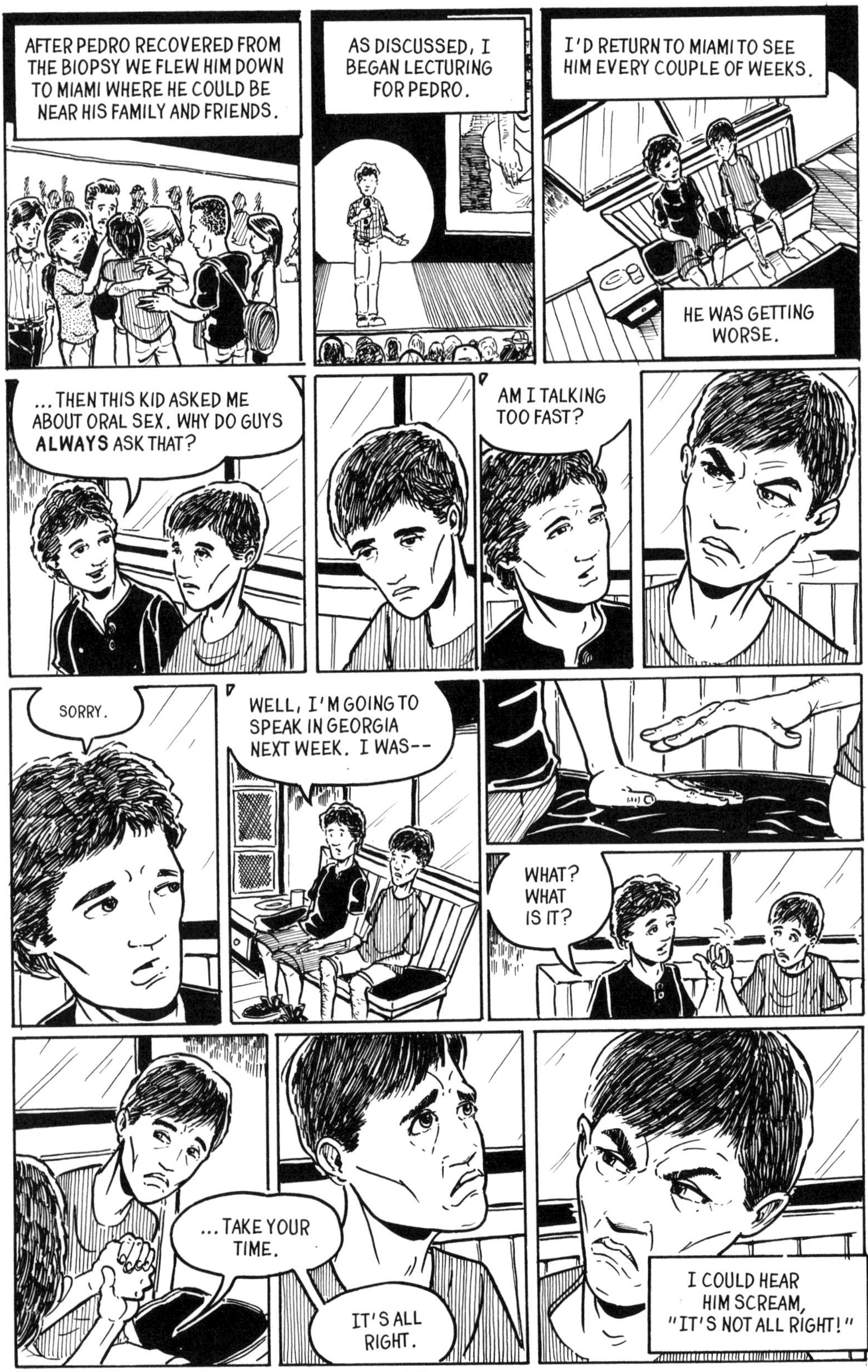
AFTER PEDRO RECOVERED FROM THE BIOPSY WE FLEW HIM DOWN TO MIAMI WHERE HE COULD BE NEAR HIS FAMILY AND FRIENDS.
AS DISCUSSED, I BEGAN LECTURING FOR PEDRO.
I'D RETURN TO MIAMI TO SEE HIM EVERY COUPLE OF WEEKS.
HE WAS GETTING WORSE.
...THEN THIS KID ASKED ME ABOUT ORAL SEX. WHY DO GUYS **ALWAYS** ASK THAT?
AM I TALKING TOO FAST?
SORRY.
WELL, I'M GOING TO SPEAK IN GEORGIA NEXT WEEK. I WAS--
WHAT? WHAT IS IT?
...TAKE YOUR TIME.
IT'S ALL RIGHT.
I COULD HEAR HIM SCREAM, "IT'S NOT ALL RIGHT!"

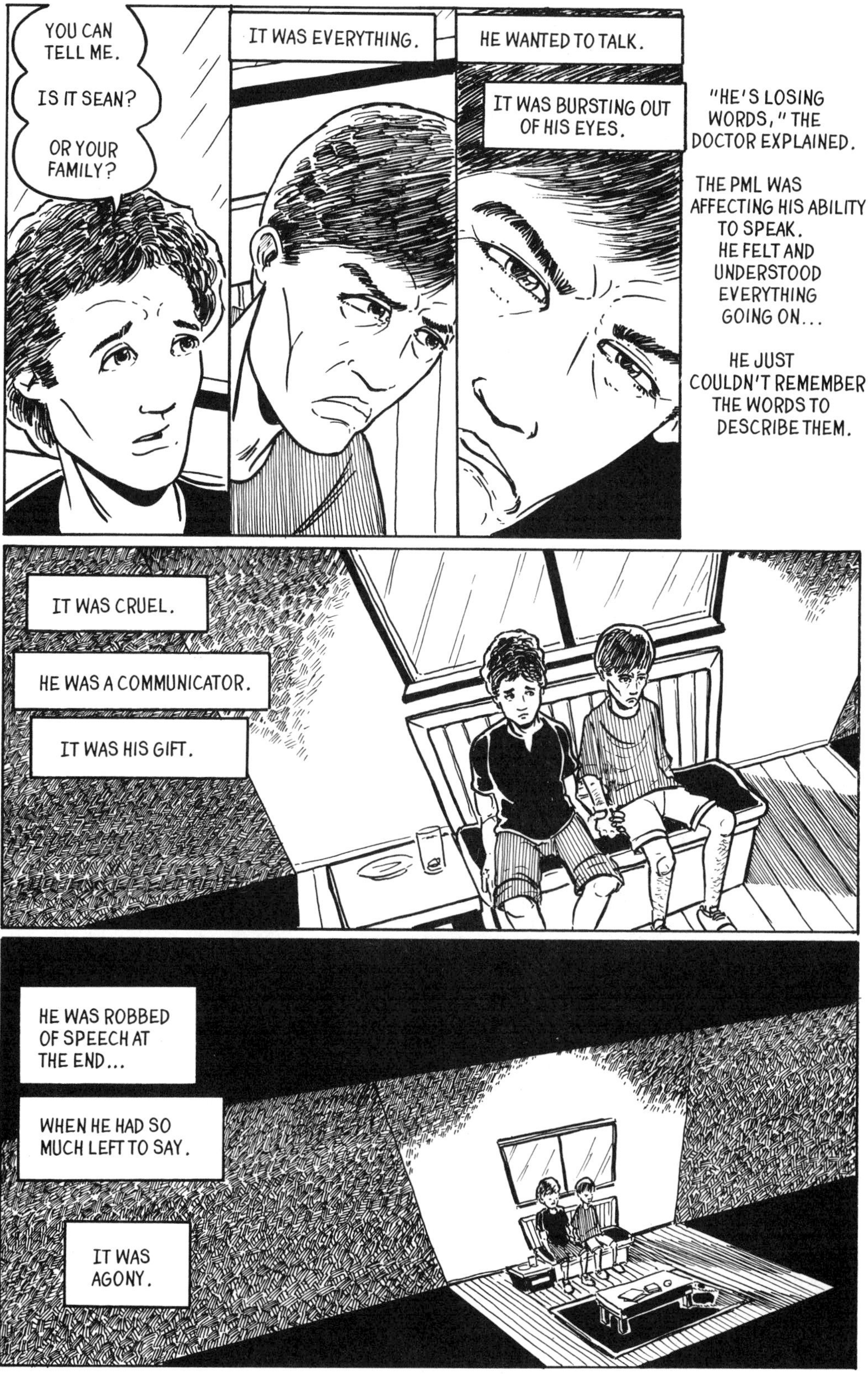
YOU CAN TELL ME.
IS IT SEAN?
OR YOUR FAMILY?
IT WAS EVERYTHING.
HE WANTED TO TALK.
IT WAS BURSTING OUT OF HIS EYES.
"HE'S LOSING WORDS," THE DOCTOR EXPLAINED.
THE PML WAS AFFECTING HIS ABILITY TO SPEAK. HE FELT AND UNDERSTOOD EVERYTHING GOING ON...
HE JUST COULDN'T REMEMBER THE WORDS TO DESCRIBE THEM.
IT WAS CRUEL.
HE WAS A COMMUNICATOR.
IT WAS HIS GIFT.
HE WAS ROBBED OF SPEECH AT THE END...
WHEN HE HAD SO MUCH LEFT TO SAY.
IT WAS AGONY.

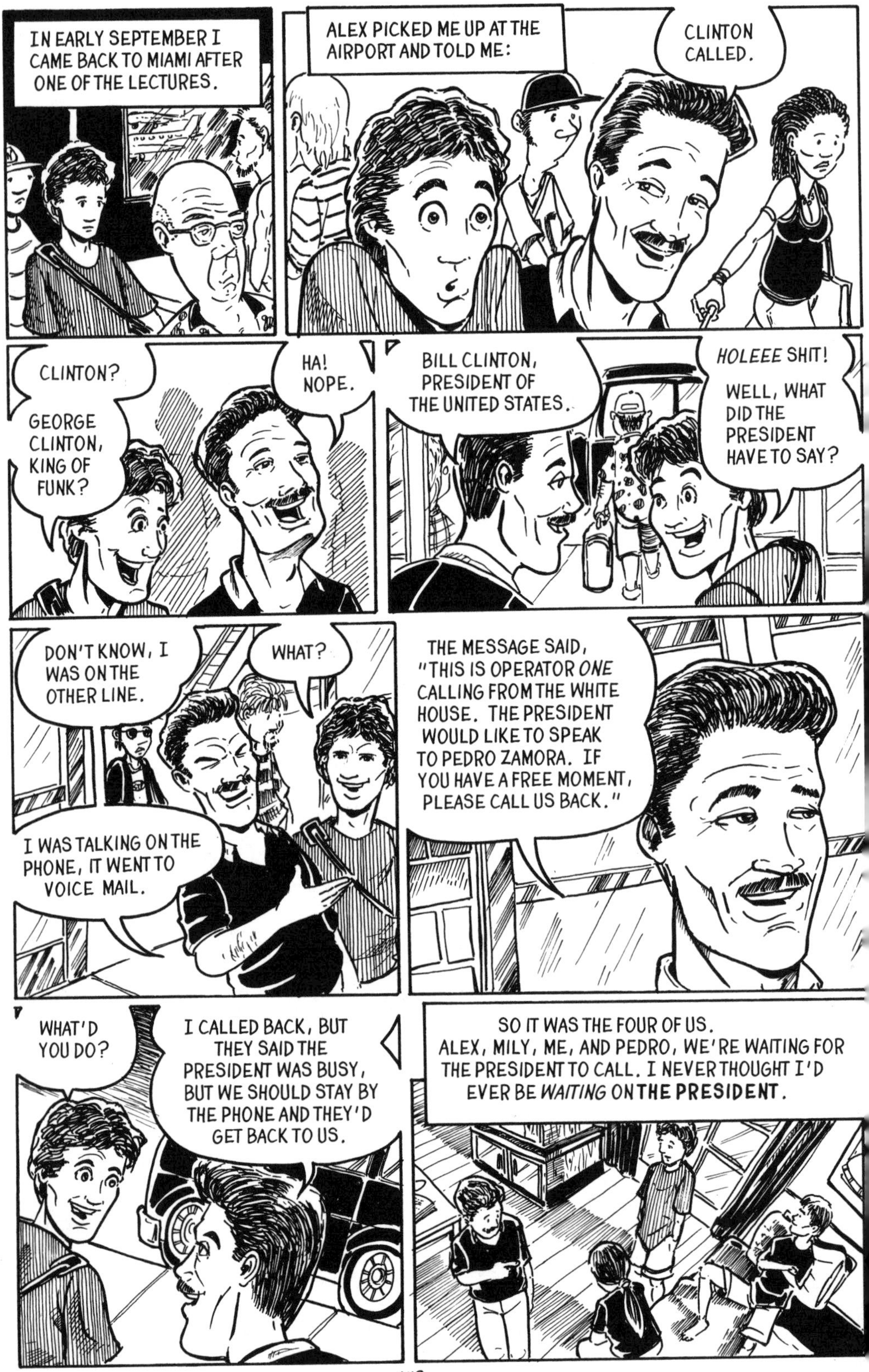
IN EARLY SEPTEMBER I CAME BACK TO MIAMI AFTER ONE OF THE LECTURES.
ALEX PICKED ME UP AT THE AIRPORT AND TOLD ME:
CLINTON CALLED.
CLINTON?
GEORGE CLINTON, KING OF FUNK?
HA! NOPE.
BILL CLINTON, PRESIDENT OF THE UNITED STATES.
HOLEEE SHIT!
WELL, WHAT DID THE PRESIDENT HAVE TO SAY?
DON'T KNOW, I WAS ON THE OTHER LINE.
WHAT?
I WAS TALKING ON THE PHONE, IT WENT TO VOICE MAIL.
THE MESSAGE SAID, "THIS IS OPERATOR *ONE* CALLING FROM THE WHITE HOUSE. THE PRESIDENT WOULD LIKE TO SPEAK TO PEDRO ZAMORA. IF YOU HAVE A FREE MOMENT, PLEASE CALL US BACK."
WHAT'D YOU DO?
I CALLED BACK, BUT THEY SAID THE PRESIDENT WAS BUSY, BUT WE SHOULD STAY BY THE PHONE AND THEY'D GET BACK TO US.
SO IT WAS THE FOUR OF US. ALEX, MILY, ME, AND PEDRO, WE'RE WAITING FOR THE PRESIDENT TO CALL. I NEVER THOUGHT I'D EVER BE *WAITING* ON **THE PRESIDENT**.

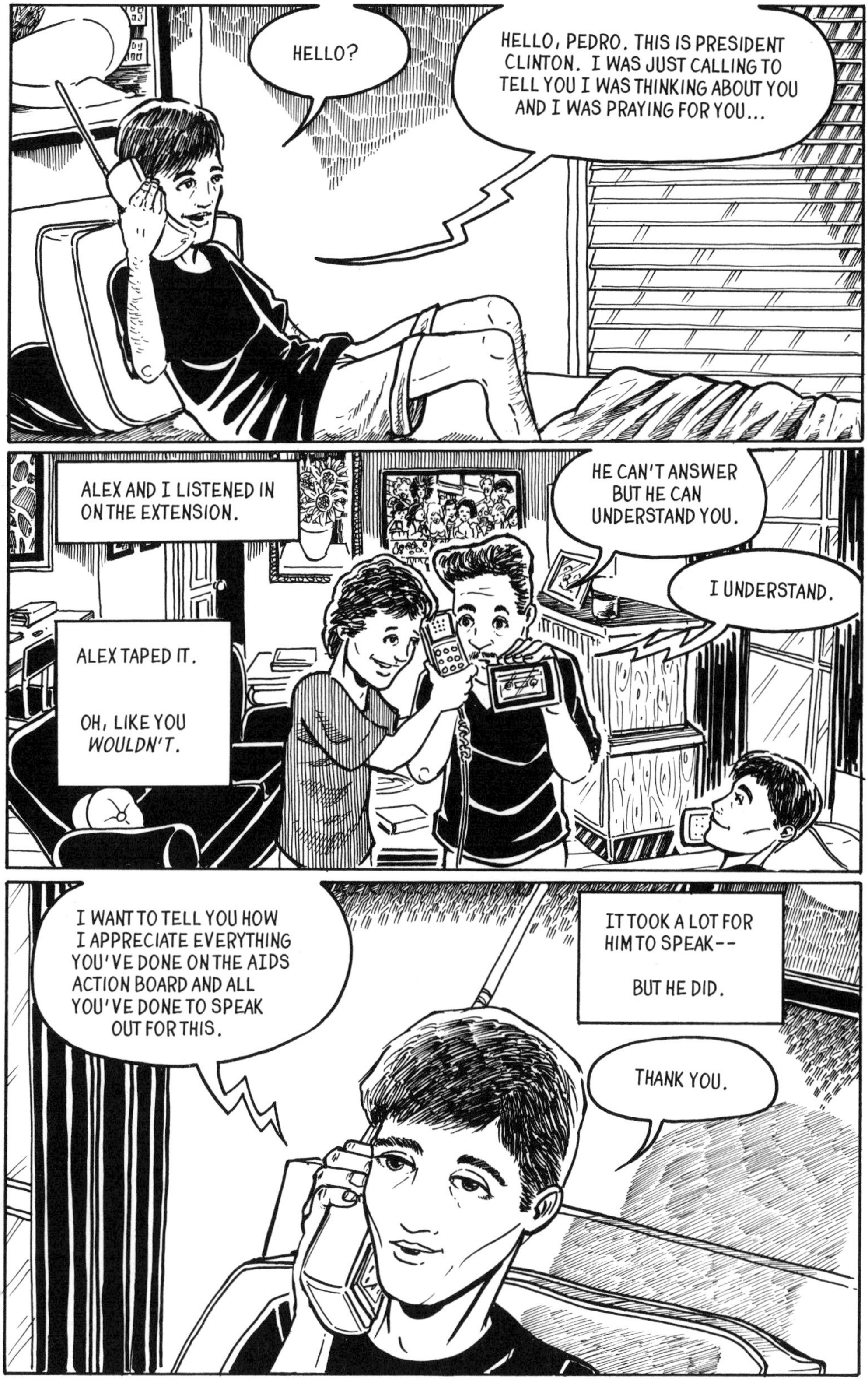
HELLO?
HELLO, PEDRO. THIS IS PRESIDENT CLINTON. I WAS JUST CALLING TO TELL YOU I WAS THINKING ABOUT YOU AND I WAS PRAYING FOR YOU...
ALEX AND I LISTENED IN ON THE EXTENSION.
HE CAN'T ANSWER BUT HE CAN UNDERSTAND YOU.
I UNDERSTAND.
ALEX TAPED IT.
OH, LIKE YOU *WOULDN'T*.
I WANT TO TELL YOU HOW I APPRECIATE EVERYTHING YOU'VE DONE ON THE AIDS ACTION BOARD AND ALL YOU'VE DONE TO SPEAK OUT FOR THIS.
IT TOOK A LOT FOR HIM TO SPEAK--
BUT HE DID.
THANK YOU.

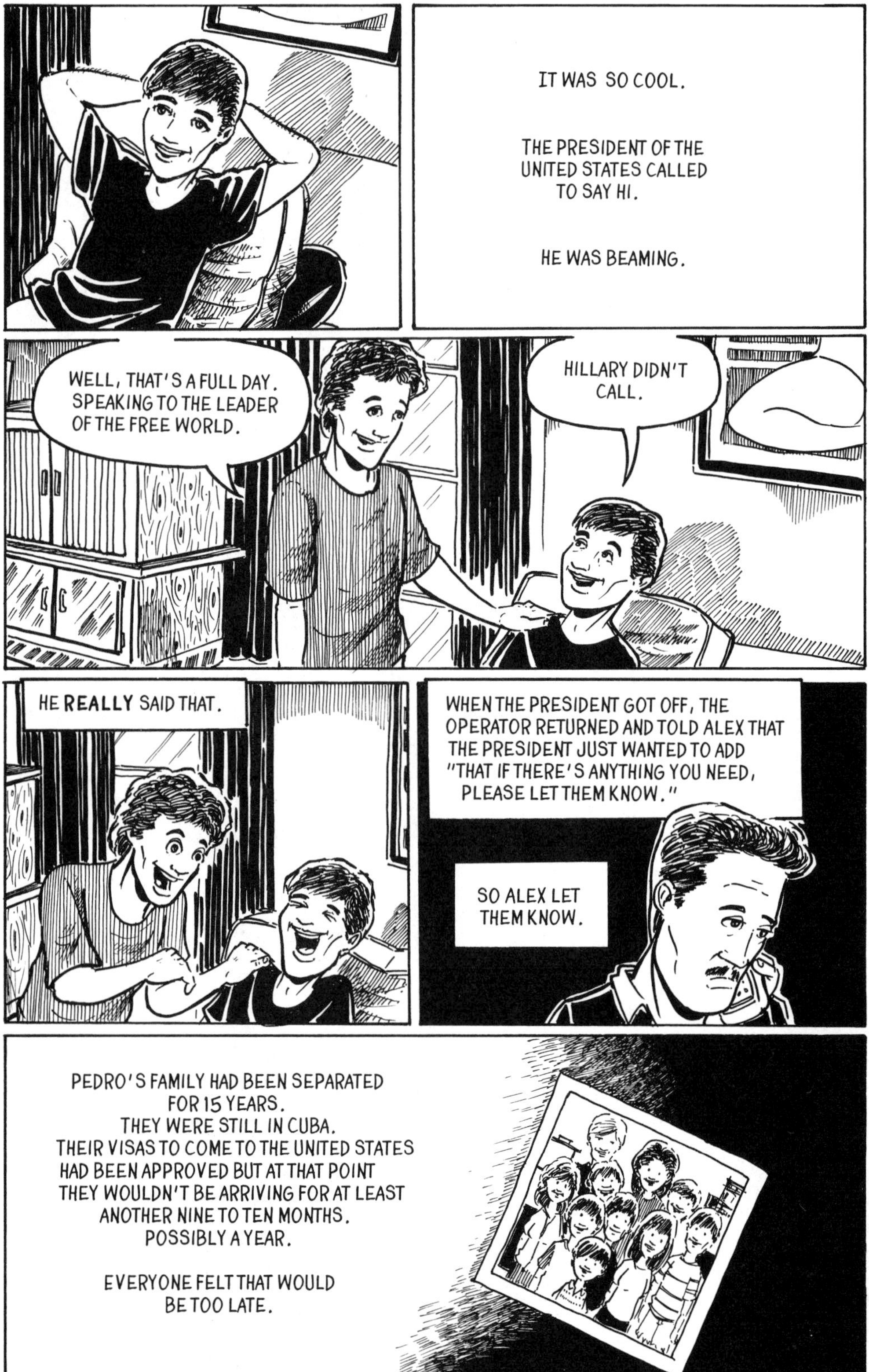
IT WAS SO COOL.
THE PRESIDENT OF THE UNITED STATES CALLED TO SAY HI.
HE WAS BEAMING.
WELL, THAT'S A FULL DAY. SPEAKING TO THE LEADER OF THE FREE WORLD.
HILLARY DIDN'T CALL.
HE **REALLY** SAID THAT.
WHEN THE PRESIDENT GOT OFF, THE OPERATOR RETURNED AND TOLD ALEX THAT THE PRESIDENT JUST WANTED TO ADD "THAT IF THERE'S ANYTHING YOU NEED, PLEASE LET THEM KNOW."
SO ALEX LET THEM KNOW.
PEDRO'S FAMILY HAD BEEN SEPARATED FOR 15 YEARS.
THEY WERE STILL IN CUBA.
THEIR VISAS TO COME TO THE UNITED STATES HAD BEEN APPROVED BUT AT THAT POINT THEY WOULDN'T BE ARRIVING FOR AT LEAST ANOTHER NINE TO TEN MONTHS.
POSSIBLY A YEAR.
EVERYONE FELT THAT WOULD BE TOO LATE.

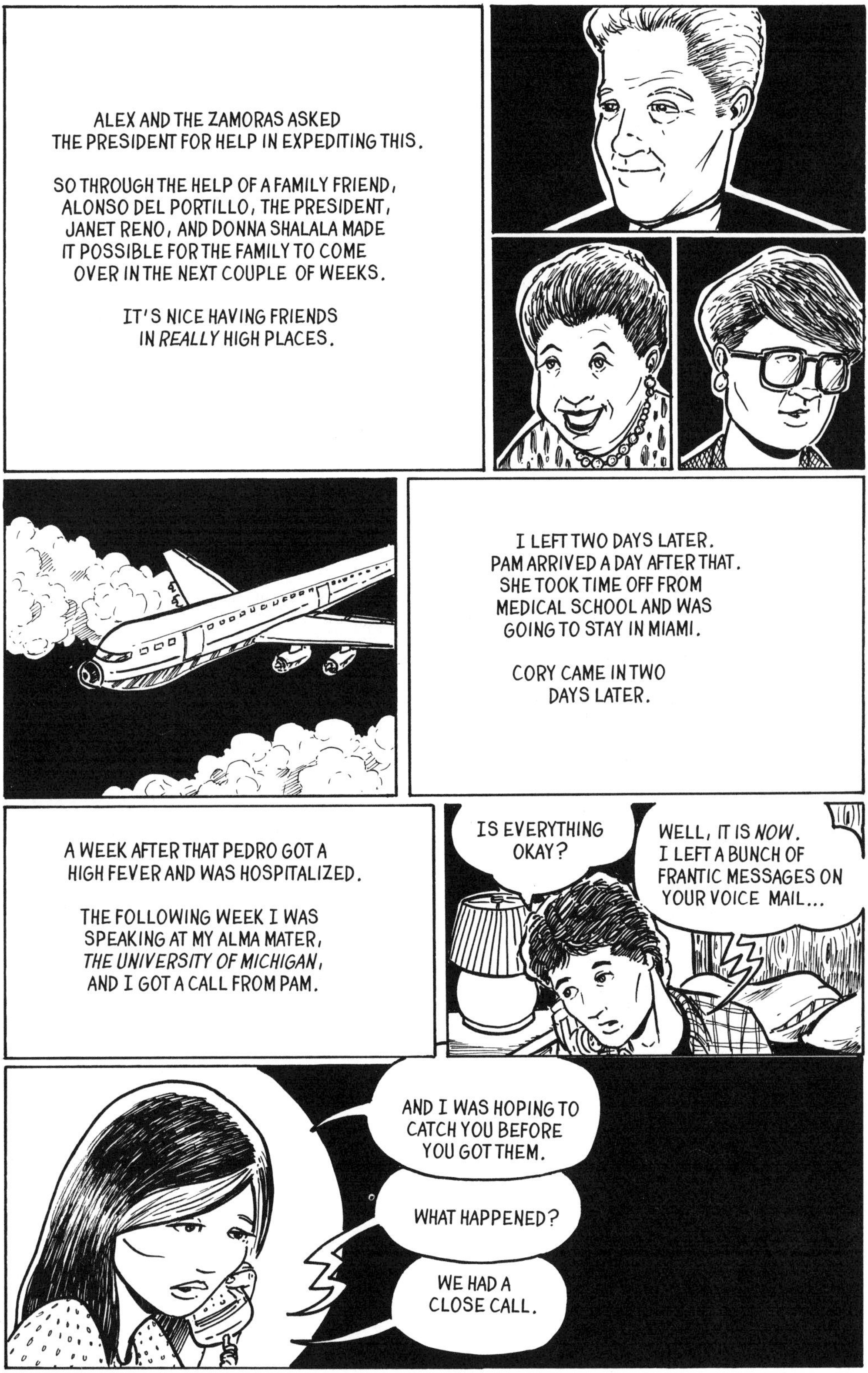
ALEX AND THE ZAMORAS ASKED THE PRESIDENT FOR HELP IN EXPEDITING THIS.
SO THROUGH THE HELP OF A FAMILY FRIEND, ALONSO DEL PORTILLO, THE PRESIDENT, JANET RENO, AND DONNA SHALALA MADE IT POSSIBLE FOR THE FAMILY TO COME OVER IN THE NEXT COUPLE OF WEEKS.
IT'S NICE HAVING FRIENDS IN *REALLY* HIGH PLACES.
I LEFT TWO DAYS LATER. PAM ARRIVED A DAY AFTER THAT. SHE TOOK TIME OFF FROM MEDICAL SCHOOL AND WAS GOING TO STAY IN MIAMI.
CORY CAME IN TWO DAYS LATER.
A WEEK AFTER THAT PEDRO GOT A HIGH FEVER AND WAS HOSPITALIZED.
THE FOLLOWING WEEK I WAS SPEAKING AT MY ALMA MATER, *THE UNIVERSITY OF MICHIGAN*, AND I GOT A CALL FROM PAM.
IS EVERYTHING OKAY?
WELL, IT IS *NOW*. I LEFT A BUNCH OF FRANTIC MESSAGES ON YOUR VOICE MAIL...
AND I WAS HOPING TO CATCH YOU BEFORE YOU GOT THEM.
WHAT HAPPENED?
WE HAD A CLOSE CALL.

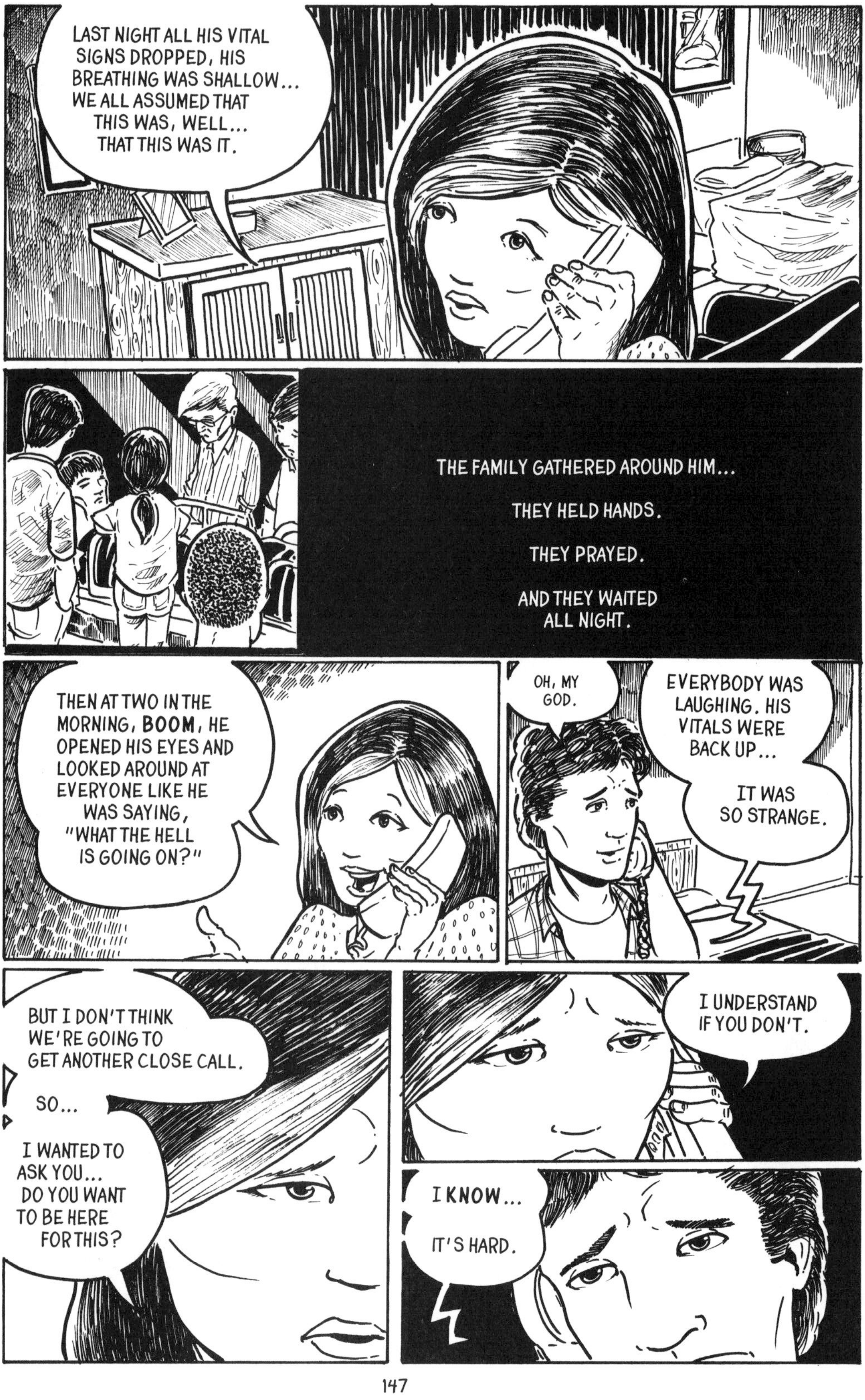
LAST NIGHT ALL HIS VITAL SIGNS DROPPED, HIS BREATHING WAS SHALLOW... WE ALL ASSUMED THAT THIS WAS, WELL... THAT THIS WAS IT.
THE FAMILY GATHERED AROUND HIM...
THEY HELD HANDS.
THEY PRAYED.
AND THEY WAITED ALL NIGHT.
THEN AT TWO IN THE MORNING, **BOOM**, HE OPENED HIS EYES AND LOOKED AROUND AT EVERYONE LIKE HE WAS SAYING, "WHAT THE HELL IS GOING ON?"
OH, MY GOD.
EVERYBODY WAS LAUGHING. HIS VITALS WERE BACK UP...
IT WAS SO STRANGE.
BUT I DON'T THINK WE'RE GOING TO GET ANOTHER CLOSE CALL.
SO...
I WANTED TO ASK YOU... DO YOU WANT TO BE HERE FOR THIS?
I UNDERSTAND IF YOU DON'T.
I KNOW...
IT'S HARD.

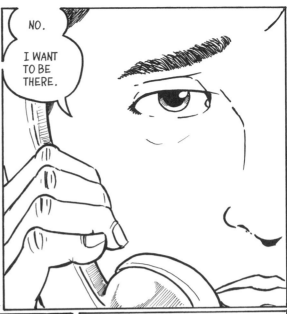

NO.

I WANT TO BE THERE.

OKAY.

THEN YOU SHOULD COME NOW.

I ARRIVED IN FLORIDA THAT NIGHT.

THREE DAYS LATER CAME PEDRO'S FAMILY FROM CUBA. PEDRO'S ELDEST SISTER, HER CHILDREN, HIS FOUR OLDER BROTHERS, THEIR WIVES, THEIR CHILDREN-- A WHOLE BUNCH OF ZAMORAS GOT OFF A PLANE IN MIAMI AND HEADED TOWARD THE HOSPITAL.

IT WAS EXTRAORDINARY. HE WAS REUNITED WITH HIS ENTIRE FAMILY.

HIS MOTHER DIDN'T LIVE TO SEE IT.

THEY WERE TOGETHER AGAIN...

BUT UNDER THE WORST OF CIRCUMSTANCES.

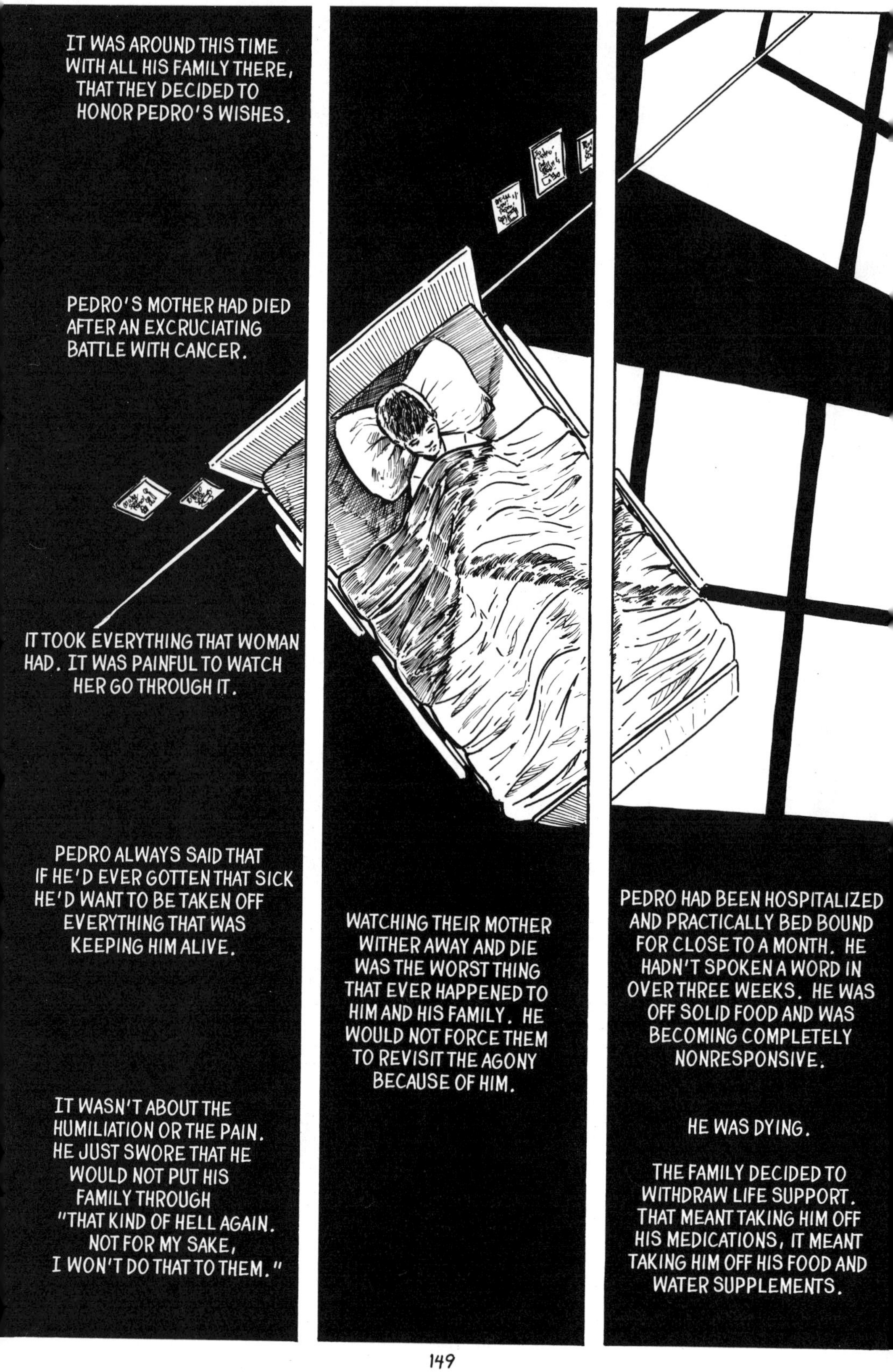

IT WAS AROUND THIS TIME WITH ALL HIS FAMILY THERE, THAT THEY DECIDED TO HONOR PEDRO'S WISHES.
PEDRO'S MOTHER HAD DIED AFTER AN EXCRUCIATING BATTLE WITH CANCER.
IT TOOK EVERYTHING THAT WOMAN HAD. IT WAS PAINFUL TO WATCH HER GO THROUGH IT.
PEDRO ALWAYS SAID THAT IF HE'D EVER GOTTEN THAT SICK HE'D WANT TO BE TAKEN OFF EVERYTHING THAT WAS KEEPING HIM ALIVE.
IT WASN'T ABOUT THE HUMILIATION OR THE PAIN. HE JUST SWORE THAT HE WOULD NOT PUT HIS FAMILY THROUGH "THAT KIND OF HELL AGAIN. NOT FOR MY SAKE, I WON'T DO THAT TO THEM."
WATCHING THEIR MOTHER WITHER AWAY AND DIE WAS THE WORST THING THAT EVER HAPPENED TO HIM AND HIS FAMILY. HE WOULD NOT FORCE THEM TO REVISIT THE AGONY BECAUSE OF HIM.
PEDRO HAD BEEN HOSPITALIZED AND PRACTICALLY BED BOUND FOR CLOSE TO A MONTH. HE HADN'T SPOKEN A WORD IN OVER THREE WEEKS. HE WAS OFF SOLID FOOD AND WAS BECOMING COMPLETELY NONRESPONSIVE.
HE WAS DYING.
THE FAMILY DECIDED TO WITHDRAW LIFE SUPPORT. THAT MEANT TAKING HIM OFF HIS MEDICATIONS, IT MEANT TAKING HIM OFF HIS FOOD AND WATER SUPPLEMENTS.

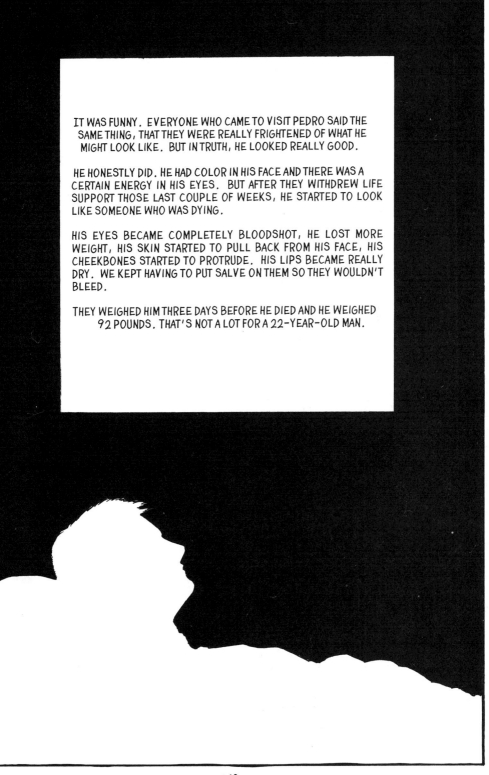

IT WAS FUNNY. EVERYONE WHO CAME TO VISIT PEDRO SAID THE SAME THING, THAT THEY WERE REALLY FRIGHTENED OF WHAT HE MIGHT LOOK LIKE. BUT IN TRUTH, HE LOOKED REALLY GOOD.

HE HONESTLY DID. HE HAD COLOR IN HIS FACE AND THERE WAS A CERTAIN ENERGY IN HIS EYES. BUT AFTER THEY WITHDREW LIFE SUPPORT THOSE LAST COUPLE OF WEEKS, HE STARTED TO LOOK LIKE SOMEONE WHO WAS DYING.

HIS EYES BECAME COMPLETELY BLOODSHOT, HE LOST MORE WEIGHT, HIS SKIN STARTED TO PULL BACK FROM HIS FACE, HIS CHEEKBONES STARTED TO PROTRUDE. HIS LIPS BECAME REALLY DRY. WE KEPT HAVING TO PUT SALVE ON THEM SO THEY WOULDN'T BLEED.

THEY WEIGHED HIM THREE DAYS BEFORE HE DIED AND HE WEIGHED 92 POUNDS. THAT'S NOT A LOT FOR A 22-YEAR-OLD MAN.

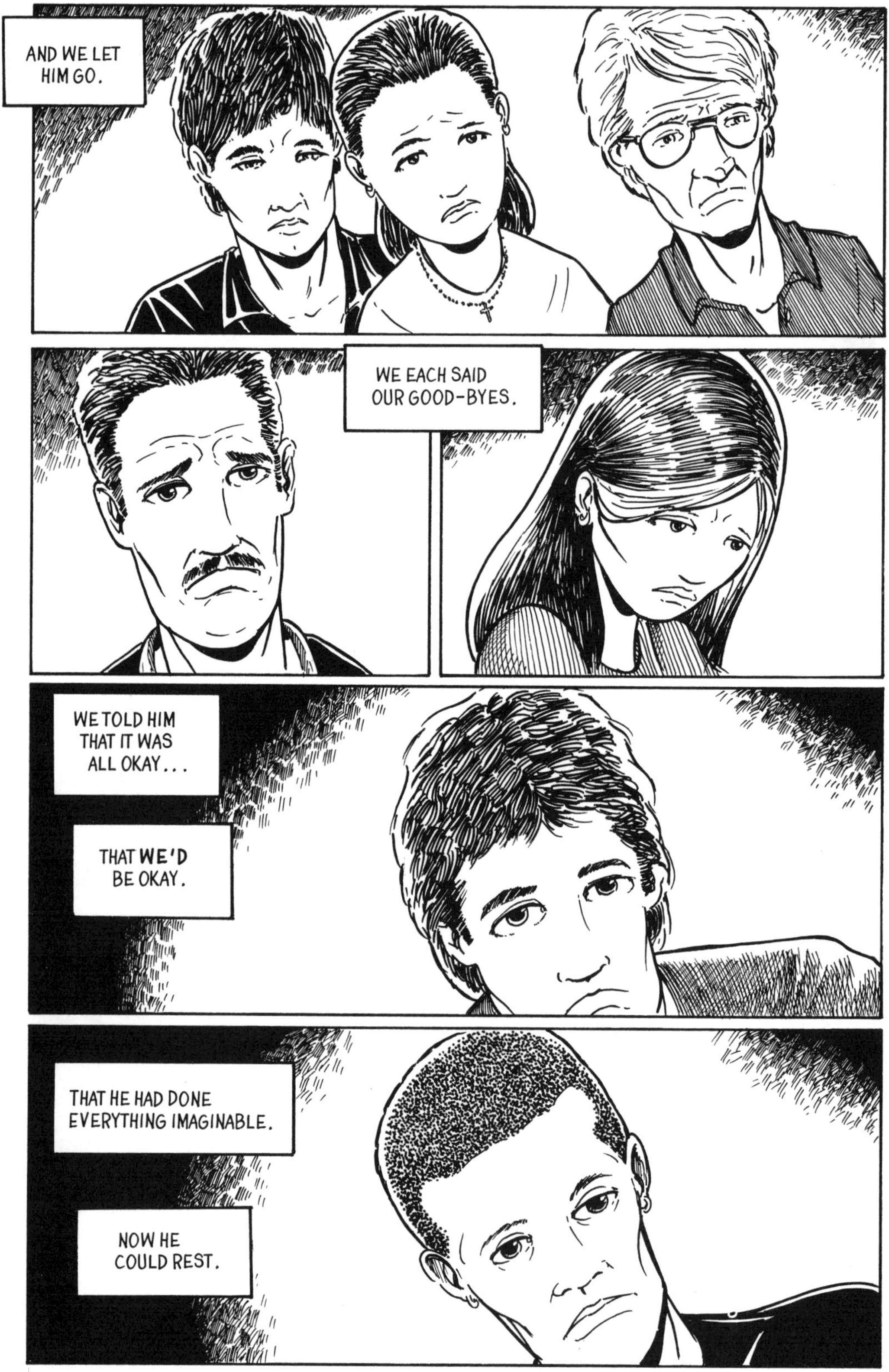
AND WE LET HIM GO.
WE EACH SAID OUR GOOD-BYES.
WE TOLD HIM THAT IT WAS ALL OKAY...
THAT **WE'D** BE OKAY.
THAT HE HAD DONE EVERYTHING IMAGINABLE.
NOW HE COULD REST.

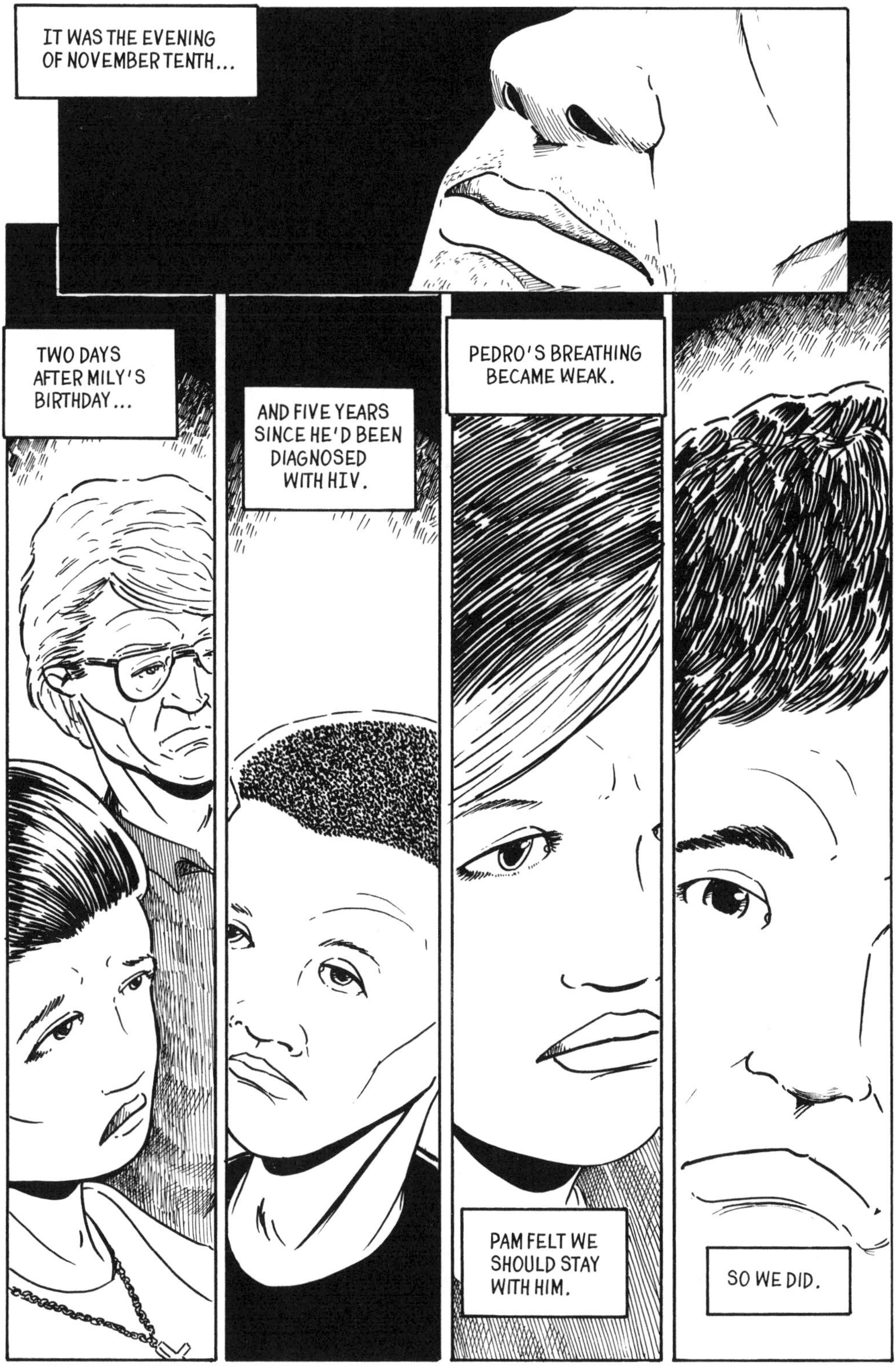
IT WAS THE EVENING OF NOVEMBER TENTH...
TWO DAYS AFTER MILY'S BIRTHDAY...
AND FIVE YEARS SINCE HE'D BEEN DIAGNOSED WITH HIV.
PEDRO'S BREATHING BECAME WEAK.
PAM FELT WE SHOULD STAY WITH HIM.
SO WE DID.

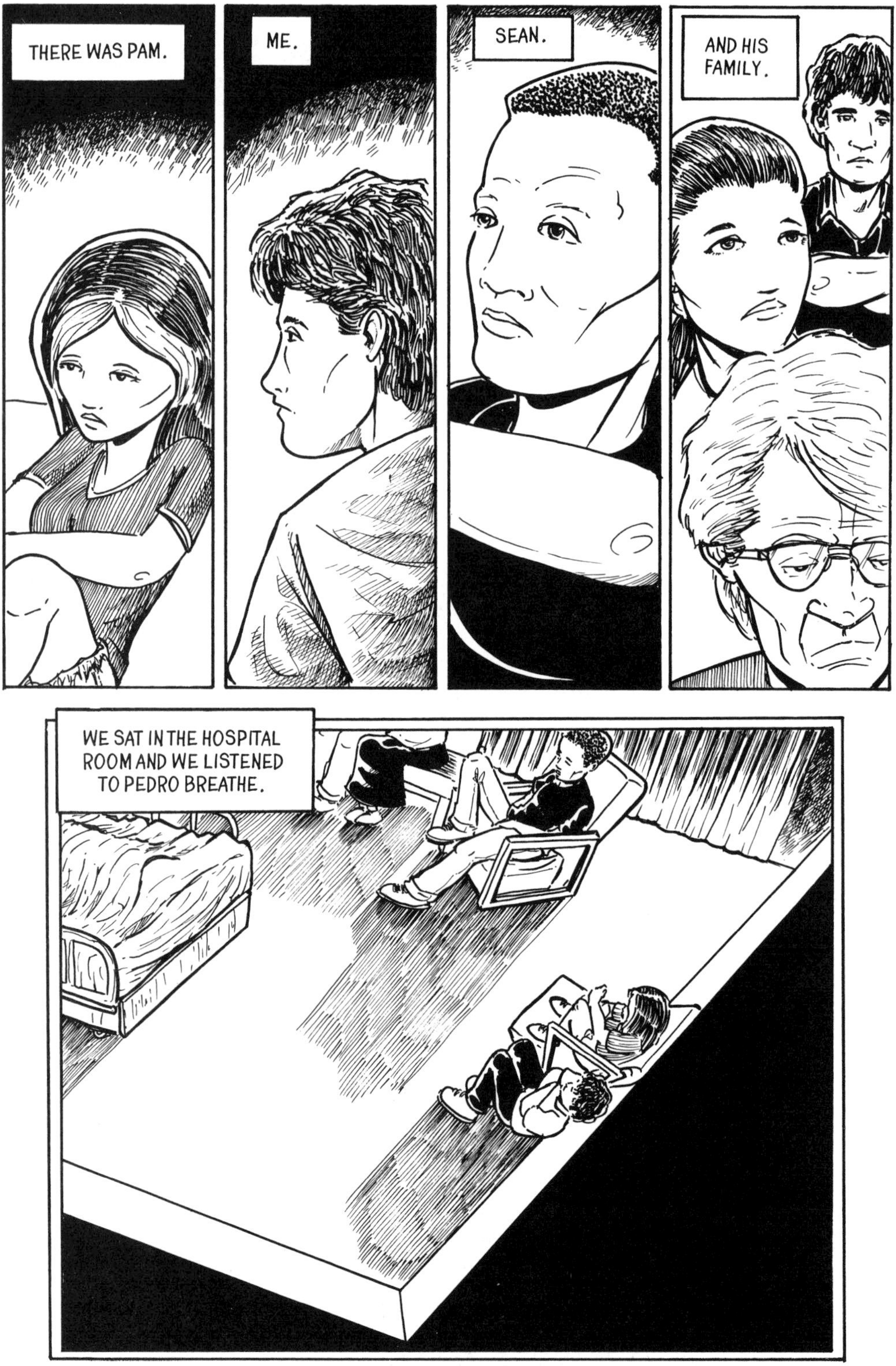
THERE WAS PAM.
ME.
SEAN.
AND HIS FAMILY.
WE SAT IN THE HOSPITAL ROOM AND WE LISTENED TO PEDRO BREATHE.

AROUND 4:30 IN THE MORNING WITH ALL OF US AROUND HIM...

THE NURSES CAME IN TO CHANGE HIS BED SHEETS.

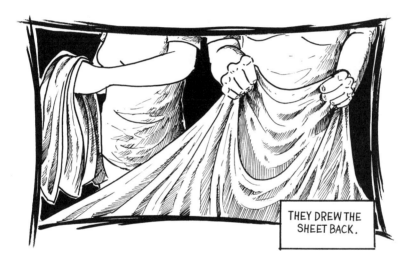

THEY DREW THE SHEET BACK.

AND HE WAS GONE.

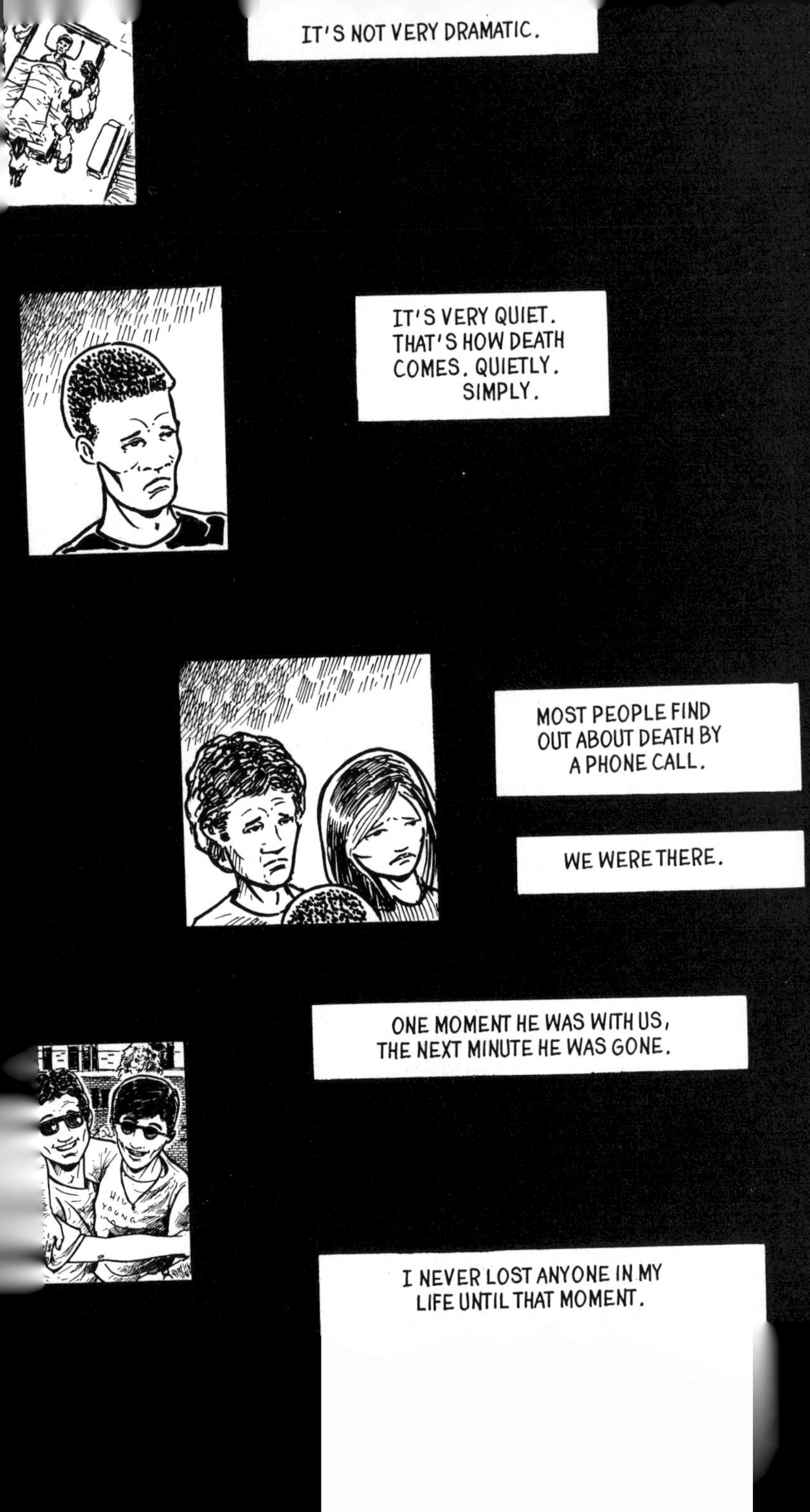
IT'S NOT VERY DRAMATIC.
IT'S VERY QUIET. THAT'S HOW DEATH COMES. QUIETLY. SIMPLY.
MOST PEOPLE FIND OUT ABOUT DEATH BY A PHONE CALL.
WE WERE THERE.
ONE MOMENT HE WAS WITH US, THE NEXT MINUTE HE WAS GONE.
I NEVER LOST ANYONE IN MY LIFE UNTIL THAT MOMENT.

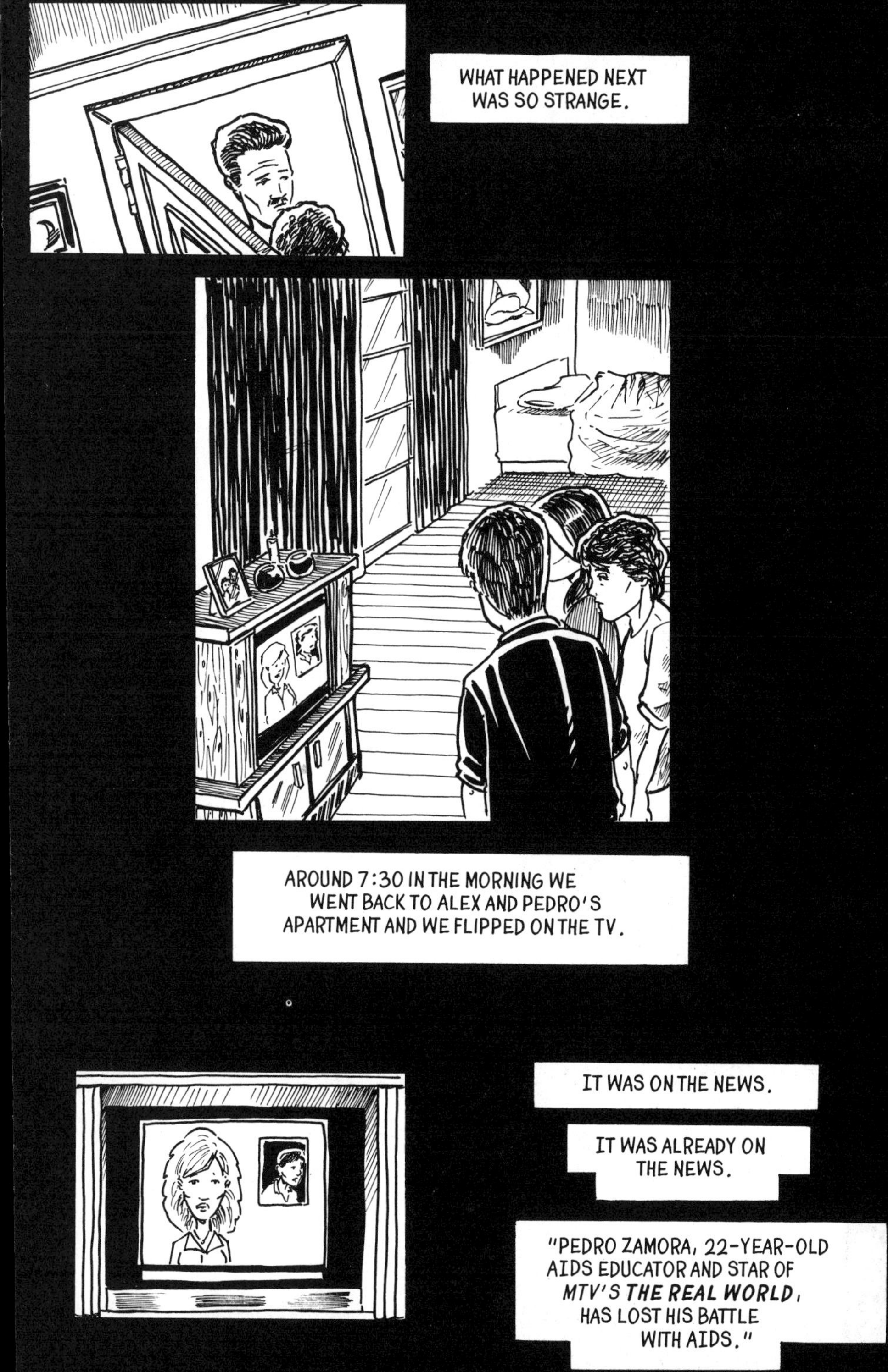
WHAT HAPPENED NEXT WAS SO STRANGE.
AROUND 7:30 IN THE MORNING WE WENT BACK TO ALEX AND PEDRO'S APARTMENT AND WE FLIPPED ON THE TV.
IT WAS ON THE NEWS.
IT WAS ALREADY ON THE NEWS.
"PEDRO ZAMORA, 22-YEAR-OLD AIDS EDUCATOR AND STAR OF MTV'S THE REAL WORLD, HAS LOST HIS BATTLE WITH AIDS."

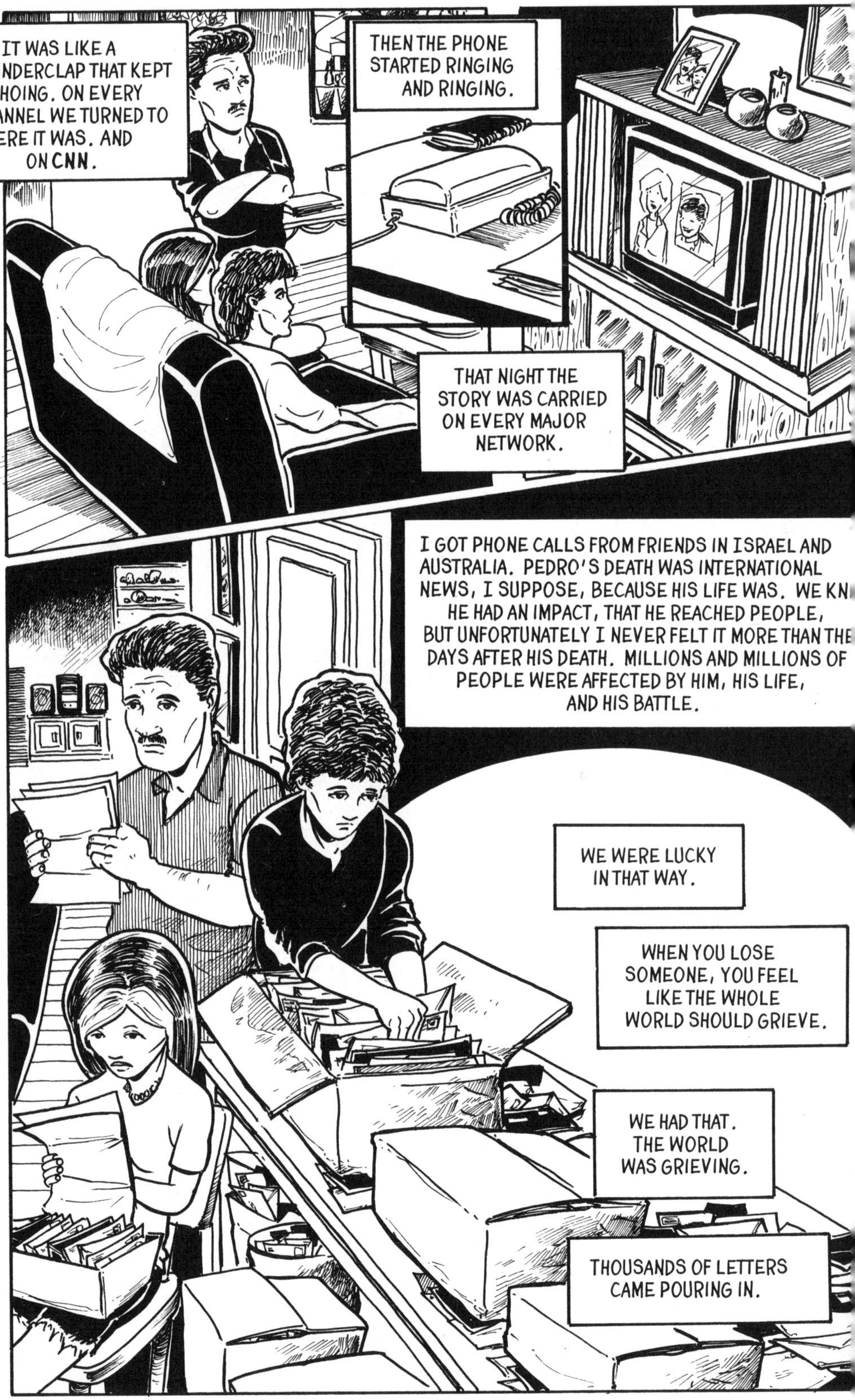
IT WAS LIKE A THUNDERCLAP THAT KEPT ECHOING. ON EVERY CHANNEL WE TURNED TO THERE IT WAS. AND ON CNN.
THEN THE PHONE STARTED RINGING AND RINGING.
THAT NIGHT THE STORY WAS CARRIED ON EVERY MAJOR NETWORK.
I GOT PHONE CALLS FROM FRIENDS IN ISRAEL AND AUSTRALIA. PEDRO'S DEATH WAS INTERNATIONAL NEWS, I SUPPOSE, BECAUSE HIS LIFE WAS. WE KN HE HAD AN IMPACT, THAT HE REACHED PEOPLE, BUT UNFORTUNATELY I NEVER FELT IT MORE THAN THE DAYS AFTER HIS DEATH. MILLIONS AND MILLIONS OF PEOPLE WERE AFFECTED BY HIM, HIS LIFE, AND HIS BATTLE.
WE WERE LUCKY IN THAT WAY.
WHEN YOU LOSE SOMEONE, YOU FEEL LIKE THE WHOLE WORLD SHOULD GRIEVE.
WE HAD THAT. THE WORLD WAS GRIEVING.
THOUSANDS OF LETTERS CAME POURING IN.

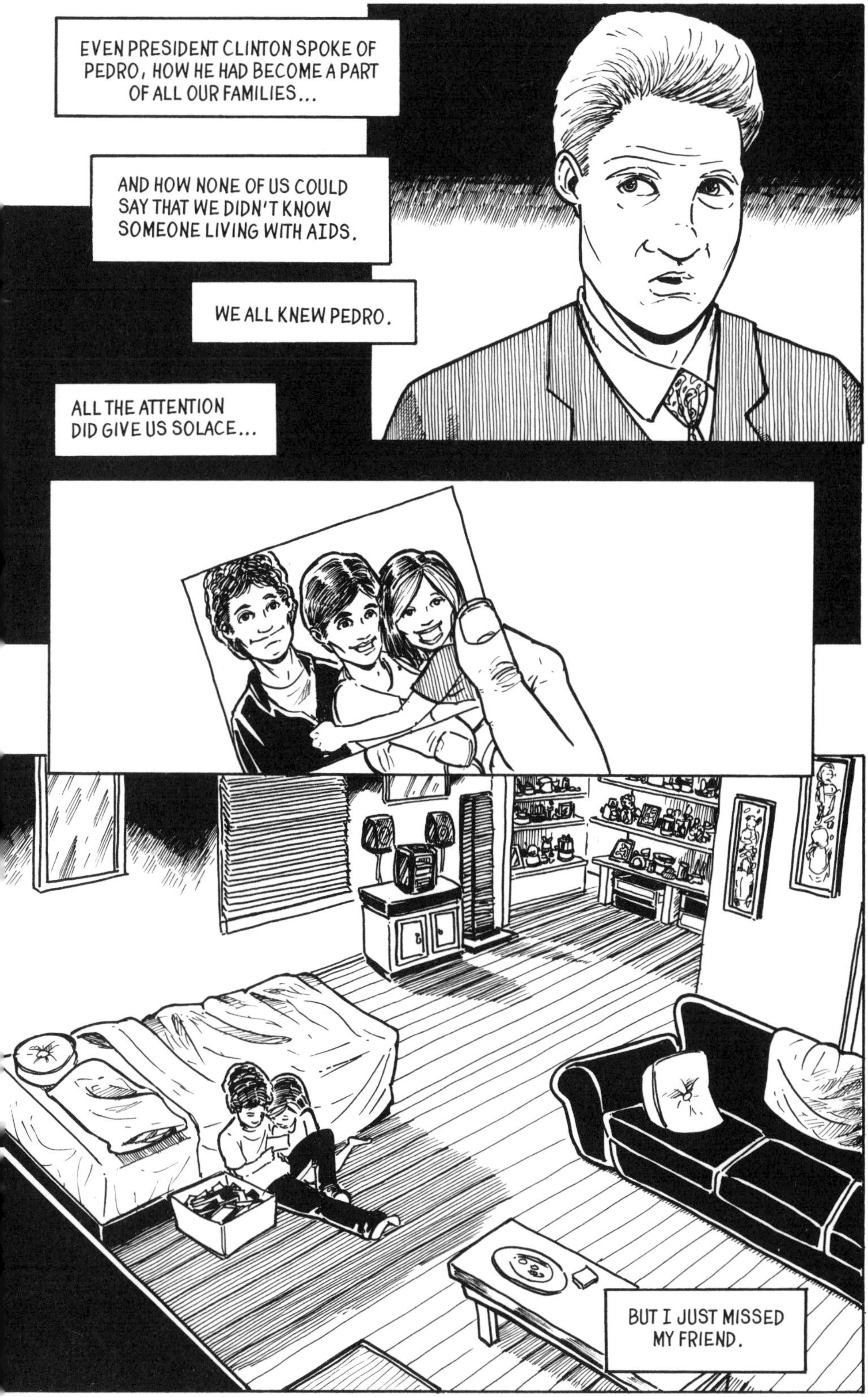
EVEN PRESIDENT CLINTON SPOKE OF PEDRO, HOW HE HAD BECOME A PART OF ALL OUR FAMILIES...
AND HOW NONE OF US COULD SAY THAT WE DIDN'T KNOW SOMEONE LIVING WITH AIDS.
WE ALL KNEW PEDRO.
ALL THE ATTENTION DID GIVE US SOLACE...
BUT I JUST MISSED MY FRIEND.

PEDRO'S FUNERAL
WAS ON NOVEMBER 13.

HE LIES NEXT
TO HIS MOTHER.

WITHOUT CATCHING MY BREATH, I WAS LECTURING THE NEXT WEEK. ANOTHER AFTER THAT, ANOTHER AFTER THAT.

I KEPT SPEAKING TO WHOEVER WOULD LISTEN.

IT WAS THE ONLY THING I COULD THINK OF TO DO.

A MONTH LATER I WAS LECTURING AT A MIDDLE SCHOOL, MY FIRST. I'D NEVER SPOKEN TO A GROUP THIS YOUNG BEFORE.

IT'S EASIER TALKING TO COLLEGE STUDENTS. THEY'RE *ALWAYS* THINKING ABOUT SEX, ANYWAY. YOU JUST HAVE TO ADD A COUPLE OF IQ POINTS TO THEIR HORMONES.

I DECIDED THAT BEING FRANK, STRAIGHTFORWARD, AND HONEST WITH THEM WAS THE ONLY WAY TO DO IT.

CONDOMS ARE LATEX SHEATHS. YOU SEE THEY KIND OF LOOK LIKE SOCKS BUT THEY DON'T GO ON YOUR FEET.

STILL, IT'S NOT EASY. YOU EVER SAY **PENIS** TO 200 SEVENTH GRADERS? IT'S LIKE THROWING WATER ON CHICKENS.

THE TEACHERS WERE ACTUALLY A LOT WORSE. YOU COULD FEEL THE MORE CONSERVATIVE ONES START TO SQUIRM AS I GOT UP TO STUFF LIKE MUTUAL MASTURBATION AND DENTAL DAMS.

DIDN'T THEY FIRE THE SURGEON GENERAL FOR CRAP LIKE THIS?

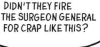

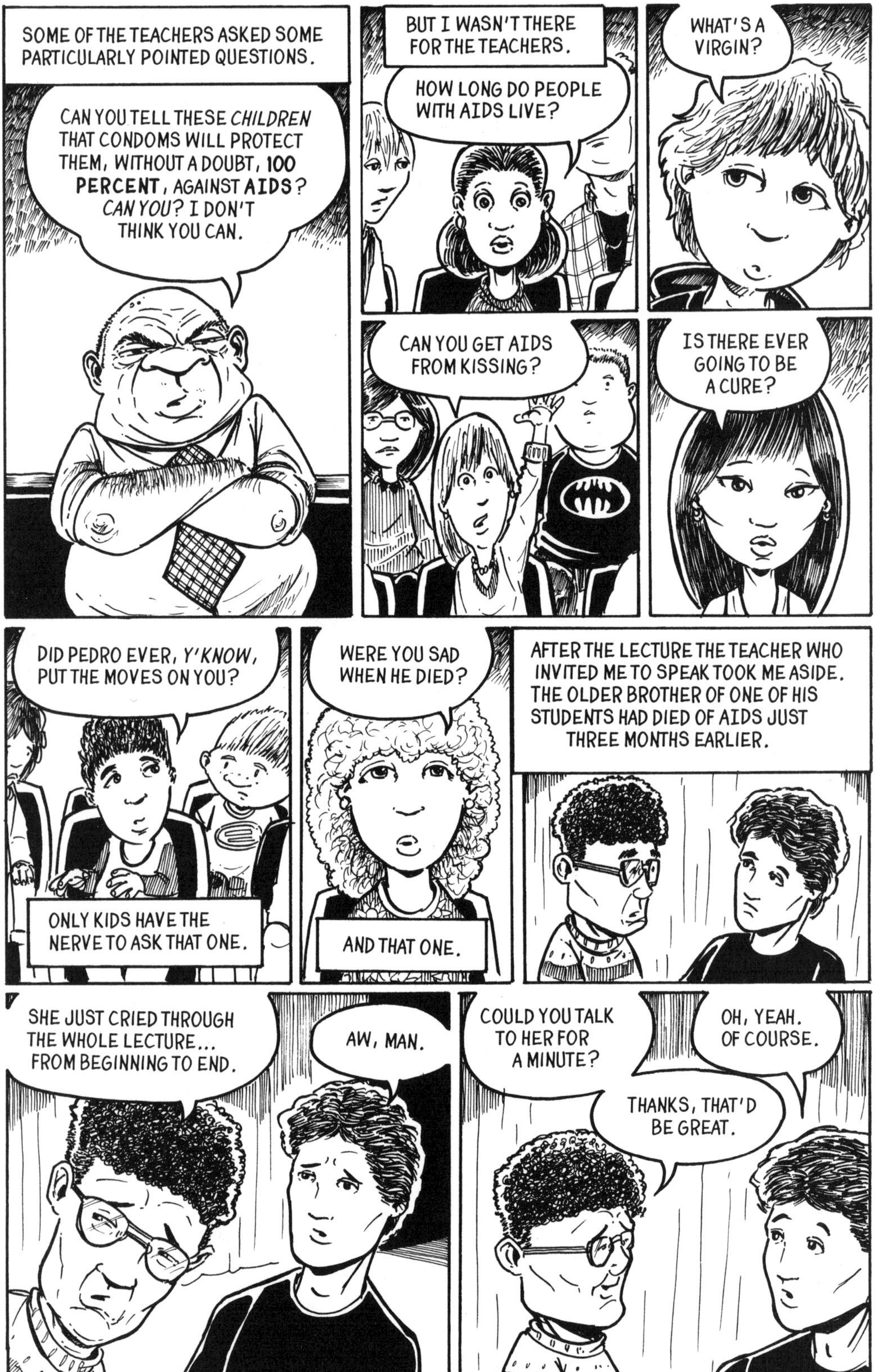
SOME OF THE TEACHERS ASKED SOME PARTICULARLY POINTED QUESTIONS.
CAN YOU TELL THESE *CHILDREN* THAT CONDOMS WILL PROTECT THEM, WITHOUT A DOUBT, **100 PERCENT**, AGAINST **AIDS**? *CAN YOU*? I DON'T THINK YOU CAN.
BUT I WASN'T THERE FOR THE TEACHERS.
HOW LONG DO PEOPLE WITH AIDS LIVE?
WHAT'S A VIRGIN?
CAN YOU GET AIDS FROM KISSING?
IS THERE EVER GOING TO BE A CURE?
DID PEDRO EVER, *Y'KNOW*, PUT THE MOVES ON YOU?
ONLY KIDS HAVE THE NERVE TO ASK THAT ONE.
WERE YOU SAD WHEN HE DIED?
AND THAT ONE.
AFTER THE LECTURE THE TEACHER WHO INVITED ME TO SPEAK TOOK ME ASIDE. THE OLDER BROTHER OF ONE OF HIS STUDENTS HAD DIED OF AIDS JUST THREE MONTHS EARLIER.
SHE JUST CRIED THROUGH THE WHOLE LECTURE... FROM BEGINNING TO END.
AW, MAN.
COULD YOU TALK TO HER FOR A MINUTE?
OH, YEAH. OF COURSE.
THANKS, THAT'D BE GREAT.

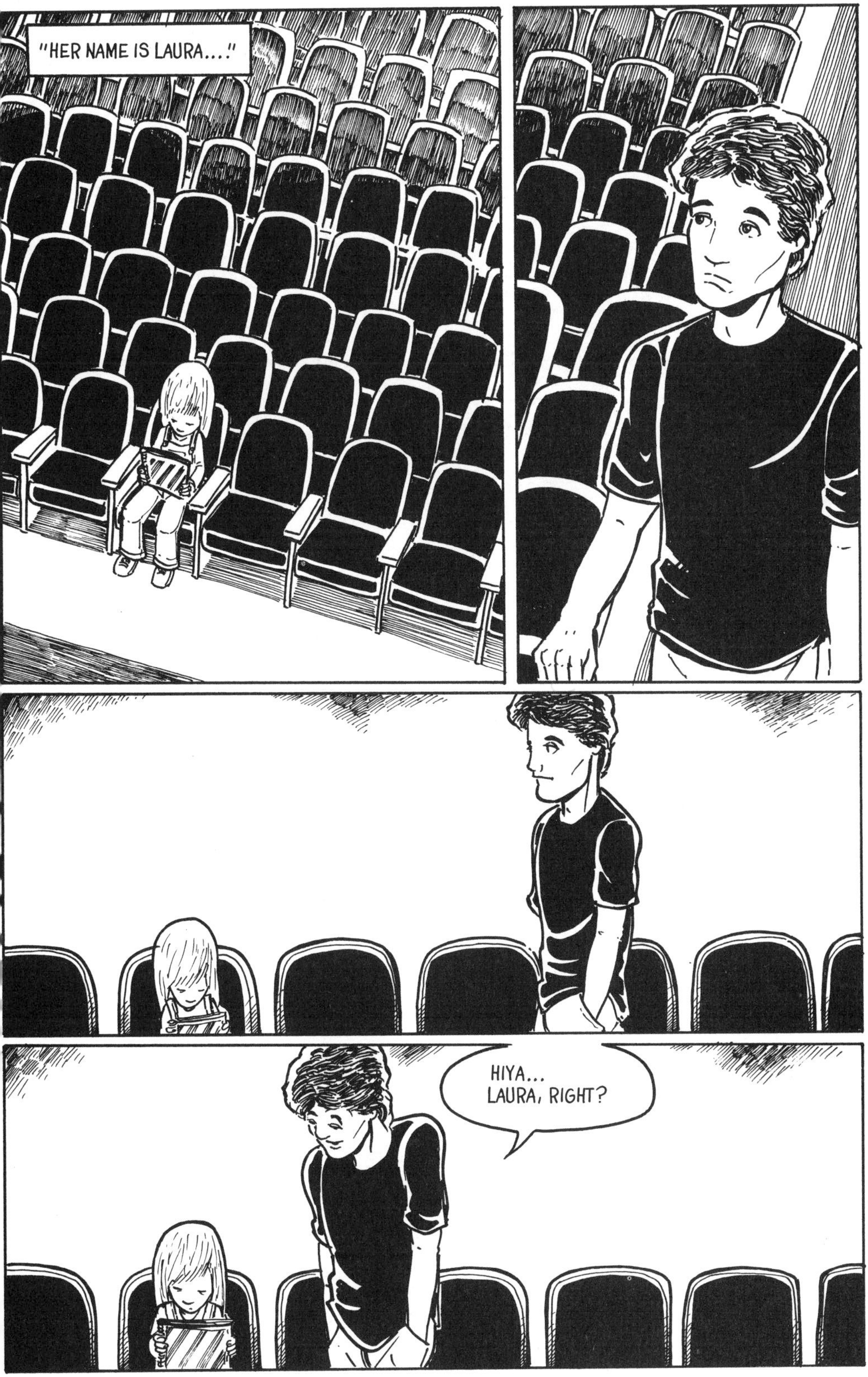
"HER NAME IS LAURA...."
HIYA...
LAURA, RIGHT?

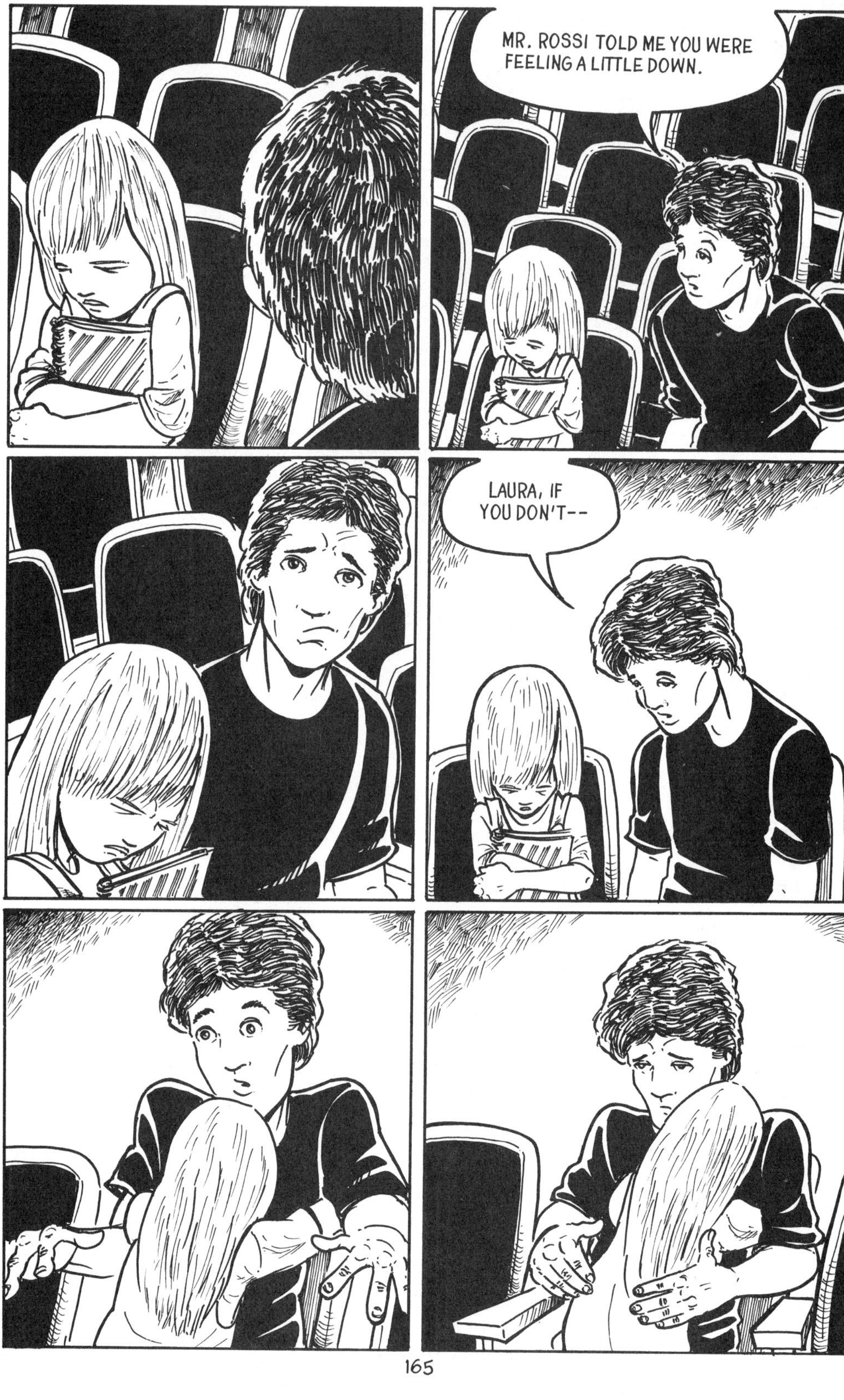
MR. ROSSI TOLD ME YOU WERE
FEELING A LITTLE DOWN.
LAURA, IF
YOU DON'T--

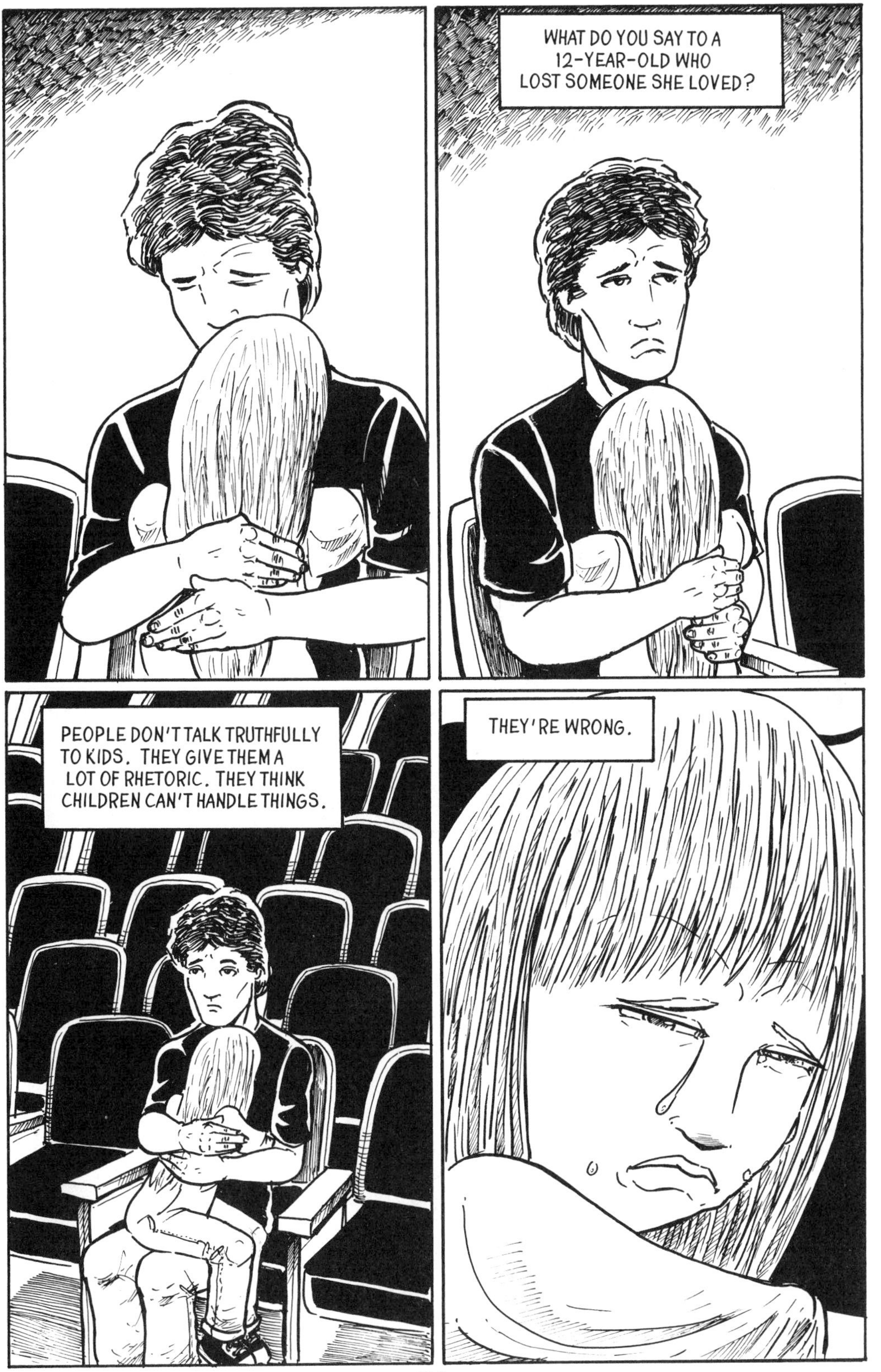
WHAT DO YOU SAY TO A 12-YEAR-OLD WHO LOST SOMEONE SHE LOVED?
PEOPLE DON'T TALK TRUTHFULLY TO KIDS. THEY GIVE THEM A LOT OF RHETORIC. THEY THINK CHILDREN CAN'T HANDLE THINGS.
THEY'RE WRONG.

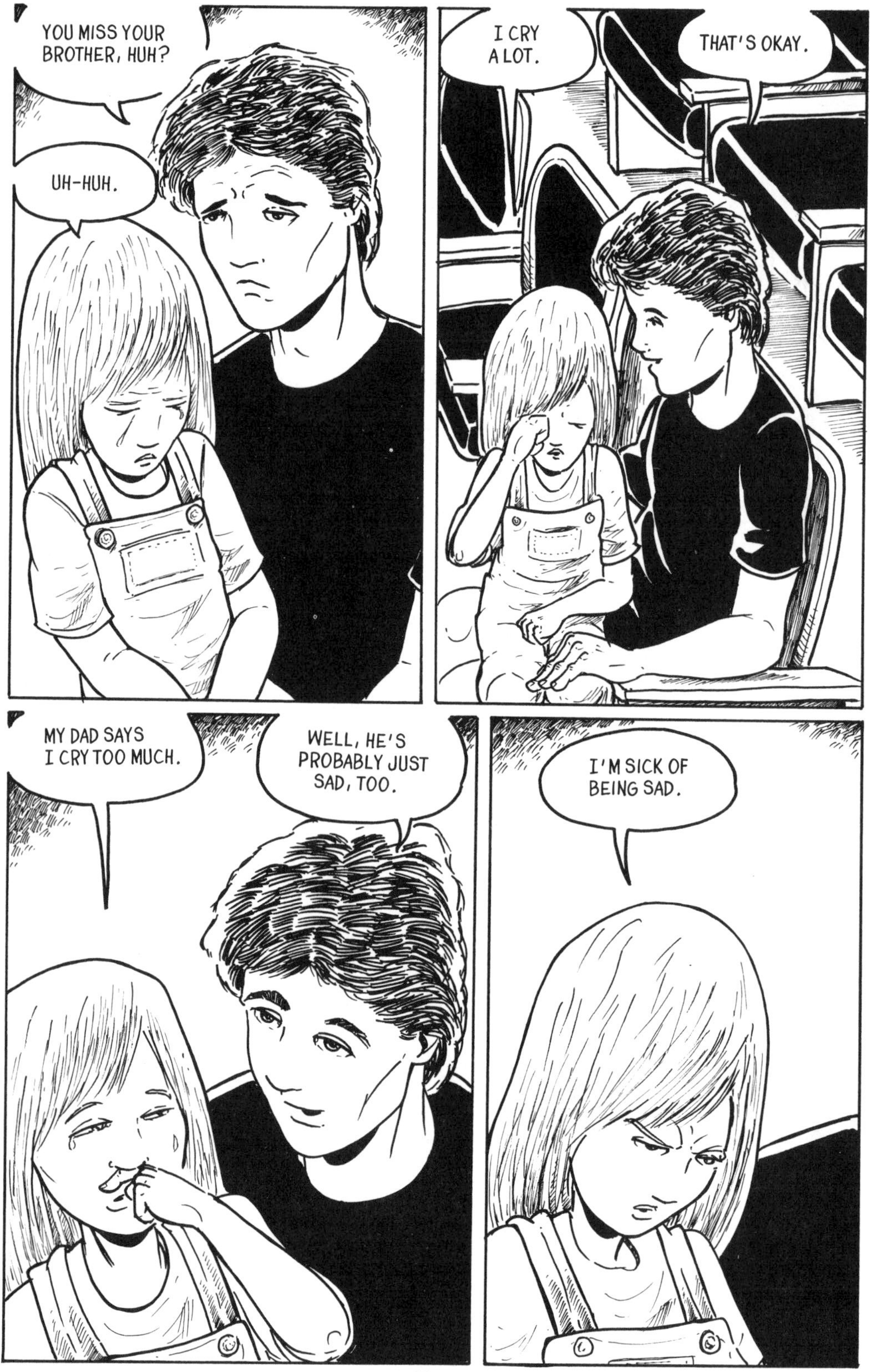
YOU MISS YOUR BROTHER, HUH?
UH-HUH.
I CRY A LOT.
THAT'S OKAY.
MY DAD SAYS I CRY TOO MUCH.
WELL, HE'S PROBABLY JUST SAD, TOO.
I'M SICK OF BEING SAD.

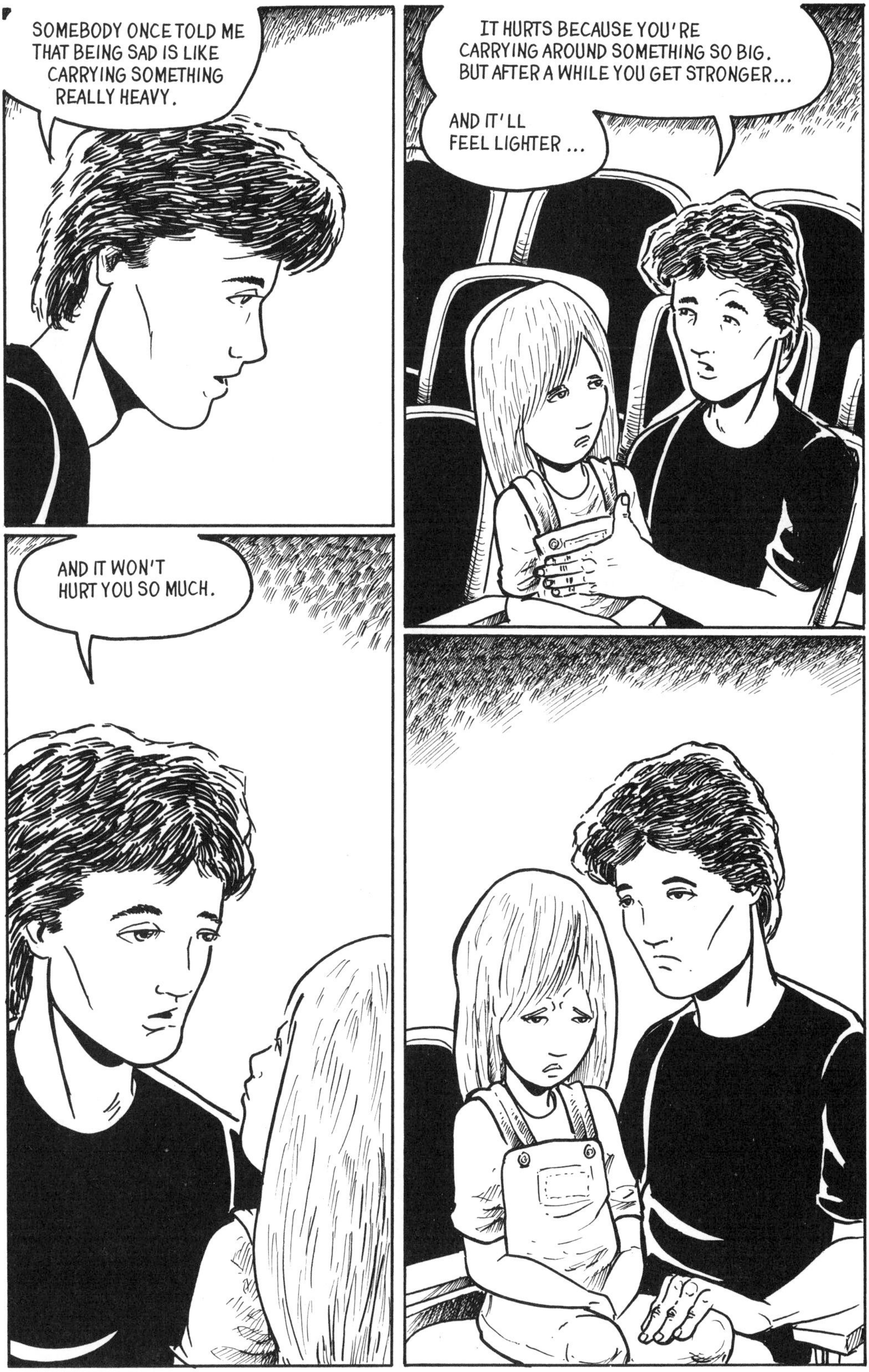
SOMEBODY ONCE TOLD ME THAT BEING SAD IS LIKE CARRYING SOMETHING REALLY HEAVY.
IT HURTS BECAUSE YOU'RE CARRYING AROUND SOMETHING SO BIG. BUT AFTER A WHILE YOU GET STRONGER...
AND IT'LL FEEL LIGHTER ...
AND IT WON'T HURT YOU SO MUCH.

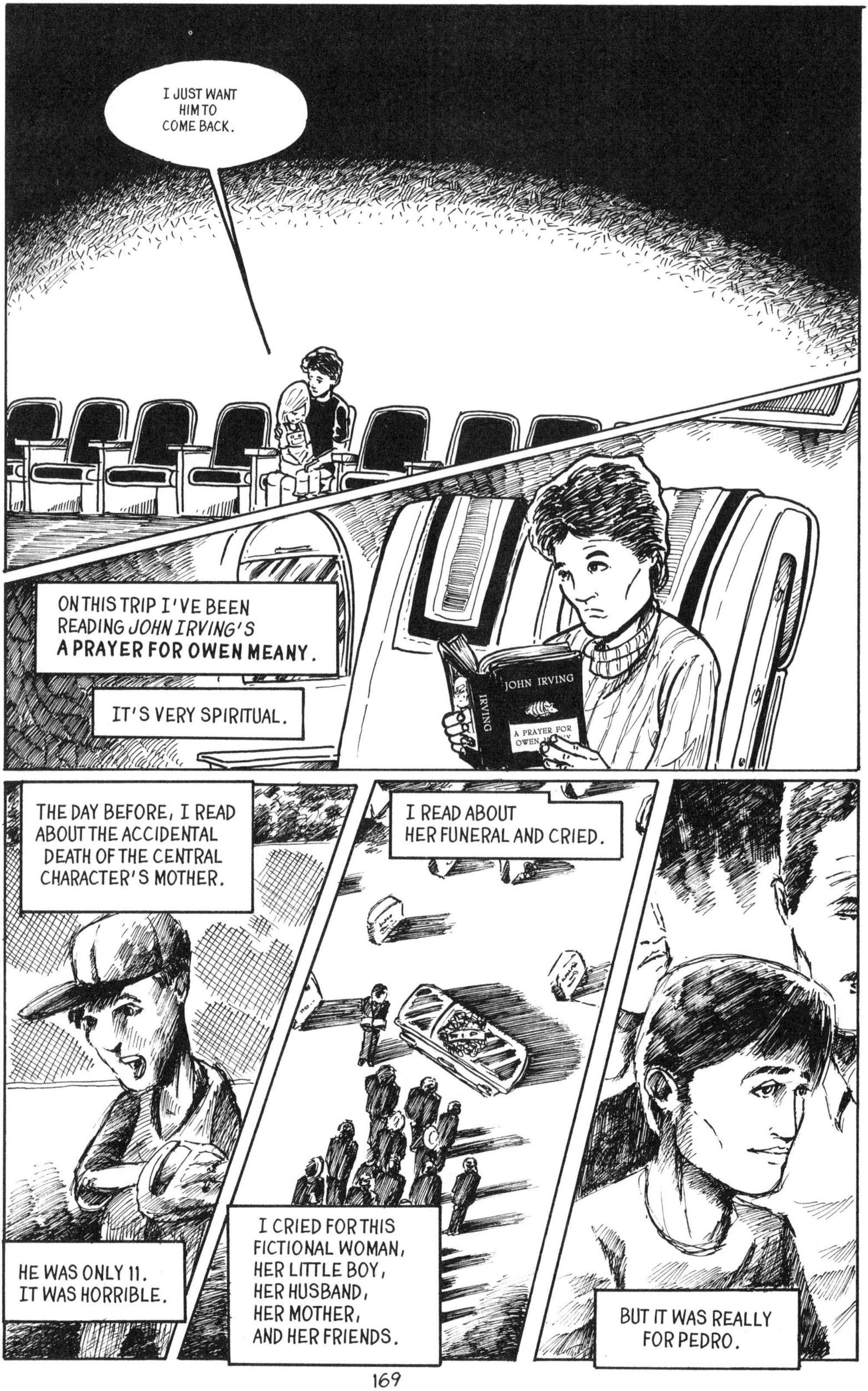
I JUST WANT HIM TO COME BACK.
ON THIS TRIP I'VE BEEN READING JOHN IRVING'S A PRAYER FOR OWEN MEANY.
IT'S VERY SPIRITUAL.
JOHN IRVING
IRVING
A PRAYER FOR
THE DAY BEFORE, I READ ABOUT THE ACCIDENTAL DEATH OF THE CENTRAL CHARACTER'S MOTHER.
HE WAS ONLY 11. IT WAS HORRIBLE.
I READ ABOUT HER FUNERAL AND CRIED.
I CRIED FOR THIS FICTIONAL WOMAN, HER LITTLE BOY, HER HUSBAND, HER MOTHER, AND HER FRIENDS.
BUT IT WAS REALLY FOR PEDRO.

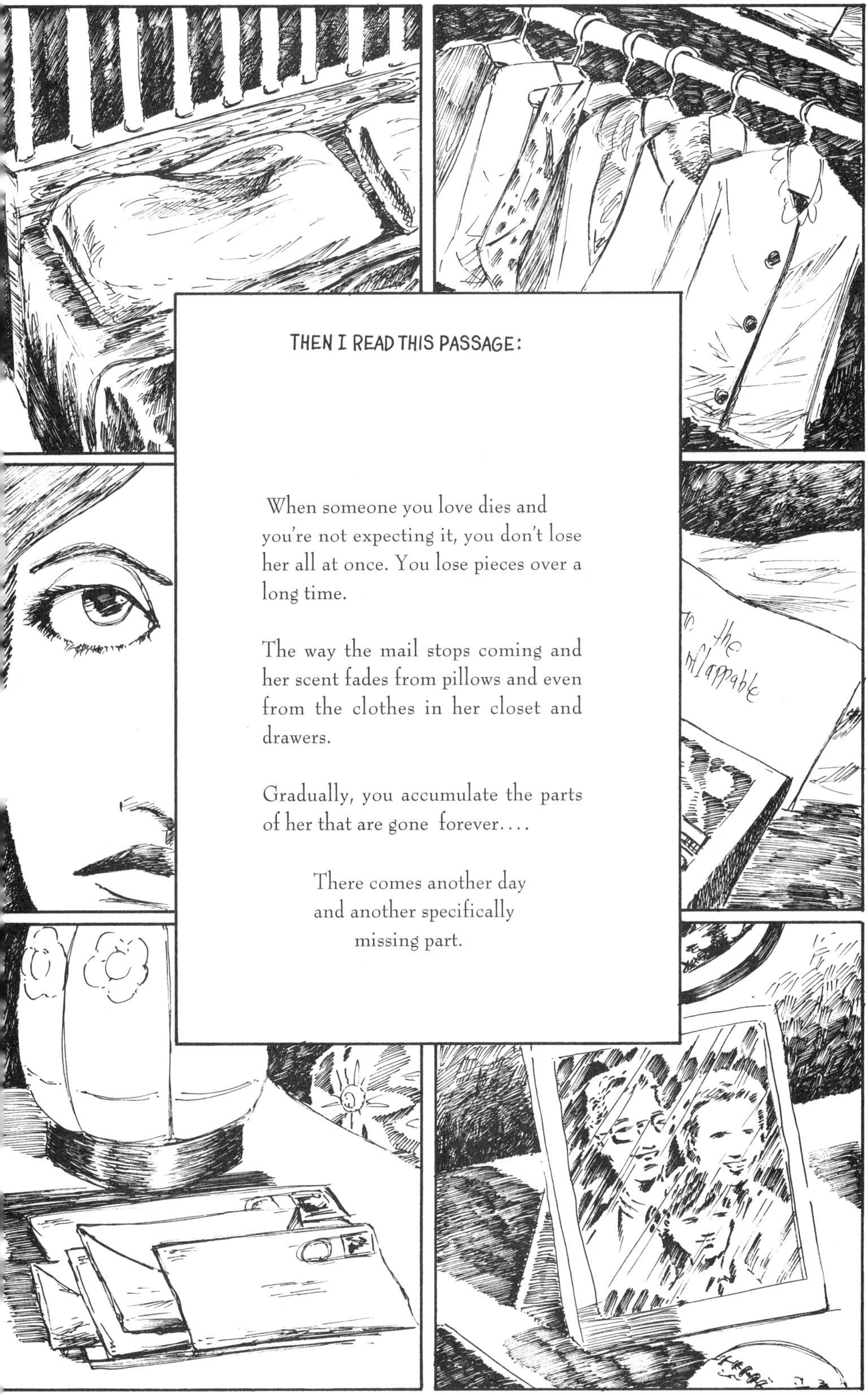
THEN I READ THIS PASSAGE:
When someone you love dies and you're not expecting it, you don't lose her all at once. You lose pieces over a long time.
The way the mail stops coming and her scent fades from pillows and even from the clothes in her closet and drawers.
Gradually, you accumulate the parts of her that are gone forever....
There comes another day and another specifically missing part.

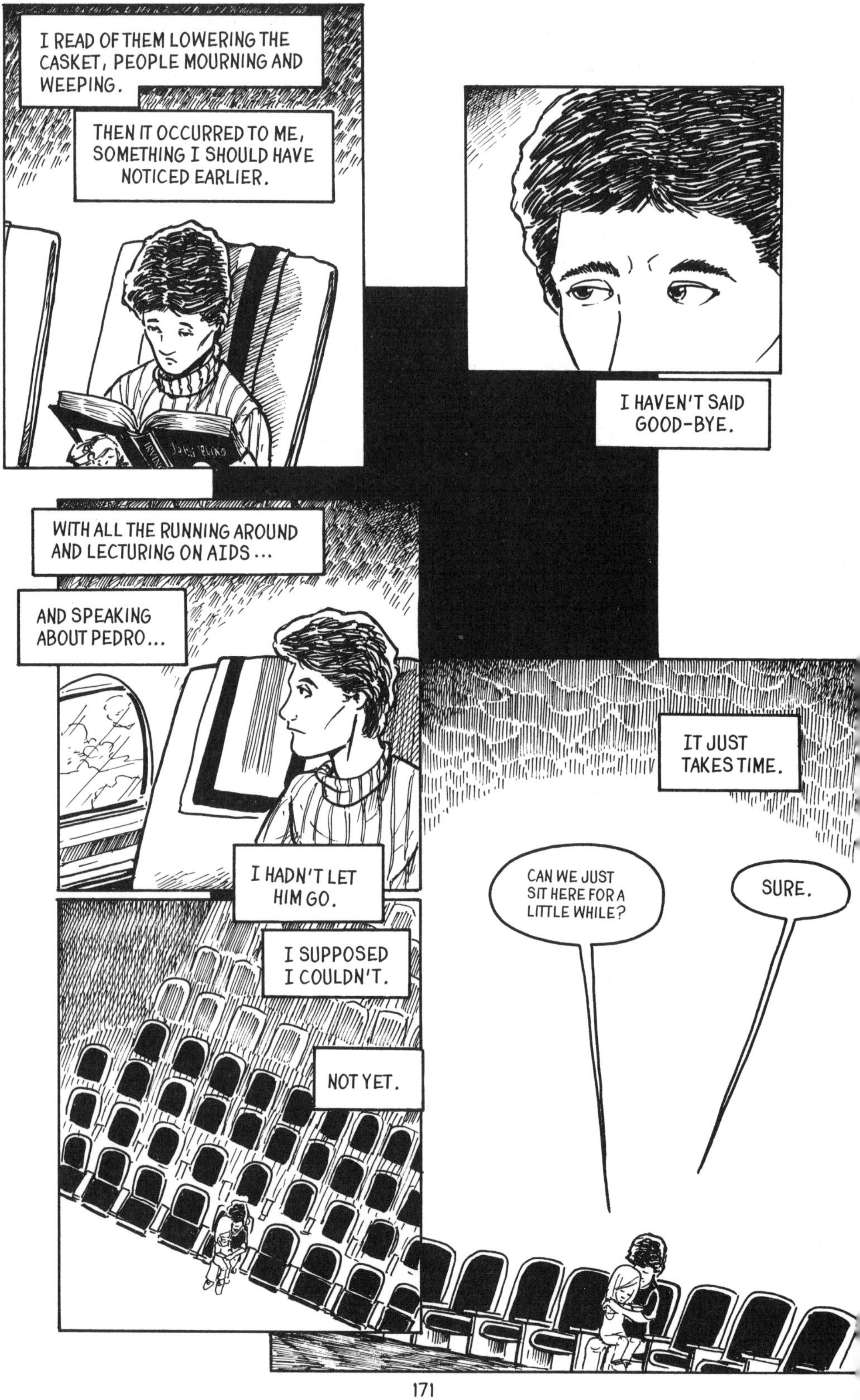

I READ OF THEM LOWERING THE CASKET, PEOPLE MOURNING AND WEEPING.
THEN IT OCCURRED TO ME, SOMETHING I SHOULD HAVE NOTICED EARLIER.
I HAVEN'T SAID GOOD-BYE.
WITH ALL THE RUNNING AROUND AND LECTURING ON AIDS...
AND SPEAKING ABOUT PEDRO...
I HADN'T LET HIM GO.
I SUPPOSED I COULDN'T.
NOT YET.
IT JUST TAKES TIME.
CAN WE JUST SIT HERE FOR A LITTLE WHILE?
SURE.

EPILOGUE

THE RETURN OF THE SHUTTLE GUY

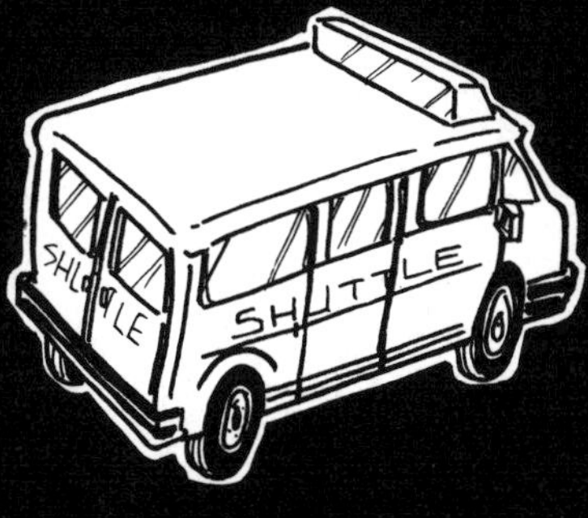
SHUTTLE
SHUTTLE

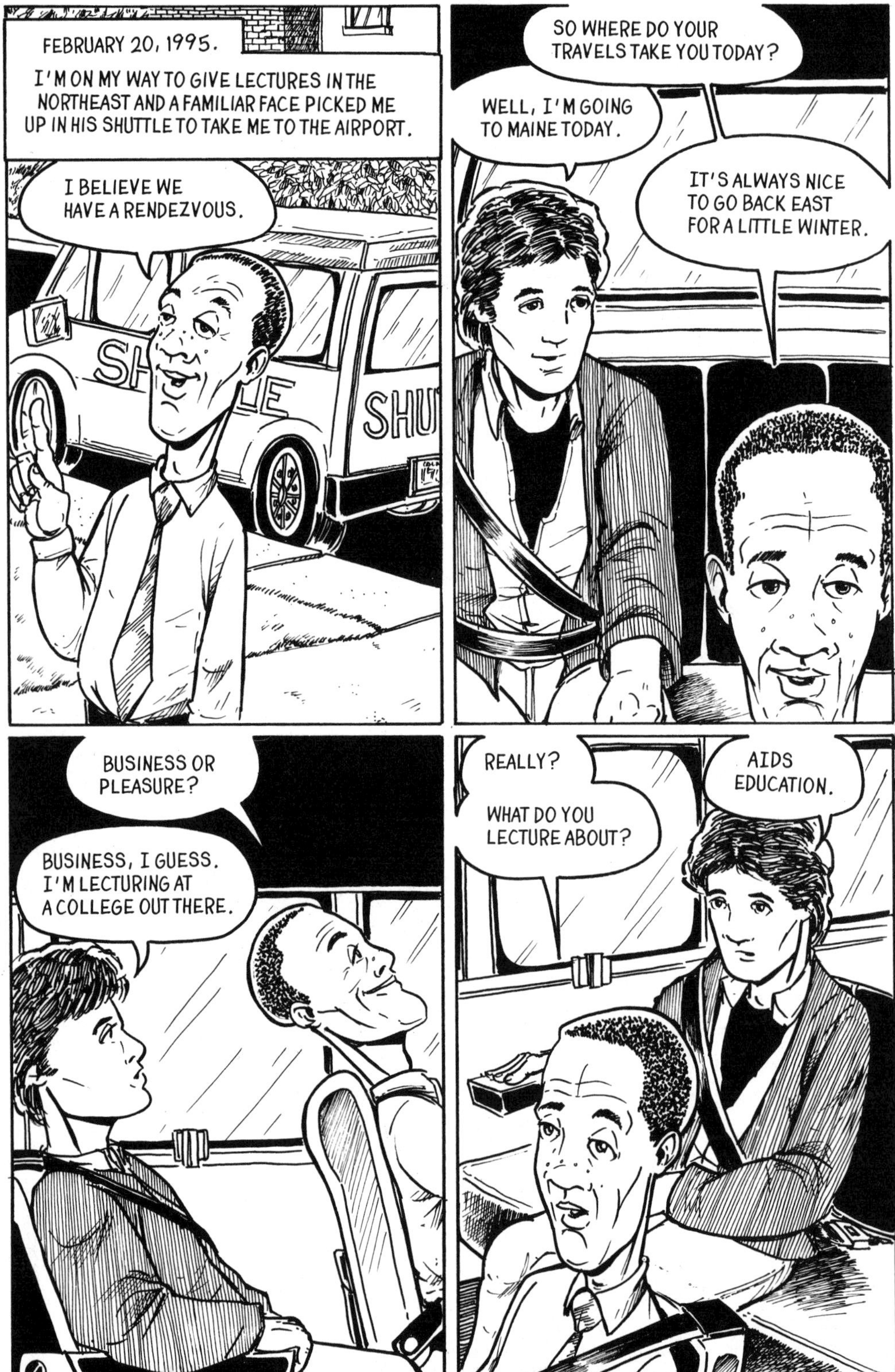
FEBRUARY 20, 1995.
I'M ON MY WAY TO GIVE LECTURES IN THE NORTHEAST AND A FAMILIAR FACE PICKED ME UP IN HIS SHUTTLE TO TAKE ME TO THE AIRPORT.
I BELIEVE WE HAVE A RENDEZVOUS.
SHUTTLE
SO WHERE DO YOUR TRAVELS TAKE YOU TODAY?
WELL, I'M GOING TO MAINE TODAY.
IT'S ALWAYS NICE TO GO BACK EAST FOR A LITTLE WINTER.
BUSINESS OR PLEASURE?
BUSINESS, I GUESS. I'M LECTURING AT A COLLEGE OUT THERE.
REALLY?
WHAT DO YOU LECTURE ABOUT?
AIDS EDUCATION.

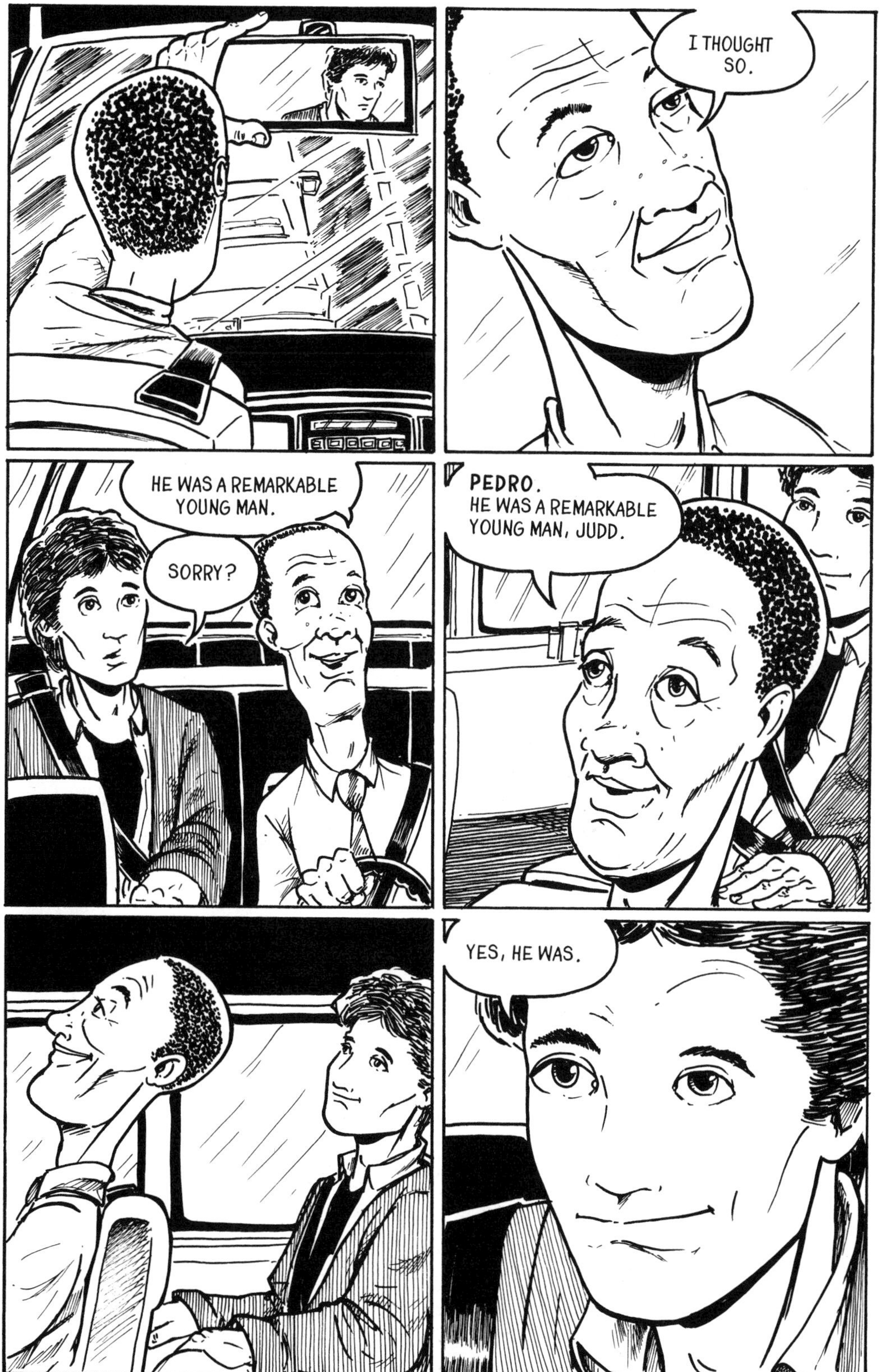
I THOUGHT SO.
HE WAS A REMARKABLE YOUNG MAN.
SORRY?
PEDRO.
HE WAS A REMARKABLE YOUNG MAN, JUDD.
YES, HE WAS.

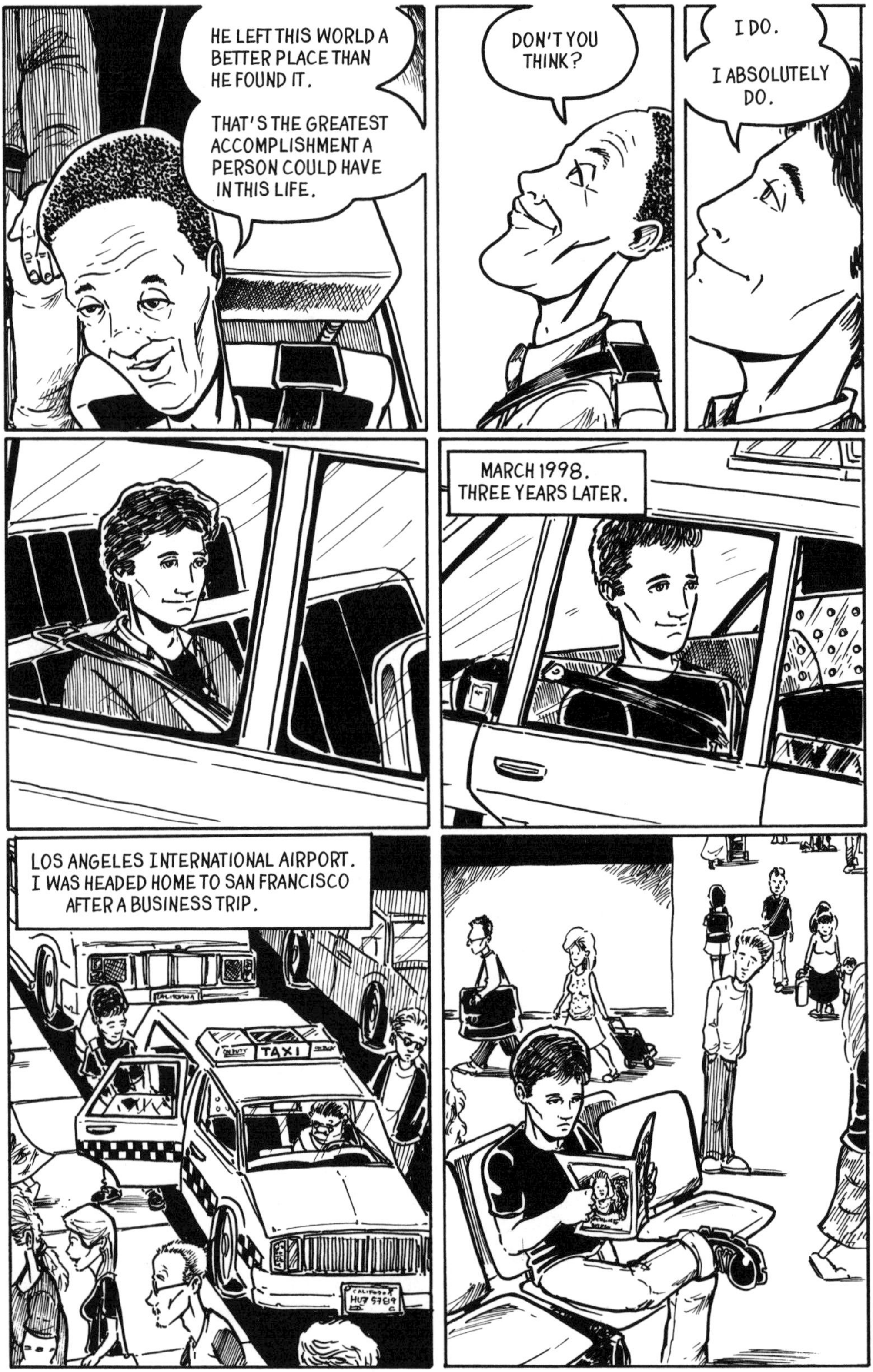
HE LEFT THIS WORLD A BETTER PLACE THAN HE FOUND IT.
THAT'S THE GREATEST ACCOMPLISHMENT A PERSON COULD HAVE IN THIS LIFE.
DON'T YOU THINK?
I DO.
I ABSOLUTELY DO.
MARCH 1998. THREE YEARS LATER.
LOS ANGELES INTERNATIONAL AIRPORT. I WAS HEADED HOME TO SAN FRANCISCO AFTER A BUSINESS TRIP.
TAXI

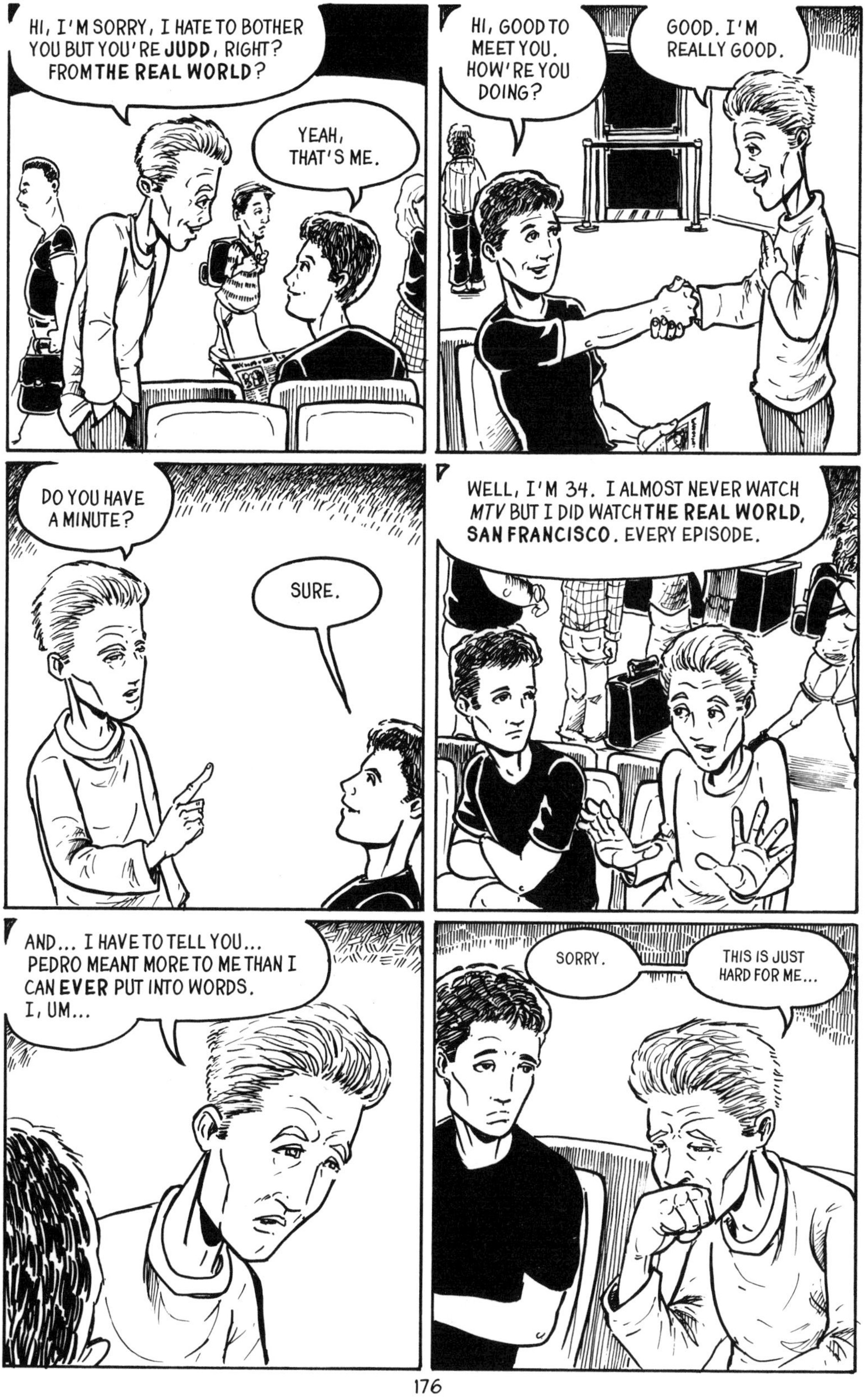
HI, I'M SORRY, I HATE TO BOTHER YOU BUT YOU'RE **JUDD**, RIGHT? FROM **THE REAL WORLD**?
YEAH, THAT'S ME.
HI, GOOD TO MEET YOU. HOW'RE YOU DOING?
GOOD. I'M REALLY GOOD.
DO YOU HAVE A MINUTE?
SURE.
WELL, I'M 34. I ALMOST NEVER WATCH *MTV* BUT I DID WATCH **THE REAL WORLD, SAN FRANCISCO**. EVERY EPISODE.
AND... I HAVE TO TELL YOU... PEDRO MEANT MORE TO ME THAN I CAN **EVER** PUT INTO WORDS. I, UM...
SORRY.
THIS IS JUST HARD FOR ME...

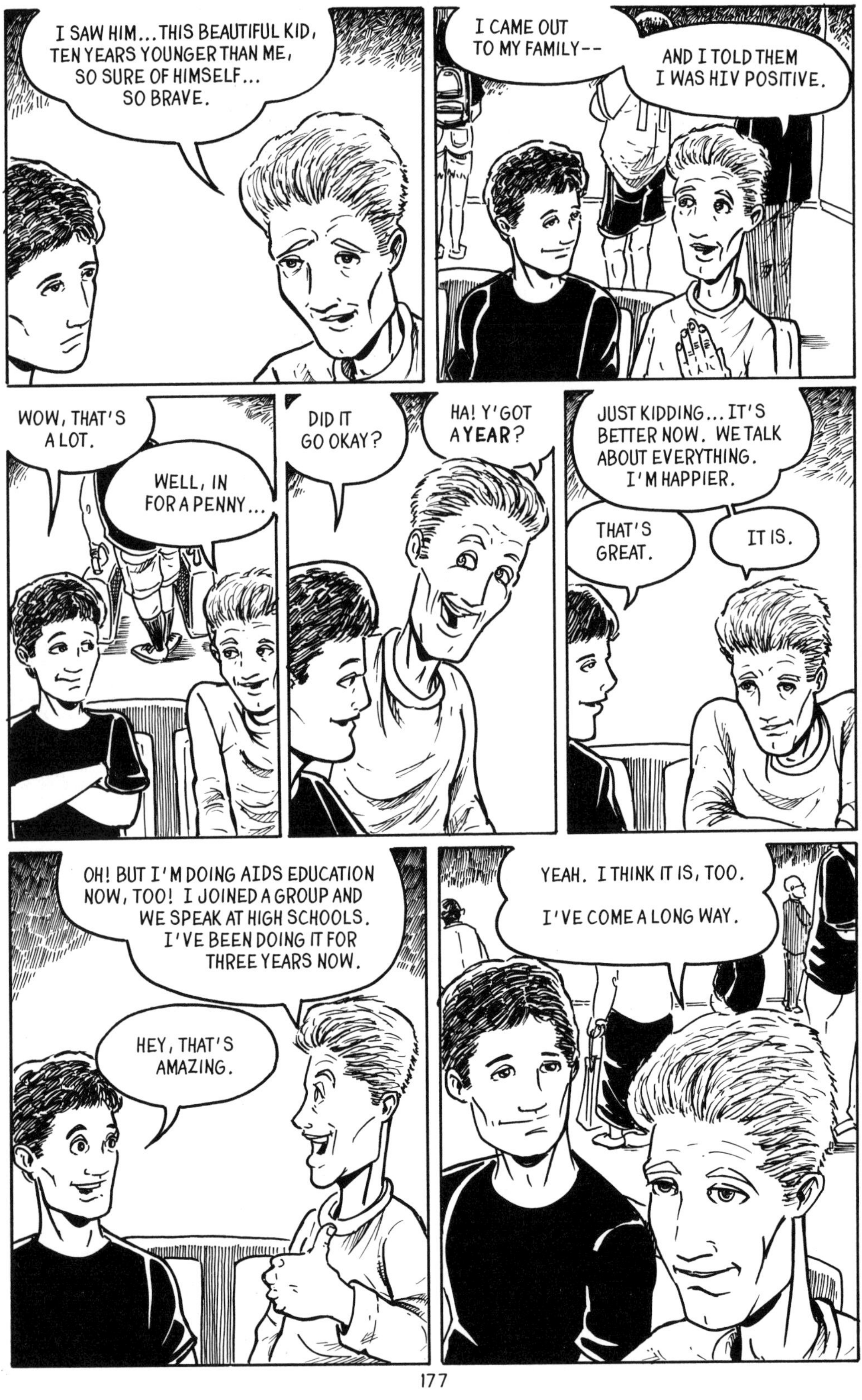
I SAW HIM... THIS BEAUTIFUL KID, TEN YEARS YOUNGER THAN ME, SO SURE OF HIMSELF... SO BRAVE.
I CAME OUT TO MY FAMILY--
AND I TOLD THEM I WAS HIV POSITIVE.
WOW, THAT'S A LOT.
WELL, IN FOR A PENNY...
DID IT GO OKAY?
HA! Y'GOT A YEAR?
JUST KIDDING... IT'S BETTER NOW. WE TALK ABOUT EVERYTHING. I'M HAPPIER.
THAT'S GREAT.
IT IS.
OH! BUT I'M DOING AIDS EDUCATION NOW, TOO! I JOINED A GROUP AND WE SPEAK AT HIGH SCHOOLS. I'VE BEEN DOING IT FOR THREE YEARS NOW.
HEY, THAT'S AMAZING.
YEAH. I THINK IT IS, TOO.
I'VE COME A LONG WAY.

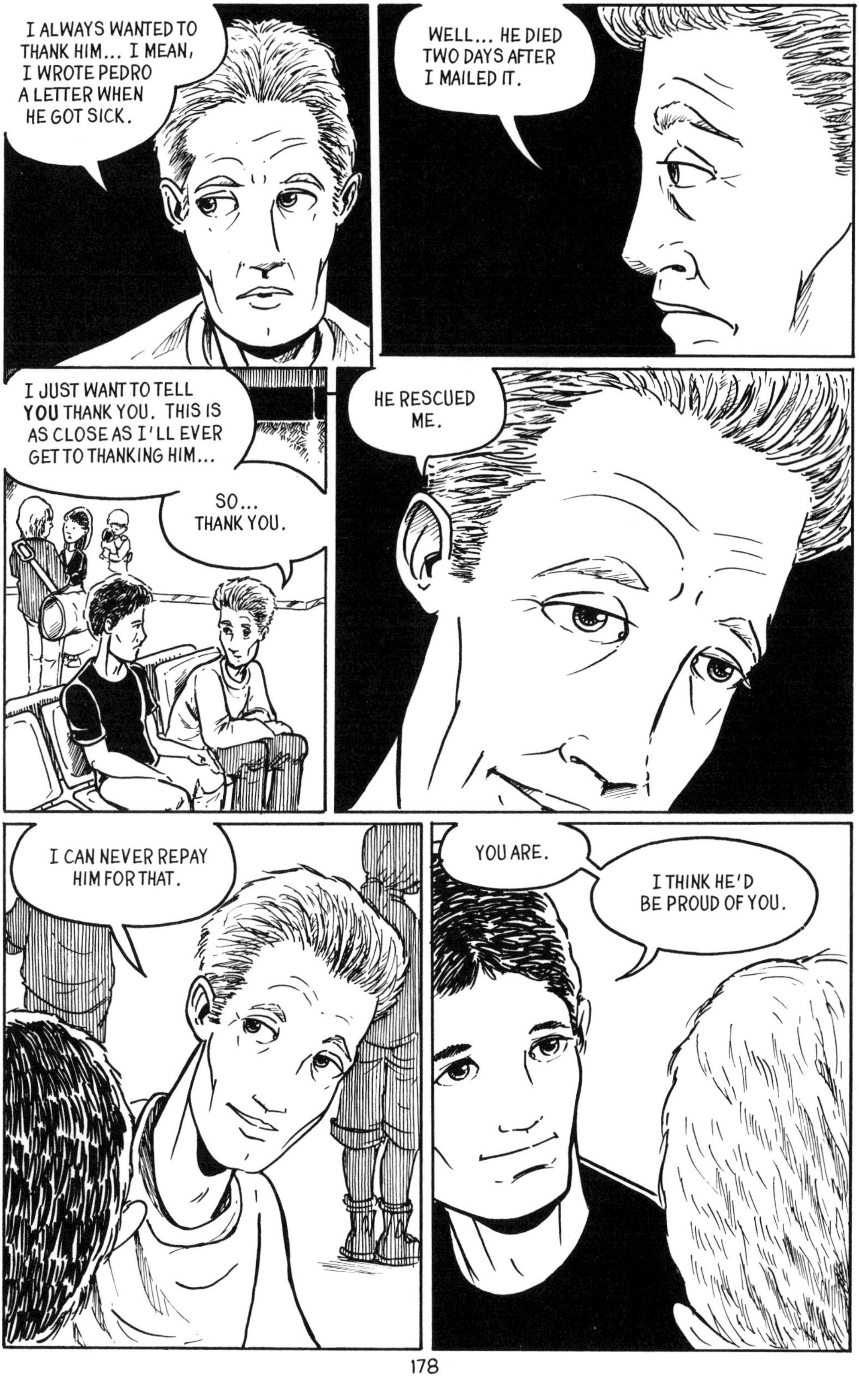
I ALWAYS WANTED TO THANK HIM... I MEAN, I WROTE PEDRO A LETTER WHEN HE GOT SICK.
WELL... HE DIED TWO DAYS AFTER I MAILED IT.
I JUST WANT TO TELL **YOU** THANK YOU. THIS IS AS CLOSE AS I'LL EVER GET TO THANKING HIM...
SO... THANK YOU.
HE RESCUED ME.
I CAN NEVER REPAY HIM FOR THAT.
YOU ARE.
I THINK HE'D BE PROUD OF YOU.

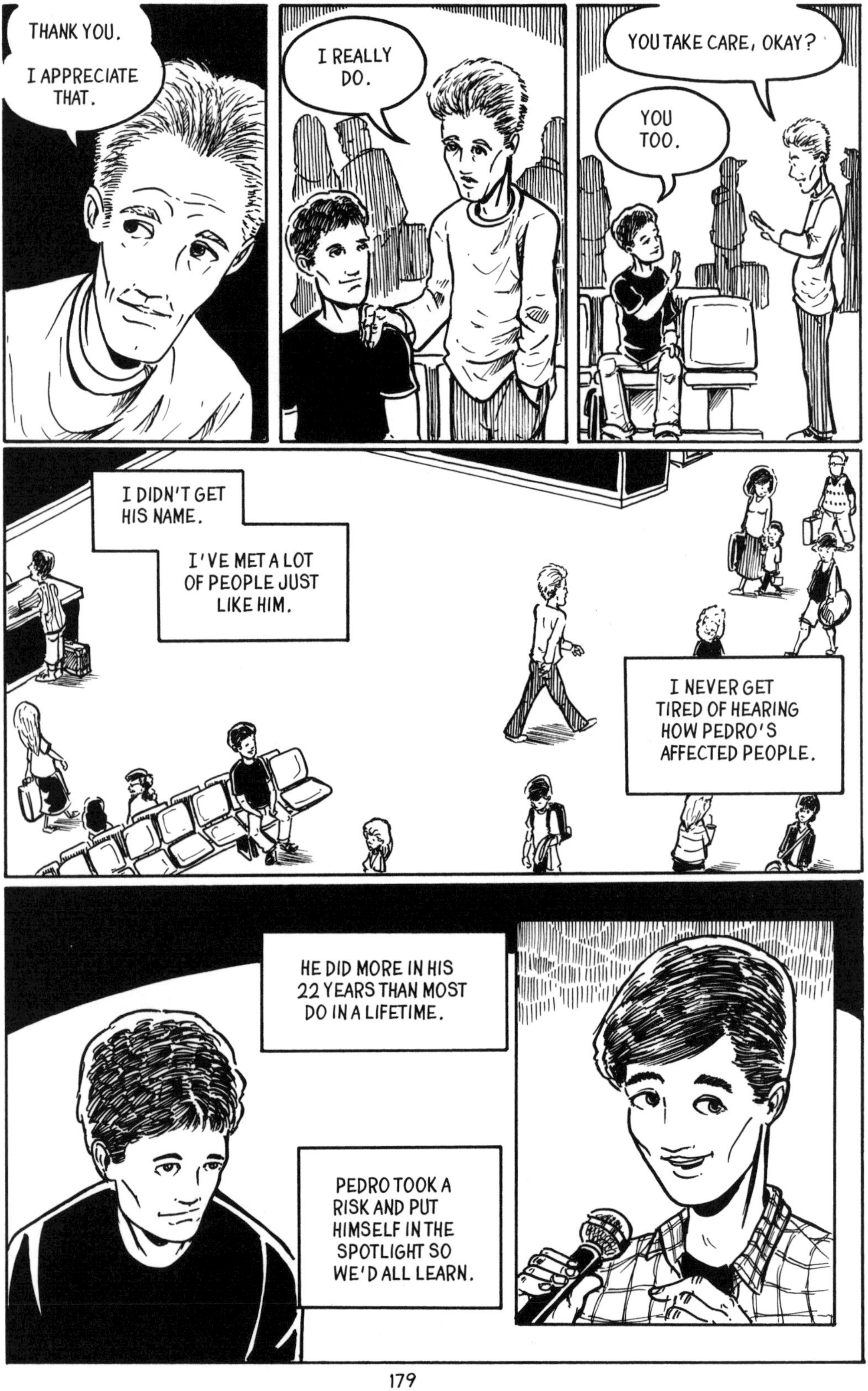
THANK YOU.
I APPRECIATE THAT.
I REALLY DO.
YOU TAKE CARE, OKAY?
YOU TOO.
I DIDN'T GET HIS NAME.
I'VE MET A LOT OF PEOPLE JUST LIKE HIM.
I NEVER GET TIRED OF HEARING HOW PEDRO'S AFFECTED PEOPLE.
HE DID MORE IN HIS 22 YEARS THAN MOST DO IN A LIFETIME.
PEDRO TOOK A RISK AND PUT HIMSELF IN THE SPOTLIGHT SO WE'D ALL LEARN.

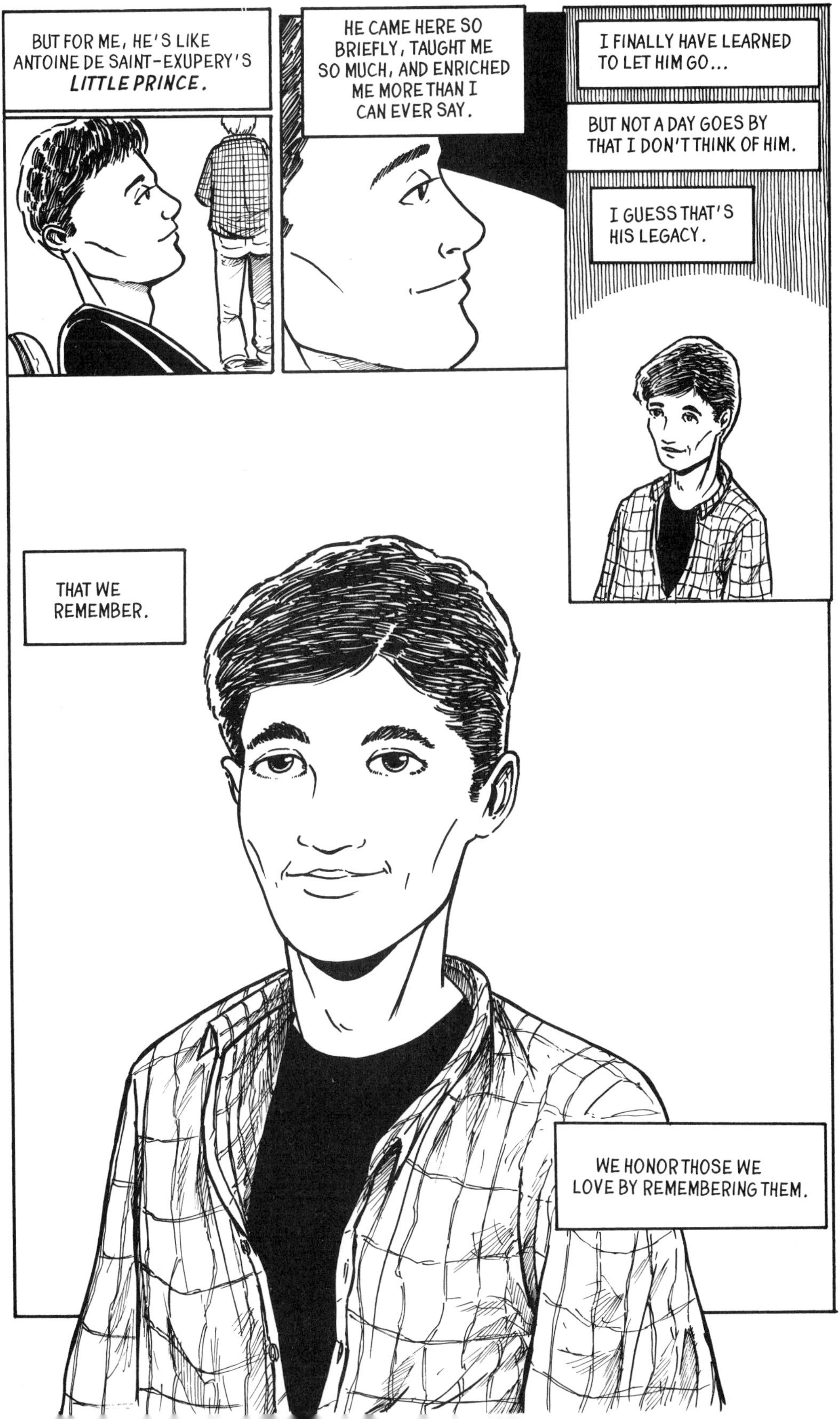
BUT FOR ME, HE'S LIKE ANTOINE DE SAINT-EXUPERY'S *LITTLE PRINCE*.
HE CAME HERE SO BRIEFLY, TAUGHT ME SO MUCH, AND ENRICHED ME MORE THAN I CAN EVER SAY.
I FINALLY HAVE LEARNED TO LET HIM GO...
BUT NOT A DAY GOES BY THAT I DON'T THINK OF HIM.
I GUESS THAT'S HIS LEGACY.
THAT WE REMEMBER.
WE HONOR THOSE WE LOVE BY REMEMBERING THEM.

ACKNOWLEDGMENTS

This book was more than two and a half years in the making. That doesn't include the time, guidance, and hand-holding that went on for me to be in a place that I could begin telling this story. There are many people to whom I owe my thanks. These are just a few of them:

I'd like to thank Pedro Zamora. I know this may seem redundant after this entire tale, but there's one more nod I'd like to give to Pedro. Aside from the friendship, love, and lessons, Pedro, thank you for giving me my voice. Before writing and drawing this book, I'd never truly found my way as a storyteller. You've given me that. So, once again, thank you. It's one more way that I can never repay you.

And thanks:

To my mom and dad, Bobbi and Michael Winick, who have supported me, cajoled me, tolerated me, and made me everything that I am. They created a home that welcomed all my creative endeavors and provided me anything that I needed to attain my goals. *Nobody* drives me crazy like you two. And I love you for it. (I know I make you nuts, too.)

To my big brother, Orin, whom I couldn't be more different from *and* more like. His love and support have been indispensable. He knew about this book before almost anyone. He quietly read and rooted for it. (Thanks, O!)

To the good folks at MTV! *The Real World* has proven to be a deeper experience than I ever could have fathomed. I have these folks to thank: Mary-Ellis Bunim and Jon Murray, the producers of *The Real World*. They were the orchestrators who possessed the guts, the finesse, the sensitivity, and the compassion to introduce Pedro to the world. We owe them—and Lisa Berger, executive producer of *RW, San Francisco*—a great debt.

To the crew, the creative workhorses we lived, sweated,

laughed, and cried with for six months while they documented all of it on video: directors George Verschoor and Bob Fisher, as well as Adam Beckman, Billy Rainey, Clay Newbill, Craig Borders, Matt Kunitz, Laura Ganis, Rick de Oliveira, Kerry Rose, Tom Wardan, John Gumina, and, of course, David Albrecht. And also Toni Gallagher, Gordon Cassidy, Scott Freeman, Wendy Battles, David Rupel, Oscar Dektyar, and Laura Folger. Also about another sixty people who put their time and strength into making our season something special.

To my *RW* housemates Cory Murphy, Rachel Campos, Jo Rhodes, and Mohammed Bilal: We all sailed on the same ship, and only we know what it was really like.

To my mentors Linda Simensky and Cathy Guisewite: two of my friends who will insist that they have yet to help me. You're both wrong. You've both been amazing.

To my two readers Elizabeth Riley and Kelli Coleman: the people who read the first draft and warmly embraced it. I kept going because of you. Thanks, ladies.

To my buddies from the underworld, the comic-book community: You all told me over and over again how important this work was; it fueled the pump, gang. Thank-yous to Jamie Rich, Joe Nozemack, Brian Hibbs, Diana Schutz, Greg Rucka, and Jen Van Meter. Special thank-yous to Phil Jimenez and Bob Schreck. When it came to praising this book, you could hear these two guys on the fifty-yard line even if they sat at the top of the bleachers, if you know what I mean.

To my friends: Barry Wein, my oldest and dearest friend; Ben Holcomb, my art-school buddy; Noah Kuttler, my earliest reader, best biased critic, and cheerleader; Jon Gardin, who aided more than I can ever say in my life lessons and learning to stay *present;* Jessica Landaw, who let me crash on her couch during the aftermath of the show and tolerated me with the patience of a saint; Greg Weinstein, who's kept an eye out for me and has always *had my back,* as they like to say.

To Alex Escarano: It pains me that Alex can't see this book. A fellow artist, but more important, a believer in something larger than himself. Bless you, Alex. We miss you dearly.

To Eric Morganthaler: Eric wrote the first in-depth and substantive piece on Pedro. It was Eric who pulled from Pedro all the wonderful and rich stories of his youth and adolescence, as well as many of the tragedies. Eric's work was an indispensable source in the creation of this book, and I humbly thank him for it. Eric, you truly did us all who knew Pedro a service in preserving these moments.

To Armistead Maupin: We rarely get the chance to meet our heroes. I'm lucky; I know all three of mine. Two of them gave me life. The third is *this* man. And he's my friend. He's been an inspiration, a constant source of advice, and an unparalleled teacher. He has both my admiration and love.

To Eric Ciasullo: Rabbi Ciasullo pushed, debated, wept with, extolled upon, and exalted me more than anyone while I was creating this work. The most emotional, painful, and heartwarming parts of this story come from Eric's impassioned counsel. I am always in awe of his energy and his love.

To the Zamora family: From the moment I met all of you, you welcomed me into your family. That sentiment and those feelings have never wavered. You gave the world a remarkable gift in Pedro. Thank you for allowing me to share his memory again. It was an honor.

To Sean Sasser: I could not have published this book without Sean's blessing. I got far more than that. He has given me his trust, his love, and his friendship.

To Kara Woodruff, who fought like hell to get me on *The Real World* and followed through by looking out for me. Kara was my guardian angel.

To all the amazing folks at Henry Holt and Company: Laura Godwin, George Wen, Beth Feldman, Martha Rago, Stephani Hughes, and all of you who have treated this work with such respect and pursued its success with an enthusiasm that seems unending. Thank you, all.

To Marc Aronson, my editor: Marc said he wanted to publish it. Then, this gentleman, this prince, took me by the hand and painstakingly helped me make it something we were both proud of. All authors should be as lucky as I am to have Marc in my corner.

To Brad Meltzer: Brad was a lunatic about this book from day one. He praised, agonized, suggested, praised some more, offered, and pulled out every stop to help me make it a reality. If I hadn't found a publisher, I'm reasonably sure Brad would have published it himself. Brad, you are my partner in crime.

Lastly, Brad introduced me to this treasure—my agent, Jill Kneerim. Jill is a marvel. She had faith in this book and in me more than I did. With her gentle spirit, her bottomless pit of support, and her sheer force of will, she found this book a home. Keep in mind that I handed Jill a two-hundred-page comic book and said, "Find a publisher." She moved mountains until we did. As long as I live, Jill, I will be attempting to pay you back for this service. You are the champion of this book.

Sitting next to Jill is just one more person. Before pencil touched paper, before I had even considered the notion of doing it, there was Pam. Pam and I lived through this entire experience together, all the joys and the horrors. Pam helped me find the courage to write it out.

This is *our* book, not mine. I wouldn't have begun it, and it would never have been finished without her patience, her consideration, and her love. For two and a half years, this project has lived in our house like a person. It was a constant. Pam always believed in it and believed in me. And I don't know if any of you will understand this, but I like the person I am because she loves me. Thank you, sweetie. I can't imagine what I'd do without you.

Thank you, all. Now, be safe, and remember to love each other.

Judd Winick
San Francisco
January 2000

UPDATES

It has been more than six years since the events in this book have taken place. Here are a few updates on some of the people featured in this work:

Hector Zamora and his children Mily, Jesus, Hector, Lazaro, Eduardo, and Francisco, as well as his thirteen grandchildren, all reside in Miami. María Elena Zamora, Pedro's eldest sister, still resides in Cuba with her two daughters. On Pedro's behalf, Mily Zamora continues to work toward better AIDS education for young people and people of color.

Alex Escarano died of AIDS complications on Sunday, August 10, 1997. Alex was forty—a true Renaissance man, a graduate of Duke University, an accomplished painter, actor, television producer, and comedy writer. Most important, he was an AIDS activist who fought tirelessly for the rights of PWAs (People with AIDS) and for the education of young people. Alex was one of the greatest people we knew. He always gave so much more than he received, and our lives are diminished with his absence. We loved him so much.

Sean Sasser still resides, happy and healthy, in San Francisco. Sean is the director of development for Health Initiatives for Youth (HIFY), a youth-oriented health organization.

Pam Ling is an M.D. and completed her residency in primary care at the University of California, San Francisco, in 1999. She is now in the second year of an AIDS-research fellowship.

Judd Winick is an Eisner award–nominated cartoonist who writes for DC Comics. He is the creator of the comic-book series *The Adventures of Barry Ween, Boy Genius* for Oni Press, and illustrates The Complete Idiot's Guide series.

Judd and Pam live together in San Francisco with their two cats, Chaka and Sleestak, and are as happy as clams.

✦RGANIZATIONS

If you wish to make a donation to help in the fight against AIDS in all its forms or to seek information about AIDS and HIV, we suggest the following (a more comprehensive list can be found on www.pedroandme.com):

The National Pedro Zamora Project
915 Cole Street
Suite 289
San Francisco, CA 94117
www.pedrozamoraproject.com

This is a 100 percent nonprofit grant-giving organization founded and run by Sean Sasser, Mily Zamora, Pam Ling, and Judd Winick.

The Pedro Zamora Memorial Fund
c/o AIDS Action Foundation
1906 Sunderland Place, NW
Washington, DC 20036
(202) 530-8030
www.aidsaction.com

The Pedro Zamora Youth HIV Clinic
c/o The L.A. Gay and Lesbian Community Services Center
1625 North Schrader Boulevard
Los Angeles, CA 90028
(323) 993-7571
www.laglc.org

National Youth Advocacy Coalition
1638 R Street, NW
Suite 300
Washington, DC 20009
(202) 319-7596
www.nyacyouth.org

Gay, Lesbian, and Straight Education Network (GLSEN)
121 West 27th Street
Suite 804
New York, NY 10001
(212) 727-0135
www.glsen.org

The Zamora family, Judd Winick, Pam Ling, and Sean Sasser have no affiliation with nor do they endorse The Pedro Zamora Foundation.